MUSIC LITERATURE OUTLINES
SERIES III

EARLY AMERICAN MUSIC

✶ ✶ ✶ ✶ ✶ ✶

Music in America from 1620 to 1920

by

Harold Gleason and Warren Becker

Second Edition

✶ ✶ ✶ ✶ ✶ ✶ ✶ ✶

Frangipani Press

P.O. Box 669
Bloomington, Indiana 47402
812-332-3307
Telex 272204

Frangipani Press books are printed in the United States of America by Tichenor Publishing Group, a division of T.I.S. Enterprises.

1986 Printing
Copyright © 1981 by Frangipani Press
All Rights Reserved

ISBN 0-89917-265-2

Library of Congress Catalog Card Number: 80-53731

ISBN 0-89917-265-2

"Low Dutch Tune" from the
Bay Psalm Book, 1698

PREFACE TO THE SECOND EDITION

This edition of *Music Literature Outlines*, Series III, *Early American Music*, is a complete revision of the first edition, 1955. The *Outlines* are designed to be a guide and a resource in the study of music in America from the time of the arrival of the early settlers at Plymouth and Jamestown to the period of World War I. Extended outlines on North American Indian music and Black folk music are beyond the limits of this *Outline*. However, Black musicians have been noted and a new section on the origins of jazz has been included.

In preparation for the United States Bicentennial activities of 1976 and as a response to the great variety of festal occasions, a deeper interest in the history of American music was aroused. To generate further interest an expanding quantity of musical materials has become available. Of particular significance is the series *Earlier American Music* under the editorship of H. Wiley Hitchcock. Not to be overlooked is the large collection of reprints of important earlier books which has been made available by many publishers in America.

Of vital interest to the student, teacher and performer are new materials which are noted in the bibliographies at the end of each *Outline*. The bibliographies have been revised and brought up to date, but they are in no way intended to be exhaustive. They give a representation of the scope of literature available in books, periodicals, anthologies, and books of music important to the efficient study of music of this period. The list of recordings has been deleted. Referral to any up-to-date catalogs of recordings will reveal an extensive list of early American compositions. Anyone studying the music of this period is encouraged to listen to recordings with score in hand, and to perform the music whenever practicable.

A considerable number of facsimiles of music is included, especially of material that is not readily available. Most of the books from which the facsimiles were made are in the Sibley Music Library of the Eastman School of Music, Rochester, New York. Acknowledgement is made to the New York Public Library for the facsimiles from the *Bay Psalm Book* and to The Library of Congress for the facsimile of the original manuscript of "My days have been so wondrous free" by Francis Hopkinson.

The authors are indebted to Dr. Ruth Watanabe, librarian, and Miss Elizabeth Smith for making valuable materials available from the Sibley Music Library for the preparation of the first edition, and to the music and reference librarians of the Honnold Library of the Claremont Colleges, and the music division of the library of the University of California, Los Angeles. Thanks are expressed to Catharine Crozier Gleason who read the final copy and gave constant support and encouragement.

August 30, 1981　　　　　　　　　　　　　　　　　　　　　　Harold Gleason
Pomona, California　　　　　　　　　　　　　　　　　　　　　Warren Becker

CONTENTS

EARLY AMERICAN MUSIC

Music in America from 1620 to 1920

ILLUSTRATIONS

ABBREVIATIONS

AH — American Hymns, Old and New, ed. Christ-Janer, Hughes and Sprague.

ANE — Daniel, Ralph T. The Anthem in New England before 1800.

ASA — Upton, William Treat. The Art-Song in America.

B — book

BCAC — The Bicentennial Collection of American Choral Music, ed. Martens

BCAK — The Bicentennial Collection of American Keyboard Music, ed. Gold.

BCAM — The Bicentennial Collection of American Music, ed. Wienandt.

c. — circa

CAO — A Century of American Organ Music, ed. Owen.

CMCA — Christmas Music from Colonial America, ed. Van Camp.

CSA — Chadwick, George. Song Album (A. P. Schmidt).

CWS — The Civil War Songbook, ed. Crawford.

EAM — Earlier American Music, ed. Hitchcock.

ed. — edited, editor, edition.

FAS — Foster, Album of Songs, ed. Milligan.

fl. — flourished.

FSB — Stephen Foster Song Book, ed. Jackson.

FVPS — Freedom's Voice in Poetry and Song, ed. Anderson.

GB — General Bibliography.

HiFi/MA — HiFi and Musical America.

Hymnal — The Hymnal of the Protestant Episcopal Church, 1940.

JAMS — Journal of the American Musicological Society.

LEAM — Landmarks of Early American Music, 1760-1800, ed. Goldman and Smith.

LU — Liber Usualis.

M — music

MA — Musical America.

MC — Musical Courier.

MDGW — Music from the Days of George Washington, ed. Strunk and Engel.

MinA — Music in America, an Anthology, ed. Marrocco and Gleason.

ML — Music and Letters.

MQ — The Musical Quarterly.

MT — The Musical Times.

n. d. — no date.

n. p. — no publisher.

p. — page (**pp.** — pages)

PAS — A Program of Early and Mid-Eighteenth Century American Songs, ed. Howard.

PCMA — Stevenson, Robert. Protestant Church Music in America.

PMA — The Royal Music Association Proceedings.

PMG — Piano Music of Louis Moreau Gottschalk, ed. Jackson.

ProMTNA — Proceedings of the Music Teachers National Association.

PW — Piano Works; Gottschalk, ed. Lawrence.

ROL — Romantic Organ Literature Series, ed. Leupold.

RRAM — Recent Researches in American Music.

SSF — Songs of Stephen Foster, ed. Earhart and Birge.

tr. — translated, translator, translation.

v. — volume (**vols.** — volumes)

WWP — Wa-Wan Press, ed. Lawrence.

YONE — Ye Olde New England Psalm-Tunes, ed. Fisher.

EARLY AMERICAN MUSIC

MUSIC IN AMERICA FROM 1620 TO 1920

OUTLINE I

INTRODUCTION

Early Exploration and Settlements — Early Protestant Monophonic Psalters
English Polyphonic Psalters

I. **Early Explorations and Settlements**

   A. There are few contemporary accounts of singing or playing music in what is now the United States before the arrival of the Pilgrims in 1620. The Indians had their primitive music, and the early Protestant French, English and Dutch explorers and settlers sang their psalms and the popular songs, ballads and folksongs of their homelands.

   B. The Spaniards under Juan Ponce de Léon (*c.* 1460-1521) settled near what is now St. Augustine, Florida, in 1513. Under the leadership of Hernando Cortés (1485-1547) Mexico City fell to the Spanish in 1521. Other Spanish explorers, including Francisco Vásquez de Coronado (1510-1554), pushed northward into what is now the southwest continental United States. The influence of early music printing (1556) in Mexico City no doubt extended throughout these newly explored areas.

      1. Missions were established in the wake of their conquests and missionaries sought to convert the Indians to the Catholic faith and teach them to sing the liturgical chants of the church (*GB-B* 51, pp. 4-8).

         a. Around 1600 the Mission of San Felipe, New Mexico, had a small organ, the first in what is now the United States. During the second quarter of the seventeenth century transportation lists from Mexico northward included other musical instruments such as shawms, trumpets and bassoons.

         b. In 1769 the first of nine missions founded by the Franciscan Fray Junípero [José Miguel] Serra (1713-1784) was established in San Diego. By 1823 more than 20 missions had been founded in "New California" where music, both vocal and instrumental, played an important part in the education of the Indians. Some of the missions boasted of flourishing instrumental ensembles of as many as thirty to forty participants.

   C. In 1564 three shiploads of French Huguenots attempted to establish Fort Caroline at the mouth of the St. Johns River, ten miles from what is now Jacksonville, Florida. As a pastime they sang psalms from one of the Geneva psalters. The Indians were immediately attracted to the strong Calvinist tunes and learned many of them by rote. After the massacre of the Huguenots by the Spanish, the Indians continued to sing portions of these psalms as greetings or signals to determine whether a wanderer was friend or foe.

      1. *Bienheureux est quiconque* (Blessed is everyone that feareth the Lord) [Psalm 128] (*GB-B* 62, p. 4)

      2. *Du fond de ma pensée* (Out of the depths have I cried unto thee) [Psalm 130] (*MinA*, p. 24)

D.   The English explorers with their psalters left traces of psalm singing on the Pacific as well as the Atlantic seacoast of North America.

   1.   The English explorer, Sir Francis Drake (1545-1596), pillaged settlements and ships in the Caribbean, sailed around South America in 1578 and in 1579 explored the coast of Spanish California up to San Francisco. His chaplain, Francis Fletcher, gives accounts of the Indians enthusiastically listening to the sailors singing psalms, no doubt from the Sternhold and Hopkins version of the psalter.

   2.   The first English settlement in America was established by the London Company at Jamestown, Virginia, in 1607. This mixed group included non-Separatist Puritans of the Church of England. They sang their psalms from the Sternhold and Hopkins Psalter, sang the secular songs they knew and played on any instrument they might have brought with them.

      a.   There are a few contemporary accounts which mention the "noyse of Trumpets" and drums and the music of the Indians.

      b.   In spite of starvation, disease and Indian attacks, Jamestown managed to survive until it was burned in 1676 and Williamsburg became the temporary capital of Virginia. When Williamsburg became the permanent capital in 1699 the rebuilt colony at Jamestown fell into decay.

E.   The Dutch, led by the Englishman Henry Hudson (d. 1611), explored the North River, later known as the Hudson River, in 1609. The Protestant Dutch colonists settled in "New Netherland" and New Amsterdam, now New York City, was established in 1624.

   1.   The Reformed Protestant Dutch Church was organized in 1628. The congregation sang their psalms in Dutch verse from their own psalter until Francis Hopkinson made an English translation (published in 1767) to fit the old melodies.

II.   Early Protestant Monophonic Psalters

A.   The followers of the Protestant Reformation in Europe, except those of Luther and the Bohemian Brethren, were persuaded that the singing of psalms was the principal mode of praising God with music. Groups from the various Protestant persuasions found sanctuary in the "New World" and thus brought their psalmody with them.

   1.   The ill-fated Huguenots brought the French Psalter to Florida; they later spread northward as far as Massachusetts. The Dutch brought their version of the French Psalter to New Amsterdam (New York); the Old Version of Sternhold and Hopkins was used by Drake on the California coast and by the settlers at Jamestown; the Ainsworth Psalter came with the Pilgrims to Plymouth; settlers of the Massachusetts Bay Colony sang from the Ravenscroft tune book.

B.   John Calvin (1509-1564), French Protestant theologian of the Reformation, was born in Paris. From 1536 he continued his work of the Reformation in Geneva.

   1.   Calvin believed that church music should consist only of unaccompanied unison singing of metrical translations of the psalms or other Biblical texts.

      a.   All other forms of church music were "popish" and associated with the uses of the Catholic Church.

   2.   The influence of Calvinism spread throughout Western Europe, particularly in Holland, Scotland, England, and from 1620 by the Puritans to New England.

      a.   Psalters were compiled in large numbers with versifications of the Psalms in the vernacular. The tunes were adapted from various sources including folk and other secular songs, hymn tunes and chants, and a few were composed. Many were taken from earlier psalters.

   3.   Almost all the psalm tunes sung by the Puritans in the Plymouth and Massachusetts Bay Colonies had their origin in early Protestant psalters.

C.   French (Genevan) Psalter, 1562

   1.   The Calvinists, following the example of the Lutherans in Germany, published for the

use of their own church their first psalter, *Aulcuns pseaulmes et cantiques mys en chant*, in 1539 at Strasbourg. Among the 18 metrical psalm translations there are six by Calvin and the remaining 12 by Clément Marot. Included also are the Ten Commandments, the Song of Simeon and the Creed.

2. With additions being made during successive years (1542, 1543, 1551, 1554, 1555) the complete Geneva Psalter, *Les Pseaumes mis en rime*, was published in Geneva in 1562 with metrical versions of the 150 Psalms, translated from the Hebrew, 50 by Marot (1496-1544) and 100 by Théodore de Bèze (1519-1605). Included are 125 tunes taken from various sources; at least 84 were compiled, adapted or composed by **Louis Bourgeois** (*c.* 1510-*c.* 1561).

   a. The texts are generally set syllabically; the meter is duple and various rhythms are used. A single phrase may encompass an interval of a fourth to a sixth; the complete melody generally remains within the range of an octave.

   b. Although harmonizing of the psalm-tunes was opposed by Calvin, inevitably part-settings were made by various composers.

3. *Du fond de ma pensée* (Out of the depths) [Ps. 130], Strasbourg, 1539 (*MinA*, p. 24)

4. *Or sus, serviteurs du Siegneur* (Ye servants of the Lord) [Psalm 34], Geneva, 1551 (*MinA*, p. 27)

D. Sternhold and Hopkins Psalter, 1562

1. Singing the rhymed translations of the Psalms is a practice that may have existed in England before the Reformation. Early in the second quarter of the sixteenth century some of the Psalms were translated by Sir Thomas Wyatt, the Earl of Surrey, and Miles Coverdale (*Goostly psalmes and spirituall songes drawen out of the Holy Scriptures, c.* 1539).

   a. In 1549 there appeared a complete psalter in metrical translation set to four-part music in chant form (*The Psalter of Dauid newely translated into English metre*, 1549, by Robert Crowley).

2. English metrical psalmody, which later became the authorized version, had its beginning about 1548 with the publication of *Certayne Psalmes chosen out of the Psalter of Dauid and drawen into Englishe metre by Thomas Sternhold, grome of yᵉ Kynges Maiesties roobes*, London. The 19 metrical psalms (17 in common meter, 2 in short meter) were composed, as he wrote, for his own "Godly Solace."

3. *The Whole Booke of Psalmes, collected into Englysh Metre by T. Starnhold [sic] I. Hopkins & others: conferred with the Ebrue, with apt Notes to synge then withal, Faithfully perused and alowed according to thordre appointed in the Quenes maiesties Iniunctions: Very mete to be vsed of all sortes of people privately for their solace & comfort: laying apart all vngodly Songes and Ballades, which tende only to the norishing of vyce, and corrupting of youth . . . Imprinted at London by John Day . . . 1562.* The psalter includes versifications of *"Hymnes & spirituall songs"* as well as the Psalms.

   a. For the 150 Psalms there are 65 tunes, many of which appeared in earlier editions (1558, 1560, 1561). Sixteen tunes were new and some no doubt were taken from a French source, possibly *The One and Fiftie Psalmes of David in Englishe metre . . .*, 1556, published in Geneva for the English and Scottish refugees who found asylum in Switzerland from the persecution by the Catholic Queen Mary I.

4. Music: *MinA*, pp. 30-32

E. Scottish Psalter, 1564

1. *The Forme of Prayers and Ministration Of The Sacraments &c. vsed in the English Church at Geneua, approued and receiued by the Churche of Scotland, whereunto besydes that was in the former bokes, are also added sondrie other prayers, with the whole Psalmes of Dauid in English meter . . . Printed At Edinburgh by Robert Lekprevik*, 1564

2. The first complete psalter, ordered for use in public and private worship in the Refor-

mation church (Presbyterian) under John Knox in Scotland, was published in 1564. Included in addition to the Psalms were other materials for congregational worship: the Genevan Form of Prayer, ministration of the sacraments, Calvin's Catechism and a calendar.

3.   The Psalter, the first music printed in Scotland, contains 105 tunes for use with the Psalms.

   a.   The association of a particular tune ("Proper" tune) with a certain Psalm became common. Only the unbarred melodies are included; indifferent congregational part-singing was less worthy than unison singing.

4.   New editions of the Psalter continued to be produced (1567, 1575, 1595, 1599, 1611).

5.   *The CL. Psalmes of David, in Prose and Meeter: With their whole usuall Tunes, newly corrected and amended. Hereunto is Added the whole Church Discipline, with many godly prayers, and an exact Kalendar for xxv. yeers: and also the Song of Moses in Meeter, never before this time in print, Edinburgh, Printed by Andro Hart, Anno, 1615.*

   a.   *The Stilt* (*MinA*, p. 29; *Hymnal*, No. 312; *M 1*, p. 20; *M 7*, No. 205)

      1)   Known as the "Yorke" tune, this melody later appears in the tenor of a four-part setting in the London Psalter, 1621, and in a two-part setting in the *Bay Psalm Book*, of 1698 (the first edition to contain music).

F.   Dutch Psalter, 1566

1.   In 1540 the Dutch Calvinists published the earliest complete vernacular translation of the Psalms in rhyme known as *Souterliedekens*. The 159 monophonic psalm tunes were taken from popular and folk tunes of the time. This continued through more than 30 editions.

2.   In 1566 the Genevan (French) Psalter of 1562 was translated into Dutch metrical verse by Peter Datheen. The French Psalter tunes by **Bourgeois** were likewise adapted to the texts. Ultimately becoming the official psalter of the Dutch Reformed Church throughout Holland, it also was the official version used in the first organized Dutch Reformed Church in America (1628).

III.   English Polyphonic Psalters

A.   Many four-part settings of the Psalms with the psalm tune in the tenor part (rarely in the cantus) were written in England, some by outstanding composers of the Elizabethan era. Protestant composers on the continent, among them **Louis Bourgeois** (1547), **Claude Goudimel** (1565), **Claude LeJeune** (1564), **Jacques Mauduit** and **Jan P. Sweelinck** (1604), wrote polyphonic psalters.

1.   The Puritans brought their psalters with them when they came to the "New Land." The metrical translations of the Psalms were sung in church and at home. Part-singing and the use of instruments by "those skilled in the art" was confined to the home or social gatherings.

B.   **William Parsons**, 1563

1.   *The Whole Psalmes in foure partes, whiche may be song [sic] to al Musical instrumentes, set forth for the encrease of vertue: and aboleshyng of other vayne and trifyling ballades*, printed by John Day, 1563

   a.   Of the 141 psalm tunes, 81 are by **William Parsons**. Included also are 27 by **Thomas Caustun**. In contrast to the simple, plain counterpoint of many of the psalm tunes, those by **Caustun** show a more elaborate treatment with short points of imitation.

      1)   *Psalm 100* (All people that on earth do dwell) (*MinA*, p. 28)

C.   **William Daman**, 1579

1.   *The Psalmes of David in English Meter, with Notes of foure partes set vnto them, by Guilielmo Damon, for Iohn Bull, to the vse of the godly Christians for recreatyng themselves, in stede of fond and vnseemly Ballades*, London, 1579

      a.   This work, not well received, contains 79 harmonized psalm tunes. **Daman** reharmonized the tunes and had them published in two parts by **Thomas East** in 1591; the first book having the tunes in the tenor and the second with the tunes in the "highest" part.

          1)   *The second Booke of the Musicke of M. William Damon, late one of her maiesties Musitions . . .*

      b.   Music

          1)   *Windsor* (*Hymnal*, Nos. 284, 462; *M 7*, No. 129); *Psalm 25* (*AH*, p. 17; *M 7*, No. 44); *Psalm 124* (*AH*, p. 18; *M 7*, No. 139)

  D.   **Thomas East [Easte, Est, Este]**, 1592

    1.   *The Whole Booke of Psalmes: with their wonted Tunes, as they are song [sic] in the Churches, composed into foure parts: All which are so placed that foure may sing ech one a seuerall part in this booke . . .* London, 1592

      a.   The tunes were taken from Anglo-Genevan, English (including **Daman's** Psalter) and Scottish sources. They were harmonized by 10 eminent men of the day, including **Richard Allison, John Dowland, John Farmer, Michael Cavendish, George Kirbye, Giles Farnaby** and **Edward Johnson.**

      b.   In this collection some of the tunes are here given distinctive names for the first time. Also this is one of the first psalters in which the harmonized parts are printed in score rather than in separate part books.

      c.   Music

          1)   *Winchester Old* (*Hymnal*, No. 13; *M 7*, No. 302); *Old 120th* (*Hymnal*, Nos. 115, 491; *M 7*, No. 135)

  E.   **Richard Allison [Alison]**, 1599

    1.   *The Psalmes of David in Meter, The plaine Song beeing the common tunne to be sung and plaid vpon the Lute, Orpharyon, Citterne, or Base Violl, seuerally or altogether, the singing part to be either Tenor or Treble to the Instrument, according to the nature of the voyce, or for fowre voyces.* London, 1599

      a.   Like *"The second Booke"* by **William Daman**, this book is one of the earlier psalters in which the psalm tune is placed in the cantus; this is also one of the earlier collections in which instrumental accompaniment is suggested.

  F.   **Thomas Ravenscroft**, 1621

    1.   *The Whole Booke of Psalmes: With the Hymnes Evangelicall, And Songs Spiritvall. Composed into 4. parts by Sundry Authors, to such severall Tunes as have beene and are usually sung in England, Scotland, Wales, Germany, Italy, France, and the Netherlands: Never as yet before in one volume published . . .* London, 1621

      a.   Although the tunes "have been or are usually sung" in many countries, most of them are to be found in earlier Anglo-Genevan, English and Scottish psalters. The **Ravenscroft** Psalter was commonly used among the Massachusetts Bay colonists. There are a number of new tunes.

          1)   Of the 100 harmonizations, 48 are by **Ravenscroft**. Among other composers represented are **John Milton**, father of the poet, **Richard Allison, John Bennett, John Dowland, Giles Farnaby, William Harrison, Thomas Morley, William Parsons, Thomas Tallis** and **John** and **Thomas Tomkins.**

      b.   Music

          1)   **Ravenscroft:** *Bristol* (*Hymnal*, No. 7; *M 7*, No. 229); *Old 104th* (*Hymnal*, No. 260; *M 7*, No. 119); *Durham* (*Hymnal*, No. 297; *M 7*, No. 236); *Da Pacem* (*AH*, p. 19; *M 7*, No. 183); *Dundee* (*AH*, p. 27; *M 7*, No. 204; *Hymnal*, Nos. 397, 497); **Farnaby:** *High Dutch* (*AH*, p. 22; *M 7*, No. 144); **Parsons:** *The Lamentation* (*AH*, p. 23; *M 7*, No. 10); **Milton, Sr.:** *Yorke* (*Hymnal*, No. 312; *M 7*, No. 205; *MinA*, p. 29, facsimile: second page following p. 246; *M 1*, p. 20)

BIBLIOGRAPHY

Books

1. Benson, Louis Fitzgerald. *The English Hymn; Its Development and Use in Worship*. Philadelphia: Presbyterian Board of Publications, 1915; reprint: Richmond: John Knox Press, 1962.
2. Douen, Orentin. *Clément Marot et le Psautier Huguenot*. Paris: Imperimerie-nationale, 1878-1879.
3. Marot, Clément, and Théodore de Bèze. *Pseaulmes Octantetrois de David*. Kent, CT: Reprint Distribution Service, 1974.
4. Nettl, Bruno. *North American Indian Musical Styles*. Philadelphia: American Folklore Society, 1954.
5. Patrick, Millar. *Four Centuries of Scottish Psalmody*. London: Oxford University Press, 1949.
6. Playford, John. *The Whole Booke of Psalms*. London: 1677; 4th edition, 1698; 20th edition with corrections and additions by Joseph Fox, London: Printed by R. Brown for C. Ware, 1757.
7. Pratt, Waldo Selden. *The Music of the French Psalter of 1562*. New York: Columbia University Press, 1939.

Articles

1. Benson, Norman Arthur. "Music in the California Missions." *Student Musicology* 3 (1968-1969), pp. 128-167.
2. Boeringer, James. "Early American Church Music in California." *Journal of Church Music* 18 (May, 1976), pp. 2-4.
3. Cudworth, Charles L. "The California Missions: 1769-1969." *MT* 110 (1969), pp. 194-196.
4. Garside, Charles W. "Calvin's Preface to the Psalter: A Re-Appraisal." *MQ* 37 (1951), pp. 566-577.
5. Goellner, Theodor. "Two Polyphonic Passions from California's Mission Period." *Inter-American Musical Research Yearbook* 6 (1970), pp. 67-76.
6. Keim, Betty. "Comparative Study of the Music of the Indians and the Spanish in Arizona and New Mexico: A Selected Bibliography." *Current Musicology* 19 (1975), pp. 117-121.
7. McGill, Anna Blanche. "Old Mission Music." *MQ* 24 (1938), pp. 186-193.
8. Pratt, Waldo Selden. "The Importance of the Early French Psalter." *MQ* 21 (1935), pp. 25-32.
9. Ryard, Herbert. "A Sternhold and Hopkins Puzzle." *MQ* 56 (1970), pp. 221-229.
10. Spiess, Lincoln Bunce. "Benavides and Church Music in New Mexico in the Early Seventeenth Century." *JAMS* 17 (1964), pp. 144-156.
11. Williams, Albert S. "America's First Book was Musical." *Music Journal* 17 (March, 1959), pp. 60-61.
12. Woodward, G. R. "The Genevan Psalter of 1562; Set in Four-Part Harmony by Claude Goudimel, in 1565." *PMA* 44 (1917-1918), pp. 167-192.

Music

1. Alison, Richard. *The Psalmes of David in Meter, 1599*, ed. Ian Howard, facsimile edition. Menston, England: The Scolar Press, 1968.
2. *Calvin's First Psalter*, ed. Richard Runciman Terry. London: E. Benn, 1932.

3. Damon, William. *The Former Booke of the Musicke of M. William Damon, Late One of Her Maiesties Musitions.* London: T. Este, 1591.

4. da Silva, Owen Francis. *Mission Music of California: A Collection of Old California Mission Hymns and Masses.* Los Angeles: W. F. Lewis, 1941; reprint: New York: Da Capo Press, 1978.

5. Day, John. *The Whole Psalmes in foure Partes.* London: John Day, 1563.

6. Este, Thomas. *The Whole Booke of Psalmes; With Their Wonted Tunes, as they are song in Churches, composed into foure parts.* London, 1592; ed. by Edward F. Rimbault for the Musical Antiquarian Society, London: Chappell, 1844.

7. Frost, Maurice. *English & Scottish Psalm & Hymn Tunes, c. 1543-1677.* London: Oxford University Press, 1953.

8. Goudimel, Claude. *Les 150 Psaumes de David mis en rime françoise, 1565,* in *Les Monuments de la Musique Française au temps de la Renaissance,* vols, 2, 4, 6, ed. Henry Expert. Paris: Maurice Senart, 1924-1930; Kassel: Bärenreiter-Verlag, 1935 (facsimile).

9. Hague, Eleanor. *Spanish-American Folk-Songs.* Lancaster, PA, and New York: American Folk-Lore Society, 1917.

10. Lawes, Henry. *Choice psalms put into Musick, for three Voices.* London: James Young, 1648.

11. Ravenscroft, Thomas. *The Whole Booke of Psalmes with the Hymnes Evangelicall and Songs Spirituall.* London: 1621.

12. Robb, John Donald. *Hispanic Folk Songs of New Mexico.* Albuquerque: University of New Mexico Press, 1954.

13. *Songs America Voted by,* ed. Irwin Silber. Harrisburg, PA: Stackpole Books, 1971.

14. Sternhold [Sterneholde], Thomas. *The Whole Booke of Psalmes; Collected into English Meeter by Thomas Sternehold, John Hopkins and others.* London: Printed for the Company of Stationers, 1624.

15. Sternhold [Sterneholde], Thomas. *One and Fiftie Psalmes.* Geneva: Printed for the English congregation at Geneva by John Crespin, 1556.

16. Tate, Naham, and Nicholas Brady. *The Psalms of David, a New Version of, Fitted to the Tunes Used in Churches.* London: M. Jenour, for the Company of Stationers, 1718.

17. Terry, Richard Runciman. *The Scottish Psalter of 1635.* New York: H. W. Gray, 1935. *The Psalmes of David in Prose and Meeter With their whole Tunes in foure or more parts.* Edinburgh: Printed by the Heiress of Andrew Hart, 1635. Facsimile following page 94.

PSALMODY IN NEW ENGLAND, 1620 - 1720

The Pilgrims – The Non-Separatist Puritans
The New Version, 1708 – Psalmody to Hymnody

I. **The Pilgrims**

A. During the reign of Queen Elizabeth (1558-1603) there was a strong movement to reform or "purify" the traditional and formal practices of the Church of England. In 1602 a group of "Puritans" separated from the Church of England and by 1606 had formed an Independent (Congregational) Church at Scrooby in Nottinghamshire. The leaders were William Brewster and John Robinson who had been educated at Cambridge. In order to maintain their strict Calvinistic beliefs and escape persecution many of the congregation fled to Amsterdam, Holland, finally settling in the university town of Leyden where they enjoyed complete religious liberty.

　　1. In 1620 a small group of the devout Separatist Puritans, now known as Pilgrims, planned to sail by way of Southampton and Plymouth, England, for the New World. After some delay they finally set sail September 16 on the Mayflower with 101 passengers. These included 35 Pilgrims ("Saincts") from Leyden and a mixed English group ("Strangers"), most of whom were not Separatists. The Mayflower reached the American shore at Cape Cod on November 21. On December 16 it entered Plymouth harbor and the first permanent settlement in New England was founded.

　　2. The singing of the Pilgrims in Holland was described by Edward Winslow (1595-1655), one of the Pilgrims on the Mayflower, who wrote, "They that stayed at Leyden feasted us that were to go at our pastor's house [it] being large, where wee refreshed our selves after our teares, with the singing of Psalmes, making joyfull melody in our hearts, as well as with the voyce, there being many of our Congregation very expert in Musick; and indeed it was the sweetest melody that ever mine eares heard (*B* 10, p. 6).

B. The *Ainsworth Psalter*, 1612

　　1. The Pilgrims brought with them a psalter which had been prepared by Rev. Henry Ainsworth (1570-1623), pastor of the Separatist Puritans in Holland.

　　　　a. The psalter was "Imprinted at Amsterdam" by Giles Thorpe in 1612. The title reads: *The Book of Psalmes: Englished both in Prose and Metre. With Annotations, opening both the words and sentences, by conference with other scriptures. By H.[enry] A.[insworth].*

　　　　　　1) In addition to Ainsworth's metrical and prose translations of the Psalms with annotations, the psalter included 39 tunes printed with the words. A second edition appeared in 1618 with the same music.

　　　　b. The Pilgrims in Plymouth followed zealously the admonition of Calvin that the only music to be used in church services was the unaccompanied singing of metrical translations of the Psalms and other Biblical passages, and they sang them with enthusiasm at home as well as in church.

　　2. Ainsworth used 15 different meters in his versifications of the Psalms and preferred the longer meters and stanzas.

　　　　a. The meters of versified Psalms are designated by the number of syllables in each line of the stanza. All stanzas have the same meter and are sung to the same music, almost invariably with one note to a syllable.

   b.   The meters used include the following:
      1)   Common Meter Double (8. 6. 8. 6. 8. 6. 8. 6.)
      2)   Long Meter Double (8. 8. 8. 8. 8. 8. 8. 8.)
      3)   Four 10's (10. 10. 10. 10.); five 10's; six 10's; eight 10's
      4)   Six 8's (8. 8. 8. 8. 8. 8.); twelve 8's
      5)   7. 6. 7. 6. Double; 5. 5. 5. 5. 6. 5. 6. 5. Double
   c.   Very few Psalms are in four-line Short Meter (6. 6. 8. 6.), Long Meter (8. 8. 8. 8.) or
         the Common (Ballad) Meter (8. 6. 8. 6) which is used almost exclusively in the
         Sternhold and Hopkins Psalter and the Bay Psalm Book.
3.   Ainsworth wrote that the 39 tunes he selected for his psalter were "most taken from
      our former Englished Psalmes [Sternhold and Hopkins, 1562], when they will fit the
      measure [meter] of the verse. And for the other long verses I have also taken (for the
      most part) the gravest and easiest tunes of the French and Dutch psalmes."
   a.   Many of the tunes in Sternhold and Hopkins and all the tunes in the Dutch psalter
         had their origin in French psalters.
   b.   The melodies are printed in diamond-shape half and whole notes and without bar-
         lines. The C clef is used throughout and time signatures, almost without exception,
         are ₵.
   c.   In addition to their length and metrical and rhythmic variety, the tunes have unusual
         melodic interest and some suggest a folksong style.
4.   The *Ainsworth Psalter* went through six editions from 1612 to 1690. It was used in
      Salem until about 1667 when, "because of the difficulty of the tunes," the popular
      Bay Psalm Book was adopted. The Puritans in the Plymouth Colony, however, clung
      steadfastly to their psalter until 1692 when the new generation, who were not so "ex-
      pert in musick," also found the Ainsworth tunes too long and difficult and turned to
      the *Bay Psalm Book* of the Boston Puritans with its many four-line common-meter
      tunes.
5.   Music
   a.   *Psalme 7* (*MinA*, p. 24); *Psalme 130* (*MinA*, p. 24); *Old 124th* (*MinA*, p. 25);
         Windsor (*MinA*, p. 26); *Old 112th* (*MinA*, p. 26); *Old 100th* (*MinA*, p. 27)
   b.   *Psalm 124* (*AH*, p. 34; *M* 6, No. 139); *The Complaint of a Sinner* (*AH*, p. 35;
         M 6, No. 185); *Benedictus* (*AH*, p. 36; *M* 6, No. 3); *Psalm 28* (*AH*, p. 37; *M* 6,
         No. 323); *De Profundis* (*AH*, p. 38; *M* 5, No. 149); *Psalm 23* (*AH*, p. 37; *M* 6,
         No. 320); *Psalm 8* (*AH*, p. 42; *M* 6, No. 321); *Psalm 100* (*AH*, p. 43; *M* 6, No.
         322); *Psalm 24* (*AH*, p. 44; *M* 6, No. 326); *Psalm 120* (*AH*, p. 46; *M* 6, No. 328)
   c.   *Old 112th* (*Hymnal*, No. 147); *Commandments* (*Hymnal*, No. 179); *Old 100th*
         (*Hymnal*, No. 277); *Windsor* (*Hymnal*, No. 284); *Old 124th* (*Hymnal*, No. 536)
C.   Merry Mount
   1.   Dancing among the Puritans was not forbidden, as John Cotton (b. England, 1548; d.
         Boston, 1652) wrote in 1625: "Dancing (yea though mixt) I would not simply con-
         demn . . . Only lascivious dancing to wanton ditties . . ."
   2.   Thomas Morton, an English adventurer, was banished from Plymouth in 1625 because
         of the Maypole festivities he espoused in a settlement at Mount Wollaston (now Brain-
         tree, Massachusetts). It was known as "Merriemount" after Morton took over the
         colony.
      a.   Not only did the Puritan settlers object to Morton and his followers because of their
            Maypole festivities but also because he paid higher prices to the Indians for furs.
            More objectionable was the fact that Morton sold guns to the Indians and gave in-
            struction for their use.
         1)   An account written in 1647 by William Bradford, Governor of Plymouth Colony,
               describes the revels at Merry Mount: "They also set up a May-pole, drinking and
               dancing aboute it . . ., inviting the Indean women, for their consorts, dancing and
               frisking togither . . . and worse practices . . .

  b.   Morton was arrested in 1630 and sent back to England, but he returned to New England and eventually was imprisoned in Boston (1644-1645). He died in Maine in 1647.

II.   Non-Separatist Puritans

  A.   The *Bay Psalm Book*, 1640
    1.   The English non-Separatist Puritans, who began the "great migration" to Massachusetts Bay in 1630 under the leadership of John Winthrop, brought with them the Sternhold and Hopkins (1562 and later) and Ravenscroft's polyphonic psalter (1621). Richard Allison's polyphonic psalter (1599), with its suggestions for performance with various instruments, was owned by William Brewster, one of the Pilgrims.
      a.   The Puritan divines had become dissatisfied with the translations of the Psalms in the Sternhold and Hopkins, and John Cotton declared that the psalter had "variations of the sense and alterations of the sacred text."
      b.   Thirty "pious and learned ministers" were therefore appointed to translate the Psalms again and set them into verse which would be more faithful to the original Hebrew than the Sternhold and Hopkins version.
        1)   The ministers evidently realized their lack of poetic gifts and explained in the Preface that "if the verses are not always so smooth and elegant as some may desire or expect; let them consider that God's Altar needs not our pollishing."
    2.   The *Bay Psalm Book*, 1640, was the first book to be printed in the English colonies of North America and was used throughout the Massachusetts Bay Colony in this and many later editions. Several editions were printed in England and Scotland. The title page reads as follows: *The Whole Booke of Psalmes Faithfully translated into English Metre. Whereunto is prefixed a discourse declaring not only the lawfullness, but also the necessity of the heavenly Ordinance of singing Scripture Psalmes in the Churches of God. Coll. III. Let the word of God dwell plenteously in you, in all wisdome, teaching and exhorting one another in Psalmes, Himnes, and Spirituall Songs, singing to the Lord with grace in your hearts. James V. If any be afflicted, let him pray, and if any be merry let him sing psalmes. Imprinted 1640* [Cambridge, Massachusetts]
    3.   The *Bay Psalm Book*, unlike the *Ainsworth Psalter*, did not include music, but "An Admonition to the Reader" states that the versifications of the Psalms had been reduced to six meters (C. M., S. M., L. M., H. M., six 8's, twelve 8's) and that almost all the Psalms are included in the first three meters.
      a.   The sources for the tunes which might be sung to the Psalms were Ravenscroft's psalter (1621) and "our english psalm booke" (Sternhold and Hopkins).
      b.   The 112 C. M. Psalm versions in the 1640 edition may be sung to any of the 39 C. M. tunes in Ravenscroft's psalter.
      c.   The 14 S. M. Psalms may be sung to the three S. M. tunes in "our english psalm booke."
  B.   The *Bay Psalm Book*, 1698
    1.   The title page of the ninth edition (1698) remained identical with that of the 1651 edition; it reads as follows: *The Psalms, Hymns, and Spiritual Songs, of the Old & New Testament: Faithfully Translated into English Meetre. For the use, Edification and Comfort of the Saints in publick and private, especially in New England. 2 Tim 3. 16, 17. Col. 6. 16. Let the word of God dwell in you richly in all wisdom, teaching and admonishing one another in Psalms, Hymns and Spiritual Songs, singing to the Lord with grace in your hearts. Eph. 5. 18, 19 Be filled with, &c. Jam. 5. 13. The Ninth Edition Boston, Printed by B. Green, and J. Allen, for Michael Perry, under the West-end of the Town house. 1698.* (facsimile: M 2, opposite p. 1; B 7, p. 30)
    2.   This edition of 1698 is the first known edition to contain music. A five-page supplement placed at the back of the psalm-book includes 13 tunes "with the Bass Set under

Tune" and a foreword which reads in part: "Some few directions for ordering the Voice in Setting [the pitch of] these following Tunes of the Psalms. First observe of how many *Notes* compass the *Tune* is. Next, the place of your first *Note*; and how many *Notes* above &c below that: so as you may begin the *Tune* of your first *Note* as the rest may be sung in the compass of your and the peoples voices, without *Squeaking* above, or *Grumbling* below."

3.   The two-part tunes (cantus and bass) no doubt were copied from the 1674 or 1679 editions of **John Playford's** *A Brief Introduction to the Skill of Musick.*

    a.   **Playford** states that the bass part might be "Play'd and Sung to the Organ, Virginals, Theorbo-Lute, or Bass-Viol."

        1)   Although instrumental music was not allowed in the New England Puritan churches, there was no objection to its "proper" secular use.

    b.   The tunes are printed from woodcuts in diamond-shape white notes with the solmization letters, f[a], s[ol], l[a], m[i], placed under the notes (facsimile: *M* 2, p. 14; *B* 7, p. 34).

        1)   This notation system was taken directly from **Playford's** *Brief Introduction*, 1672 edition, the only edition of the *Brief Introduction* utilizing the fasola notation.

    c.   Nine of the tunes are in Common Meter (one in C. M. D.) and the remaining four meters are S. M., L. M., twelve 8's and H. M.

        1)   It will be noted that only three of the tunes have more than four lines.

4.   The foreword, copied from **Playford's** *Brief Introduction*, 1667, groups the tunes according to the pitch on which they should begin, the meters, and the character of the Psalms to which the tunes should be sung. Each of the tunes is identified with a particular Psalm (facsimile: *M* 2, pp. 10, 12; *B* 11, p. 33)

    a.   *Oxford, Litchfield* and *Low Dutch* "To Psalms Consolatory." Psalms 4, 69, 23 (C. M.)

    b.   *York* and *Windsor* "To Psalms of Prayer, Confession & Funerals." Psalms 73, 116 (C. M.)

    c.   *Cambridge Short* "To peculiar Psalms." Psalm 70 (S. M.)

        1)   The above six tunes begin the first note with a "cheerful high pitch, in regard their whole compass from the lowest Note, the highest is not above five or six Notes."

    d.   *St. David's* and *Martyrs* "To Psalms of Praise and Thanksgiving." Psalms 95, 39 (C. M.). "These two Tunes are eight Notes compass above the first Note, and therefore begin first Note low."

    e.   *Hackney*, Psalm 67 (C. M.) and Psalm 119 (C. M. D.). "Begin your first note low."

    f.   *100th Psalm* (L. M.) "begin the first Note indifferent high, in regard you are to fall four Notes lower than your first pitch Note."

    g.   *115th Psalm* (twelve 8's) and *148th Psalm* (H. M.) "begin your first Note low, in regard the Tune ascends eight Notes above it."

5.   The *Bay Psalm Book*, 1698, was the beginning of a development in eighteenth-century New England that led from music instruction books and singing schools to the first native American composers and compilers of tune books.

6.   Music

    a.   *Oxford* (*MinA*, p. 33; *M* 2, p. 14); *Low Dutch* (*MinA*, p. 34; *M* 2, p. 18); *Martyrs* (*MinA*, p. 35; *M* 2, p. 28); *Psalm 100* (*MinA*, p. 36; *M* 2, p. 34); *Psalm 119* (*MinA*, p. 37; *M* 2, p. 32)

    b.   *London* (*AH*, p. 38; *M* 6, No. 45); *Old 148th* (*AH*, p. 49; *M* 6, No. 174); *Old 100th* (*AH*, p. 52; *M* 6, No. 114); *Old 113th* (*AH*, p. 50; *M* 6, No. 125); *Pater Noster* or *Old 112th* (*AH*, p. 53; *M* 6, No. 180); *York* (*AH*, p. 54; *M* 6, No. 205); *Windsor* (*AH*, p. 55; *M* 6, No. 129); *Nunc Dimittis* (*AH*, No. 56; *M* 6, No. 37); *Old 119th* (*AH*, p. 57; *M* 6, No. 132); *Song 34* (*AH*, p. 58; *M* 6, No. 362a); *Psalm 69* (*AH*, p. 59; *M* 6, No. 86)

III. The New Version

A. The changing literary taste in England during the seventeenth century led to many efforts to produce freer, more singable and, above all, more poetic versions of the Psalms.

B. In 1696 **Nahum Tate** (1651-1715), poet laureate and librettist of **Purcell's** *Dido and Aeneas*, and **Nicholas Brady** (1650-1726), an Anglican clergyman, published in London *A New Version of the Psalms of David, Fitted to the Tunes Used in Churches* (revised edition, 1698). Tunes were not included.

  1. The *New Version*, also known as the "Tate and Brady" was "permitted to be used in all churches" by King William III as an alternate to the Sternhold and Hopkins, which now became known as the "Old Version."

C. *A Supplement to the New Version of Psalms by Dr. Brady and Mr. Tate* was published in London in 1700; included were six hymns and several tunes in two and three voices. In 1708 the sixth edition appeared which contained 63 tunes for the 150 Psalms and 12 tunes for the Hymns of the Church, all set in two parts, melody and bass.

  1. Also included were "Plain Instructions for all those who are desirous to learn to improve themselves in Psalmody."

  2. Among the fine tunes selected by Tate and Brady for the 1708 *Supplement* are *St. Anne's Tune* and *Psalm 149* (*"Hanover"*), both by **William Croft** and *While Shepherds Watched Their Flocks by Night*, set to a tune taken from **Thomas East's** *Whole Booke of Psalms*, 1592.

D. The *New Version* was not used in church services by the New England Puritans until after the middle of the eighteenth century, but was adopted by many Episcopalian churches in Boston, New York, Philadelphia and elsewhere. In 1740 in Boston the Baptists changed to the *New Version*.

  1. In 1713 Brady and Tate's *Psalms for the Use of His Majesty's Chappell of America*, now King's Chapel, was published in Boston. Nine tunes were included.

  2. Judge Sewall noted in his *Diary*, 1720, that at a singing-school in Boston "the singing [was] extraordinarily Excellent, such as has hardly been heard before in Boston. Sung four times out of Tate and Brady."

    a. **John Tufts**, in his *Introduction to the Singing of Psalm-Tunes*, 1726, used a text from the *New Version*, 1698.

  3. In 1755 a tune supplement for the *New Version* was engraved and sold by Thomas Johnston in Boston. It included the famous tune *"Mear"* in a three-part setting which found its way into Southern folk hymnody as well as many twentieth-century hymnals (*MinA*, p. 41).

E. Music and/or texts, selected from various editions of the *New Version*, were published in many hymnals during the eighteenth and nineteenth centuries and are found in hymnals today.

F. Music

  1. *St. Anne's Tune* (*MinA*, p. 39); *Song of the Angels [Winchester]* (*MinA*, p. 40); *Mear* (*MinA*, p. 41)

  2. *Psalm 42* (*Hymnal*, No. 450); *Psalm 122* (*Hymnal*, No. 390); *Psalm 130* (*Hymnal*, No. 439)

IV. Psalmody to Hymnody (Isaac Watts)

A. The Reverend Dr. **Isaac Watts** (1674-1748), a non-conformist English clergyman, was the first important writer of hymns for the English Protestant church. He strongly disapproved of the old metrical translations of the Psalms and sought to write freer and more poetic versions in the "Spirit of the Gospel."

B. **Watts** published his *Hymns and Spiritual Songs*, including Psalm paraphrases, in London in 1707, and they were republished in Boston in 1739. The *Psalms of David Imitated*, London, 1719, were republished by Benjamin Franklin in Philadelphia in 1729.

   1.   The 454 *Hymns* were known in New England even before their publication in Boston. **Cotton Mather** wrote in his *Diary* in 1711 that "the religious, ingenious and sweet-spirited *Isaac Watts*, hath sent me the new Edition of his *Hymns*."

C.   The hymns and Psalms of **Dr. Watts** began to be widely used during the eighteenth century, although the Puritan churches were reluctant to give up their metrical psalmody. The few hymn texts which had been added to their Psalm books, including those of **Watts**, were first used as devotional literature in the home.

D.   Hymnody spread with increasing rapidity through the evangelistic efforts of four men: **John** (1703-1791) and **Charles Wesley** (1707-1788) in the South (1735 and later), **Jonathan Edwards** (1703-1758), who started the "Great Awakening" in Northampton, Massachusetts, in 1734, and **George Whitefield** (1714-1770), the Calvinist Methodist who came to the Colonies in 1738.

   1.   **John Wesley's** first *Collection of Psalms and Hymns* was printed in Charleston, South Carolina, in 1737.

   2.   The hymns and free paraphrases of the Psalms by **Watts** achieved extraordinary popularity and were the chief sources of texts for hymns composed well into the nineteenth century.

E.   Hymn and Psalm texts by **Watts**

   1.   *MinA*, pp. 58, 107, 124, 126, 138, 142, 147, 148, 151, 156, 165, 237, 247, 249, 250, 255

   2.   *Hymnal*, Nos. 289, 319, 337, 369, 542, 550

   3.   *AH*, pp. 119, 120, 223, 224

BIBLIOGRAPHY

Books

1.   Cotton, John. *A Brief Exposition with Practical Observations Upon the Whole Book of Canticles.* London, 1655; reprint: New York: Arno Press, 1972.

2.   ——————*Singing of Psalms a Gospel Ordinance.* Boston: M. S. Crowne, 1647.

3.   Fischer, William Arms. *Notes on Music in Old Boston.* Boston: Oliver Ditson, 1918; reprint: New York: AMS Press, 1977.

4.   Foote, Henry Wilder. *An Account of the Bay Psalm Book.* New York: The Hymn Society of America, 1940.

5.   Hood, George. *A History of Music in New England.* Boston: Wilkens, Carter and Co., 1846; reprint: New York: Johnson Reprint Corporation, 1970.

6.   Lowens, Irving. "The Bay Psalm Book in 17th-Century New England," in *Music and Musicians in Early America.* New York: W. W. Norton, 1964, pp. 25-38.

7.   MacDougall, Hamilton Crawford. *Early New England Psalmody, An Historical Appreciation, 1620-1820.* Brattleboro: Stephen Daye Press, 1940; reprint: New York: Da Capo Press, 1969.

8.   Mather, Cotton. *Magnalia Christi Americana: or The Ecclesiastical History of New-England From Its First Planting in the Year 1620 Unto the Year . . . 1698,* 7 vols. London: T. Parkhurst, 1702; in 2 vols., Hartford: S. Andrus and Son, 1853.

9.   Metcalf, Frank J. *American Psalmody: or, Titles of Books, Containing Tunes Printed in America from 1721-1820.* New York: C. F. Heartmann, 1917; reprint: New York: Da Capo Press, 1968.

10.   Pratt, Waldo Selden. *The Music of the Pilgrims; A Description of the Psalm Book Brought to Plymouth in 1620 [Ainsworth Psalter].* Boston: Oliver Ditson, 1921; reprint: New York: Russell & Russell, 1971; New York: AMS Press, 1966.

11.   Scholes, Percy Alfred. *The Puritans and Music in England and New England.* New York: Oxford University Press, 1934; reprint: New York: Oxford University Press, 1969.

12. Simpson, Christopher. *A Compendium of Practical Music in Five Parts*. London, 1665; reprint: Oxford, England: B. Blackwell, 1970.
13. Thomas, Isaiah. *A History of Music Printing in America*, 2nd edition. Albany, New York: J. Munsell, 1874; reprint: New York: Burt Franklin & Co., 1967.
14. Warrington, James. *Short Titles of Books Relating to Or Illustrating the History and Practice of Psalmody in the U. S. (1620-1820)*. Philadelphia: Privately Printed, 1898; reprint: New York: Burt Franklin & Co., 1971
15. Wright, Louis B. *The Cultural Life of the American Colonies, 1607-1763*, ed. Henry Steele Commager and Richard B. Morris. New York: Harper & Row, 1962.

Articles

1. Appel, Richard Gilmore. "The Bay Psalm Book and Its Music—1640-1773." *Consort* 30 (1974), pp. 72-76.
2. Bennett, Joseph. "Psalm Singing. An Old-Time Controversy. *MT* 42 (1901), pp. 453-455.
3. Britton, Allen P., and Irving Lowens. "Unlocated Titles in Early Sacred American Music." *Notes* 11 (1953), pp. 33-48.
4. Fox, Frederic E. "Stephen Daye, First Printer in the U. S. A." *The Hymn* 7 (April, 1956), pp. 61-63.
5. Lowens, Irving. "The Bay Psalm Book in 17th-Century New England." *JAMS* 8 (1955), pp. 22-29.
6. Maurer, Maurer. "The 'Professor of Musick' in Colonial America." *MQ* 36 (1950), pp. 511-524.
7. Truro, The Bishop [Walterus Truron]. "The Rhythm of Metrical Psalm-Tunes." *ML* 9 (1928), pp. 29-33.

Music

1. Ainsworth, Henry. *The Psalmes in Metre*. Amsterdam, 1612.
2. Appel, Richard G. *The Music of the Bay Psalm Book, 9th edition (1698)*. Brooklyn: Institute for Studies in American Music, 1975. (ISAM Monograph, No. 5)
3. *Bay Psalm Book: Being a Facsimile Reprint*, ed. Wilberforce Eames. New York: Dodd, Mead and Co., 1903.
4. *A Collection of the Psalm and Hymn Tunes, Used by the Reformed Protestant Dutch Church of the City of New-York, agreeable to their Psalm Book, published in English. In Four Parts, Viz. Tenor, Bass, Treble, and Counter*. New York: Hodge and Shober, 1774.
5. *Early Psalmody in America*, Series I, ed. Carleton Sprague Smith. New York: The New York Public Library, 1938. (*The Ainsworth Psalter. Psalm 65* with settings by Claude Goudimel)
6. Frost, Maurice. *English & Scottish Psalm & Hymn Tunes, c. 1543-1677*. London: Oxford University Press, 1953.

Pfal.XCix.C.

For he hath wrought throughout the
  his wonders great and ftrong.   (world,
2 With his right hand full worthily
  he doth his foes deuoure:
And get himfelfe the victory,
  with his owne hand and power.

3 The Lord doth make the people know
  his fauing health and might:
The Lord doth eke his iuftice fhew,
  in all the peoples fight.
4 His grace and truth to Ifrael,
  in mind he doth record,
That all the earth hath feene right well,
  the goodneffe of the Lord.

5 Be glad in him with ioyfull voyce,
  all people on the earth:
Giue thankes to God, fing, and reioyce,
  to him with ioy and mirth.
6 Vpon the Harpe vnto him fing,
  giue thankes to him with Pfalmes:
Reioyce before the Lord our King,
  with Trumpets and with Shalmes.

7 Yea, let the Sea and all therein,
  for ioy both rore and fwell:
The earth likewife let it begin
  with all that therein dwell.
8 And let the flouds reioyce their fills,
  and clap their hands apace:
And eke the mountaines and the hils,
  before the Lord his face.

9 For he fhall come to iudge and try
  the world and euerie wight:
And rule the people mightily,
  with iuftice and with might.

Dom.regnauit. Pfalm.XCix.I.H.

He commendeth the power, equity, and excel-
lency of the Kingdome of God by Chrift, ouer
the Iewes and Gentiles, prouoking him to
magnifie the fame, and to feare the Lord, as
the ancient Fathers, Mofes, Aaron, and Sa-
muel, who calling vpon God, were heard in
their prayers.

Sing this as
·be 95.
Pfalme.

THe Lord doth raigne, although at it
  the people rage full fore:
Yea he on Cherubins doth fit,
  though all the world doe roare.
2 The Lord that doth in Sion dwell,
  is high and wondrous great:
Aboue all folke he doth excell,
  and he aloft is fet.

3 Let all men praife thy mighty Name,
  for it is fearefull fure:
And let them magnifie the fame,
  that holy is and pure.
4 The princely power of the King,
  doth loue iudgement and right:

Thou rightly ruleft euery thing,
  in Iacob through thy might.

5 To praife the Lord our God deuife,
  all honour to him doe:
His footftoole worfhip him before,
  for he is holy too.
6 Mofes, Aaron, and Samuel,
  as priefts on him did call:
When they did pray, he heard them well,
  and gaue them anfwere all.

7 Within the cloud to them he fpake,
  then did they labour ftill:
To keepe fuch lawes as he did make,
  and poynted them vntill.
8 O Lord our God, thou didft them heare,
  and anfweredft them againe:
Thy mercy did on them appeare,
  their deeds thou didft maintaine.

9 O laud and praife our God and Lord,
  within his holy hill:
For why, our God throughout the world,
  is holy euer ftill.

Iubilate Deo omnis.Pfal.C.I.H.

He exhorteth all men to ferue the Lord, who
hath made vs to enter into his Courts and Af-
fembly, to praife his name.

All people that on earth doe dwell,
Sing to the Lord with chearefull voyce:
him ferue with feare, his praife forth tell,
Come ye before him and reioyce.

2 The Lord, ye know, is God indeed,
  without our ayde he did vs make:
3 We are his flocke, he doth vs feede,
  and for his fheepe he doth vs take.

4 O enter then his gates with praife,
  approch with ioy his Courts vnto:
Praife, laud, and bleffe his name alwayes,
  for it is feemely fo to doe.

5 For why the Lord our God is good,
  his mercy is for euer fure:
His truth at all times firmely ftood,
  and fhall from age to age endure.

Another of the fame.

IN God the Lord be glad and light,
  praife him throughout the earth:
Serue him and come before his fight,
  with finging and with mirth.

Sing this as
the 67.
Pfalme.

2 Know

From **The Whole Booke of Psalmes**
by Thomas Sternhold, John Hopkins, and others, 1624

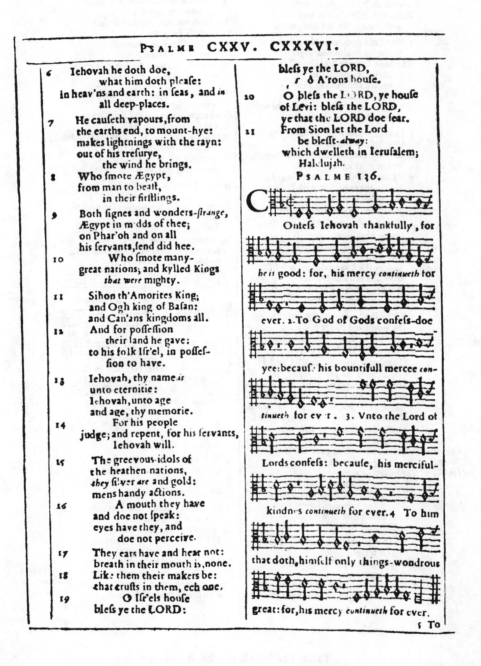

From **The Psalmes in Metre** by Henry Ainsworth, 1618

PSALME xxiii, xxiiii.

2 Hee in the folds of tender-graffe,
  doth caufe mee downe to lie:
  To waters calme me gently leads
3 Reftore my foule doth hee:
  he doth in paths of righteoufnes:
  for his names fake leade mee.
4 Yea though in valley of deaths fhade
  I walk, none ill I'le feare:
  becaufe thou art with mee, thy rod,
  and ftaffe my comfort are.
5 For mee a table thou haft fpread,
  in prefence of my foes:
  thou doft annoynt my head with oyle,
  my cup it over-flowes.
6 Goodnes & mercy furely fhall
  all my dayes follow mee:
  and in the Lords houfe I fhall dwell
  fo long as dayes fhall bee.

Pfalme 24
A pfalme of david.

THe earth Iehovahs is,
  and the fulneffe of it:
  the habitable world, & they
  that there upon doe fit.
2 Becaufe upon the feas,
  hee hath it firmly layd:
  and it upon the water-floods
  moft follidly hath ftayd.
3 The mountaine of the Lord,
  who fhall thereto afcend?
  and in his place of holynes,

E 5

PSALM xxii, xxiii.

25 Concerning thee fhall be my prayfe
  in the great affembly:
  before them that him reverence
  performe my vowes will I.
26 The meek fhall eat & oe fuffic'd:
  Iehovah prayfe fhall they
  that doe him feek: your heart fhall live
  unto perpetuall aye.
27 All ends of th'earth remember fhall
  and turne unto the Lord:
  and thee all heathen-families
  to worfhip fhall accord.
28 Becaufe unto Iehovah doth
  the kingdome appertaine
  and he among the nations
  is ruler Soveraigne.
29 Earths-fat-ones, eat & worfhip fhall:
  all who to duft defcend,
  (though none can make alive his foule)
  before his face fhall bend.
30 With fervice a pofterity
  him fhall attend upon;
  to God it fhall accounted bee
  a generation.
31 Come fhall they, & his righteoufnes
  by them declar'd fhall bee,
  unto a people yet unborne,
  that done this thing hath hee.

23 A Pfalme of David.

THe Lord to mee a fhepheard is,
  want therefore fhall not I.

2 Hee

Psalm 23 from the **Bay Psalm Book**, 1640

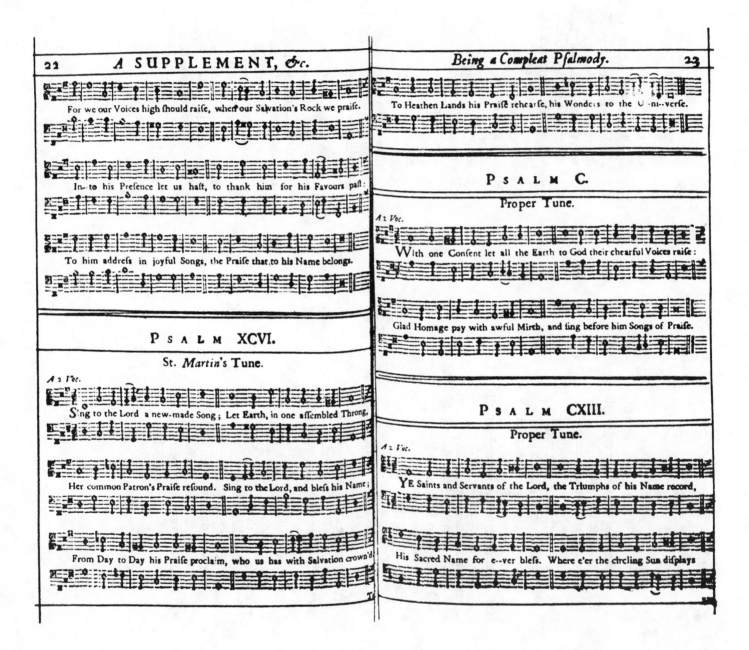

From **A Supplement to the New Version of Psalms**
by Dr. Brady and Mr. Tate, seventh edition, 1717

Frontispiece from **The Royal Melody Compleat** by William Tans'ur, 1764

From **The American Harmony or Royal Melody Compleat** by William Tans'ur, 1773

OUTLINE III

MUSIC IN NEW ENGLAND, 1720 – 1770

The Decline of Psalm-Singing – Singing by Note
The First Music Instruction Books
Collections of Psalm-Tunes and Anthems before 1770
Instruments – Concerts

I.   The Decline of Psalm-Singing

A.   The quality of psalm singing in the Puritan churches, particularly in the rural areas, declined during the seventeenth century and by 1700 had reached a deplorable state.

    1.   The Plymouth Colony had their *Ainsworth Psalter* with music. There were no printed tunes in the *Bay Psalm Book* until 1698. By that time very few in the congregations could read music and many did not have psalters.

    2.   The poor quality of the poetry, the monotony of singing the same few tunes and meters, the "lining-out" of the psalms and singing by rote, the adding of "Turns and Flourishes," and the fact that instruments to support the singing were not allowed in church, culminated in the early eighteenth century in a strong movement by the Puritan ministers to "reform" the singing.

B.   The lining-out of the psalms (a custom adopted in England as early as 1644) was introduced in an effort to teach the congregation the words and tunes of the psalms.

    1.   The Reverend John Cotton wrote in his *Singing of Psalms a Gospel Ordinance*, 1647, that for those who did not have psalm books, could not read or say the psalms by heart " it will be a necessary helpe, that the lines of the *Psalme*, be openly read beforehand, line after line, or two lines together, so that they who want either books or skill to reade may know what is to be sung, and joyne with the rest in the dutie of singing."

    2.   In lining-out a psalm the clerk would read one or two lines and then the "precentor," often a deacon, would "set the pitch" and sing what had been read. He then led the congregation in singing what had been learned.

        a.   Even the precentors became confused; Deacon Samuel Sewall (1652-1730) recorded in his *Diary* on December 28, 1705, that he "intended to set Windsor and fell into High-Dutch, and then essaying to set another Tune, went into a key too high." Again on July 5, 1713, he wrote, "try'd to set Low-Dutch Tune and fail'd. Try'd again and fell into the tune of the 119th Psalm."

    3.   Lining-out the psalms resulted in a slow tempo in contrast to the lively singing of the early settlers; no two congregations sang the tunes the same way.

        a.   Lining-out also afforded the more ambitious and skilled to have opportunity to add embellishments, a style generally enjoyed. In 1728 the Reverend Nathaniel Chauncey wrote in his *Regular Singing Defended, and proved to be the only true way of singing the songs of the Lord*, "They use many Quavers and Semiquavers, &c. And on this very account it is they are pleased with it, and so very loath to part with it."

II.   Singing by Note

A.   The ministers who led the movement to "reform" psalm-singing in the Puritan churches preached sermons, published pamphlets and encouraged singing schools in order to teach the congregation to "Sing by Note," (in the "Regular Way"). Among these progressive ministers were Cotton Mather (1663-1728), Thomas Symmes (1677-1725), John Cotton

(1685-1752), Nathaniel Chauncey (1681-1756), John Tufts (1689-1750) and Thomas Walter (1696-1725).

    1.   Many congregations in the rural areas resisted the efforts of the ministers and continued to sing in the "Common" or "Usual Way."

  B.   Singing by Note and the Usual Way were defined by Thomas Symmes, a Harvard graduate and pastor of churches in Boxford and Bradford: "Singing by Note is giving every note its proper pitch, and turning the voice in its proper place, and giving every note its true length and sound. Whereas, the Usual Way varies much from this. In it, some notes are sung too high, others too low, and most too long, and many turnings or flourishings with the voice (as they call them) are made where they should not be, and some are wanting where they should have been . . ."

III. The First Music Instruction Books

  A.   In 1720 the only printed music readily available in New England were the 13 tunes in the *Bay Psalm Book*, 1698, and the nine tunes in Brady and Tate's *New Version*, 1713.

    1.   The publication in 1721 of instruction books with text and music by the Reverend **John Tufts** and the Reverend **Thomas Walter** provided a means of teaching "even Children" to sing by note and marked the beginning of the development of the singing-school and music education in the United States.

  B.   **John Tufts** (1689-1750)

    1.   **Tufts** was born in Medford, Massachusetts, on February 26 and died in Amesbury, Massachusetts. He graduated from Harvard College, 1708, and became a Congregational minister in Newbury in 1714. In 1738 he retired from the ministry to Amesbury where he became a shopkeeper.

    2.   The first music instruction book published in the English Colonies was advertised in the *Boston News-Letter*, January 2/9, 1721, as "A Small Book containing 20 Psalm Tunes, with Directions how to Sing them, contrived in the most easy Method ever yet Invented, for the ease of Learners, whereby even Children, or People of the meanest Capacities, may come to Sing them by Rule . . ."

      a.   **Tufts** was undoubtedly the author although his name was not mentioned. The 20 tunes appear only as one-part melodies. Succeeding editions incorporated more tunes although there are no known copies of the first four editions.

    3.   The title page of the fifth edition, 1726, reads as follows: *An Introduction to the Singing of Psalm-Tunes, in a plain & easy Method. With a Collection of Tunes in Three Parts. By the Rev. Mr. TUFTS. The Fifth Edition, printed from Copper-Plates, Neatly Engraved. BOSTON, In N. E. Printed for Samuel Gerrish, at the Lower End of Cornhill. 1726.* (facsimile: *B* 7, p. 48)

    4.   **Tufts'** *Introduction* includes a "Short Introduction" in which he explains the notation and rudiments of music, followed by a few "Lessons for Tuning Ye Voice" and 37 tunes set in three parts with the melody in the cantus.

      a.   The "plain & easy Method" of notation is based on the "fasola" system, probably taken from **John Playford's** *Brief Introduction*, 1672. This system which spread rapidly utilized the capital letters F, S, L, M (Fa, Sol, La, Mi) located on the staff in place of notes. The system was also used in the *Bay Psalm Book* by placing the letters underneath the notes. Note values are determined by punctuation marks. Letters without a period indicate a quarter note; one period, a half note; a colon, a whole note. Barlines are used only at the end of phrases.

    5.   Twenty-two of the tunes used by **Tufts** may be found in both **John Playford's** *Whole Book of Psalms* (1677) and in **Thomas Walter's** *The Grounds and Rules of Musick Explained* (1721, 1723). Five of the remaining tunes were also from English sources. The *100 Psalm Tune New* included in the collection may have been composed by **Tufts** and thus may be the first original American composition or it may have been reworked from another setting.

6. Music
   a. *Northampton* (*MinA*, p. 48); *Psalm 149 [Hanover]* (*MinA*, p. 49); *100th Psalm Tune New* (*MinA*, p. 50)
   b. *M* 8, Nos. 1, 25, 36, 42, 45, 99, 114, 121, 125, 129, 132, 174, 178, 180, 186, 200, 204, 205, 209, 222, 235, 239c, 244, 246b, 251, 333a, 362c

C. **Thomas Walter** (1696-1725)

1. **Walter** was born in Roxbury, Massachusetts, on December 13; he died there of tuberculosis. He graduated from Harvard College in 1713 and became an ordained minister in 1718. He was a grandson of Increase Mather and a nephew of Cotton Mather.

2. Soon after **Tufts'** first book appeared in 1721 the second music instruction book was published by the Reverend **Thomas Walter** with the following title: *The Grounds and Rules of Musick Explained, or an Introduction to the Art of Singing by Note. Fitted to the meanest Capacities. Boston. Printed by J. Franklin* [the elder brother of Benjamin] *for S. Gerrish, 1721.*

3. *"The Grounds and Rules"* includes a "Recommendatory Preface," signed by 15 ministers, where **Walter** makes many of the frequently quoted comments about the tunes which once "were sung according to the Rules of the *Scale of Musick* (by the early New England settlers), but are now miserably tortured, and twisted, and quavered, in some Churches, into a horrid Medly of confused and disorderly Noises . . ."
   a. Also included are "Some brief and very plain Instructions for Singing by Note."

4. The music consists of 24 psalm-tunes set in three parts, without texts, and engraved on copper in diamond-shape notes. Regular barlines and three-part settings are here published for the first time in the Colonies.
   a. In his "Sermon on Regular Singing," 1722, **Walter** justifies his use of three parts by saying that "The Music of the Temple, as it was under the Management and Direction of our *Sweet Psalmist* of Israel, was a *Chorus of Parts.*"

5. The following well-known psalm-tunes are included in **Walter's** *Grounds and Rules*, 1721, and also in **Playford's** *Whole Book of Psalms*, 1677, the *Bay Psalm Book*, 1698, and **Tufts'** *Introduction*, 1726: *Canterbury* (*M* 8, No. 19b); *St. Mary's* (*M* 8, No. 333a); *St. Davids* (*M* 8, No. 235); *Windsor* (*M* 8, No. 129; *Hymnal*, No. 284); *York* (*M* 8, No. 205; *Hymnal*, No. 312); *Psalm 100* (*M* 8, No. 114); *Hymnal*, No. 139); *Psalm 102* (*M* 8, No. 115); *Psalm 113* (*M* 8, No. 125); *Psalm 148* (*M* 8, No. 174); *Psalm 103* (*M* 8, No. 117)

6. Music
   a. *London [Litchfield]* (*MinA*, p. 51); *Southwell, New* (*MinA*, p. 52); *100 Psalm* (*MinA*, p. 53; facsimile: third page following p. 246)
   b. *M* 8, Nos. 25, 42, 45, 99, 121, 178, 180, 186, 209, 222, 239c, 244, 362c

IV. Collections of Psalm-Tunes and Anthems before 1770

A. The popular music instruction books by **Tufts** (last edition, 1744) and **Walter** (last edition, 1764) were used in New England singing schools for many years. By 1770 the singing school had become a flourishing institution. The demand for instruction and music was met by **William Billings** and many later native New England composers.

1. There were several influential collections of English music, published in New England before 1770, which introduced the anthem and "fuging" tune to the New England composers.

2. **James Lyon's** *Urania*, published in Philadelphia, 1761, includes two anthems by **Lyon** and six examples of English fuging psalm-tunes.

B. Fuging psalm-tunes

1. The typical American fuging tune, a style in its own right, follows the idiom current in England during the eighteenth century. Contemporaneous with **William Billings** in Boston were many composer-compilers of fuging tunes throughout New England who

no doubt exerted some influence on **Billings**.

2.   The fuging tune is usually divided into two parts: first a homophonic treatment of the tune and second, a free imitative form in which each voice enters successively according to the wish of the composer; this "fuge" section is normally repeated.

   a.   **Tans'ur** in his *A Compleat Melody, or Harmony of Sion*, London, 1738, defines the fuge as "a quantity of *Notes* of any Number; which is begun by any *single Part* and carried on; and afterward is sounded again, by some other Part; which repeats the same (or such like *Notes*) either in the *Unison* or 8th; but more commonly in the latter; in a 4th, or 5th, or 8th, above, or below the leading Part."

   b.   **Tans'ur's** further influence on the "fuging" idiom in America is expressed in his *A New Musical Grammar*, London, 1746, when he says "two *Fifths*, or two *Eighths* (and no more) may be taken together in *Three*, or more *Parts* (when it cannot be well avoided) rather than spoil the Air."

C.   **Josiah Flagg** (1738-1794)

   1.   **Flagg** was born in Woburn, Massachusetts, on May 28. He was a teacher, director of a military band, publisher of two collections of music and an impresario who introduced many foreign musicians including the English organist **William Selby** to American audiences. He settled in Providence, Rhode Island, organized concerts (including the music of **Bach** and **Handel**) and fought in the Revolution.

   2.   **Flagg's** tune book is entitled: *A Collection of the best Psalm Tunes, in two, three and four Parts: From the most approv'd Authors, fitted to all Measures [meters], and approv'd of by the best Masters in Boston, New England; to which are added some Hymns and Anthems the greater part of them never before Printed in America. By Josiah Flagg. Engrav'd by Paul Revere; Printed & sold by him and Josiah Flagg, Boston, 1764.*

   a.   The *"Collection,"* taken from English sources, contains 116 psalm tunes and two anthems, one by **Tans'ur**. These are the first anthems published in New England. Included also is **Handel's** "March" from *Richard III*.

   b.   *Hallelujah,* a chorus for five voices (*MinA*, p. 59)

   3.   A second collection, the first extensive compilation of anthems printed in America, was first published by **Flagg** in 1766 and later often reprinted. The various editions include from 16 to 20 anthems (a few psalm tunes) by identified composers. The title reads: *A Collection of All Tans'ur's and a number of other Anthems from [Aaron] Williams, [William] Knapp, [Caleb] Ashworth and [Joseph] Stephenson.*

   a.   Eleven anthems by **Tans'ur**, one by **Williams**, four by **Knapp**, one by **Ashworth** and two by **Stephenson** are included.

D.   **William Tans'ur [Tanzer]** (1706-1783)

   1.   **Tans'ur** was born in Dunchurch, Warwickshire, on about November 6; he died in St. Noets, Huntingdonshire. He was a theoretician, teacher, composer-compiler of popular psalm tunes and anthems and a bookbinder.

   2.   In 1735 **Tans'ur's** *A Compleat Melody; or The Harmony of Sion* was published in London with music in 2, 3 and 4 parts. A new, enlarged edition appeared in London in 1755 entitled *The Royal Melody Complete, or The New Harmony of Zion*.

   a.   *Westerham Tune*, Psalm 81 (Be light and glad, in God rejoice), 1755 (*MinA*, p. 54)

   3.   In 1767 the first American edition, a reprint of the 1755 edition, was printed and sold in Boston by William M'Alpine, in Salem by M. Williams and in Newbury-Port by Daniel Bayley.

   a.   A copy of this edition, which includes 14 anthems by **Tans'ur**, was owned by **William Billings** and contains the only known holograph by **Billings**.

   4.   The "fifth" edition entitled *The American Harmony; or Royal Melody Compleat* was published by Daniel Bayley in Newbury-Port in 1769 in combination with **Aaron Williams'** *The Universal Psalmodist*, London, 1763.

   a.   *St. Martin's* (Hear, O my people, to my law), 1755 (*MinA*, p. 57; *AH*, p. 151)

    b.   Anthem: *Psalm 47* (O clap your hands) (*GB-B* 13, p. 175)

E. **Joseph Stephenson** (1723-1810)

  1.   **Stephenson** was an English psalmodist and a clerk in the Unitarian Church at Poole, Dorsetshire.

  2.   **Stephenson** published two undated collections, *Church Harmony, Sacred to Devotion* (third edition, 1760) and *The Musical Companion . . . for the use of country choirs.*

  3.   A few of **Stephenson's** anthems were published in New England collections including **Flagg's** *Sixteen Anthems*, 1766, and **Aaron Williams'** *Universal Psalmodist*, 1769.

    a.   The "Thirty-fourth" Psalm (*c.* 1755) from the *Church Harmony* introduced the fuging tune idiom to many New England composers (facsimile: *B* 8, p. 240).

    b.   Anthem: *Behold I bring you glad tidings* (*GB-B* 13, p. 194)

F. **Aaron Williams** (1731-1776)

  1.   **Williams** was born and died in London. He was a music teacher, engraver, publisher, composer and a clerk at the Scottish Church in London Wall.

  2.   **Williams'** *The Universal Psalmodist*, published in London in 1763, was "calculated to promote and improve the most excellent Part of Social Worship."

    a.   *St. Thomas* (Great is the Lord our God) (*MinA*, p. 58; *AH*, p. 448)

  3.   An altered version with the title *The American Harmony; or Universal Psalmodist* was published by Daniel Bailey [Bayley] in Newbury-Port in 1769. Included with this edition was a reprint of **Tans'ur's** *Royal Melody Complete*. This became very generally used throughout New England.

    a.   Anthem: *Psalm 122* (I was glad when they said unto me) (*GB-B* 13, p. 185)

  4.   An anthem by **Williams** was published in **Flagg's** *Sixteen Anthems*, 1766, and two in **Williams'** *American Harmony*, 1769. As late as 1853 **Williams** is represented in **Lowell Mason's** *The New Carmina Sacra*.

V.   Instruments

A.   Although instruments were not allowed in Puritan Church services, the Reverend **John Cotton**, in his *Singing of Psalms a Gospel Ordinance*, 1647, wrote, "Nor doe we forbid the private use of any instrument of musick, therewithall."

  1.   There are contemporary references to a few instruments during the early seventeenth century including the drum, trumpet, jew's-harp, guitar, treble "viall," bass "Vyol," virginal and hoeboy [oboe].

  2.   The *Boston News-Letter* of April 16-23, 1716, advertised "that there is lately sent over from London, a choice Collection of Musickal Instruments, consisting of Flageolets, Flutes, Haut-Boys, Bass-Viols, Violins, Bows, Strings, Reads for Haut-Boys, Books of Instructions for all these Instruments, Books of ruled Paper. To be Sold at the Dancing School of Mr. [Edward] Enstone in Sudbury Street near the Orange Tree, Boston. NOTE. Any person may have all Instruments of Musick mended, or Virginalls and Spinnets Strung and Tuned at a reasonable Rate, and likewise may be taught to Play on any of these Instruments above mention'd; dancing taught by a true and easier method than has been heretofore."

B.   Organs in New England

  1.   In 1713 a Boston merchant, Thomas Brattle, willed a small one-manual organ of six stops to the dissenting Brattle Square Church (the Anglican Church), now King's Chapel. The organ was not accepted by the Brattle Square Church. It remained packed on the porch for seven months before installation in Queen's [King's] Chapel in 1714, the first pipe organ in a church in the colonies.

    a.   William Price played the organ for several months before Mr. Edward Enstone of London was imported to "play skillfully there with a loud noise." There were many objections to the use of an organ in church; it was denounced by Cotton Mather and other ministers.

2. A large organ built by Richard Bridge of London for Trinity Church, Newport, Rhode Island, was installed in 1733 with the help of **Charles Theodore Pachelbel**, son of the well-known German organist-composer.

3. In 1736 an organ built or imported by William Claggett, a clock-maker in Newport, Rhode Island, was installed in Old North Church (Christ Church), Boston. It was replaced in 1752 by an organ from the shop of the first organ builder in Boston, Thomas Johnston (1708-1767).

   a. A small one-manual six-stop organ was built by Johnston for St. Peter's Church, Salem, in 1754.

4. In 1744 Trinity Church, Boston, imported from London a "moderate size" two-manual organ built by Abraham Jordan, who first used the "swell" in English organs, *c.* 1712. Before leaving London the organ was played and approved by **Handel**.

5. In 1756 a new three-manual organ built by the English Richard Bridge was installed in King's Chapel. The Brattle organ was moved to St. Paul's Church, Newburyport, and in 1836 was sold to St. John's Church, Portsmouth, New Hampshire.

VI. Concerts

A. The first public paid concert in the Colonies was advertised in the *Boston Weekly News-Letter* December 16/23, 1731; in 1744 "a number of gentlemen" requested "the use of Faneuil Hall for a Concert of Musick."

B. In 1771 **Josiah Flagg** put on the following program of "vocal and instrumental musick accompanied by French horns, hautboys, etc. by the band of the 64th Regiment."

Act I.	Overture Ptolemy . . . . Handel
	Song 'From the East breaks the morn'
	Concerto Ist . . . . .Stanley
	Symphony 3d. . . . . Bach
Act II.	Overture Ist . . . . Swindl
	Duet to 'Turn fair Clora'
	Organ concerto
	Periodical Symphony . . . . Stamitz
Act III.	Overture Ist . . . . Abel
	Duetto 'When Phoebus the tops of the hills'
	Solo Violin
	A new Hunting Song, set to music by Mr. Morgan
	Periodical Symphony . . . . Pasquale Ricci

C. Before the Revolution European musicians began arriving in America to give concerts; among them was **Charles Theodore Pachelbel** who played in New York in 1736. Following the Revolution the musical life of the Colonies from Massachusetts to Virginia was virtually dominated by European musicians and the native American composers and musicians became almost totally obscured.

1. Nevertheless the rapid development of the singing school, the first music instruction books, the publication of collections of English psalm-tunes, anthems and fuging tunes, and the increased interest in secular music prepared the way for the first native composers in New England.

BIBLIOGRAPHY

Books

1. Brooks, Henry Mason. *Olden-Time Music*. Boston: Ticknor and Co., 1888; reprint: New York: AMS Press, 1973.

2. Foote, Henry Wilder. *Musical Life in Boston in the Eighteenth Century*. Worcester, MA: American Antiquarian Society, 1940.

3. Fuld, James J., and Mary Wallace Davidson. *18th-Century American Secular Music Manuscripts: an Inventory*. Philadelphia: Music Library Association, 1980.

4. Goldin, Milton. *The Music Merchants*. London: Macmillan, 1969.

5. Howard, John Tasker. *A Program Outline of American Music*. New York: Thomas Y. Crowell, 1931.

6. Lowens, Irving. "The American Tradition of Church Song," in *Music and Musicians in Early America*. New York: W. W. Norton, 1964, pp. 279-286.

7. ——————"John Tufts's *Introduction to the Singing of Psalm-Tunes (1721-1744)*: The First American Music Textbook," in *Music and Musicians in Early America*. New York: W. W. Norton, 1964, pp. 39-57.

8. ——————"The Origins of the American Fuging-Tune," in *Music and Musicians in Early America*. New York: W. W. Norton, 1964, pp. 237-248.

9. Metcalf, Frank J. *American Writers and Compilers of Sacred Music*. New York: Abingdon Press, 1925; reprint: New York: Russell & Russell, 1967.

10. ——————*Stories of Hymn Tunes*. New York: Abingdon Press, 1928.

11. Pichierri, Louis. *Music in New Hampshire, 1623-1800*. New York: Columbia University Press, 1960.

12. Sewall, Samuel. *Diary*, ed. Mark Van Doren. New York: Macy-Masius, 1927; reprint: *Diary of Samuel Sewall*. New York: Arno Press, 1972; *Samuel Sewall's Diary*. New York: Russell & Russell, 1963.

13. Symmes, Thomas. *Utile Dulci. Or, A Joco-Serious Dialogue, concerning regular singing: calculated for a particular town (where it was publicly had, on Friday, Oct. 12, 1772.) but may serve some other places in the same climate*. Boston: Printed by B. Green, for S. Gerrish, in Cornhill, 1723.

14. Tufts, John. "The Complete Text of John Tufts's *Short Introduction to the Singing of Psalm-Tunes* (1726)," in Irving Lowens. *Music and Musicians in Early America*. New York: W. W. Norton, 1964, pp. 289-291.

Articles

1. Anderson, Simon Vance. "Ignored by Historians, Obscured by Military Records—The Unofficial Bands of the American Revolution." *Music Educators Journal* 61 (December, 1974), pp. 26-33.

2. Brandon, George. "A Plea for Early American Tunes." *The Hymn* 18 (1967), pp. 50-51.

3. Butler, John Harrison. "John Tufts: Aurora Unaware." *Music Educators Journal* 55 (1969), pp. 44-46.

4. Camus, Raoul François. "Band Music of Colonial America." *Music Journal* 29 (June, 1971), pp. 18-20.

5. Colles, Henry Cope. "Some Musical Instruction Books of the Seventeenth Century." *PMA* 55 (1928-1929), pp. 31-49, 55-59.

6. Covey, Cyclone. "Did Puritanism or the Frontier Cause the Decline of Colonial Music? Debated in a Dialogue between Mr. Quaver and Mr. Crotchet." *Journal of Research in Music Education* 6 (1958), pp. 68-78.

7. Cowell, William King. "The Organs of Trinity Church, Newport, R. I., U. S. A." *The Organ* 14 (1935), pp. 245-255.

8. Daniel, Ralph T. "English Models for the First American Anthems." *JAMS* 12 (1959), pp. 49-58.

9. ——————"Handel Publications in 18th-Century America." *MQ* 45 (1959), pp. 168-174.

10. Davis, Josephine K. R. "Early American Singing Schools." *Music Journal* 20 (1962), pp. 19-20.

11. Demarest, Alison. "Paul Revere's Music Engraving." *Music Journal* 22 (1964), pp. 58-59.

12. Dinneen, William. "Early American Manuscript Music-Books." *MQ* 30 (1944), pp. 50-62.

13. Ellinwood, Leonard. "Revolutionary Hymnody." *Journal of Church Music* 17 (November, 1975), pp. 2-5.

14. Finney, Theodore Mitchell. "The Third Edition of Tufts' Introduction to the Art of Singing Psalm-Tunes." *Journal of Research in Music Education* 14 (1966), pp. 163-170.

15. Freeman, Andrew. "John Snetzler and His Organs." *The Organ* 14 (1934-1935), pp. 34-42, 92, 101, 163-171.

16. Frischmann, Charles. "Organs and Organ Music in Colonial America." *Journal of Church Music* 17 (December, 1975), pp. 2-4.

17. Gordon, Edgar B. "Instrumental Music in the Pioneer Days." *Music Educators Journal* 46 (1960), pp. 34, 37.

18. Hamblen, David. "Early Boston Bands." *Music Journal* 24 (December, 1966), pp. 32-34.

19. Hooper, William Loyd. "The Story of Baptist Hymnody in Colonial America." *Church Music* 15 (March, 1964), p. 10.

20. Jones, Matt B. "Biographical Notes on Thomas Walter's 'Grounds and Rules of Music Explained'." *Proceedings of the American Antiquarian Society*, October, 1932.

21. Lowens, Irving. "Tune Books, Tunesmiths and Singing Schools." *Etude* 74 (November, 1956), pp. 20, 59, 62-64.

22. McManis, Charles W. "David Tannenberg and the Old Salem Restoration." *The American Organist* 48 (May, 1965), pp. 15-20.

23. Myers, Gordon. "Songs of Early America." *Music Journal* 27 (September, 1969), p. 36.

24. Owen, Barbara. "American Organ Music and Playing, from 1700." *Organ Institute Quarterly* 10 (1963), pp. 7-13.

25. ——————"The Organ in Colonial America." *Journal of Church Music* 18 (April, 1976). pp. 2-4.

26. Poladian, Sirvart. "The Reverend John Tufts and Three-Part Psalmody in America." *JAMS* 4 (1951), p. 276.

27. Ray, Sister Mary Dominic. "Drums, Wigs & Six Wax Lights." [Early American Opera] *HiFi/MA* 25 (August, 1975), pp. MA 14-17.

28. Redway, Virginia Larkin. "Charles Theodore Pachelbell, Musical Emigrant." *JAMS* 5 (1952), pp. 32-36.

29. ——————"A New York Concert in 1736." *MQ* 22 (1936), pp. 170-177.

30. Riedel, Johannes. "Early American Music." *Journal of Church Music* 5 (November, 1963), pp. 2-4.

31. Robinson, Albert F. "Choral Music and Choirs in Early America." *Journal of Church Music* 18 (February, 1976), pp. 2-5.

32. ——————"Historic American Organ Builders." *Music (AGO)* 10 (1976), pp. 34-37.

33. Scholten, James William. "Amzi Chapin: Frontier Singing Master and Folk Hymn Composer." *Journal of Research in Music Education* 23 (1975), pp. 109-119.

34. Stainer, Sir John. "On the Musical Introductions Found in Certain Metrical Psalters." *PMA* 27 (1900), pp. 1-50.

35. Steinberg, Judith Tick. "Old Folks Concerts and the Revival of New England Psalmody." *MQ* 59 (1973), pp. 602-619.

36. Symmes, Thomas. "The Reasonableness of Regular Singing (or, Singing by Note, 1720)." *Choral Journal* 16, No. 1 (1975), p. 23; No. 2 (1975), pp. 23-24.

37. Taricani, Jo Ann. "Music in Colonial Philadelphia: Some New Documents." *MQ* 65 (1979), pp. 185-199.

38.   Van Camp, Leonard W. "Choral Balance and the Alto Part in Early American Choral Music." *Choral Journal* 15, No. 9 (1975), pp. 7-9.

39.   Woodall, W. L. "Early American Psalm Singers." *Church Music* 13 (September, 1962), pp. 14-16.

40.   Woodword, Henry. "February 18, 1729: A Neglected Date in Boston Concert Life." *Notes* 33 (1976), pp. 243-252.

Music

1.   "A Folio of Pages from Early American Songbooks." *Church Music* (St. Louis) 1 (1976), pp. 38-40.

2.   Pachelbel, Carl Theodore. *Magnificat, for eight voices and organ*, ed. Hans T. David. New York: New York Public Library, 1937.

3.   Tans'ur, William. *The American Harmony or, Royal Melody Complete*, 2 vols. Newbury-Port, MA: Daniel Bayley, 1773.

4.   ––––––*The Royal Melody Compleat; or the New Harmony of Sion*. London: Brown, 1764.

5.   Tufts, John. *A Very Plain and Easy Introduction to the Singing of Psalm-Tunes*, 5th edition. Boston: Published and sold by Samuel Gerrish, 1726. (Facsimile ed. Harry Dichter. Philadelphia: Musical Americana, 1954)

6.   ––––––*An Introduction to the Singing of Psalm Tunes*, 8th edition. Boston: Printed for Gerrish, 1731.

7.   Walter, Thomas. *The Grounds and Rules of Musick Explained; or, An Introduction to the Art of Singing by Note*. Boston: Thomas Johnston, 1721.

8.   Frost, Maurice. *English & Scottish Psalm & Hymn Tunes, c. 1543-1677*. London: Oxford University Press, 1953.

OUTLINE IV

GERMAN SECTS IN PENNSYLVANIA

Early Settlers – German Pietists
Ephrata Cloister – Moravians

I. **Early Settlers**

    A. The province established in Philadelphia in 1682 by the English Quaker, William Penn, became a haven for dissenting German Protestants during the better part of the eighteenth century.
        1. The Quakers (Society of Friends) were opposed to all forms of the "vain pastime" of music, but granted religious freedom to all sects and denominations.
    B. Many of the small, German-speaking sects who came to Pennsylvania first settled in Germantown (founded in 1683), near Philadelphia, in the late seventeenth and early eighteenth centuries.
        1. These groups included the Mennonites (1683), Labadists from North Netherlands (1684), German Pietists (Wissahickon Mystics or Hermits, 1694), German Baptists (Dunkards [Dunkers], 1719), Ephrata Community (1720), Schwenkfelders (1734) and Moravians or Bohemian Brethren (1735-1741).
            a. The various sects were closely knit and differed in their religious beliefs and in the simple or elaborate use of music in their worship services, but all sang the chorales and hymns of their homelands.
        2. The sects who were most active musically include the German Pietists, Ephrata Community and, above all, the Moravians.

II. **German Pietists**

    A. **Johann Kelpius** (1673-1708)
        1. **Kelpius**, a scholar and musician, at the age of twenty-one led a group of Pietists who settled in the Wissahickon Valley not far from Philadelphia.
            a. Music was an important part of their worship services and instruments, which were brought with them from London, were used with the singing of hymns, psalms and anthems.
        2. In 1703 the "Wissahickon Hermits" furnished music for the ordination of the German Lutheran pastor, Justus Falckner, of the Gloria Dei Church in Philadelphia.
            a. In addition to the singing of a hymn and an anthem the service "opened with a voluntary on the little organ in the gallery . . . supplemented with instrumental music by the Mystics on the viol, hautboy, trumpets and kettle-drums."
        3. A manuscript of hymn texts, probably compiled by **Kelpius**, includes ten melodies from German sources, seven with figured basses. The title of the collection reads: *The Lamenting Voice of the Hidden Love at the time when She Lay in Misery & forsaken; and oprest by the multitude of Her Enemies* . . . 1705 (*B* 17, v. 1)
            a. *Ich liebe Jesus noch allein* (I love my Jesus quite alone) (*AH*, p. 242)

III. **Ephrata Cloister**

    A. **Conrad Beissel** (1690/91-1768)
        1. **Beissel** apprenticed as a baker under his father, became a violinist and a Pietist mystic;

he migrated from the Rhineland to Germantown in 1720. He first joined the German Baptists (Dunkards), but in 1727 he organized a new sect called Seventh-day Baptists or "New Dunkards" and was joined by some of the German Pietists.

2.   In 1732 **Beissel** and his semi-monastic, celibate "solitary Brothers and Sisters" founded the Ephrata ("the beautiful") Cloister on the banks of the Cocalico River not far from Lancaster, Pennsylvania.

   a.   Vocal music was an essential part of the austere life in the cloister, and under **Beissel's** leadership a choir and singing school were established. The community numbered about 300.

   1)   In its most prosperous days the choir consisted of 15 women and 10 men.

   b.   **Beissel** organized the entire life of the Brothers and Sisters, including their dress and diet. Meat and also eggs "which arouse numerous capricious cravings" were forbidden.

3.   In the early 1740's **Beissel**, a self-taught musician, turned to composition. During the next 25 years he composed over 1,000 unaccompanied hymns and anthems in four to eight parts; he also set to music complete chapters of the Old Testament and two versions of the Song of Songs.

   a.   **Beissel's** most notable manuscript collection of 750 hymns, completed in 1747, was titled *Das Gesäng der einsamen und verlassenen Turtel-Taube Nemlich der Christlichen Kirche* (The Song of the Solitary and Forsaken Turtle-Dove namely the Christian Church).

   1)   The music is in **Beissel's** own original notation, and the manuscript was copied "by many of the younger Sisters" into a beautifully illuminated songbook.

   2)   *Die Sonn ist wieder Aufgegangen* (The Sun now risen) (*AH*, p. 256)

   3)   Hymns: *B* 17, v. 2

   4)   *Ich werde aufs Neue* (*GB-B* 62, p. 37)

   5)   *Gott ein Herrscher aller Heyden* (God, ruler of all) (*MinA*, p. 64; facsimile: p. 4 following p. 246)

   b.   A number of other works by **Beissel** were printed by Benjamin Franklin and on two presses acquired by the Cloister in 1742.

   c.   **Beissel's** last collection (2nd ed., 1766) includes over 700 hymns, many by members of the Cloister.

4.   **Beissel** devised his own rules of composition which resulted mainly in a series of consonances in major keys, with frequent parallel fifths and octaves.

   a.   Another tune book containing 375 hymns was copied by Sisters Anastasia and Iphigenia in 1747 and shows variety in changing keys in the circle of major keys from three sharps to three flats.

   b.   Suspensions and dissonant harmonies are avoided, as modulations generally are also; the music was sung in a free rhythm based on the accents of the German words. Second inversion chords are interpolated in various progressions.

   1)   The accented syllables are placed on notes of the major triad ("masters") in longer values.

   2)   The unaccented syllables are placed on the other notes ("servants") in shorter values.

5.   The Cloister under Peter Miller, **Beissel's** successor, continued; during the nineteenth and early twentieth centuries the buildings were used by the Seventh-day Baptist Church. Since 1941 it has been a museum.

IV.   The Moravians

A.   The *Unitas Fratrum* (Unity of Brethren, now the Moravian Church) was founded in 1457 by the followers of the Bohemian reformer, John Hus.

1.   A small group of persecuted Moravians, descendants of the Unity of Brethren, fled to

Saxony in 1722 under the protection of Count Nicholas von Zinzendorf (1700-1760). There they developed a thriving musical life based on choral singing with instrumental accompaniment, composing their own music and using the music of their contemporaries.

2. The Moravians first came to America in 1735, established a settlement in Savannah, Georgia, and began their missionary work among the Indians and Blacks.

3. In 1740 the "Moravian Brethren" moved to Nazareth, Pennsylvania, and in 1741 established a permanent settlement at Bethlehem.

    a. Groups also settled in Lititz (1740) and, most importantly, in Salem [Winston-Salem], North Carolina (1753).

B. Music (1750-1810)

1. The Moravians had traditionally been a singing group and the singing of hymns and chorales was an important part of their religious and community life.

2. Sacred music of high quality for voices with instrumental accompaniment and chamber music was composed by outstanding Moravian musicians who generally followed European models.

3. A *Collegium Musicum* was organized about 1744 and performed the instrumental accompaniments for the sacred choral music. By the end of the century the small orchestra had performed chamber music and symphonies by **Johann Christoph Bach, Johann Stamitz, Handel, Johann Gottlieb Graun, Haydn,** and **Mozart**, as well as ensemble works by the Moravian composers.

    a. In 1780 the orchestra consisted of 4 violins, 1 viola, 2 cellos, 2 flutes, 2 oboes, 2 horns, and 2 trumpets.

4. The traditional trombone "choir" (treble, alto, tenor and bass trombones) played for community and religious events, including funerals, weddings and special days in the church year.

C. Moravian composers (1766-1850)

1. The Moravian composers wrote principally for the church and had been well trained in their native land, with the exception of **John Antes** who was born in Pennsylvania.

2. The composers wrote sacred anthems, arias and chorales with instrumental accompaniments. These usually included strings and *continuo* (organ), rarely woodwinds or brass. Music for instruments alone played a minor role.

    a. *Bohemian Brethren* (*Hymnal*, No. 522)

3. **Jeremias Dencke** (1725-1795)

    a. **Dencke** arrived in Bethlehem from Germany in 1760 and wrote sacred music with instrumental accompaniment as early as 1766. He was probably the first Moravian to write music of quality and high rank.

    b. *Canto Primo* from *Doxologie* (facsimile: *B* 5, Plate B)

    c. *Christmas Music*, 1767 (facsimile: *B* 5, Plates C, D, E))

    d. *Freuet euch, ihr Töchter Seines Volks* (Oh, be glad, ye daughters of his people) (*M* 12); *Gehet in der Geruch Seines Bräutigams-Namens* (Go ye forth in his name) (*M* 12); *Ich will singen von einem Könige* (I will sing of the King) (*M* 12); *Meine Seele erhebet den Herrn* (My soul doth magnify the Lord) (*M* 12)

    e. *O blessed art ye my folk* (*M* 7)

4. **Johannes Herbst** (1735-1812)

    a. **Herbst** was educated in Herrnhut, Bohemia, where he learned the watchmaker trade. In 1787 he came to Lancaster, Pennsylvania, was a preacher in Lititz (1791-1811) and then moved to Salem where he died the following year. **Herbst** was the most prolific composer among the Moravians; he wrote some 125 anthems and sacred songs in addition to copying an enormous amount of music by other Moravians and European composers.

        1) *I will go in the strength of the Lord* (*M* 7); Three sacred songs for soprano (*M* 7).

5.   **John Antes** (1740-1811)

    a.   **Antes** was the first native-born Moravian composer, although he spent much of his life in Germany, Egypt and England (1781). A gifted composer of accompanied anthems and arias, **Antes**, while in Cairo also composed *Three Trios for 2 Violins and Violoncello* (1779-1781).

    b.   *Tre Trii, per due Violini e Violoncello, Obligato*, Allegro (*MinA*, p. 74)

    c.   *Surely He has borne our griefs, c.* 1795 (SATB and strings) (*MinA*, p. 70; *M* 9)

    d.   *Go, Congregation, Go! c.* 1795, (aria for soprano and strings) (*M* 9, 12)

    e.   *O welch ein Licht* (What splendid rays) (*AH*, p. 267)

6.   **John Frederick Peter** (1746-1813)

    a.   **Peter** was born of German parents and came to Bethlehem from Holland in 1770. An outstanding composer, **Peter** composed more than a hundred arias and anthems, some for double chorus, and six *Quintetti à Due Violini, Due Viole e Violoncello* written in Salem in 1789, the first chamber music written by an American composer. Like **Herbst**, he also copied much European music for use in America.

    b.   *Quintet V*, Adagio (*MinA*, p. 81; *M* 11)

    c.   *I will make an everlasting covenant*, 1782 (aria for soprano and strings) (*MinA*, p. 84; *M* 9)

    d.   *Leite mich in Deiner Wahrheit* (Lead me in Thy truth), 1770 (facsimile: *B* 5, Plates F, G; *M* 12)

7.   **David Moritz Michael** (1751-1825)

    a.   In addition to anthems and sacred arias, **Michael** is known for his 14 ensemble suites (*Parthien*) for clarinets, horns, bassoon, trumpet or flute (*c.* 1807). He also composed a cantata on Psalm 130 in 1805 and conducted a performance of **Haydn's** *Creation* in 1811.

    b.   *Parthia*, No. 1, Allegro for 2 clarinets, trumpet, 2 horns, bassoon (*MinA*, p. 87; *M* 9)

    c.   *Hearken! Stay close to Jesus Christ* (soprano with SATB and strings) (*M* 1)

8.   **Georg Gottfried Müller** (1762-1821)

    a.   **Müller**, a composer of arias with string accompaniment, was the last of the main group of Moravian composers.

    b.   *Lamb of God Thou shalt remain forever*

    c.   *Mein Heiland geht ins Leiden* (My Saviour lies in anguish) (*M* 12)

D.   Early organs

  1.   **Johann Gottlob Klemm** (1690-1762)

    a.   **Klemm**, a Separatist, came from Germany to Philadelphia in 1733; he possibly had learned the art of organ building from **Gottfried Silbermann**. In 1739 **Klemm** installed an organ for Trinity Parish, New York. With Gustaff Hesselius he installed an organ in the Moravian Church in Bethlehem in 1746. **Klemm** moved to New York and later (1757) retired to Bethlehem and became associated with **David Tannenberg**.

  2.   **David Tannenberg** (1728-1804)

    a.   **Tannenberg**, a Moravian who became known as the "best organ builder in the Colonies," designed and built about 50 organs. He migrated to Bethlehem in 1749 and became associated with **Klemm** in 1758; the two moved to Nazareth where they built two small organs.

E.   The tradition of Moravian music was handed down to the present generation by **John Christian Till** (1762-1844) and **Peter Wolle** (1792-1871), both pupils of **John Frederick Peter**. It was not until the 1930's, however, that interest in the larger collections of Moravian music began to be investigated, gradually published, performed and eventually catalogued.

BIBLIOGRAPHY

Books

1. Armstrong, William H. *Organs for America: The Life and Work of David Tannenberg*. Philadelphia: University of Pennsylvania Press, 1967.
2. *The Catalog of the Johannes Herbst Collection*, ed. Marilyn Gombosi. Chapel Hill: The University of North Carolina Press, 1970.
3. *Catalog of the Salem Congregation Music*, ed. Frances Cumnock. Chapel Hill: The University of North Carolina Press, 1980.
4. David, Hans Theodore. *Musical Life in the Pennsylvania Settlements of the Unitas Fratrum*. Winston-Salem, NC: The Moravian Music Foundation, 1959.
5. David, Hans T., and Albert G. Rau. *A Catalog of Music by American Moravians, 1742-1842*. Bethlehem: The Moravian Seminary and College for Women, 1938; reprint: New York: AMS Press, 1970.
6. Drummond, Robert Rutherford. *Early German Music in Philadelphia*. New York: D. Appleton & Co., 1910; reprint: New York: Da Capo Press, 1970.
7. Eliason, Robert E. *Early American Brass Makers*. Nashville: The Brass Press, 1979.
8. Friedman, Robert. *Mennonite Piety through the Centuries: Its Genius and Its Literature*. Goshen, IN: The Mennonite Historical Society, 1949.
9. Gerson, Robert A. *Music in Philadelphia*. Philadelphia: Theodore Presser, 1940; reprint: Westport, CT: Greenwood Press, 1970.
10. Gollin, Gillian L. *Moravians in Two Worlds: A Study in Changing Communities*. New York: Columbia University Press, 1967.
11. Good, Mary Bigler. *Some Musical Background of Pennsylvania*. Carrolltown, PA: Carrolltown News Press, 1932.
12. Grider, Rufus A. *Historical Notes on Music in Bethlehem, Pa. (1741-1871)*. Winston-Salem, NC: The Moravian Music Foundation, 1957.
13. Kriebel, Howard Wiegner. *The Schwenkfelders in Pennsylvania, A Historical Sketch*. Lancaster, PA: Pennsylvania German Society, 1904; reprint: New York: AMS Press, 1971.
14. Levering, Joseph M. *A History of Bethlehem, Pennsylvania, 1741-1892*. Bethlehem, PA: Times Publishing Co., 1903.
15. Mann, Thomas. *Doctor Faustus; the Life of a German Composer, Adrian Leverkühn, as Told by a Friend*, tr. Helen Tracy Lowe-Porter. New York: Alfred A. Knopf, 1948.
16. McCorkle, Donald M. *The Collegium Musicum Salem: Musicians and Importance*. Salem, NC: Moravian Music Foundation, 1956.
17. National Society of the Colonial Dames of America (Pennsylvania). *Music and Musical Life in Pennsylvania in the Eighteenth Century*, 3 vols. Philadelphia: Printed for the Society, 1926-1947; New York: AMS Press, 1972. (Includes facsimiles of "The Hymn Book of Magister Johannes Kelpius," translated by Dr. Christopher Witt and the libretto of "The Fool's Opera" by Anthony Aston)
18. *Records of the Mormons in North Carolina*. Raleigh, NC: Publications of the North Carolina Historical Commission, 1922.
19. Rohrer, Gertrude M. *Music and Musicians of Pennsylvania*. Philadelphia: Pennsylvania Federation of Music Clubs, 1940; reprint: Port Washington, NY: Kennikat Press, 1971.
20. Sachse, Julius Friedrich. *The Music of the Ephrata Cloister* (also Conrad Beissel's Treatise On Music as Set Forth in a Preface to the "Turtel Taube" of 1747). Lancaster, PA: Printed for the Author, 1903; reprint: New York: AMS Press, 1971.
21. Seipt, Allen Anders. *Schwenkfelder Hymnology*. Philadelphia: Americana Germanica Press, 1909.
22. Smith, C. Henry. *The Story of the Mennonites*, 5th edition revised. Newton, KS: Mennonite Publication Office, 1957.

23.   Walters, Raymond. *The Bethlehem Bach Choir. An Historical and Interpretative Sketch*. Boston: 1918; reprint: New York: AMS Press, 1971.

Articles

1.   Blakely, Lloyd G. "Johann Conrad Beissel and Music of the Ephrata Cloister" (includes translation of the Treatise from the '*Turtel-Taube*'). *Journal of Research in Music Education* 15 (1967), pp. 120-138.

2.   Bornemann, Robert. "Johannes Kelpius, Mystic Hymn Writer (Wissahickon Brotherhood)." *Journal of Church Music* 18 (June, 1976), pp. 13-14.

3.   Carlson, Charles Howard. "The Ephrata Cloister's Music of Yesteryear." *Music Journal* 22 (1964), pp. 52, 118-120.

4.   David, Hans Theodore. "Background for Bethlehem." *Magazine of Art* 32 (1939), pp. 222-225.

5.   ––––––"Ephrata and Bethlehem in Pennsylvania: A Comparison." *Papers of the American Musicological Society* (Annual meeting, 1941), pp. 97-104.

6.   Engel, Carl. "Views and Reviews (*Turtel-Taube*)." *MQ* 14 (1928), pp. 301-303.

7.   Finney, Theodore M. "The Collegium Musicum at Lititz, Pennsylvania, during the 18th Century." *Papers of the American Musicological Society*, 1937.

8.   Griffin, Francis. "The Moravian Musical Heritage." *The Hymn* 19 (1968), pp. 101-103.

9.   Hall, Harry H. "Early Sounds of Moravian Brass Music in America: A Cultural Note From Colonial Georgia." *Brass Quarterly* 7 (1964), pp. 115-123.

10.   ––––––"The Moravian Wind Ensemble Tradition in America." *Journal of Band Research* 1 (1965), pp. 27-29.

11.   Hess, Albert G. "John F. Peter." *MQ* 23 (1937), p. 306.

12.   ––––––"Observations on *The Lamenting Voice of the Hidden Love*." *JAMS* 5 (1952), pp. 211-223.

13.   Lowens, Irving: "Moravian Music–Neglected American Heritage." *MA* 78 (February, 1958), pp. 30-31.

14.   Marrocco, W. Thomas. "The Notation in American Sacred Music Collections." *Acta Musicologica* 36 (1964), pp. 136-142.

15.   Mauer, Joseph A. "Moravian Church Music (1457-1957)." *American Guild of Organists Quarterly* 2 (1957), p. 6.

16.   McCorkle, Donald M. "Early American Moravian Music." *Music Joural* 13 (November, 1955), pp. 11, 45-47.

17.   ––––––"John Antes, American Dilittante." *MQ* 42 (1956), pp. 486-499.

18.   ––––––"The Moravian Contribution to American Music." *Notes* 13 (1956), pp. 597-606.

19.   Nolte, Ewald Valentin. "Early Moravian Music in America." *Journal of Church Music* 8 (April, 1966), pp. 2-4; *Choral Journal* 8, No. 2 (1967), p. 11.

20.   Rau, Albert G. "John Frederick Peter." *MQ* 23 (1937), pp. 306-313.

21.   Redway, Virginia Larkin. "James Parker and the 'Dutch Church'." *MQ* 24 (1938), pp. 481-500.

22.   Stolba, K Marie. "Evidence for Quartets by John Antes, American-Born Moravian Composer." *JAMS* 33 (1980), pp. 565-574.

23.   William, George W. "Jacob Eckhard and His Choirmaster's Book." *JAMS* 7 (1954), pp. 41-47.

Music

1. *Early American Moravian Church Music*, ed. Clarence Dickinson. Melville, NY: Belwin-Mills (H. W. Gray), 1954.
2. *Ephrata Cloister Chorales; A Collection of Hymns and Anthems Composed by Conrad Beissel*, ed. Russell Paul Getz. New York: G. Schirmer, 1971.
3. *Hymnal and Liturgies for the Moravian Church (Unitas Fratrum)*. Bethlehem, PA: Provincial Synod, 1920.
4. Hohmann, Walter, H., and Lester Hostetler. *The Mennonite Hymnary*. Newton, KS: The Mennonite Publication Office, 1940.
5. *The Johannes Herbst Collection.* New York: University Music Editions, 1976- (manuscript reproductions on microfiche)
6. *The Moravian Music Series*, ed. Karl Kroeger. New York: Carl Fischer.
7. *A Moravian Sampler*, ed. Karl Kroeger. Winston-Salem, NC: The Moravian Music Foundation, 1974. (Moravian Music Foundation Publication, No. 7)
8. *Music of the Moravians*, ed. Hans T. David. New York: New York Public Library, 1938-1939.
9. *New Moramus Editions of the Moravian Music Foundation*, ed. Karl Kroeger. Oceanside, NY: , 1976.
10. *Old Melodies of the South*, compiled by Carrie Jacobs Bond, tr. Mary Gillen and Oliver Chalifoux. Chicago: Jacobs-Bond & Son, 1918; reprint: New York: Gordon Press.
11. Peter, John Frederick. *Six Quintets*, ed. Hans T. David. New York: New York Public Library, 1939; New York: C. F. Peters, 1955. (Music of the Moravians, No. 2)
12. *Ten Sacred Songs*, ed. Hans T. David. New York: New York Public Library, 1947; New York: C. F. Peters, 1954.
13. *Three Sacred Songs for Soprano*, ed. Thor Johnson and Donald M. McCorkle. New York: Boosey & Hawkes, 1958.
14. *Twelve Moravian Chorales*, ed. Thor Johnson and Donald M. McCorkle. New York: Boosey & Hawkes, 1957.

Original of the seven-part motet
Gott ein Herrscher aller Heiden from the **Wunder-Spiel**
by Conrad Beissel (Ephrata, 1754)

Modern edition of the seven-part motet
Gott ein Herrscher aller Heiden from the **Wunder-Spiel**
by Conrad Beissel (Ephrata, 1754)

THE FIRST AMERICAN COMPOSERS (1759-1800)

Francis Hopkinson – James Lyon

I. **Francis Hopkinson** (1737-1791)

A. **Hopkinson**, born in Philadelphia on September 21, was a man of many talents.
  1. He became a lawyer in 1761, was a delegate to the Continental Congress (1776), was one of the signers of the Declaration of Independence and served as a judge from 1779 to his death. Among his personal friends were George Washington and Thomas Jefferson. In addition to writing many poems, essays and pamphlets, he was a skilled designer and draftsman.
  2. **Hopkinson's** interest in the harpsichord, which he learned at the age of 17, resulted in his inventing a new method of quilling a harpsichord. As a cultivated amateur musician he often joined music ensembles and gave concerts. He was particularly attracted to and copied the music of **Handel, Corelli, Galuppi, Geminiani, Stamitz** and **Arne**. In 1770 he succeeded **James Bremner**, his harpsichord teacher, as organist of Christ Church, Philadelphia.
  3. **Hopkinson** not only taught psalmody but also compiled a tune book for congregational singing. He also composed many songs.
      a. *My days have been so wondrous free*, 1759, on a text by Thomas Parnell (*MinA*, p. 103; *B* 17, p. 199; *M* 7; *M* 5)
          1) In 1759-1760 **Hopkinson** compiled in his own hand a collection (never printed) of 109 pieces, many of which are songs from operas and cantatas of known composers (**Handel, Arne, Pepusch, Boyce, Purcell**), anthems and hymns. Among them are several compositions by **Hopkinson**, one of which is the famous song, said to be the first musical composition by a native American.
          2) The music is written in two parts in the style of English composers of the time.
      b. Other songs by **Hopkinson** (initialed "F. H.") in the manuscript collection are:
          1) *The Garland* (*B* 17, p. 79)
          2) *Oh! come to Mason boroughs grove* (*B* 17, p. 79)
          3) *With pleasure have I past [sic] my days* (*B* 17, p. 80)
          4) *The 23rd Psalm* (*B* 17, p. 92; *M* 95
          5) *An Anthem from the 114th Psalm*, dated "F. H. 1760" (*B* 17, p. 200; *BCAC*, p. 6)
  4. *A Collection of Psalm Tunes with a few Anthems and Hymns. Some of them Entirely New: for the Use of the United Churches of Christ Church and St. Peter's Church in Philadelphia 1763*
      a. A short introduction to this collection gives instruction on note values, clefs, keeping time and intonation. Included also are 21 anonymous pieces, most of which are in three voices.
      b. *Philadelphia* (Arise and see the glorious sun) (*AH*, p. 198)
  5. *The Psalms of David, with the Ten Commandments, Creed, Lord's Prayer, &c. In Metre Also the Catechism, Confession of Faith, Liturgy &c. Translated from the Dutch. For the Use of the Reformed Protestant Dutch Church of the City of New York.* (Philadelphia, 1767)
      a. In 1764 **Hopkinson** was employed by the Consistory of the Dutch Reformed Church of New York to make an English translation of the Psalms. The task, completed by

December, 1765, was to adopt the common meter texts of the popular Tate and Brady *"A New Version of the Psalms"* to the meters of the Dutch Psalter which were mostly ten syllables to a line, four to six lines to a stanza.

6.   *Seven Songs for the Harpsichord or Forte Piano. The Words and Music Composed by Francis Hopkinson* (M 1)

   a.   In 1788 Thomas Dobson of Philadelphia published and sold a collection of eight songs (one was added after the title-page was printed) dedicated to George Washington. In the dedication **Hopkinson** wrote: "However small the Reputation may be that I shall derive from this Work I cannot, I believe, be refused the Credit of being the first Native of the United States who has produced a Music Composition." Washington replied (in part): "I can neither sing one of the songs, nor raise a single note on any instrument to convince the unbelieving. But I have, however, one argument which will prevail with persons of true taste (at least in America)—I can tell them that *it is the production of Mr. Hopkinson*" (February 5, 1789). A copy was also sent to **Hopkinson's** friend, Thomas Jefferson, then in Paris.

      1)   As stated in an advertisement in the *Federal Gazette* of November 29, 1788: "These songs are composed in an easy, familiar style, intended for young Practioners on the Harpsichord or Forte Piano, and is the first Work of this kind attempted in the United States."

   b.   *My gen'rous heart disdains the slave of love to be* (B 17, p. 204; *GB-B* 30, p. 41)

7.   *A Toast*, 1778 (*MinA*, p. 105; *FVPS*, p. 711; *LEAM*, p. 72; *M* 4; *M* 6)

   a.   George Washington, leader of the new nation, was the subject of many songs. This one, set by **Francis Hopkinson**, apparently has several musical fragments borrowed from the English national anthem.

II.   James Lyon (1735-1794)

A.   **James Lyon**, composer and editor of church music, was born in Newark, "East New Jersey," on July 1. He graduated from New Jersey College (later known as Princeton) in 1759, taught in a singing school in Philadelphia in 1760 and became a Presbyterian minister in 1762. In 1764 he moved to Nova Scotia and after eight years (1772) settled in Machias, Maine, where he spent the remainder of his life.

   1.   *Urania or A Choice Collection of Psalm-Tunes, Anthems, and Hymns*, 1761   (M 2)

      a.   According to an advertisement which appeared both in the *Pennsylvania Gazette* and *Pennsylvania Journal* of May 22, 1760, "this is the first Attempt of the kind to spread the Art of Psalmody, in its Perfection, thro' our American Colonies."

      b.   The important compilation of American psalmody is larger than any previous American tune book; it is the first to include English "fuging-tunes," the first set generally for four voices (two- and three-voice pieces are included) and the first to identify native (American) compositions; in it appear the first printed examples of music by **Lyon, Hopkinson** and **William Tuckey**. Neverthless it is deeply rooted in the tradition of English-American psalmody, not at all new in the musical life of the Colonists; the book was widely used.

      c.   A twelve-page introduction outlines the "Gamut or Scale of Music," explains the values of notes and rests, syncopation, transposition and ornaments. Singing exercises defining all the intervals are included.

      d.   There is a total of 96 compositions including hymns (52), psalm tunes (32) and anthems (12).

         1)   Five of **Lyon's** own compositions appear: 1) *The 8th Psalm Tune* (p. 44; *LEAM*, p. 29), 2) *The 95th Psalm Tune* (p. 63), 3) *The 104th Psalm by Dr. Watts* (p. 194; *AH*, p. 209), 4) the anthem *The Lord descended from above* (*Two Celebrated Verses by Sternhold & Hopkins set to Music*) (p. 125) and 5) *Let the shrill trumpets* (*An Anthem taken from the 150th Psalm*) (p. 165).

a) In *"The Lord descended from above"* note the suggested text-painting on the words "rode," "cherubs," "cherubim" and "flying" (pp. 129, 130).

2) **Francis Hopkinson** is represented once with his arrangement of *"The 23rd Psalm Tune"* (p. 50) and **John Tufts** once, *"The New 100. Psalm Tune"* (p. 66).

3) There are several examples of the British fuging-tune: *"The 12th Psalm Tune"* (p. 46), *"The 15th Psalm Tune"* (p. 18) and *"The V Psalm Tune"* (p. 42; *GB-B* 30, p. 9). Note the fuging in pairs of parallel sixths and thirds (pp. 52-53).

4) The tune called *"Whitefield's,"* which is known as *"America,"* is set to the words "Come, Thou Almighty King" (p. 190; *MinA*, p. 106).

2. **Lyon's** continuing activity as a composer is further evidenced by the publication of two new compositions in **John Stickney's** (1744-1827) *Gentleman and Lady's Musical Companion*, 1774: *"Friendship"* and *"Machias."*

a. *Friendship* (*MinA*, p. 107; *BCAC*, p. 10)

1) One of **Lyon's** most important works, the ode, divided into three parts, makes use of unique florid passages.

b. *Chorus from the Military Glory of Great Britain* (*BCAM*, p. 22)

c. *Glory, Triumph, Vict'ry, Fame* (*LEAM*, p. 71)

d. *A Marriage Hymn* (*LEAM*, p. 30)

BIBLIOGRAPHY

Books

1. Benton, Rita. "The Early Piano in the United States," in *Music Libraries and Instruments*. London: Hinrichsen's Eleventh Music Book, 1961, pp. 200-204.

2. Brown, Thomas Allston. *History of the New York Stage, From the First Performance in 1732 to 1901*, 3 vols. New York: Dodd, Mead & Co., 1903; reprint: New York: Burt Franklin, 1969; New York: Blom, 1969.

3. Cripe, Helen Louise Petts. *Thomas Jefferson and Music*. Charlottesville: University Press of Virginia, 1974.

4. Dichter, Harry, and Elliott Shapiro. *Early American Sheet Music: Its Lure and Its Lore, 1768-1889*. New York: R. R. Bowker, 1941; New York: Dover Publications, 1977.

5. Fisher, William Arms. *One Hundred and Fifty Years of Music Publishing in the United States, 1783-1933*. Boston: Oliver Ditson, 1933.

6. Graf, Herbert. *The Opera and Its Future in America*. New York: W. W. Norton, 1941; reprint: Port Washington, NY: Kennikat Press, 1973.

7. Hastings, George Everett. *The Life and Works of Francis Hopkinson*. Chicago: University of Chicago Press, 1926; reprint: New York: Russell & Russell, 1968.

8. Hopkinson, Francis. "Dedication to His Excellency George Washington, Esquire," in *The American Composer Speaks; A Historical Anthology, 1770-1965*, ed. Gilbert Chase. Baton Rouge: Louisiana State University Press, 1966, pp. 38-40.

9. Howard, John Tasker. *The Music of George Washington's Time*. Washington, DC: United States Government, 1931.

10. Johnson, H. Earle. *Musical Interludes in Boston, 1795-1830*. New York: Columbia University Press, 1943; reprint: New York: AMS Press, 1967.

11. Lawrence, Vera Brodsky. *Music for Patriots, Politicians and Presidents: Harmonies and Discords of the First Hundred Years*. New York: Macmillan, 1975.

12. Madeira, Louis C. *Annals of Music in Philadelphia and History of the Musical Fund Society*. Philadelphia: J. B. Lippincott, 1896; reprint: New York: Da Capo Press, 1973.

13. Messiter, Arthur Henry. *A History of the Choir and Music of Trinity Church, New York*. New York: E. S. Gorham, 1906; reprint: New York: AMS Press, 1971.

14. *The Psalms of David . . . Translated from the Dutch. For the Use of the Reformed Protes-*

tant Dutch Church of the City of New-York, tr. Francis Hopkinson. New York: James Parker, 1767.

15. Sonneck, Oscar George Theodore. *Early Opera in America*. New York: Benjamin Blom, 1915; reprint: New York: Benjamin Blom, 1963.

16. ———"Early American Opera," in *Miscellaneous Studies in the History of Music*. New York: Macmillan, 1921; reprint: New York: Da Capo Press, 1968, pp. 16-92.

17. ———*Francis Hopkinson and James Lyon*. Washington, DC: H. L. McQueen, 1905; reprint: New York: Da Capo Press, 1967.

18. ———"Benjamin Franklin's Musical Side," in *Suum Cuique Essays in Music*. New York: G. Schirmer, 1916, 1944; reprint: Freeport, NY: Books for Libraries Press, 1969.

19. ———"The Musical Side of Our First Presidents," in *Suum Cuique Essays in Music*. New York: G. Schirmer, 1916, 1944; reprint: Freeport, NY: Books for Libraries Press, 1969.

20. Stoutamire, Albert. *Music of the Old South: Colony to Confederacy*. Rutherford: Fairleigh Dickinson University Press, 1972.

Articles

1. Aaron, Amy. "William Tuckey, A Choirmaster in Colonial New York." *MQ* 64 (1978), pp. 79-97.

2. Albrecht, Otto E. "Francis Hopkinson, Musician, Poet and Patriot." *Library Chronicle of the University of Pennsylvania* 6 (1938), p. 3.

3. ———"Opera in Philadelphia, 1800-1830." *JAMS* 32 (1979), pp. 499-515.

4. Cumming, Robert E. "Francis Hopkinson, America's First Composer." *Music Clubs Magazine* 46, No. 4 (1967), pp. 18-19.

5. Davis, Josephine K. R. "Young Opera in Young America." *Music Journal* 21 (October, 1963), pp. 68-69.

6. Eaton, Quaintance. " 'A Yankee Trick' (First American Opera on a Native Subject)." *Opera News* 31 (April 1, 1967), pp. 6-7.

7. Goldberg, Isaac. "The First American Musician." *American Mercury* 14 (May, 1928), pp. 67-75.

8. Mahan, Katherine Hines. "Hopkinson and Reinagle: Patriot-Musicians of Washington's Time." *Music Educators Journal* 62 (April, 1976), pp. 40-50.

9. McKay, David. "*The Fashionable Lady*: The First Opera by an American." *MQ* 65 (1979), pp. 360-367.

10. Maurer, Maurer. "A Musical Family in Colonial Virginia." *MQ* 34 (1948), pp. 358-364.

11. Merkling, Frank. "Yankee Doodle opera—How an Immigrant Art Form Took to the Rich Soil of the New World." *Opera News* 40 (June, 1976), pp. 10-13; 41 (July, 1976), pp. 8-12.

12. Molnar, John W. "A Collection of Music in Colonial Virginia; the Ogle Inventory." *MQ* 49 (1963), pp. 150-162.

13. Norton, M. D. Herter. "Haydn in America (Before 1820)." *MQ* 18 (1932), pp. 309-337.

14. Pierce, Edwin Hall. "On Some Old Bugle-Calls of the U. S. Navy." *MQ* 18 (1932), pp. 134-139.

15. Redway, Virginia Larkin. "A New York Concert in 1736." *MQ* 22 (1936), pp. 170-177.

16. Smith, Carleton Sprague. "The 1774 Psalm Book of the Reformed Protestant Dutch Church in New York City." *MQ* 34 (1948), pp. 84-96.

17. Williams, George W. "Charleston Church Music, 1562-1833." *JAMS* 7 (1954), pp. 35-40.

18. Winter, Marian Hannah. "American Theatrical Dancing from 1750 to 1800." *MQ* 24 (1938), pp. 58-73.

19. Wright, Edith A. "James Lyon's 'Friendship'." *Notes* 4 (1947), pp. 293-295.

Music

1. Hopkinson, Francis. *Seven Songs for the Harpsichord or Forte Piano* (1788). Philadelphia: Musical Americana, 1954, 1959.
2. Lyon, James. *Urania. A Choice Collection of Psalm-Tunes, Anthems, and Hymns.* Philadelphia: Henry Dawkins, 1761; reprint: New York: Da Capo Press, 1974.
3. *Music of the American Revolution*, arr. Richard Bales. New York: Peer International Corporation, 1953 (Suite No. 1); 1956 (Suite No. 2).
4. *Music from the Days of George Washington*, ed. Carl Engel and W. Oliver Strunk. Washington, DC: United States George Washington Bicentennial Commission, 1931; reprint: New York: AMS Press, 1970.
5. *The Music Washington Knew*, ed. William Arms Fisher and N. Clifford Page. Boston: Oliver Ditson, 1931; reprint: Bryn Mawr, PA: Theodore Presser, 1976.
6. *Songbook of the American Revolution*, ed. Carolyn Rabson. Peaks Island, ME: NEO Press, 1974.
7. *Songs by Francis Hopkinson*, arr. Oliver Daniel. New York: Carl Fischer, 1951.
8. *Songs from the Williamsburg Theatre: A Selection of Fifty Songs Performed on the Stage in Williamsburg in the Eighteenth Century*, ed. John W. Molnar. Charlottesville: University Press of Virginia, 1972.
9. *A Williamsburg Songbook*, ed. John Edmunds. New York: Holt, Rinehart and Winston, 1964.
10. Yerbury, Grace D. *Song in America from Early Times to About 1850*. Metuchen, NJ: The Scarecrow Press, 1971.

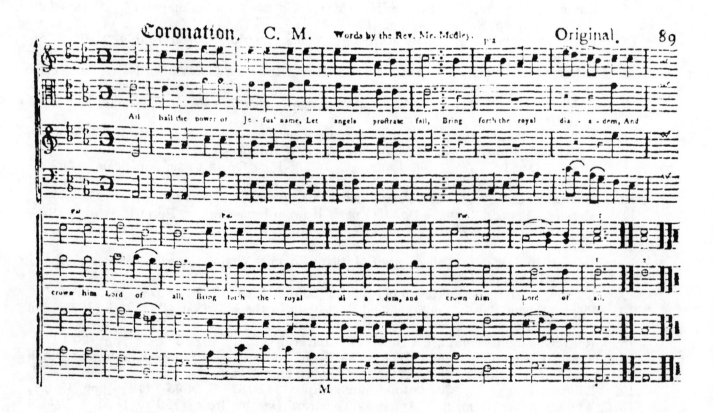

From **The Union Harmony** by Oliver Holden, 1793

Original MS of Hopkinson's "My days have been so wondrous free," 1759

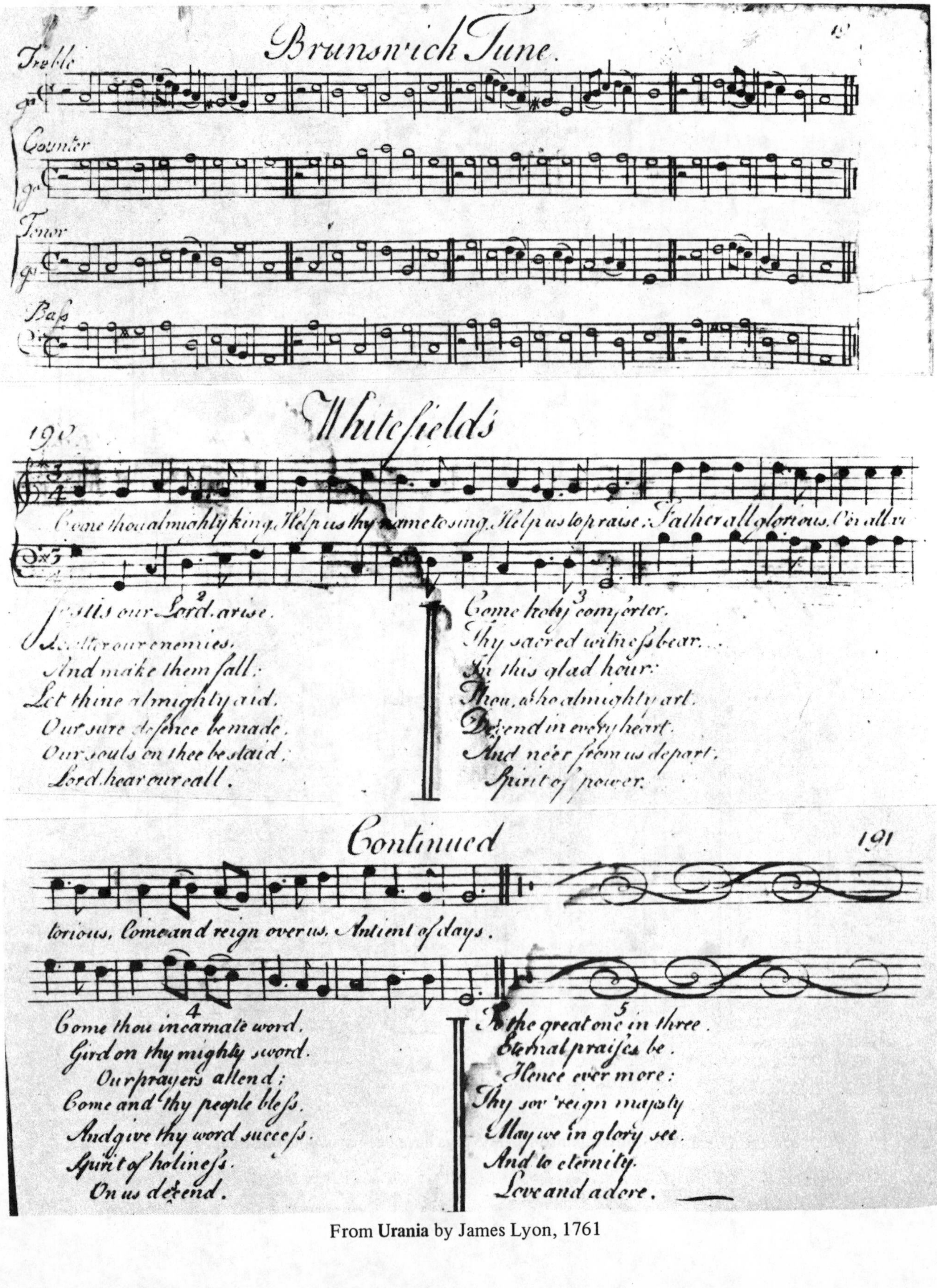

From **Urania** by James Lyon, 1761

MUSIC IN NEW ENGLAND (1770-1820)

New England Singing Schools
William Billings — Andrew Law
Other Composers — Secular Music

I. New England Singing Schools

A. In the early eighteenth century the singing schools resulted from a desire among Puritan ministers to improve the singing in their churches. As has been noted (*Outline*, p. 20) the publishing of tune books, generally with instructional introductions, began in the 1720's and continued well into the nineteenth century. Although the singing schools began mainly as church related activities, they nevertheless were as much secular institutions providing for secular and social outlets.

  1. Boston boasted of a "Society for Promoting Regular Singing" early in 1722.

  2. By the mid-eighteenth century the singing school idea had spread southward to New York (1754), Pennsylvania (late 1750's), South Carolina (1730) and Maryland (1765).

  3. The itinerant singing master, after holding classes on how to sing correctly, would often close his series by presenting a choral concert; he would move on to a new location to begin a new singing school and thus propagate his method and books to a new constituency.

  4. Singing schools of the mid-eighteenth century relied principally on tune books (**Tufts** and **Walter**) based on English psalters and hymnals. Even **Lyon's** *Urania* (1761) was largely indebted to English tune books circulating in the Colonies at the time.

  5. The first New England "tunesmiths" appeared in the 1770's with the compositions of **William Billings**.

    a. Before and during the Revolutionary War (1775-1783) considerable prejudice developed against everything English; music by American composers was particularly welcome. Sacred and secular music continued to develop, especially after the Revolutionary War; concerts became frequent; there were many music teachers and the folk-like music of the self-taught New England composers was extraordinarily popular.

    b. By the turn of the nineteenth century, with the coming to America of foreign musicians and the importation of European music, a strong reaction to the "crudities" of the music of New England composers set in.

II. William Billings (1746-1800)

A. **Billings**, a Boston tanner, patriot and self-taught musician, believed in American music for Americans. In spite of physical deformities, his energy and enthusiasm was extraordinary.

  1. An entry in the diary of Reverend William Bentley of Salem, Massachusetts, points up the main characteristics of **Billings'** life, his humble beginning, physical appearance, education and originality, early success and later decline: "He may justly be considered as the father of our New England music. Many who have imitated have excelled him, but none of them had better original powers . . . He was a singular man, of moderate size, short of one leg, with one eye, without any address, & with an uncommon negligence of person. Still he spake & sung & thought as a man above the common abilities. He died poor & neglected & and perhaps did too much neglect himself."

    2.   **Billings** died in poverty and was buried in an unmarked grave. His music continued to live in the folk hymn collections which sprang up in the South.

    3.   **Billings** made many contributions to musical life in America, stimulating the second revival of singing by founding singing societies and church choirs. He held a singing school in Weymouth in 1771; his singing class held in Stoughton in 1774 no doubt was in cooperation with Ye Olde Musical Society founded in 1762. The offshoot organization, Old Stoughton Musical Society, formed in 1786 probably profitted from **Billings'** earlier instruction.

    4.   **Billings** advocated the use of a pitch-pipe to pitch a tune, was wholeheartedly opposed to the "lining out" of tunes and the doleful psalm singing, and encouraged the use of a bass viol to reinforce a strong bass line.

B.   Musical style

    1.   **Billings** wrote in *The New England Psalm-Singer* concerning rules for composition "that Nature is the best Dictator, for all the hard, dry, studied rules that ever was prescribed, will not enable any person to form an air . . . without a Genius. It must be Nature, Nature must lay the Foundation, Nature must inspire the Thought." Furthermore he did not think himself "confined to any Rules for Composition, laid down by any that went before me."

    2.   **Billings** was strongly influenced by **William Tans'ur's** *Royal Melody Complete* in several of his volumes.

       a.   He made use of but did not invent the lively fuging style. The term "fuging" was used in its older meaning of free polyphonic imitation (rudimentary in his works) and not in the sense of "fugue."

       b.   His music is direct and strongly rhythmic, with effective use of syncopation.

       c.   His sturdy melodies are composed of simple intervals and modulation is rare.

         1)   The principal melody, generally in the tenor part, was usually sung by both sopranos and tenors.

       d.   The harmony is square cut and triads are used on any degree of the scale, in any order, giving a strong primitive quality to much of his music. Inversions of chords are frequent, but the seventh chord is not used. Parallel fifths are common.

C.   **Billings** published six volumes of music which include some 375 pieces; the second edition of one volume was extensively enlarged. A few single anthems were published during his lifetime. **Billings** also was editor for one issue of the *Boston Magazine*, October, 1783.

    1.   *The New England Psalm-Singer: or American Chorister*, 1770 (*CE* v. 1)

       a.   This is the first collection of sacred music composed wholly by an American. Although Paul Revere engraved the frontispiece, in all likelihood the engraving of the remainder of the book was done by **Josiah Flagg**.

       b.   It includes a chart showing the musical scale and solmization ("Gamut"), the terms and signs used in notation ("Musical Characters") and an "Explanation." "An Introduction to the Rules of Musick" and additional instructions are given.

       c.   There are 126 compositions, including 4 anthems, 4 canons, 3 fuging tunes and one set-piece. Most of the pieces are without text.

        1)   The text of the anthem is prose, whereas the text of the set-piece is verse.

       d.   *America* (*AH*, p. 138); *Sudbury* (*AH*, p. 156); *Amherst* (*AH*, p. 234)

    2.   *The Singing Master's Assistant, or Key to Practical Music*, 1778; 2nd edition, 1779; 3rd edition, 1781; 4th edition, *c.* 1786-1789 (*CE*, v. 2)

       a.   Having gone through four editions, this book appears to have been one of the most impressive tune books of the eighteenth century and is called "Billings' Best." It is the first tune book printed in America after the outbreak of the Revolutionary War. Evidence of its popularity may be noted in the fact that 44 of the compositions appeared in tune books by other compilers.

       b.   In all, the collection contains 71 pieces, including 8 anthems, one set-piece and 10 fuging tunes, "music with more than twenty times the power of the old slow tunes."

The majority of pieces are psalm and hymn tunes.

   1)   In response to the critics of his first book (1770) who complained that the harmonies were too sweet and the tunes too simple, **Billings** composed his famous *"Jargon;"* this contains no concords and shows that he could write dissonant music.

      a)   *Jargon* (*CE* v. 2, p. 263)

  c.   Tempo indications are given in various ways, based on the four "moods" of common time. Tempos were determined by counting the number of beats per second, relating the tempos to each other, and measuring the length of a pendulum that would swing the correct speed. (Refer to *The Continental Harmony*)

  d.   *Chester* (*CE*, v. 2, p. 72; *AH*, p. 143; *YONE*, p. 7)

   1)   This is probably **Billings'** most famous tune and became very popular as a Revolutionary War song. In this, as in other pieces by **Billings**, the principal melody is in the tenor part and was usually sung by sopranos and tenors.

  e.   *Savannah* (*AH*, p. 158); *Sullivan* (*AH*, p. 231); *Majesty* (*AH*, p. 24; *YONE*, p. 11)

3.   *Music in Miniature*, 1779 (*CE*, v. 2)

  a.   This textless compilation of 74 short pieces is printed on only 32 pages; it is the only book published by **Billings** in which he included music of other composers than himself (11 pieces). Of these 11 pieces one is attributed to **Abraham Wood** and the remaining 10 are popular pieces by European composers.

  b.   To confirm the idea that the fuge section is optional, in this volume **Billings** includes five pieces without a fuge which appear in other volumes with a fuge.

  c.   *Paris* (*AH*, p. 142)

4.   *The Psalm-Singer's Amusement Containing a number of fuging pieces and anthems*, 1781 (*CE*, v. 3; *EAM*, v. 20)

  a.   The collection contains 24 pieces spread over 101 pages; included in the volume are 7 anthems, 5 fuging tunes, 4 set-pieces and 8 tunes, some being extended.

   1)   **Billings** apparently refers to the fuging as a technique rather than a specific form since at least 16 pieces demonstrate fuging.

  b.   A later edition, evidently published posthumously by an anonymous compiler, includes a 16-page supplement of 26 psalm tunes and a short preface of instructions. The title page of the earlier edition was replaced by the following: *The Psalm-Singer's Amusement. Containing, I. A gamut and explanations of the rules of music, &c. II. A number of plain, easy and useful tunes, from the best authors, ancient and modern, and well adapted to schools, churches and families, in the United States.*

  c.   *Modern Music* (We are met for a concert of modern music) (*MinA*, p. 114; *EAM*, v. 2, p. 72; *BCAC*, p. 17)

   1)   The text, probably by **Billings**, gives his ideas of composition. This piece is said to be the "crowning achievement in his secular music." A prefatory note reads: "NB. after the Audience are seated & the Performers have taken the pitch slyly from the Leader the Song begins." It no doubt was frequently used at singing schools and concerts.

  d.   *Consonance* (*EAM*, v. 20, p. 81)

   1)   This song in praise of music, and one of **Billings'** few secular pieces, was called an anthem. The text is by Dr. Mather Byles.

  e.   *Thomas-Town* (*AH*, p. 175); *Jordan* (*AH*, p. 211)

5.   *The Suffolk Harmony consisting of psalm tunes, fuges and anthems*, 1786 (*CE* v. 3)

  a.   The book, without preface, contains 32 pieces; it opens with **Billings'** 10-stanza setting *"Shiloh for Christmas."* **Billings** documented each element of the text with scriptural verses in no less than 24 footnotes. This might have been done to dispel some of the Puritan antagonism against Christmas celebrations which persisted into the mid-nineteenth century in New England.

    b.   *Conquest* (*MinA*, p. 119); *The Lord is Risen Indeed* (*YONE*, p. 18)

    6.   *The Continental Harmony, containing, A Number of Anthems, Fuges, and Choruses, in several Parts, Never before published,* 1794 (*CE*, v. 4)

        a.   This book of 51 pieces includes 17 anthems and one set-piece.

        b.   After the title page is a chart of "Musical Characters," a series of 8 short lessons and "A Commentary on the preceding Rules; by way of Dialogue, between Master and Scholar." Here again **Billings** discusses major and minor as "sharp" and "flat" keys and observes that "the female part of the creation are much the greatest lovers of music . . . and I am very positive that nine tenths of them are much more pleased and entertained with a flat, than a sharp air."

        c.   In "Lesson VI" **Billings** determines tempos by the length and speed of a pendulum.

1)	C	Adagio	quarter note	60
2)	¢	Largo	quarter note	80
3)	2/2	Allegro	half note	60
4)	2/4		quarter note	120
5)	3/2		half note	60
6)	3/4		quarter note	80
7)	6/8		dotted quarter note	80
8)	6/4		dotted half note	80

           9)   Tempos indicated as 80 above are given as 75, but **Billings** probably preferred the faster tempos.

III. Andrew Law (1748-1821)

    A.   Born in Milford, Connecticut, on March 21, **Law** was the grandson of Governor Law of Connecticut; he graduated from Rhode Island College (later Brown University) in 1775, received a Master's degree in 1782 and an honorary Master's degree from Yale College in 1786. Having studied theology privately, he began preaching (1776) and was ordained at Hartford in 1787. Because of his interest in music, he spent most of his time composing, teaching in singing schools and compiling song books. He conducted singing schools in New England, New York, New Jersey, Pennsylvania, Maryland and as far south as the Carolinas.

        1.   Although an advocate of the florid fuging tune, later in life **Law** spoke and wrote disparagingly of the creativity of the American musical pioneers and actively opposed the music of **William Billings**; he worked to promote "better music" by letting anyone become "acquainted with the sublime and beautiful compositions of the great Masters of Music."

        2.   **Law** encouraged the establishment of copyright laws; like **Billings** he was among the first to be granted legal copyrights for his music.

        3.   **Law** introduced to America, following the fashion of European composers, the idea of setting the melody in the soprano instead of the tenor as was customary. The soprano thus was often indicated by the use of the word "Air."

        4.   **Law** also introduced in 1803 the use of "shape" or "character" notes without staff lines; his system never became popular.

           a.   Another plan of notation did, however, become very successful. In 1801 **William Smith** and **William Little**, singing school teachers in Philadelphia, published their *The Easy Instructor, or A New Method of Teaching Sacred Harmony* in which they promoted the use of the same "shape" notes (in reversed order to those of **Law**) but located on staff lines which no doubt insured their success.

        5.   Included in **Law's** output are at least eight major publications which went through many editions and revisions. During the years 1777 to 1785 **Law** published books to satisfy the needs of almost all levels of American musical participation: *Select Har-*

mony (1779, 1782) is a general compilation which contains all the important styles and forms of American sacred music; *A Select Number of Plain Tunes* (1781) contains tunes to which the metrical psalms may be sung; *Rudiments of Music* (1783) is an inexpensive instruction book with simple tunes for practice to be used in the singing schools for beginners; and *A Collection of Hymns* (1783) is focused toward more skilled singers who preferred modern hymns over the psalm tunes and European-styled music over the native American music.

a.   *A Select Number of Plain Tunes Adapted to Congregational Worship*, Cheshire, 1781
  1)   The collection contains 54 psalm tunes and was designed to be a tune supplement to the standard psalm book.
  2)   *Bunker Hill* (*LEAM*, p. 90; *AH*, p. 140; *MinA*, p. 120)
    a)   The tune displays several "primitive" Yankee characteristics: modal chord progressions, open and parallel fifths, minor triads on the fifth degree of the scale and lack of harmonic progression toward a tonic.

b.   *Select Harmony*, Cheshire, December, 1778
  1)   Within a few months of the December publication, **Law** republished the *Select Harmony* and more than doubled the contents (totaling 100 pages) and added to the introduction; the new title reads: *Select Harmony, Containing in a plain and concise Manner, the Rules of Singing: Together with A Collection of Psalm Tunes, Hymns and Anthems*, 1779. Later editions appeared in 1782 and 1812.
    a)   With respect to his deep concern for copyrights, the drawing on the new title page is exactly the same as that of **John Lyon's** *Urania*, 1761.
  2)   *A Hymn on Peace* (*FVPS*, p. 840); *Portsmouth* (*YONE*, p. 21); *Blendon* (*LEAM*, p. 43)

c.   *The Art of Singing*, 1794
  1)   This work is composed of three separate works: 1) *The Musical Primer*, 2) *The Christian Harmony* and 3) *The Musical Magazine*. As separate works they did not always appear as parts of *The Art of Singing* and there is some confusion on the edition numbering (*B* 5, pp. 271-282).
    a)   *The Musical Primer* was printed singly in 1793, 1810 and 1817, and the first two issues of *The Musical Magazine* had been published respectively in 1792 and 1793.
  2)   The first edition of *The Art of Singing* was published in 1794; each of the three parts was paged separately. This included the second edition of *The Musical Primer* and only the first volume of *The Christian Harmony*; a second volume of *The Christian Harmony* was published in 1796.
  3)   The second edition of *The Art of Singing* (called by **Law** the third edition) was published in 1800; it contains 208 pages with consecutive pagination and includes 137 compositions.
  4)   *The Art of Singing*, third edition, 1803 (called the fourth edition by **Law**) contains "additions and improvements" and is "Printed upon a new plan." Shape-notes are used without staff lines, but the notes are placed relatively higher or lower.
    a)   Major keys are called "sharp" keys and minor keys are called "flat."
    (1)   The "sharp" key of F requires one flat and the "flat" key of B requires two sharps. The seventh degree in "flat" keys is raised by an accidental placed before the note.
    b)   Four syllables are used with the following shape notes:

"faw" □   "sol" ○   "law" ◺   "mi" ◇

    (1)   "Mi" is the seventh degree of the "sharp" keys and second degree of the "flat" keys; this constitutes a "movable do" system.

(2)   Major ("sharp") keys:

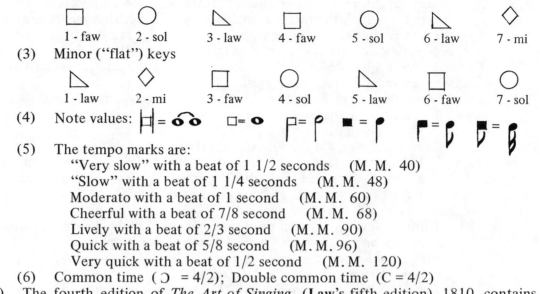

   1 - faw   2 - sol   3 - law   4 - faw   5 - sol   6 - law   7 - mi

(3)   Minor ("flat") keys

   1 - law   2 - mi   3 - faw   4 - sol   5 - law   6 - faw   7 - sol

(4)   Note values:

(5)   The tempo marks are:
    "Very slow" with a beat of 1 1/2 seconds   (M.M. 40)
    "Slow" with a beat of 1 1/4 seconds   (M.M. 48)
    Moderato with a beat of 1 second   (M.M. 60)
    Cheerful with a beat of 7/8 second   (M.M. 68)
    Lively with a beat of 2/3 second   (M.M. 90)
    Quick with a beat of 5/8 second   (M.M. 96)
    Very quick with a beat of 1/2 second   (M.M. 120)

(6)   Common time (◡ = 4/2); Double common time (C = 4/2)

5)   The fourth edition of *The Art of Singing* (**Law's** fifth edition), 1810, contains only *The Musical Magazine* since Parts I and II were incorporated into the *Harmonic Companion*, 1807.

d.   *A Collection of Hymns for Social Worship*, Cheshire, 1783

1)   This contains 48 pages and was often bound together with *A Collection of Hymn Tunes* and referred to by **Law** as "Hymns and Tunes." The "Hymn Tune" collection includes 38 tunes.

e.   *Rudiments of Music*, Cheshire, 1783, 1785, 1791, 1792

1)   This is a short treatise on the rules of psalmody to which was added a number of plain tunes and chants. The fourth edition (1792) contains 89 pages of music using round notes. In the last three editions there are included 15 fuging tunes and the eight chants included in the first two editions are deleted from the last two editions. The first edition includes only 31 compositions, but each edition has an increased number of pieces culminating with 90 in the fourth edition.

f.   *Harmonic Companion, and Guide to Social Worship: Being a Choice Selection of Tunes, Adapted to the Various Psalms and Hymns*, Philadelphia, 1807, 1810, 1813, 1819

1)   The first and second parts of *The Art of Singing* are contained in the *Harmonic Companion*, which is a volume of 112 pages. It is made up of the rules of psalmody and 139 psalm and hymn tunes, including 8 set-pieces. The second edition (1810) was slightly enlarged, 120 pages with 149 tunes.

2)   In his dedication to "ministers, singing masters, clerks and choristers," **Law** complains about the low state of church music and suggests that the ministers have the power to raise the standard.

3)   He uses his shape-note system with some improvements. A dot is added over or under the shape-notes for "faw," "sol," and "law" in the upper part of the scale.

g.   *The Art of Playing the Organ and Piano Forte or Characters Adapted to Instruments*, Philadelphia, 1809

1)   This small pamphlet of 8 pages without any tunes is not a method of playing, but rather gives the principles of his seven shape-note notation system as applied to the keyboard.

h.   *Essays on Music*, Philadelphia, 1814; Hartford, 1821

1)   **Law** intended to publish a series of essays on general music and reviews of new publications of music; only two issues were put out. In all there are four essays and two reviews.

IV. Other Composers

A. **Oliver Holden** (1765-1844)
   1. **Holden** was born in Shirley, Massachusetts, on September 18; he lived an active life as a carpenter, real estate broker, preacher, singing teacher, compiler and editor of song books and composer of hymns and anthems. He settled in Charlestown in 1787 and later served as a representative in the Massachusetts House of Representatives (1818-1833).
   2. **Holden's** musical training was limited, and he was a conservative composer. Like **Law**, **Holden** was opposed to the lively fuging-tune style of **William Billings**.
   3. Among **Holden's** works there are several compilations of hymns and anthems for special occasions.
      a. *The American Harmony*, Boston, 1792
         1) Verse anthem: *The Lord is good to all* (*ANE*, p. 263)
         2) *Ordination Anthem* (*BCAM*, p. 104)
      b. *The Union Harmony, or, Universal Collection of Sacred Music*, 1793, 1796, 1801
         1) Among **Holden's** 21 hymns is *"Coronation"* which is the first American tune to have been used continuously from its first printing to the present. Expression was generally conveyed by the conductor, therefore it was rarely indicated. "Piano" and "forte" are, however, indicated in *Coronation*.
         2) *Coronation* (*Hymnal*, No. 355; *MinA*, p. 143; *AH*, p. 419); *Fairlee* (*AH*, p. 216); *Hopkinton* (*AH*, p. 130); *Aberdeen* (*AH*, p. 217); *Holley* (*AH*, p. 429)
      c. *Sacred Dirges, Hymns and Anthems*, 1800
         1) This collection was "commemorative of the death of General George Washington [died December 14, 1799], the guardian of his country and the friend of man. An original composition by a citizen of Massachusetts."
         2) The tributory service to George Washington held at Old South Meeting Hall in Boston, January, 1800, closed with **Holden's** composition *"From Vernon's Mount Behold the Hero Rise"* (*BCAM*, p. 227).
         3) *Dirge, or Sepulchral Service commemorating the sublime virtues and distinguished talents of George Washington.* "Composed and set to music at the request of the Mechanic's Association, for performance on Saturday the 22 inst." (February, 1800).
            a) Organized in several varied sections, the dirge opens with a recitative and includes *"Lo! sorrow reigneth, and the nation mourns,"* an air with instrumental bass, a three-part choral section and a duet.
            b) *Funeral Hymn* (*LEAM*, p. 100)
      d. *The Charlestown Collection of Sacred Songs*, Boston, 1803
      e. *The Worcester Collection of Sacred Harmony*, 6th edition, 1803
         1) **Holden** became editor of the extensively used collection for the sixth edition and continued for two more editions.
         2) *Confidence* (*YONE*, p. 33)
      f. *The Massachusetts Compiler*, 1795
         1) This appears as one of the most progressive works on psalmody before 1800. Edited by **Holden** in cooperation with **Samuel Holyoke** and **Hans Gram**, it includes theoretical and practical explanations of sacred music and a musical dictionary. It has also been described as the "first American theory manual to espouse 'modern' European principles."
B. **Samuel Holyoke** (1762-1820)
   1. **Holyoke** was born in Boxford, Massachusetts, October 15; he was a composer and teacher of vocal and instrumental music. He graduated from Harvard College (1789) and organized Groton (late Lawrence) Academy of higher education (1793). He promoted choral concerts about Boston and Salem.

2.   **Holyoke** was opposed to the fuging style because, as noted in the Preface of his *Harmonia Americana*, of "the trifling effect produced by that sort of music; for the parts, falling in, one after another, each conveying a different idea, confound the sense, and render the performance a mere jargon of words."

3.   Several of **Holyoke's** compositions were published in *The Massachusetts Magazine*, including *Washington*; *The Pensive Shepherd*; *Salley, a Pastoral*; and *Terraminta*.

4.   Collections of music

   a.   *Harmonia Americana*, Boston, 1791

     1)   *Sunbury* (*AH*, p. 160); *Cyrene* (*AH*, p. 162); *Andover* (*LEAM*, p. 59); *Delhi* (*AH*, p. 208)

   b.   *The Columbian Repository of Sacred Harmony*, Exeter, 1802, 1805, 1809

     1)   This contains 734 tunes, many by **Holyoke**, after the style of Dr. **Isaac Watts'** psalms and hymns.

     2)   *Arnheim* (*MinA*, p. 165; *AH*, p. 170)

       a)   This, composed at the age of 16, is probably **Holyoke's** most famous tune.

     3)   *Confidence* (*AH*, p. 456); *Amoskeag* (*YONE*, p. 38); *Kennebunk* (*YONE*, p. 40); *Warsaw* (*CMCA*, p. 11)

   c.   *The Christian Harmonist*, Salem, 1804

     1)   Designed for use by the Baptist Churches of America, this includes hymns, two anthems and a funeral dirge.

     2)   *Suncook* (*AH*, p. 417); *Keswick* (*AH*, p. 418)

     3)   *Hear our prayer, O Lord* (*BCAC*, p. 52)

   d.   *The Instrumental Assistant*, vol. I, 1800; vol. II, 1807

     1)   This includes instruction for violin, flute, clarinet, bass viol and oboe compiled from European publications (marches, airs, duets, rondos, minuets) and arranged progressively. Volume II includes instruction for bassoon and French horn.

     2)   *Handel's Water Piece* (*BCAM*, p. 231)

   e.   *Hark from the Tomb* and *Beneath the Honors*, both adapted from **Isaac Watts**, were anthems performed at Newburyport, January 2, 1800, "the day on which the citizens unitedly expressed their unbounded veneration for the memory of our beloved Washington."

C.   **Daniel Read** (1757-1836)

  1.   **Read** was born in Attleboro, Massachusetts, on November 16; he studied mechanics and later became a surveyor (1775). After serving in the Continental Army he settled at New Haven. He conducted a singing school (1782-1783), became a manufacturer of ivory combs and developed a sales and publishing business. He left a collection of about 400 tunes by himself and others; he was fond of the fuging tune.

  2.   Collections of music

   a.   *The American Singing Book, or a New and Easy Guide to the Art of Psalmody, devised for the use of Singing Schools in America*, 1785, 1786, 1792, 1793, 1795

     1)   Anthem: *Down Steers the Bass* (*MinA*, p. 127); *Windham* (*MinA*, p. 126; *AH*, p. 223)

   b.   *The American Musical Magazine*, 1786-1787

     1)   **Read**, in collaboration with **Amos Doolittle**, edited 12 numbers of this magazine which are compilations of church music.

   c.   *The Columbian Harmonist*

     1)   This was first published in three separate books: volume I , New Haven, 1793; volume II, New Haven, 1794, with additions being made in two succeeding editions, 1798, 1801; volume III, New Haven, 1795.

     2)   All three books were published in one volume in 1795 in New Haven. In 1804 a completely revised edition was brought out in Dedham. The third edition (Dedham, 1806) and the corrected, improved and enlarged fourth edition (1810) was published in Boston.

3)   Anthem: *O be joyful in the Lord* (*ANE*, p. 257)
4)   *Greenwich* (*YONE*, p. 26); *Victory* (*YONE*, p. 27); *Newport* (*LEAM*, p. 47)

D.   **Timothy Swan** (1758-1842)
1.   **Swan** was born in Worcester, Massachusetts, on July 23; his only musical training was a few weeks of singing school; he began to teach music at the age of 17 and learned to play the flute while serving in the Continental Army. **Swan** composed some music of considerable originality. Several of his tunes are still in use today, such as *China, Ocean, Poland* and *Pownall*.
   a.   *The Songster's Assistant, c.* 1800
      1)   This book includes a unique decoration which shows a two-voice canon on a staff in the shape of a French horn.
   b.   *The New England Harmony*, Northampton, 1801
      1)   *China* (*AH*, p. 224; *MinA*, p. 142); *Christmas* (*CMCA*, p. 35); *Montague* (*YONE*, p. 37); *Leghorn* (*LEAM*, p. 49); *London* (*LEAM*, p. 52)
   c.   *Federal Harmony*, 1785
   d.   *The Songster's Museum; or, A Trip to Elysium*, Northampton, 1803

E.   **Jacob Kimball**, Jr. (1761-1826)
1.   **Kimball** was born in Topsfield, Massachusetts, on February 22; he graduated from Harvard with a degree in law in 1780. He was admitted to the bar in Stratford, New Hampshire, but soon gave up the law profession to devote his life to music, singing schools and promoting his own music collections. His music, which includes fuges, is somewhat in the style of **Billings** and a few of his tunes achieved popularity.
   a.   When tunes are in three parts, the melody is placed between the tenor and the bass.
2.   *The Rural Harmony*, Boston, 1793
   a.   In addition to the 71 original compositions, an introduction discussing music fundamentals opens the collection. **Kimball** suggests in order to produce a soft effect for greater contrast some of the singers should "be silent." In fuging music there is an increase of sound "as the parts fall in."
   b.   *Invitation* (*MinA*, p. 144; *AH*, p. 180; *YONE*, p. 29)
      1)   Note how the words "over the hills" are reflected in the music.
   c.   *Woburn* (*MinA*, p. 147; *YONE*, p. 30)
      1)   In the fuging section each one-measure entrance is terminated on a pedal point which builds up a sustained chord.
   d.   *Stoneham* (*AH*, p. 132); *Stockholm* (*AH*, p. 206); *Bradford* (*YONE*, p. 28)
3.   *The Essex Harmony*, Exeter, 1880
   a.   **Holyoke** is a co-editor of this collection which contains an introduction, 42 tunes and two anthems.
   b.   *Plainfield* (*AH*, p. 230); *O come, sing unto the Lord* (*BCAC*, p. 33)

F.   **Supply Belcher** (1751-1836)
1.   **Belcher** was born in Stoughton, Massachusetts, on March 29; he was a hymn writer, violinist, school teacher and choir leader, was also a Justice of the Peace and a state legislator; he served under George Washington in the Revolutionary War. With **Billings** he was one of the original members of the Stoughton Musical Society and was called "the Handel of Maine." He left only one music collection.
2.   *The Harmony of Maine*, Boston, 1794 (*EAM*, v. 6)
   a.   As a collection of psalm and hymn tunes, fuging tunes and anthems, including a section on the rudiments of music, it was practical for use in singing schools and musical societies.
   b.   *Jubilant* (*MinA*, p. 154; *LEAM*, p. 44; *EAM*, v. 6, p. 39); *Union* (*AH*, p. 126; *EAM*, v. 6); *Rapture* (*CMCA*, p. 19; *EAM*, v. 6)

G.   **Daniel Belknap** (1771-1815)
1.   Born in Framingham, Massachusetts, on February 9, **Belknap** remained there most of his life as a farmer and mechanic. From the age of 18 he also taught singing schools.

Of his five known publications, only the first contains an original anthem; his other pieces are hymns and secular tunes.

2. *The Harmonist's Companion*, Boston, 1797
   a. The *"Companion"* includes a number of airs for divine worship, an Easter anthem and a Masonic ode.
   b. *Spring* (He sends his word and melts the snow) (*MinA*, p. 159)
      1) Note the fuging section and the music reflecting the word "blow."
   c. *Summer* (How soon, alas! must Summer's sweets decay) (*MinA*, p. 160)
3. *The Evangelical Harmony*, Boston, 1800
   a. This contains a great variety of airs for divine worship and other favorite pieces. "To the grounds of music" is a practical introduction to the rudiments of music.
   b. *Autumn* ('Twas spring, 'twas summer) (*MinA*, p. 162)
   c. *Winter* (Now clouds the wintry skies deform) (*MinA*, p. 164)
      1) Although dynamic indications are rare in the music of this period, **Belknap** does indicate "piano" and "forte" in this tune.
   d. *Blue Hill* (*AH*, p. 630; *YONE*, p. 36); *Redemption* (*LEAM*, p. 62)
4. *The Middlesex Collection of Sacred Harmony*, Boston, 1802
5. *The Village Compilation of Sacred Musick*, Boston, 1806
6. *The Middlesex Songster, Containing a Collection of the Most Approved Songs Now in Use*, Dedham, 1809
   a. The *"Songster"* is a collection of 22 secular tunes.

H. **Jacob French** (1754-1817)
1. **French**, one of the most gifted of early American psalm tune composers, was born in Stoughton, Massachusetts, on July 15. With **Billings** and **Belcher**, he was among those who established the Stoughton Musical Society in 1774. He fought in the battle of Bunker Hill and was one of the few who survived the massacre of Cherry Valley. After the war **French** established himself as a singing teacher and published three collections of music.
2. *The New American Melody*, Boston, 1789
   a. An introduction opens this book of songs and five anthems.
   b. Anthems: *O sing unto the Lord* (*ANE*, p. 252); *My friends, I am going on a long and tedious journey* (*BCAC*, p. 28)
3. *The Psalmodist's Companion*, Worcester, 1793
   a. **French** divides the book into four sections: 1) rudiments of music; 2) psalm tunes, 3) choruses and fuging tunes, and 4) two anthems.
   b. Few non-American anthems were included in the American compilations of the late eighteenth century. However, **French** did include **Handel's** anthem *"Already see the daughters of the Lord* from *Saul*. Before the Revolution, **Josiah Flagg** had published this same anthem in his *Sixteen Anthems*, 1766.
   c. *Harmony* (*MinA*, p. 148); *The death of George Washington* (*LEAM*, p. 94); **Daniel Read's** *Russia* (*AH*, p. 182)
4. *Harmony of Harmony*, Northampton, 1802
   a. *Ascension* (*AH*, p. 184); *Babylon* (*AH*, p. 228)

I. **Simeon Jocelin [Jocelyn]** (1746-1823)
1. **Jocelin** was born on October 22. He was not a composer but rather a compiler, engraver and publisher; he collaborated with **Amos Doolittle**, another engraver, on the publication of many collections of music.
2. *The Chorister's Companion*, New Haven, 1782
   a. The compilation includes plain and fuging tunes along with the rules of psalmody. Some suggestions on tone production are given: "Let the voice be clear and smooth . . . neither forcing the sound through the nose, nor blowing through the teeth . . . the notes . . . should be begun and ended soft, swelling greatly as the air of the tune requires . . . High notes should be sung soft, but not faint; low notes full but not harsh."

b.   *Psalm 146* (I'll praise my maker) (*MinA*, p. 121)
c.   **Lewis Edson**, Sr. (1748-1820), *Lenox* (*MinA*, p. 124)
d.   **William Tuckey** (1708-1781), *Knighton* (*MinA*, p. 181)

3.   *A Collection of Favorite Psalm Tunes, from Late and Approved British Authors*, 1787
a.   *89th Psalm* (*LEAM*, p. 37); *146th Psalm* (*LEAM*, p. 39)

J.   **Eliakim Doolittle** (1772-1850)

1.   **Eliakim**, the younger brother of **Amos**, was born in Connecticut on August 29; he studied at Yale College and taught singing classes in the evenings. In response to the sinking of the Peacock, a British warship, by the American Hornet during the War of 1812, **Doolittle** wrote the war song *"The Hornet stung the Peacock."*

2.   *Exhortation* (*MinA*, p. 156), from **William Little** and **William Smith**, *The Easy Instructor, c.* 1809.

3.   *Solemnity* (*AH*, p. 214), printed in **Asahel Benham's** *Social Harmony*, 1798

K.   **Stephen Jenks** (1772-1856)

1.   **Jenks**, born in New Canaan, Connecticut, was well known through his tunes which were quite broadly used, even in the South. His work was centered in Connecticut until 1829 when he went west to Ohio employed as a maker of tambourines and drums.

2.   *The Musical Harmonist* (first issued as *The New England Harmony*), Danbury, 1800, 1803
a.   *Desolation* (*AH*, p. 127); *Evening Shade* (*AH*, p. 164); *Variety* (*AH*, p. 172); *Liberty* (*AH*, p. 283)

3.   *The American Compiler of Sacred Harmony*, No. 1, Northampton, 1803
a.   The rules of psalmody are included in this collection of sacred music.

4.   *The Delights of Harmony; or, Norfolk Compiler*, Dedham and New Haven, 1805
a.   A collection of psalm and hymn tunes.
b.   *Evening Shade* (*MinA*, p. 158; *AH*, p. 164), a three-part fuging tune.
   1)   *Evening Shade* was first published in *The New England Harmony* under the title *"Mount Vernon,"* possibly in commemoration of the death of George Washington.

L.   **Abraham Wood** (1752-1804)

1.   **Wood**, born on July 30, spent his life in Northboro, Massachusetts, and was a prolific hymn and tune writer. Dissimilar to most New England composers of this period, he apparently did not conduct singing schools. During the Revolution he was involved with military duties.

a.   *A Hymn [An Anthem] on Peace*, Worcester, 1784
b.   *The Worcester Collection of Sacred Harmony*, Worcester, 1786
   1)   *Worcester* (*MinA*, p. 138; *CMCA*, p. 25)
c.   *Divine Songs, extracted from Mr. J. Hart's Hymns, and set to musick in three and four parts*, Boston, 1789
d.   *The Columbian Harmony*, Boston, 1793
   1)   The pieces in this collection, issued in collaboration with **Joseph Stone**, show frequent use of the dotted rhythm with two notes to a syllable and some use of text painting.
   2)   *Worcester* (*YONE*, p. 24)
e.   *A Funeral Elegy on the Death of General George Washington,* Boston, 1800 (*BCAM*, p. 218)
   1)   The *"Elegy"* was republished and used on the occasion of President William Henry Harrison's death, 1841.

M.   **Abraham Maxim** (1773-1829)

1.   **Maxim** was born on January 3 in Carver, Massachusetts; he studied with **William Billings.**

2.   *The Oriental Harmony; Being an Original Composition*, Exeter, New Hampshire, 1802

      a.   Thirty-nine tunes are included in this collection.

   3.   *The Northern Harmony; being a Collection from the Works of Many Approved Authors of Sacred Music*, Exeter, 1805; fifth edition, 1819

      a.   *Columbia* (*AH*, p. 284); *Turner* (*YONE*, p. 47)

N. **Bartholomew Brown** (1772-1854)

   1.   **Brown** was born in Sterling, Massachusetts, on September 8; he graduated from Harvard in 1799 and became a lawyer. He was one of the most accomplished musicians in New England. **Brown** wrote the calendars in the *American Farmers Almanac* for some 50 years.

   2.   *Columbian and European Harmony; or, Bridgewater Collection of Sacred Music*, Boston, 1802; second edition, 1804; third edition, 1810

V. Secular Music

A. **Hans Gram** (*fl*. 1785-1795)

   1.   Born in Denmark and educated in Stockholm, **Gram** came to America and settled in Boston around 1789. In 1793 and for several years after he was organist of the Brattle Street Church; he taught many of the native American composers of his time, among them **Samuel Holyoke, Jacob Kimball** and **Oliver Holden**.

   2.   Little of **Gram's** music is extant, indeed, it is possible that he wrote very little.

      a.   *The Death Song of an Indian Chief*, for tenor and orchestra (*MinA*, pp. 222, 225)

         1)   This song first appeared in *The Massachusetts Magazine*, March, 1791, and apparently is the first orchestral score published in America. It is scored for 2 clarinets, 2 E-flat horns and strings.

      b.   *Ode to the President of the United States* (The season sheds its mildest rays), for solo voice and chorus, was printed in *The Massachusetts Magazine*, October, 1789.

      c.   *Ode for the New Year* (On the top of a mountain), for voice and piano, was published in *The Massachusetts Magazine*, January, 1791.

      d.   *America. A New March* in three-part open score appeared in the July, 1791, issue of *The Massachusetts Magazine*.

      e.   *Sacred Lines for Thanksgiving Day* (November 7, 1793) (*BCAM*, p. 120)

         1)   This anthem is patterned after the English "verse anthem" in which solo parts are interpolated between the choral sections.

      f.   Anthem: *Praise ye the Lord* (*ANE*, p. 217)

   3.   **Gram** is also known as a co-editor with **Samuel Holyoke** and **Oliver Holden** of *The Massachusetts Compiler*, 1795 (see above under **Holden**).

B. **William Selby** (1738-1798)

   1.   Born in England, **Selby** came to America about 1771; then about 1774 he settled in Newport, Rhode Island, where he was organist at Trinity Church. Around 1776 he made his home in Boston and became organist of King's Chapel. Due to the Revolution his musical activities were curtailed so he made his living as a liquor dealer and grocer. By 1783 he was able to resume his musical career, taught and served as an impresario.

      a.   His concert programs included music by himself, **Bach, Corelli** and **Handel**, pieces for band and chorus, and solos for voice and various instruments, including organ, and a *Concerto for Organ*.

   2.   Among his compositions are songs, anthems and instrumental pieces for piano and organ.

      a.   *A Fuge or Voluntary*, for organ (*CAO*, p. 10)

      b.   *Apollo, and the Muse's Musical Compositions*

         1)   This collection was advertised in the *Columbian Centinel* of Boston, June 16, 1790. It was to include anthems in four parts, voluntaries or fuges for organ or harpsichord, sonatas or lessons for harpsichord or pianoforte, a piece with var-

iations, an organ concerto with instruments and a sonata for two violins and cello. Evidently no copy of this remains.

      c.   *Ptalaemon to Pastora* is "a new air" published in *The Gentlemen and Ladies Town & Country Magazine*, Boston, March, 1789.

      d.   *Voluntary VIII*, for organ or harpsichord (*MinA*, p. 186)

      e.   *Ode for the New Year* (January 1, 1790) (*MinA*, p. 189), from *The Massachusetts Magazine*, January, 1790.

      f.   Anthem: *O be joyful in the Lord* (*ANE*, p. 210)

C.   Plays with incidental music were given in Boston; the anti-theatre law of 1750 was often avoided by using the terms "moral lecture" or "readings." By the end of the century the law was no longer enforced, and ballad-operas were regularly performed in the two Boston theatres (the New Federal Street Theatre and the Haymarket).

   1.   To aid in musical development the theatre became the means by which many music leaders were introduced to the Boston audiences.

BIBLIOGRAPHY

Books

1.   Barbour, J. Murray. *The Church Music of William Billings*. Lansing: Michigan State University Press, 1960.

2.   Billings, William. "To All Musical Practitioners" and "Dialogue, between Master and Scholar," in *The American Composer Speaks; A Historical Anthology, 1770-1965*, ed. Gilbert Chase. Baton Rouge: Louisiana State University Press, 1966, pp. 28-37.

3.   Clark, Garry E. "Yankee Tunesmiths," in *Essays on American Music*. Westport, CT: Greenwood Press, 1977, pp. 17-47.

4.   Cleveland, Catherine C. *The Great Revival in the West, 1797-1805*. Chicago: University of Chicago Press, 1916.

5.   Crawford, Richard A. *Andrew Law, American Psalmodist*. Evanston: Northwestern University Press, 1968.

6.   Edwards, George Thornton. *Music and Musicians of Maine*. Portland: The Southworth Press, 1928; reprint: New York: AMS Press, 1970.

7.   Gould, Nathaniel Duren. *Church Music in America*. Boston: A. N. Johnson, 1853; reprint: New York: AMS Press, 1972

8.   Lowens, Irving. "Andrew Law and the Pirates," in *Music and Musicians in Early America*. New York: W. W. Norton, 1964, pp. 58-88.

9.   ——————"Daniel Read's World: The Letters of an Early American Composer," in *Music and Musicians in Early America*. New York: W. W. Norton, 1964, pp. 159-177.

10.   ——————"*The Easy Instructor* (1789-1831): A History and Bibliography of the First Shape-Note Tune-Book," in *Music and Musicians in Early America*. New York: W. W. Norton, 1964, pp. 115-137.

11.   ——————"*The Easy Instructor* (1801-1831): A Check-List of Editions and Issues," in *Music and Musicians in Early America*. New York: W. W. Norton, 1964, pp. 292-310.

12.   ——————"The Musical Edsons of Shady: Early American Tunesmiths," in *Music and Musicians in Early America*. New York: W. W. Norton, 1964, pp. 178-193.

13.   Mangler, Joyce Ellen. *Rhode Island Music and Musicians, 1733-1850*. Detroit: Information Services, 1965.

14.   McKay, David P., and Richard Crawford. *William Billings of Boston: Eighteenth-Century Composer*. Princeton: Princeton University Press, 1975.

15.   Owen, Earl McLain. *The Life and Music of Supply Belcher*, 2 vols. Ann Arbor: University Microfilms, 1969.

16.   Seybolt, Robert F. *The Private Schools of Colonial Boston*. Cambridge, MA: Harvard

University Press, 1935; reprint: New York: Arno Press.

17. Stanislaw, Richard J. *A Checklist of Four-Shape Shape-Note Tunebooks*. Brooklyn: Institute for Studies in American Music, 1978. (ISAM Monograph, No. 10)

18. *William Billings: Data and Documents*, ed. Hans Nathan. Detroit: Information Coordinators, 1976.

Articles

1. Britton, Allen P. "The Musical Idiom in Early American Tunebooks." *JAMS* 3 (1950), p. 286.

2. Cowell, Sidney Robertson. "The 'Shape-Note Singers' and Their Music." *Score* 12 (June, 1955), pp. 9-14.

3. Crawford, Richard, and H. Wiley Hitchcock. "Andrew Law *Tunesmith*." *University of Michigan Library Bulletin* 68 (May, 1961).

4. Held, Jerrold. "Abraham Wood, an Early American Composer." *American Choral Review* 7 (September, 1964), pp. 1, 14-16; (December, 1964), pp. 8-10.

5. Hitchcock, H. Wiley. "William Billings and the Yankee Tunesmiths" (includes discography). *HiFi Review* 16 (February, 1966), pp. 55-65.

6. Jackson, George Pullen. "Buckwheat Notes." *MQ* 19 (1933), pp. 393-400.

7. Lindstrom, Carl E. "William Billings and His Times." *MQ* 25 (1939), pp. 479-497.

8. Lowens, Irving. "Andrew Law and the Pirates." *JAMS* 13 (1960), pp. 206-223.

9. ———————"Daniel Read's World: The Letters of an Early American Composer." *Notes* 9 (1952), pp. 233-248.

10. ———————"Tune Books, Tunesmiths and Singing Schools." *Etude* 74 (November, 1956), pp. 20, 59, 62-64.

11. Marrocco, W. Thomas. "The 'Set Piece'." *JAMS* 15 (1962), pp. 348-352.

12. McKay, David. "William Selby, Musical Émigré in Colonial Boston." *MQ* 57 (1971), pp. 609-627.

13. Moore, Lillian. "Ballet Music in Washington's Time." *Etude* 74 (September, 1956), pp. 17, 47, 51.

14. Perrin, Phil D. "Systems of Scale Notation in Nineteenth-Century American Tunebooks." *Journal of Research in Music Education* 18 (1970), pp. 257-264.

15. Pierce, Edwin Hall. "The Rise and Fall of the 'Fugue-Tune' in America." *MQ* 16 (1930), pp. 214-228.

16. Scholten, James William. "Lucius Chapin: a New England Singing Master on the Frontier." *Contributions to Music Education* 4 (Winter, 1976), pp. 64-76.

17. Scott, John Anthony. "Ballads and Broadsides of the American Revolution." *Sing Out!* 16, No. 2 (1966), pp. 18-23.

18. Stoutamire, Albert L. "Musical Life in Late Eighteenth Century Richmond." *Journal of Research in Music Education* 11 (1963), pp. 99-109.

Music

1. Belcher, Supply. *The Harmony of Maine*, Boston, 1794; reprint: New York: Da Capo Press, 1972. (Earlier American Music, v. 6)

2. *The Best of Billings*, ed. Richard C. Pisano. New York: Walton Music, 1968.

3. Billings, William. *(CE) The Complete Works of William Billings*, 4 vols., ed. Hans Nathan. Charlottesville, VA: The American Musicological Society & The Colonial Society of Massachusetts, Boston, 1977.
   Volume I: *New-England Psalm-Singer*
   Volume II: *The Singing Master's Assistant* and *Music in Miniature*
   Volume III: *The Psalm-Singer's Amusement* and *The Suffolk Harmony*
   Volume IV: *The Continental Harmony*

4.   Billings, William. *The Continental Harmony*. Boston: Isaiah Thomas and Ebenezer T. Andrews, 1794; reprint: ed. Hans Nathan. Cambridge, MA: The Belknap Press of Harvard University Press, 1961.

5.   ––––––*The Psalm-Singer's Amusement*. Boston: 1781; reprint: New York: Da Capo Press, 1974. (Early American Music, v. 20)

6.   ––––––*Sacred Choral Music from Colonial America by William Billings*, ed. Leonard Van Camp. St. Louis, MO: Concordia Publishing House, 1973.

7.   ––––––*William Billings (1746-1800)*, ed. Oliver Daniel. New York: C. F. Peters, 1970.

8.   *Choral Music of the American Folk Tradition: Fuging Tunes*, ed. Jeanne Behrend. Philadelphia: Elkan-Vogel, 1954.

9.   *Freedom's Voice in Poetry and Song*, ed. Gillian B. Anderson. Wilmington, DE: Scholarly Resources, 1977.   (Part I: An Inventory of Political and Patriotic Lyrics in Colonial American Newspapers, 1773-1783. Part II: Song Book)

10.   *Songs of Praise from Early America*, ed. Don McAfee. New York: Bourne Press, 1967.

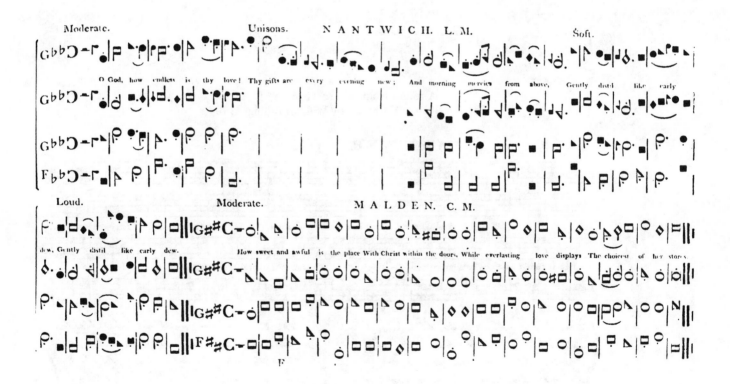

From **Harmonic Companion, and Guide to Social Worship**
by Andrew Law, 1807

A round from the frontispiece of
The Continental Harmony by William Billings, 1794

"Chester" from **The Singing Master's Assistant**
by William Billings, 1778

From **The Art of Singing** by Andrew Law, 1794

From **The Art of Singing** by Andrew Law, 1803

OUTLINE VII

FOREIGN MUSICIANS IN NEW YORK AND PHILADELPHIA (1780-1825)

The State of Music — Composers
National Airs

I. The State of Music

A. There was little musical activity in Philadelphia during the Revolution (1775-1783). In New York, however, the British militia was in control from 1776 to 1783 and they not only patronized concerts and theatrical performances but also presented them.

1. In 1781 to 1783 a regular concert series prospered, being supported by British Army and Navy personnel, as well as local British sympathizers.

2. In New York on April 27, 1782, a program to be presented by the British was announced:

THEATRE
(By Permission)

This evening will be performed, a Concert of Vocal and Instrumental Musick, for the benefit of two distressed Refugee Families;

It is hoped the humanity of the respectable public will, on this laudable occasion, be particularly shewn, as they may depend upon every pains being taken to render the evening's amusement agreeable.

Act I

Sinfonie of. . . . . Toeschi
Quartetto of Davaux for violins
Song by Mrs. Hyde 'Soldiers tir'd of Wars alarms'
Violino Solo Concerto of . . . . .Borchny
Quintetto of C. Bach for Flauto.
Sinfonie of Stamitz.

Act II

Sinfonie of Haydn
Quartetto of Kammell, for violino
Song by Mrs. Hyde, 'The Lark's shrill notes'
Hoboy Solo Concerto of C. Fischer
Quartetto of Vanhall, for Flauto
Sinfonie of. . . . . Haydn

Act III

Sinfonie of. . . . . Bach
Quartetto of Davaux, for violino
Song by Mrs. Hyde 'If 'tis joy to wound a lover'
Clarinetto Solo Concerto of. . . . . .Mahoy
Quartetto of Toeschi, for Flauto
Sinfonie of Mardino [Martini?]

Tickets to be had of the different printers, at Mr. Strachan's Coffee House, and Mr. James M'Ewer's No. 242 Queenstreet. Boxes 8 s. Pit 8 s. Gallery 4 s.

B.   At the end of the Revolutionary War in 1783, foreign composers, performers and teachers from England, France, Germany and Italy began to arrive in large numbers and soon took over the musical life; they became the principal source of secular music in America.

   1.   Their activities were centered chiefly in New York, Philadelphia, Charlestown and Boston.

   2.   The music of the first native American composers, such as **Hopkinson**, **Lyon** and **Billings**, ceased to appear on programs.

   3.   The foreign musicians often appeared on the programs as composer, performer and concert manager, but the music of **Haydn, Mozart, Beethoven, Gossec, Stamitz, Pleyel, Gretry, J. C. Bach, Handel** and other well-known European masters was also performed.

   4.   In New York in 1785, **William Brown** began a series of subscription concerts which lasted at least ten seasons. **John Bentley** began a series of concerts in Philadelphia which, likewise, continued for ten years. However, in both cases, theatrical performances became more popular and finally caused the concert series to close.

   5.   Church music, including hymns, anthems and Mass settings, continued to be written and compiled for use in both Protestant and Catholic churches.

      a.   John Aitken printed *A Compilation of the Litanies and Vespers, Hymns and Anthems as They are Sung in the Catholic Church*, Philadelphia, 1787.

C.   The Musical Fund Society of Philadelphia was organized January 7, 1820, for "the relief and support of decayed musicians and their families." Concerts and lectures were given to raise funds.

   1.   Among musicians connected with the Society in its early days were **Benjamin Carr**, **Raynor Taylor** and **Francis Hopkinson**.

   2.   The programs were often of the mixed variety, but such ambitious works as **Haydn's** *Creation* (1822), **Beethoven's** *Mount of Olives*, **Handel's** *Messiah* and the *Dettingen Te Deum* (1823, 1824) were performed.

   3.   Ballad-operas continued to be performed.

      a.   **Stephen Storace** (1763-1796), an English composer of operas and theater music

         1)   *No Song No Supper*, 1790

         2)   *Poor Black Boy*, 1794 (*BCAM*, p. 166)

         3)   *The Pirates*, 1792

            a)   *Lullaby* (*MDGW*, p. 54)

      b.   **William Shield** (1748-1829), composer of about 40 light operas

         1)   *The bud of the rose*, from *Rosina*, 1782 (*MDGW*, p. 56)

      c.   **Samuel Arnold** (1740-1802), an English composer of light operas

         1)   *The wayworn traveller*, from *The Mountaineers*, 1793 (*MDGW*, p. 58)

      d.   **Henry Rowley Bishop** (1786-1855), an English composer of ballad-operas

         1)   *Clari, or, The Maid of Milan*, 1823

            a)   This ballad-opera includes the original version of *Home, Sweet Home*; it appears several times in the opera (*MinA*, p. 310).

II.   Composers

A.   **Peter Albrecht Van Hagen, Sr.** (1750-1803)

   1.   **Van Hagen** was born in Holland of German parentage; he settled in Charlestown, South Carolina, in 1774, where he established himself as a music teacher. His son, **Peter, Jr.**, who became a virtuoso pianist, was born there in 1781. **Van Hagen, Sr.**, taught string and keyboard instruments and composition. In 1789 this musical family

moved to New York and in October made their début there with the following program:

Act I

Symphony of	Pleyel
Concerto on the Violin	Mr. Van Hagen
Song	Mr. Van Hagen, junior
	[eight years of age]
Quartetto of	Pleyel
Concerto on the Tenor	Mr. Van Hagen
Concerto on the Piano Forte	Mr. Van Hagen, jun.

Act II

Concerto on the Violin	Mr. Van Hagen
Trio, Piano Forte	
Song Duet	Messrs. Frobel and Van Hagen
Solo upon iron nails, called Violin Harmonika	
	[never performed]
Symphony De Chasse, Finale	C. Stamitz

2. **Mrs. Van Hagen** also participated in the program and later advertised that she would be available for teaching the theory and practice of the harpsichord and "Piano Forte" with thoroughbass and the principles of singing. Since she had been an organist in several churches in the Netherlands she also taught organ and church music.

3. In 1792 **Van Hagen** joined **Henri Capron** and **George Saliment** in managing concerts in New York. The following year **Capron** broke off and moved to Philadelphia to manage concerts there.

4. The **Van Hagen** family moved to Boston in 1796. **Senior** and **Junior Van Hagen** opened a "Musical Magazine and Warranted Piano Forte Warehouse." They began to publish music in 1799. **Van Hagen** conducted the Haymarket Theatre orchestra and was organist at Stone Chapel.

5. **Van Hagen's** compositions are principally arrangements of ballad-operas, incidental music to stage performances and accompaniments adapted to the specific instrumentation of the orchestra.
    a. Ballad-opera: *The Adopted Child, or The Baron of Milford Castle*
    b. Incidental music: *The Battle of Hexham*; *Columbus, or The Discovery of America*; *Zorinski, or Freedom to the Slaves*
    c. His original compositions include *The Federal Overture* performed in 1797 and *A Funeral Dirge on the Death of George Washington* (Assembled round the patriot's grave), Boston, 1799 (*MinA*, p. 227).

B. **Peter Albrecht Van Hagen, Jr.** (1781-1837)
    1. In Boston **Van Hagen, Jr.**, continued his virtuoso piano career and composed some songs and instrumental pieces.
        a. *Adams and Washington* (*LEAM*, p. 101)

C. **Alexander Reinagle** (1756-1809)
    1. Born in Portsmouth, England, of Austrian parents, **Reinagle** moved to Edinburgh, Scotland, where he became a student of **Raynor Taylor**. On a visit to Hamburg he became a friend of **C. P. E. Bach**. He traveled considerably on the continent and then in 1786 settled in Philadelphia; he was active there and in New York as a teacher, singer, pianist, conductor, composer and concert manager. In 1793 **Reinagle** opened the Philadelphia New Theatre with Thomas Wignell. Until 1809 regular subscription concerts

known as "City Concerts" were given, which included stage plays, pianoforte and string ensembles and short popular songs and airs. **Reinagle** frequently appeared in concert with **Henri Capron**, **John Christopher Moller** and the Belgian violinst and composer, **Joseph [Jean] Gehot** (1756-*c*. 1820).

2. **Reinagle's** music shows the influence of **C. P. E. Bach** and, to some extent, **Haydn**. The Viennese style in his arrangements makes use of simple harmony, much repetition of the Alberti bass, some ornamentation and occasional cadences.

3. *A Select Collection of the Most Favourite Scots Tunes. With Variations for the Piano Forte or Harpsichord*, Philadelphia, 1787
   a. Technical devices found in these eleven pieces include grace notes, neighboring tones, passing tones for melodic embellishment and the melody in the left hand (bass) with the accompaniment in the right hand.

4. *Federal March* for pianoforte, violin and German flute, Philadelphia, 1788 (*BCAM*, p. 95; *LEAM*, p. 96)
   a. This was originally written for and performed at the Grand Procession in Philadelphia on July 4, 1788; only the piano part remains in microprint.

5. *A Chorus [A Sonata] sung by a number of young girls before Washington on April 21, 1789*, Philadelphia, 1789

6. *A Collection of Favorite Songs*, two books, Philadelphia, 1789
   a. Book II seems never to have been published. The 20 songs which make up Book I are written on two staves, the melody and the bass line.

7. *A Collection of Favorite Songs*, Philadelphia, 1789
   a. The collection of 11 songs are piano and voice arrangements of pieces by **J. C. Bach**, **William Boyce**, **Giovanni Paesiello** [*sic*] and others.

8. *Twelve Favorite Pieces, Arranged for Piano Forte*, Philadelphia, 1789
   a. This includes pieces by **Carlo Antonio Campioni**, **William Brown**, **William Shield**, **F. Staes** and **Niccolò Piccinni**.

9. *Sonata* (*MDGW*, p. 22)

10. *Two Minuets, Danced before General and Mrs. Washington*, 1792 (*MDGW*, p. 32)

11. Arrangements for piano include *My soul is thine, sweet Nora*; *Tantivy Hark Forward Huzza*; *'Tis not the bloom on Damon's cheek* and *Indian March* from the historical play *Columbus*.

12. Incidental music for the play *Columbus*

13. *La Chasse*, for piano (*BCAK*, p. 4)

14. *Finale*, from *Volunteers*, a ballad-opera, 1795 (*BCAM*, p. 170)

D. **Raynor Taylor** (1747-1825)
1. **Taylor** was born in England and received early musical training in the Chapel Royal. He was appointed music director of the London Sadler Wells Theatre in 1765. **Taylor** was one of the teachers of **Alexander Reinagle** in Edinburgh.

2. In 1792 **Taylor** came to New York and was active as a composer, violinist, organist, singer, conductor and impresario. After living for short periods of time in Baltimore and Annapolis, he settled in Philadelphia in 1793 and became organist of St. Peter's Church; in 1820 he helped establish the Musical Fund Society to promote chamber music. As an accomplished singer he also composed and produced many operetta-like humorous musical entertainments known as "olios."

3. **Taylor's** works, mostly secular, include cantatas, songs, instrumental pieces and ballad-operas.

4. Ballad-operas: *The Iron Chest*, 1797; *The Shipwrecked Mariner Preserved*, 1797; *Pizarro, or The Spaniards in Peru*, 1800

5. *An Easy and Familiar Lesson for Two Performers on One Piano Forte*, Philadelphia, *c*. 1793 (*BCAM*, p. 116)

6. *Sonata for the Piano Forte with an Accompaniment for a Violin*, Philadelphia, 1797 (*MinA*, p. 204)

7. *Divertimento II*, 1797 (*RRAM*, v. 1, p. 35)
8. *Tigris* (*AH*, p. 202)

E. **William Brown** [possibly **Wilhelm Braun** of Kassel] (*fl.* 1783-1787)
1. **Brown**, a composer and flute player, settled in America in the last quarter of the eighteenth century. He gave flute concerts in New York in 1783 and in Baltimore in 1784. That same year he went to Philadelphia and participated in benefit concerts. In 1785, in collaboration with **Henri Capron** and **Alexander Reinagle**, he sponsored a series of Subscription Concerts in Philadelphia and New York.
2. *Three Rondos for the Pianoforte or Harpsichord*, Philadelphia, 1787
    a. The rondos, dedicated to **Francis Hopkinson**, seem to be the first keyboard music published in America. Dynamics and ornaments are indicated; contrasting sections in minor mode suggest European influence.
    b. *Rondo* (*RRAM*, v. 1, p. 1; *MDGW*, p. 36; *BCAM*, p. 66)

F. **James Hewitt** (1770-1827)
1. **Hewitt** was born in Dartmoor, England, and studied violin with the famous Italian violinist and opera conductor, **Giovanni Batista Viotti** (1755-1824). He came to New York in 1792 and was active as a composer, violinist, organist, concert manager and publisher. In 1794 he joined **Henri Capron** in promoting the "City Concerts" and in 1798 he purchased **Benjamin Carr's** Musical Repository, a publishing business. **Hewitt** went to Boston in 1811, became organist at the Trinity Episcopal Church and was put in charge of the music at the Federal Street Theatre. In 1818 he returned to New York to become director of the Park Theatre. Between 1821 and 1823 he took part in a series of theatrical tours to a number of cities in the South.
2. **Hewitt's** extant music comprises 92 vocal and 75 instrumental pieces.
3. *Tammany*, New York, 1794
    a. This ballad-opera is probably the first one composed in America. With political connotations, the opera is named for a Cherokee Indian chief who allegorically portrays the stoicism of the Indians in view of the aristocratic theories of the anti-Federalists.
    b. *Alknomook* (The death song of the Cherokee Indians) (*MinA*, p. 213)
    c. *Three Sonatas for the Piano Forte* (D, C, F), New York, *c*. 1795
        1) *Sonata I* (*RRAM*, v. 7, p. 82)
    d. *The Battle of Trenton, a Favorite Historical Military Sonata* dedicated to George Washington, New York, 1797 (*RRAM*, v. 7, p. 88; *MDGW*, p. 8; *BCAM*, p. 198)
    e. *The New Federal Overture*, 1797 (*RRAM*, v. 1, p. 23)
    f. *A Complete Instructor for the Pianoforte*, New York, *c*. 1805
    g. *Theme with 30 Variations*, 1803-1806 (*RRAM*, v. 1, p. 65)
    h. *Yankee Doodle with Variations*, 1807-1810 (*RRAM*, v. 1, p. 91; *BCAK*, p. 7)
    i. *Harmonia Sacra*, 1812
        1) *Lang* (*AH*, p. 212)
    j. *Trip to Nahant, a favorite Rondo*, 1811 (*RRAM*, v. 1, p. 108)
    k. *The Federal Constitution and Liberty Forever* (*BCAM*, p. 192)
4. **Mrs. Mary Ann Pownall** and **James Hewitt**: *Six Songs for the Harpsichord or Piano Forte*, New York, 1794
    a. **Mrs. Pownall** (1751-1796) from England is apparently the first woman composer to have music printed in America.
        1) *The Straw Bonnet* (*BCAM*, p. 159)

G. **John Hill Hewitt** (1801-1890)
1. **John**, eldest son of **James Hewitt**, studied at West Point and ultimately became a drillmaster for recruits in the Confederate army during the Civil War. He was also active as a newspaper journalist, composer and theatrical manager. Among his music works are some 300 songs, four cantatas, four ballad-operas and an oratorio.
2. *All Quiet along the Potomac To-Night*, 1861 (*MinA*, p. 297; *CWS*, p. 62; *PAS*, p. 34)
    a. Although written as a Confederate song, this ballad was popular in the North also.

3.   *The Knight of the Raven Black Plume* (*PAS*, p. 31)

4.   *The Minstrel* (*PAS*, p. 28)

H. **Victor Pelissier** (*fl.* 1792-1811)

    1.   **Pelissier**, a composer and horn virtuoso, was born in France, emigrated to America and first appeared in Philadelphia in 1792. The following year he went to New York where he attached himself to the Old American Company as principal horn player in their traveling opera orchestra; he also was their composer and arranger. Among his works is incidental music for some 18 plays, mostly between 1794 and 1796, some pantomimes and several ballad-operas.

    2.   Operas: *Edwin and Angelina* or *The Banditti*, New York, 1796; *Ariadne Abandoned by Theseus in the Isle of Naxos*, New York, 1797; *Sterne's Maria* or *The Vintage*, 1799

    3.   *Columbian Melodies*, Philadelphia, 1811

      a.   This collection includes three songs from *Sterne's Maria* and one from *Edwin and Angelina*.

    4.   Incidental music: *Fourth of July* or *Temple of American Independence*, 1799

    5.   *Washington and Independence* (*BCAM*, p. 189)

    6.   *Few are the joys*, from *Edwin and Angelina* (*MinA*, p. 214)

I. **Benjamin Carr** (1768-1831)

    1.   Born in England **Carr** had his early musical training with **Samuel Arnold** (1740-1802) and **Charles Wesley** (1757-1834). In 1793 he came to Philadelphia with his father Joseph and brother Thomas and established one of the earliest music stores and publishing houses. **Carr's** father and brother opened a comparable store in Baltimore in 1794.

      a.   The "Musical Repository of B. Carr and Co." (July, 1793) has often been termed the earliest music store in America, but it was antedated by similar firms of Michael Hillegas (*c.* 1759), **John C. Moller** and **Henri Capron** (March, 1793) and others.

    2.   In 1820 **Carr** was one of the founders of the Musical Fund Society, an organization which promoted chamber music and sponsored benefit concerts for needy musicians; he was one of the early conductors of its orchestra.

    3.   **Benjamin Carr** is generally considered the foremost professional musician in Philadelphia during the early nineteenth century. His works include songs, piano pieces, psalms, motets, Masses, and at least one ballad-opera.

    4.   *A New Assistant for the Piano-forte or Harpsichord, containing the Necessary Rudiments for Beginners, with Twelve Airs Progressively Arrang'd to Which is Added Six Sonatas*, Baltimore, 1796

      a.   Fingering is marked in this instruction book.

    5.   *Musical Journal for the Piano*, in 5 volumes, Philadelphia, 1800 (*M* 9)

      a.   Each of the five volumes is divided into a "Vocal Section" and an "Instrumental Section" and is paged separately. Not only did **Carr** include some original works but other composers represented are **Reinagle**, **James Hook**, **Raynor Taylor**, **Viotti**, **Pleyel**, **Mozart**, **Haydn** and **Clementi**.

      b.   *The Welch Lullaby* (*M* 9, v. 1, vocal section, p. 13)

        1)   Small notes fill in the harmony; large notes outline only the melody and bass.

      c.   *The Wood Robin* (*M* 9, v. 1, vocal section, p. 23)

        1)   A flute part is added to imitate the sounds of a bird. A footnote suggests, "NB the Flute Part may be play'd on the upper part of the Piano by a second Person."

      d.   *Andante d'Haydn* (from the "Surprise" Symphony) (*M* 9, v. 6, instrumental section, p. 29)

      e.   *The Lullaby of Correlli [sic]* "Selected from the celebrated 8th Concerto Composed purposely for the Celebration of the Nativity of our Saviour" (*M* 9, v. 2, instrumental section, p. 5)

      f.   *Little Boy Blue* and *Shakespeare's Willow* (*BCAM*, p. 235)

6. *The Archers, or, Mountaineers of Switzerland*
   a. Based on the story of William Tell, this ballad-opera was first performed in New York in 1796 and in Boston the following year. Only two of the musical numbers have been preserved.
   b. *Why, Huntress, Why?* (*MinA*, p. 211)
7. *The Federal Overture*, 1794
   a. This medley of patriotic airs includes the first American printing of *Yankee Doodle*. Other tunes included are *Ca Ira*; *O dear, what can the matter be?*; *Rose Tree*; *Carmagnole* and *The President's March*.
8. Piano sonata: *The History of England*, Op. 11
9. *Sonata VI*, 1796 (*RRAM*, v. 1, p. 17)
10. *The Siege of Tripoli, an Historical Naval Sonata for the piano forte*, 1805 (*RRAM*, v. 1, p. 77)
11. *The Maid of Lodi, with variations*, 1809 (*RRAM*, v. 1, p. 105)
12. *Voluntary for the Organ*, 1801 (*RRAM*, v. 1, p. 49)
13. *Evening Amusement containing Fifty Airs, Songs, . . . Marches and Minuets*, 1796
    a. *Money Musk* for flute or violin (*BCAM*, p. 178); *Martini's March* for two flutes or violins (*BCAM*, p. 180)
14. *Music of the Church*, 1828
    a. *Philadelphia* (*AH*, p. 514)
15. *Masses, Vespers, Litanies, Hymns, Psalms, Anthems and Motets* "for use of the Catholic Churches in the United States of America," 1805
    a. *Dies Irae, Dies Illa* (*AH*, p. 441)
16. *The Chorister: A Collection of Chants & Melodies Adapted to the Psalms and Hymns of the Episcopal Church*, Philadelphia, 1820
    a. *Eroica* (*AH*, p. 192)
17. *Federal Street* (*LEAM*, p. 61)
18. Organ music: *Flute Voluntary* (*CAO*, p. 26); *Variations to the Sicilian Hymn* (*CAO*, p. 30)

J. **Henri Capron** (*fl.* late eighteenth century)
   1. **Capron**, a prominent cellist in America, was a pupil of the French cellist and composer **Pierre Gaviniès** (1728-1800) in Paris; he first appeared in Philadelphia in 1785. With **Alexander Reinagle** and **William Brown** he managed the "Subscription Concerts" in New York and Philadelphia. From 1788 to 1792 he performed with the orchestra of the Old American Company. In 1794 **Capron** settled in Philadelphia and later became director of a French boarding school.
   2. One of the three "Subscription Concerts" in the 1789 season was the following "under the direction of Messrs. Reinagle and Capron:"

FIRST CONCERT

Act 1st

Overture of	Giordani
Song by	Mrs. Sewell
Concerto Violoncello	Mr. Capron
Overture of	Guglielmi

Act 2nd

Overture of	Stamitz
Song by	Mrs. Sewell
Sonata Piano Forte	Mr. Reinagle
Overture of	Gossec

After the first act will be performed a Chorus to the words that were sung, as Gen. Washington passed the bridge at Trenton—the Music now composed by Mr. Reinagle.

3.   **Capron** composed many songs and the very popular *New Contredances*.

4.   *Delia*, 1793 (*MDGW*, p. 44)

K.   **John Christopher Moller** (1755-1803)

1.   **Moller**, a German composer and organist, came to America by way of England and first appeared in New York as a harpsichordist in 1790. He left immediately for Philadelphia where he became organist of the Zion German Lutheran Church. In 1791 and 1792 he took part in the City Concerts with **Reinagle** and **Capron** as both manager and performer. He and **Capron** opened a music store and a music school in conjunction with it. In 1795 he returned to New York and in the following year succeeded **James Hewitt** as manager of the City Concerts with the **Van Hagens**.

2.   Several of **Moller's** works had been published in England: *Six Quartettos*; *Progressive Lessons for the Harpsichord*; *Compleat Book of Instructions for the Pianoforte*; *Six Sonatas for the Forte Piano or Harpsichord, with a Violin or Violoncello Accompaniment*.

3.   In Philadelphia in 1793 **Moller** published with **Capron** three issues of *Monthly Numbers* which includes a *Sinfonie* arranged for piano (*MinA*, p. 218), *Rondo, Overture, Quartetto* for glass harmonica, two violas and cello, and *Duetti* for clarinet and piano.

4.   *Meddley with the most favorite Airs and Variations*, 1797 (*RRAM*, v. 1, p. 8)

5.   *Rondo*, 1800 (*RRAM*, v. 1, p. 42)

L.   Other lesser known European musicians found a ready market for their talents in America.

1.   **Francis Linley** (1771-1800), a blind English organist, spent about three years (1796-1799) in America and then returned to England. His *A New Assistant for the Piano-Forte*, Baltimore, 1796 (*BCAM*, p. 174), opens with a beginning lesson and continues with six sonatas. The fourth sonata is for four hands; fingering is indicated throughout all the sonatas.

a.   Organ works: *Introductory Voluntary* (*CAO*, p. 14); *Trumpet Voluntary* (*CAO*, p. 16)

2.   *The Battle of Prague, A Favourite Sonata for the Piano Forte* (*BCAM*, p. 142) by the Bohemian composer **Franz Kotzwara** (1720-1791) was published in Philadelphia by **Benjamin Carr** in 1793. **Kotzwara** never came to America but he became famous due solely to the tremendous popularity of this one piano sonata.

a.   The virtuoso piece reflects signal cannons, bugle calls, flying bullets, galloping horses, cries of the wounded and triumphant strains of "God, Save the King." Crossing hands, tremolandos and precipitous scale passages are effectively used.

III.   National Airs

A.   The first national airs, *Yankee Doodle* and *Hail! Columbia*, appeared in the latter part of the eighteenth century; *America* and *The Star Spangled Banner* were written early in the nineteenth century.

1.   *Yankee Doodle* (*MinA*, p. 282)

a.   The origin of the tune is uncertain; it may be traced to the time of Charles I (1600-1649) of England; another suggestion is that it was popular in Holland as a harvest tune in the early sixteenth century and thus was brought to America by Dutch settlers. The tune first appeared in *Selection of Scotch, English, Irish and Foreign Airs* edited by James Aird in England about 1775.

b.   The song as known in America was written by Richard Schuckbaugh and was used by the British to make fun of the inexperienced Yankee recruits who made up the Army. The Yankees soon took it over as their own song with new words.

1)   The best known verse, "Yankee Doodle came to town Riding on a pony, Stuck a feather in his cap, And called it macaroni," was known around 1764.

a)   The word "Doodle" may have been a corruption of "Do-little" and "macaroni" means a "dandy."

c. The first printed notice of the song was in the October 12, 1768, issue of the *New York Journal*. In the 1780's it was published in England with the title, *Yankee Doodle, or (as now Christened by the Saints of New England) The Lexington March*. A ridiculing note was added: "NB. The Words to be Sung thro' the Nose & in the West Country drawl & dialect."

d. The first known print of the music in America appeared as part of **Benjamin Carr's** medley of patriotic airs, *Federal Overture*, Baltimore, 1795.

2. *Hail! Columbia* (*MinA*, p. 283)

a. The verses were written in 1798 by Judge Joseph Hopkinson, son of Francis, as requested by the actor Gilbert Fox. First sung in a theater by a friend, the song was to be used to stir up American spirit at the time when a war with France was being considered.

b. The verses are set by **Philip Phile** (*c*. 1734-1793) to *The President's March* (*MinA*, p. 286), written after Washington's inauguration in 1789 but not published until about 1794.

c. *The Favorite New Federal Song Hail! Columbia* was first published "For the Voice, Piano Forte, Guittar and Clarinet" by **Benjamin Carr** in Philadelphia in 1798.

3. *The Star Spangled Banner* (*MinA*, p. 291; *Hymnal*, No. 142)

a. The verses were written by the American lawyer, Francis Scott Key (1780-1843), during the War of 1812 after the bombardment of Fort McHenry (1814) by the British.

b. The words were soon adapted to the "theme song" of the Anacreontic Society of London (from about 1766).

1) *The Anacreontic Song* (*MinA*, p. 287), written by the Society's former president, Ralph Tomlinson, the music by member John Stafford Smith (1750-1836) and first printed in the *Vocal Magazine* of August 1, 1778, was used to open (after a concert and supper) the evening entertainment of the Society.

c. Francis Scott Key knew the tune and had used it nine years before (1805) to set the text "When the warrior returns from the battle afar." Between 1790 and 1818 there were no less than 85 parodies made of the song.

d. Since 1865 *The Star Spangled Banner* has been used by the United States military bands. It was officially proclaimed the United States National Anthem on March 3, 1931, by President Herbert Hoover.

4. *America* (*MinA*, p. 293; *Hymnal*, No. 141)

a. The words of *"My Country! 'Tis of Thee"* were written in 1831 by Samuel Francis Smith (1808-1895) at the suggestion of **Lowell Mason** (1792-1872). **Mason's** children's choir sang the new song on July 4, 1831, at the Park Street Church in Boston. The song was adapted to the music of the British National Anthem, *"God Save the King."*

b. Some of the other texts set by this tune are "God Save America" and "God Save Great Washington."

c. The tune was first printed in America in **Lyon's** *Urania*, 1761 (*MinA*, p. 106); earlier it had appeared in London in *Harmonia Anglicana*, 1744.

BIBLIOGRAPHY

Books

1. Camus, Raoul François. *Military Music of the American Revolution*. Chapel Hill: The University of North Carolina Press, 1976.

2. *Catalog of Orchestral and Choral Compositions Published and in Manuscript Between 1790 and 1840*. Philadelphia: The Musical Fund Society of Philadelphia, 1974.

3. Delaplaine, Edward S. *Francis Scott Key and the National Anthem*. Washington, DC: Wilson-Epes Press, 1947.

4. *Early Songs of Uncle Sam* (1825-1850), ed. George Stuyvesant Jackson. Boston: Bruce Humphries, 1933; reprint: 1964.

5. Elson, Louis Charles. *The National Music of America and Its Sources*. Boston: L. C. Page, 1899; reprint: Detroit: Gale Research Co., 1975.

6. Engel, Lehman. *The American Musical Theatre: A Consideration*. New York: Collier Books, 1975.

7. Ewen, David. *The Story of America's Musical Theater*. Philadelphia: Chilton Books, 1961.

8. Filby, P. William, and Edward G. Howard, compilers. *Star-Spangled Books: Books, Sheet Music, Newspapers, Manuscripts, and Persons Associated with "The Star Spangled Banner."* Baltimore: Maryland Historical Society, 1972.

9. Hewitt, John Hill. "From *Shadows on the Wall*," in *The American Composer Speaks, A Historical Anthology, 1770-1965*, ed. Gilbert Chase. Baton Rouge: Louisiana State University Press, 1966, pp. 70-76.

10. Hill, Richard S. "The Melody of 'The Star Spangled Banner' in the United States Before 1820," in *Essays Honoring Lawrence C. Wroth*. Portland, ME: Anthoensen, 1951, pp. 151-193.

11. Keefer, Kubov. *Baltimore's Music: the Haven of the American Composer*. Baltimore: J. H. Furst Co., 1962.

12. Kobbé, Gustav. *Famous American Songs*. New York: Thomas Y. Crowell Co., 1906.

13. Lowens, Irving. "Benjamin Carr's *Federal Overture* (1794)," in *Music and Musicians in Early America*. New York: W. W. Norton, 1964, pp. 89-114.

14. ———————*Haydn in America*, with Otto E. Albrecht. *Haydn Autographs in the U. S.* Detroit: Information Coordinators, 1979.

15. ———————"James Hewitt: Professional Musician," in *Music and Musicians in Early America*. New York: W. W. Norton, 1964, pp. 194-202.

16. Mates, Julian. *The American Musical Stage Before 1800*. New Brunswick, NJ: Rutgers University Press, 1962.

17. Muller, Joseph. *The Star-Spangled Banner: Words and Music Issued Between 1814-1864*. New York: G. A. Baker, 1935; reprint: New York: Da Capo Press, 1973.

18. Nye, Russell Blaine. *The Cultural Life of the New Nation 1776-1830*, ed. Henry Steele Commager and Richard B. Morris. New York: Harper & Row, 1962.

19. Sonneck, Oscar George Theodore. "The First Edition of 'Hail, Columbia!'," in *Miscellaneous Studies in the History of Music*. New York: Macmillan, 1921; reprint: New York: Da Capo Press, 1968, pp. 180-189.

20. ———————*Report on the "The Star-Spangled Banner," "Hail Columbia," "America," "Yankee Doodle."* Washington, DC: Government Printing Office, 1909; reprint: New York: Dover Publications, 1972.

21. ———————*The Star Spangled Banner*. Washington, DC: Government Printing Office, 1914; reprint: New York: Da Capo Press, 1969.

22. Spaeth, Sigmund G. *A History of Popular Music in America*. New York: Random House, 1948, 1958.

23. Stetzel, Ronald Delbert. *John Christopher Moller, 1755-1803, and His Role in Early American Music*. Ann Arbor: University Microfilms, 1965.

Articles

1. Coppage, Noel. "Oh Say! Can You Sing The Star-Spangled Banner." *Sterio Review* 24 (February 1970), pp. 78-80.
2. Davis, Josephine K. R. "Program Music of Early America." *Music Journal* 33 (May, 1975), pp. 14-15.
3. Engel, Carl. "Introducing Mr. Braun." *MQ* 30 (1944), pp. 63-83.
4. Gilbert, Donald K. "Military Drumming During the American Revolution, 1775-1783." *Percussionist* 9, No. 1 (1971), pp. 1-5.
5. Higginson, Joseph Vincent. "John Aitken's Compilations–1787 and 1791 (Catholics in Philadelphia)." *The Hymn* 27 (1976), pp. 68-75.
6. Hill, Thomas Clifford. " 'The Star-Spangled Banner': Yesterday and To-day." *MA* 27 (July 6, 1918), pp. 11, 13.
7. Howard, John Tasker. "The Hewitt Family in American Music." *MQ* 17 (1931), pp. 25-39.
8. Keast, Laury S. "The Songs of America 1775-1840 (The First 65 Years of America's Popular Music)." *Music Journal* (Annual, 1969), pp. 50-51.
9. Kidson, Frank. "Some Guesses about 'Yankee Doodle'." *MQ* 3 (1917), pp. 98-103.
10. Kouwenhoven, John Atlee, and Lawton M. Patten. "New Light on 'The Star-Spangled Banner'." *MQ* 23 (1937), pp. 198-200.
11. Krohn, Ernst C. "Alexander Reinagle as Sonatist." *MQ* 18 (1932), pp. 140-149.
12. La Laurencie, Lionel de. "America in the French Music of the Seventeenth and Eighteenth Centuries." *MQ* 7 (1921), pp. 284-302.
13. Levy, Lester S., and James J. Fuld. "Unrecorded Printings of *The Star Spangled Banner*." *Notes* 27 (1970-1971), pp. 245-251.
14. Lichtenwanger, William. "The Music of 'The Star-Spangled Banner'." *Library of Congress Quarterly Journal* 34 (1977), pp. 136-170.
15. –––––––" 'Star Spangled' Bibliography." *College Music* 12 (1972), pp. 94-102.
16. Maginty, Edward A. " 'America': The Origin of Its Melody." *MQ* 20 (1934), pp. 259-266.
17. Marrocco, W. Thomas. "The 'Set Piece'." *JAMS* 15 (1962), pp. 348-352.
18. Meyer, Eve R. "Benjamin Carr's *Musical Miscellany*." *Notes* 33 (1976), pp. 253-265.
19. Murray, Sterling E. "A Checklist of Funeral Dirges in Honor of General Washington." *Notes* 36 (1979), pp. 326-344.
20. Ratner, Leonard G. "Eighteenth Century Theories of Musical Period Structure." *MQ* 42 (1956), pp. 439-454.
21. Redway, Virginia Larkin. "The Carrs, American Music Publishers." *MQ* 18 (1932), pp. 150-177.
22. –––––––"Handel in Colonial and Post-Colonial America." *MQ* 21 (1935), pp. 190-207.
23. Wagner, John Waldorf. "James Hewitt, 1770-1827." *MQ* 58 (1972), pp. 259-276.
24. –––––––"The Music of James Hewitt: A Supplement to the Sonneck-Upton and Wolfe Bibliographies." *Notes* 29 (1972), pp. 224-227.
25. Wolf, Edward C. "Music in Old Zion, Philadelphia, 1750-1850." *MQ* 58 (1972), pp. 622-652.

Music

1. Aitken, John. *A Compilation of the Litanies and Vespers, Hymns and Anthems as They are Sung in the Catholic Church*. Philadelphia: Thomas Dobson, 1787; reprint: Philadelphia: Musical Americana, 1954.
2. *The American Musical Magazine*, v. 1, nos. 1-12 [May, 1786–September, 1787]. New Haven: A[mos] Doolittle and D[aniel] Read; reprint: Ann Arbor: University Microfilms, 1961; Scarsdale, NY: Annemarie Schnase, 1961.

3. *The American Musical Miscellany. A Collection of the Newest and Most Approved Songs, Set to Music.* Northampton, MA: 1798; reprint: New York: Da Capo Press, 1972. (Earlier American Music, v. 9)

4. *Anthology of Early American Keyboard Music 1787-1830*, Parts I and II, ed. J. Busker Clark. Madison, WI: A–R Editions, 1977. (Recent Researches in American Music, vols. 1 and 2)

5. Carr, Benjamin R. *Musical Miscellany in Occasional Numbers Compiled.* New York: Da Capo Press, 1981. (Earlier American Music, v. 21)

6. Hewitt, James. *Selected Compositions*, ed. John W. Wagner. Madison, WI: A–R Editions, 1980.

7. Howard, John Tasker. *A Program of Early American Piano Music*. New York: J. Fischer, 1931.

8. ––––––*A Program of Early and Mid-Nineteenth Century Songs*. New York: J. Fischer, 1931.

9. *Musical Journal for the Piano*, 5 vols. Philadelphia: Carr & Schetky, 1800; reprint: in 2 vols., Wilmington, DE: Scholarly Resources, 1972.

10. Taylor, Raynor. *Buxom Joan*, burletta in one act, ed. Gregory Sandow. Bryn Mawr, PA: Theodore Presser, 1975.

From **The Rural Harmony** by Jacob Kimball, 1793

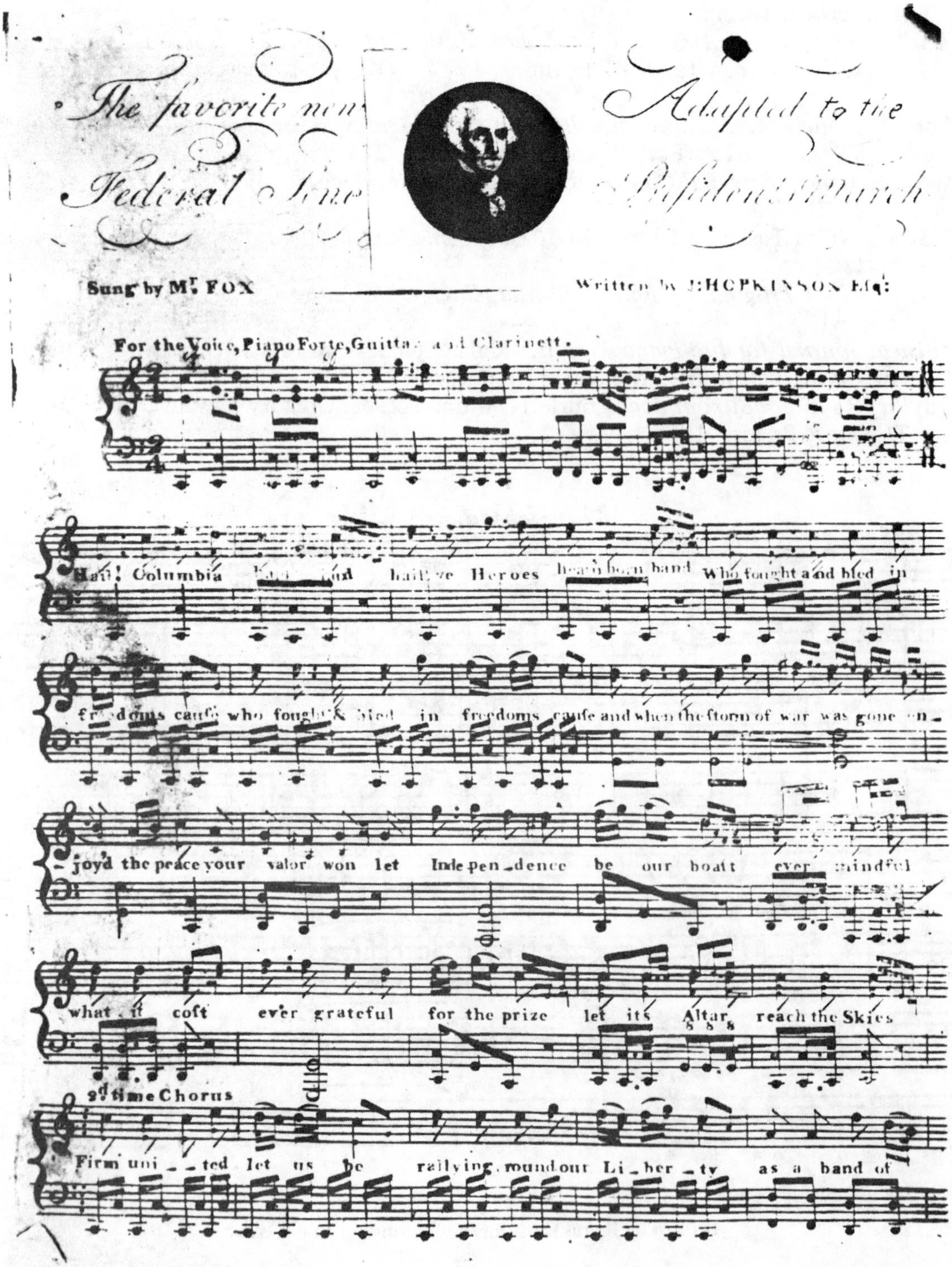

"Hail! Columbia" by Joseph Hopkinson, 1798

Brothers join'd peace and saf'ty we shall find.

2

Immortal Patriots rise once more
Defend your rights — defend your shore
Let no rude foe with impious hand
Let no rude foe with impious hand
Invade the shrine where sacred lies
Of toil and blood the well earnd prize
While offering peace sincere and just
In heavn we place a manly trust
That truth and justice will prevail
And every scheme of bondage fail
Firm — united &c

3

Sound sound the trump of fame
Let Washingtons great name
Ring thro the world with loud applause
Ring thro the world with loud applause
Let every clime to Freedom dear
Listen with a joyful ear —
With equal skill with godlike powr
He governs in the fearful hour.
Of horrid war or guides with ease
The happier times of honest peace —
Firm — united &c

4

Behold the Chief who now commands
Once more to serve his Country stands
The rock on which the storm will beat
The rock on which the storm will beat
But arm'd in virtue firm and true
His hopes are fix'd on heavn and you —
When hope was sinking in dismay
When glooms obscur'd Columbias day
His steady mind from changes free
Resolved on Death or Liberty —
Firm — united &c

For the FLUTE or VIOLIN

2 time Chorus

A Song by Alexander Reinagle

2ᵈ VERSE.

Love has bow & arrows   gentle cousin   John   Should he aim a shaft at you,

Arrows mortal every one   gentle cousin John.

...me shaft may wound me too. When that cruel deed is done, Then good evning, then good evning

cousin, cousin John.

3ᵈ

Love has chains and fetters, gentle cousin John.

Hymen is a cruel knave,

For he puts those fetters on, gentle cousin John;

Makes his best of friends his slave.

Farewell love when that is done;

Then good night ah, then good night dear cousin, cousin John.

OUTLINE VIII

LOWELL MASON AND HIS CONTEMPORARIES

The Early Nineteemth Century
Lowell Mason
Contemporaries of Lowell Mason

I. **The Early Nineteenth Century**

   A. In the early nineteenth century foreign musicians still controlled music in America, but many of the younger musicians became naturalized and were identified with music in the United States during their entire artistic careers. These early musicians and their immediate predecessors, both foreign and native American, paved the way for **Lowell Mason** and other American composers.

      1. **Filippo [Philip] Traetta** (1777-1854)

         a. Typical among these European musicians was **Traetta**; born in Venice on January 8, at an early age he received a professsional background in music in Italy, later studied with **Niccolò Piccinni** (1728-1800) in Naples and at the age of 22 sailed for Boston (1799). With his musical experience he entered right into a blossoming environment of musical activities found in an artistically developing city. He spent some years in New York (1808-1817) and Charlestown before establishing himself in Philadelphia in 1822.

         b. To further point up the foreign leadership in the musical community, in 1801 **Traetta**, in conjunction with the German **Gottlieb Graupner** and the French **François Mallet** (1750-1834) founded a very successful music school. Although **Traetta** soon moved on, the educational venture continued as an adjunct to a thriving printing business carried on by **Graupner**. After **Traetta** settled in Philadelphia he opened his "American Conservatorio" in 1828.

         c. Included in **Traetta's** works are oratorios, cantatas, songs and instrumental and vocal chamber music.

      2. **Johann Christian Gottlieb Graupner** (1767-1836)

         a. Son of **Johann Georg Graupner** of Hanover, Germany, **Gottlieb**, like his father, became a professional oboist. While in London he played in **Haydn's** orchestra (1791). He emigrated to Charlestown, South Carolina, where on March 21, 1795, he played his oboe concerto. Two years later he went to Boston where in 1800 he opened a music store and taught piano and orchestral instruments. He became an American citizen in 1808.

         b. **Graupner** founded the Boston Philharmonic Society in 1810. This small orchestra of amateurs and professionals met for the playing of **Haydn's** symphonies and other works and eventually gave concerts, the last one in November, 1824.

           1) In addition to presenting **Haydn** symphonies in concert, the Philharmonic Society presented **Handel's** *Messiah* in 1818 and **Haydn's** *Creation* in 1819, only 20 years after its first performance in Vienna.

         c. **Graupner** was also one of the organizers of a musical organization which became the Boston Handel and Haydn Society (1815). This Society sang the works of **Handel, Haydn** and other "eminent composers," raised the standard of choral singing and helped in the formation of other choral societies. A festival was established in 1865 and was subsequently held every three years.

         d. *Rudiments of the Art of Playing the Piano-Forte, Containing the Elements of Music*, Boston, 1806.

1) The Preface of the 1819 edition is largely taken from **Clementi's** *Introduction to the Art of Playing on the Piano Forte*, London, 1801.
2) The explanations for the performance of ornaments generally follow Baroque practices.

3. **George K. Jackson** (1745-1822)

   a. **Jackson**, born in Oxford, England, and a schoolmate of **Raynor Taylor**, received the Doctor of Music degree from St. Andrews College in 1791. Five years later **Jackson** emigrated to Norfolk, Virginia, and visited several cities for indefinite periods of time on his way to Boston, where he arrived in 1812. He spent some time as music director of St. George's Chapel in New York in 1804. In Boston he was organist at different churches: Brattle Square, King's Chapel, Trinity and St. Paul's. **Jackson** also became the first organist of the Boston Handel and Haydn Society and, with **Graupner** and **Mallet**, organized a series of oratorio concerts.

   b. While **Lowell Mason** was living in Savannah, he unsuccessfully sought a publisher for his new collection of church music until he met **Dr. Jackson** in Boston. **Jackson** became interested in the compilation and encouraged the Boston Handel and Haydn Society to sponsor it; *The Boston Handel and Haydn Society Collection of Church Music* was then published (1822) and subsequently went through many editions.

   c. *David's Psalms*, New York, 1804
   1) This 60-page psalter includes psalm tunes "selected from the best Ancient and Modern Authors."
   2) *Aberford* (*AH*, p. 183)

   d. *A Choice Collection of Chants*, Boston, 1816
   1) This contains 38 four-voice chants with figured bass, a *Gloria Patri* and a *Sanctus*.

4. **Oliver Shaw** (1779-1848)

   a. **Shaw** was born in Middleboro, Massachusetts, on March 13; he was a pupil of **Gottlieb Graupner**; he became known as a singing teacher, organist, compiler and composer of psalm tunes and ballads. At the age of 17 he enrolled as one of the first students of Bristol Academy; at the age of 21 he was totally blind. In 1807 he moved to Providence, Rhode Island, where he built up a thriving music class, was organist of the local First Congregational Church and organized several bands of music. In 1809 **Shaw** was instrumental in organizing the Psallonian Society for improving themselves in psalmody and sacred music; he remained its "guiding light" for the 23 years of its existence.

   b. **Shaw** composed many vocal and instrumental pieces, and compiled several books of songs and hymns.
   1) *The Gentleman's Favorite Selection of Instrumental Music*, Dedham, 1805
   2) *The Musical Olio*, Providence, 1814
   3) Providence Selection of *Psalms and Hymns*, Dedham, 1815 (110 pieces)
      a) *Benevolent Street* (*AH*, p. 426)
   4) *The Melodia Sacra*, Providence, 1819
      a) *Hymn for New Year* (*YONE*, p. 48)
   5) *Original Pieces*, 1823
      a) *Welcome the Nation's Guest, a Military Divertimento for the piano forte composed & respectfully dedicated to Genl. Lafayette on his visit to Providence* (*RRAM*, v. 2, p. 75)
   6) *Original Melodies*, 1832
   7) *Instruction for the Piano Forte*, 1831
   8) *The Social Sacred Melodist*, 1835
   9) *Thanksgiving Anthem* (O Give Thanks unto the Lord) (*MinA*, p. 169)
      a) The four-part anthem is accompanied with organ and instrumental ensemble (clarinet and strings) doubling the voice parts. Instrumental sinfonia introduce and separate the sections; expression indications (rare at this time) include "dolce," "espressivo," "f" and "p." Voices sing in pairs; contrast of key,

tempo and rhythm, and a bass solo define the second section.
10)   *The Lord is My Shepherd*, 1835 (*BCAC*, p. 76)

II.   Lowell Mason (1792-1872)

A.   Born January 8 in Medfield, Massachusetts, **Mason** began his career at the age of 16 and became an outstanding organist, conductor, music educator, composer, compiler of music collections and organizer of singing schools.

B.   At the age of 20 he traveled to Savannah, Georgia, where he became a bank clerk. Remaining there for the next 14 years (1812-1826) he was organist and choirmaster of the Presbyterian Church and continued his studying, composing and compiling of hymn tunes and anthems.

1.   *The Boston Handel and Haydn Society Collection of Church Music*, Boston, 1822 (*EAM*, v. 15)

a.   On the recommendation of **George K. Jackson**, this first of **Mason's** many compilations was published under the auspices of the Boston Handel and Haydn Society. Not only did this prove a financial success to **Mason** but also assured the financial solvency of the Society. It also drew the attention of the public to **Mason** and caused him to change to music as a profession. The publishing of this collection had a remarkable influence on the repertoire and performance of church music throughout the country. During the succeeding 35 years it went through at least 19 editions and sold approximately 50,000 copies.

b.   **Mason's** name did not appear as editor until the ninth edition in 1831, although he was mentioned in the Preface. He later said, "I was then a bank officer in Savannah and did not wish to be known as a musical man, and I had not the least thought of making music my profession."

c.   *Benson* (*AH*, p. 599); *Hamburg* (*AH*, p. 604)

C.   In 1827 **Mason** moved to Boston where he was well known through his "Handel and Haydn Society Collection." He became choir director at Lyman Beecher's Bowdoin Square Church where he remained 14 years. However, for a steady income he was employed as a bank teller at the American Bank. **Mason** was also elected president and conductor of the Boston Handel and Haydn Society.

1.   **Mason** organized the first children's singing school to train children to sing alto parts in church choirs, which rarely had altos.

2.   Collections of music for children's choirs soon began to appear. Among these is *The Juvenile Psalmist, or The Child's Introduction to Sacred Music*, Boston, 1829, the first music book for Sunday Schools. The *Juvenile Lyre; or Hymns and Songs, Religious, Moral, and Cheerful, Set to Appropriate Music, for the Use of Primary and Common Schools*, Boston, 1831, compiled in cooperation with **Elam Ives**, is "the first school song book published in this country," a book of secular school songs.

D.   In August, 1830, William C. Woodbridge, the editor of *American Annals of Education*, lectured to the American Institute of Instruction in Boston. He had spent several years in Europe (Germany and Switzerland) studying and observing the method of Johann Heinrich Pestalozzi (1746-1827) and was advocating the introduction of music into the common schools. Although **Mason** had been advocating music in the public schools for some four years, he evidently was not familiar with the Pestalozzian system of education until he met Woodbridge. To demonstrate for Woodbridge's lecture, **Mason** supplied his children's choir.

1.   **Mason** did not abandon his principles of teaching until he was convinced by Woodbridge of the superiority of the Pestalozzian theories. The children's concerts of the school year 1832-1833, trained in the new theories, proved very successful and after that time **Mason** used the new theories extensively.

a.   Pestalozzi stressed the inductive method of instruction, "*building* up instead of *patching* up."

2. After his class concerts **Mason** established the Boston Academy of Music on January 8, 1833. Because of the demands on **Mason's** time, **George J. Webb** was employed as an associate professor. Several private schools introduced music classes.

E. The Boston Academy of Music

1. **Mason** organized an annual teacher-training class at the Academy in 1834. This idea soon extended throughout New England and the Middle Atlantic States by means of "conventions" and teacher education institutes. He traveled as far west as Rochester, New York, often meeting groups of several hundred singers and teachers. The festivals which developed from these conventions helped to spread his creed of "music for the masses."

2. *Manual of the Boston Academy of Music, for Instruction in the Elements of Vocal Music, on the System of Pestalozzi*, Boston, 1834 (several editions to 1861)

   a. In the *"Manual"* **Mason** states: "It is not so much the object of education to store the mind with knowledge, as to discipline it. That person is not the best educated *who has learned the most*, but he who knows best how to learn."

   b. The *"Manual"* is divided into four sections: 1) reasons for and advantages of general and continued cultivating of vocal music, qualifications and duties of teachers, 2) rhythm, melody, dynamics (about 4/5 of the book), 3) expression and 4) types of voices, a short collection of vocalises and rounds.

F. **Mason** made a short visit to Europe in 1837. He studied musical instruction in the schools, heard much music and met many musicians. Among the latter was **Mendelssohn**, who was rehearsing his oratorio *St. Paul* in London.

G. **Mason** worked toward the establishment of music teaching in the public schools. In 1837 the Boston public schools did not receive an appropriation from the City Council to teach music in the schools; the plan was almost lost until **Mason** "offered to give instruction gratuitously in one of the schools." This he did in the Hawes Grammar School. Because of **Mason's** success in this school, on August 28, 1838, the Boston school committee voted the introduction of music as a branch of popular education in the city schools.

1. **Mason** taught in some schools and hired assistants for other schools. Early assistants were **A. N. Johnson, George F. Root, Albert Drake** and **James A. Johnson**.

2. The first classes were held in the two upper grammar grades; music was introduced into the primary grades in 1854, into the lower grammar grades and some high schools in 1868, and by 1874 all the grades, including the remaining high schools, were enjoying music classes.

3. For ten years, 1845-1855, **Mason** was on the Massachusetts State Board of Education.

H. In 1851 **Mason** went to Europe for the second time and on his return in 1853 settled in Orange, New Jersey, where he took an active part in community life.

1. In London he gave lectures on "Music for the Church" and "Pestalozzianism," directed singing schools and music classes for children.

I. **Mason** held the first teacher training music institute (The New York Musical Normal Institute) for three months during the summer of 1853 in New York City. His faculty included **George Root, Thomas Hastings** and **William B. Bradbury**.

1. The curriculum included theory, composition, instrumental and vocal training and choral practice.

2. **Mason's** teacher classes, conventions and teacher-training institutes provided well-trained music teachers for over a quarter of a century.

   a. The concept of training the children as a means of educating the parents was clearly understood, thoroughly believed, encouraged and practiced by **Mason**. The concept was stated in the Preface of his *Book of Chants*: "Let chanting be introduced into the Sabbath School . . . and it will not be long before it may be successfully introduced into the congregation.

J. In 1855 New York University awarded **Mason** the second honorary Doctor of Music degree to be conferred in this country.

    1.   The first honorary Doctor of Music degree had been awarded in 1849 by Georgetown University to Henry Dielman.

K.   **Lowell Mason's** elder sons, **Daniel Gregory** and **Lowell, Jr.**, established the publishing firm known as Mason Brothers. His son **Henry** was one of the founders of the Mason and Hamlin Company, makers of reed organs. They began the construction of pianos in 1882. Another son, **William**, became a famous piano pedagogue. **Daniel Gregory Mason (1873-1953)**, son of **Henry**, was **Lowell's** grandson.

L.   **Mason** led the reaction against the cheap "gospel song" type of hymn which had begun to appear after the fuging tunes of **Billings** were discarded.

    1.   His hymns are characterized by a religious feeling. The tunes are smooth, devoid of wide skips, limited in range and of a moderate tessitura for the average congregation.

    2.   The harmony is simple, generally of closely related chords with few modulations; the inner voices are often stationary. The reaction to the fuging tune is obvious in the lack of counterpoint; the style is basically homophonic.

    3.   The tune is conceived to serve the text; the music should not draw attention away from the text but rather reinforce the text in a spirit of worship.

    4.   **Mason** produced about 1,700 hymn tunes, about 1,210 of his own and the remaining as arrangements.

        a.   Airs or parts of compositions by well-known composers, such as **Handel, Mozart, Haydn, Palestrina, Rossini, Corelli, Schubert, Beethoven** and Gregorian chant were often adapted and arranged with religious texts.

M.   **Mason** published over a hundred different collections for a variety of organizations; many were in collaboration with his contemporaries, **Hastings, Webb, Bradbury** and **Oliver**; over a million copies were sold.

    1.   The collections usually contain sacred and secular music and an introduction called "The Singing School." This section includes the elements of music, exercises, rounds, part-songs, hymns and anthems.

        a.   The syllables, *do - re - mi*, are used in place of the old *faw - sol - law - mi* syllables.

        b.   The usual order of voices in open score is from top to bottom: tenor, alto, treble, "base." **Mason** also advocates placing the melody in the position of the top voice.

        c.   Figured bass is used in many collections.

        d.   Among **Mason's** most famous tunes are : *Olivet* (My faith looks up to Thee) (*AH*, p. 464; *Hymnal*, No. 449); *Bethany* (Nearer, my God, to Thee) (*AH*, p. 562; *Hymnal*, No. 465); *Missionary Hymn* (From Greenland's icy mountains) (*AH*, p. 335; *Hymnal* No. 254); *Watchman* (Watchman, tell us of the night) (*Hymnal*, No. 440).

        e.   *O praise God in his holiness* (*BCAC*, p. 73)

N.   Collections

    1.   *The Boston Academy's Collection of Church Music*, Boston 1835

        a.   *Downs* (*AH*, p. 607); *Federal Street* (*AH*, p. 606); *Chadwick* (*AH*, p. 638)

    2.   *The Modern Psalmist*, 1839

        a.   *Meribah* (*AH*, pp. 504, 550)

    3.   *The Boston School Song Book Published under the Sanction of the Boston Academy of Music*, Boston, Philadelphia and New York, 1841

        a.   In addition to songs, this book contains 31 rounds, 11 sentences and lessons. The book closes with 27 sets of questions on various aspects of music elements.

    4.   *The Boston Glee Book*, Boston, 1844 (**Mason** and **Webb**)

        a.   In addition to several English madrigals, compositions by **Weber, Mozart, Rossini** and **Martini** are included. "Objectionable texts have been changed."

        b.   Madrigal: **John Wilbye**, *Flora gave me fairest flowers*, p. 5

        c.   Madrigal: **Thomas Morley**, *Now is the month of Maying*, p. 55

        d.   Madrigal for two men's voices: **Michael Este**, *How merrily we live*, p. 228

    5.   *The Psaltery, A New Collection of Church Music*, Boston, 1846, by **Lowell Mason** and **George J. Webb**, "Professors at the Boston Academy of Music."

      a.   "Elements of Vocal Music," pp. 4-30; "Explanation of Musical Terms," p. 34. Figured bass is used, expression marks are indicated and tempo is suggested: "In a gentle and solemn manner," "With fervor and solemnity."

      b.   *Amboy* (*AH*, p. 458); *Bazetta* (*AH*, p. 520)

  6. *The Cherokee Singing Book*, Boston, 1846, prepared for the American Board of Commissioners for Foreign Missions.

      a.   With the texts in the Cherokee language, this book was compiled with the aid of **George Guess [Sequoie]** (1760-*c*. 1843), a Cherokee Indian of mixed blood.

  7. *New Carmina Sacra*, 1850

      a.   *Ernan* (*AH*, p. 359)

  8. *The Hallelujah*, 1854

      a.   *Alvan* (*AH*, p. 482); *Laban* (*AH*, p. 485); *Henley* (*AH*, p. 523)

III. Contemporaries of Lowell Mason

A. Thomas Hastings (1784-1872)

  1. **Hastings**, born on October 15 in Washington, Connecticut, was a self-taught composer of hymn tunes and a compiler of many successful hymn-tune collections. In 1796 he moved to Clinton, New York, and on to Utica in 1823, where he became a member of the Handel and Haydn Society and edited the religious weekly, *The Western Recorder*, for nine years. In 1832 he moved to New York City to develop choirs in several churches. In association with **Lowell Mason**, **Hastings** assisted in the first teacher training institute held in New York in 1853. New York University conferred on **Hastings** in 1858 what was probably the third honorary Doctor of Music degree presented in the United States.

  2. **Hastings** published about 50 collections including more than 1,000 hymns of his own composing. At times other compilers, such as **William Bradbury**, **Lowell Mason**, **Solomon Warriner** and **William Patton**, collaborated with **Hastings**. The success of these collections is due in no small part to the fact that **Hastings** directed the content of his compilations toward certain general groups: nursery children, mothers, vocal students, choirs and congregations in general. His writings also include some instruction books.

      a.   *Musica Sacra: or, Utica and Springfield Collection United*, Utica, 1816

         1) **Hastings'** first collection, in combination with **Solomon Warriner's** *The Springfield Collection* included psalm- and hymn-tunes, anthems and chants arranged for two, three and four voices. European composers were liberally represented. By 1836 the compilation had gone through ten editions.

      b.   *The Musical Reader, or, Practical Lessons for the Voice*, Utica, 1817

      c.   *Flute, New and Complete Preceptor for the German Flute*, Utica, 1819

      d.   *Dissertation on Musical Taste*, Albany, 1822, 1853

      e.   *The Christian Psalmist: or, Watts' Psalms and Hymns, with Copious Selections from other Sources*, New York, 1830 (with **William Patton**)

      f.   *Spiritual Songs for Social Worship*, 1831 (with **Lowell Mason**)

         1) *Toplady* (*AH*, p. 560); **Mason:** *Wesley* (*AH*, p. 334)

      g.   *The Mothers Hymn Book*, New York, 1834

      h.   *The Mothers Nursery Songs*, New York 1834

      i.   *The Manhattan Collection of Psalm and Hymn Tunes and Anthems*, New York, 1837

         1) *Luther* (*AH*, p. 556)

      j.   *The New York Choralist*, 1847

         1) *Eldridge* (*AH*, p. 424); *Zephyr* (*AH*, p. 438)

      k.   *The Mendelssohn Collection, or, Hastings' and Bradbury's Third Book of Psalmody*, New York, 1849

         1) *Woodworth* (*AH*, pp. 463-473)

l.   *Devotional Hymns and Religious Poems*, New York, 1850

m. *The Psalmista; or, Choir Melodies*, New York and Chicago, 1851 (with **William B. Bradbury**)

   l)   *Passaic* (*AH*, p. 430); *Rolland* (*AH*, p. 434)

n.   *The History of Forty Choirs*, New York, 1854

o.   *Sacred Praise: an earnest appeal to Christian Worshipers in Behalf of a Neglected Duty*, New York, 1856

  3. Several of **Hastings'** hymns are still in common use: *Retreat* (From every stormy wind that blows) (*Hymnal*, No. 421); *Toplady* (Rock of Ages) (*AH*, p. 560; *Hymnal*, No. 471; *MinA*, p. 238)

  4. *Deep is the sleep of the hero* (*BCAC*, p. 65)

B. **George James Webb** (1803-1887)

  1. **Webb** was born near Salisbury, England, on June 24; in boarding school he came under the musical influence of **Alexander Lucas** whose son became the principal of the Royal Academy of Music. In 1830 **Webb** arrived in Boston, became organist at Old South Church and played an important part in the musical life of Boston. In 1833 **Mason** appointed **Webb** as an assistant in carrying on the activities of the newly established Boston Academy of Music; **Mason** and **Webb** maintained a lifelong association and friendship.

  2. In 1840 **Webb** was elected president of the Boston Handel and Haydn Society. He edited with **Mason** *The Musical Library* (1835-1836) which includes all types of vocal music and also dance music with directions for its performance. **Webb** edited another musical periodical with T. B. Hayward, *The Musical Cabinet*, 1841-1842. In 1870 **Webb** followed **Mason** to Orange, New Jersey, and also taught in New York and held summer Normal Schools in Binghamton, New York, and other places, frequently with **Mason**.

  3. Although **Webb** composed many hymn-tunes, only one has remained in the hymnic repertoire, the tune *"Webb."* Originally it was used with the secular words "Tis dawn, the lark is singing." As a church tune it first appeared in **Mason's** *Spiritual Songs* to a text by Samuel Francis Smith, "The Morning light is breaking" (*Hymnal*, No. 264; *AH*, p. 336). Another text, "Stand up, stand up for Jesus," is frequently used with this tune (*Hymnal*, No. 562; *AH*, p. 565).

  4. **Webb's** collections show a great variety of interests and purposes.

    a. *The Little Songster: Consisting of Original Songs for Children, Together with Directions for Teachers*, Boston, 1840

    b. *The Massachusetts Collection of Psalmody*, Boston, 1840

    c. *The Odeon: A Collection of Secular Melodies*, Boston, 1837 (with **Mason**)

    d. *The American Glee Book*, Boston, 1841

    e. *The Young Ladies' Vocal Class-Book*, Boston, 1842

    f. *The Glee Hive*, New York, 1851 (with **Mason**)

    g. *The New Odeon*, New York, 1855 (with **Mason**)

    h. *Vocal Technics: A Progressive Course of 75 Exercises*, Boston, n. d. (with Chester G. Allen)

    i. *Vocal Culture: A complete Method of Theory and Practice*, New York, 1871 (with Chester G. Allen)

C. **William Batchelder Bradbury** (1816-1868)

  1. **Bradbury** was born on October 6 to musical parents in York, Maine; before he was 14 years old he learned to play most instruments. As a young man he went to Boston, entered the Boston Academy of Music and came under the influence of **Mason**. He sang in **Mason's** choir at the Bowdoin Street Church and for three months was organist there, "performing the double duty of pressing the keys to make the music, and pulling them up again to stop the sound." **Mason** recommended that **Bradbury** go to Machias, Maine, where he spent about 18 months teaching piano and conducting sing-

        ing schools. No doubt many of the townspeople still remembered **James Lyon** there (1771-1794) and singing from his *Urania* (1761).

2.   After spending some time as organist at the First Baptist Church and directing singing schools in New York, **Bradbury** sailed for Europe (1847), stopped in England and then spent two years in Germany. In Leipzig he studied piano with **Moritz Hauptmann** (1792-1868), cantor at St. Thomas School, and **Ignaz Moscheles** (1794-1870), a teacher of **Mendelssohn**. On November 4, 1847, **Mendelssohn** died and **Bradbury** attended the funeral.

3.   On returning to America **Bradbury** held his first music convention in 1851 in New Jersey and later joined **Mason**, **Hastings** and **Root** in conducting Normal Institutes. In 1854 the two **Bradbury** brothers began a piano manufacturing business along with a German maker named **Leuchte** [light]; the firm name became Lighte and Bradbury. Eventually it was absorbed by the Knabe piano company.

4.   **Bradbury** edited some 50 collections of songs, hymns and instrumental pieces. He composed at least two cantatas.
   - a.   *Musical Gems for School and Home*, New York, 1847
   - b.   *Flora's Festival; a Musical Recreation for Schools, Juvenile Singing Classes, etc.*, New York, 1847
     - 1)   *Fulton* (*AH*, p. 467)
   - c.   *The Alpine Glee Singer, A Complete Collection of Secular and Sacred Music*, New York, 1850
   - d.   *The Shawm*, 1853 (with **George F. Root**)
     - 1)   *Olive's Brow* (*AH*, p. 455)
   - e.   *The Musical Bouquet, and Institute Choir*, New York, 1856 (with **Charles C. Converse**)
   - f.   *Esther, the Beautiful Queen*, New York, 1856 (a sacred cantata)
   - g.   *Daniel; or, The Captivity and Restoration*, Boston, 1860 (a sacred cantata)
   - h.   *The Golden Chain*, 1861
     - 1)   *Sweetest Name* (*AH*, p. 500)
   - i.   *The Golden Shower of Sunday School Melodies*, New York, 1862
     - 1) *Jesus Loves Me* (*AH*, p. 360); *The Land of Beulah* (*AH*, p. 381)
   - j.   *The Golden Censer*, 1864
     - 1)   *He Leadeth Me* (*AH*, p. 382)
   - k.   *Temperance Chimes . . . Designed for the Use of Temperance Meetings*, New York, 1867 (with **J. B. Stearns**)
   - l.   *Fresh Laurels for the Sabbath School*, New York, 1867
     - 1)   This sold at least 1,200,000 copies.
   - m.   *Bright Jewels for the Sunday School*, New York, 1869

5.   Three hymns have remained common to singing congregations in America: *Luke* (I think when I read that sweet story of old) (*Hymnal*, No. 246); *Woodworth* (Just as I am) (*Hymnal*, No. 409; *MinA*, p. 241; *AH*, p. 473); *Aughton* (He leadeth me!) (*Hymnal*, No. 426; *AH*, p. 382)

6.   *Seek ye the Lord* (*BCAC*, p. 104)

D. **Henry Kemble Oliver** (1800-1885)

1.   **Oliver** was born on November 24 in Beverly, Massachusetts, and studied at Boston Latin School and Phillips Andover Academy; two years of his college work were done at Harvard and the final two years at Dartmouth, graduating in 1818. He taught school for 24 years, to 1844. During his life he played the organ in various churches in Boston and Salem. In 1826 he founded the Salem Mozart Association. This civic-minded man was mayor of Lawrence, Massachusetts (1859), during the Civil War was treasurer of the State of Massachusetts (1861-1865), and later was in charge of the Bureau of Labor and mayor of Salem. In 1862 Harvard conferred both the Bachelor's and Master's degrees on him and Dartmouth presented him with a Doctor of Music

degree in 1883.

2.   Among **Oliver's** works are many not related to music, but he also wrote hymn tunes, chants, motets and a *Te Deum in F.*

    a.   *Oliver's Collection of Hymn and Psalm Tunes*, Boston, 1860

       1)   *Vingrove* (*AH*, p. 596)

    b.   *Original Hymn Tunes*, Boston, 1875

       1)   *Clonberne* (*AH*, p. 623); *Wyeford* (*AH*, p. 635); *Leverett* (*AH*, p. 591); *Crown Point* (*AH*, p. 610); *Caton* (*AH*, p. 617); *Sydney* (*AH*, p. 621)

3.   **Oliver's** hymn tune *Federal Street* (*Hymnal*, No. 423) was originally written for another text. The tune was named for the Boston street where **Oliver's** boyhood church once stood.

E.   **Benjamin Franklin Baker** (1811-1889)

1.   **Baker** was born in Wenham, Massachusetts, on July 10; he succeeded **Lowell Mason** as a teacher in the Boston public schools. **Baker** sang and directed choirs in churches in Salem, Portland (Maine) and Boston; he became vice-president of the Boston Handel and Haydn Society; for a time he was editor of the music periodical *Boston Musical Journal*. He founded his own music school, the "Boston Music School," where he acted as director and singing teacher for 17 years. Among his students was **George F. Root**.

2.   **Baker** collaborated with other musicians in compiling at least 29 collections of songs, hymns, glees and chants; the collections also included music by **Handel, Haydn, Beethoven** and other recognized composers.

    a.   *The Boston Musical Education Society's Collection of Church Music*, Boston, 1842 (later editions with **I. B. Woodbury**)

    b.   *The Haydn Collection of Church Music*, 1850 (with **Lucien H. Southard**)

    c.   *Baker's Church Music*, Boston, 1855

    d.   *Baker's Theoretical and Practical Harmony*, Boston, 1870

    e.   Three cantatas: *The Storm King!* Boston, 1856; *The Burning Ship*, Boston, 1858, *Camillus, the Roman Conqueror*, Boston, 1865

    f.   *Wallingford* (*AH*, p. 598)

F.   **Isaac Baker Woodbury** (1819-1858)

1.   **Woodbury** was born in Beverly, Massachusetts, on October 23; he was originally a blacksmith but at the age of 13 began the study of music in Boston. In 1838 he studied in London and Paris, after which he settled in Boston where he taught for six years. He toured throughout New England with the Bay State Glee Club; in Vermont he was prevailed upon to remain for awhile; there he organized and conducted The New Hampshire and Vermont Musical Association. In New York in 1850 **Woodbury** became editor of the music magazine *The American Monthly Musical Record*. In 1852 he again went to Europe to regain his health and also to collect new music for his periodical. In 1858 he went south for his health and died in Columbia, South Carolina.

2.   **Woodbury** wrote songs for church, sabbath schools, singing schools and the family circle. *The Day Spring*, published after his death, was widely used in singing schools.

    a.   *The Elements of Musical Composition and Thorough-base [sic] Together with Rules for Arranging Music for the Full Orchestra and Military Bands*, Boston, 1842

    b.   *The Choral, A Collection of Church Music Adapted to the Worship of All Denominations*, Boston, 1845 (with **B. F. Baker**)

    c.   *The Self-Instructor in Musical Composition and Thorough-Bass*, New York, 1849

    d.   *The Dulcimer, or, The New York Collection of Sacred Music*, New York, 1850

       1)   *Tamar* (*AH*, p. 548); *Talmar* (*AH*, p. 566); *Selena* (*AH*, p. 611)

    e.   *Absalom*, a cantata, New York, 1850

    f.   *The Harp of the South*, 1853

    g.   *The Cythara*, New York, 1854

       1)   *Lake Enon* (*AH*, p. 536); *Trumpet* (*AH*, p. 586)

    h.   *The Casket*, Charleston, South Carolina, 1855

    i.   *The New Lute of Zion*, 1856

G. **George Frederick Root** (1820-1895)

    1.   Another contemporary of **Mason** associated with the "better music" movement centered in Boston was **G. F. Root**, born in Sheffield, Massachusetts, on August 30. His interest in music stems from childhood; he became a student of **George Webb** and **Benjamin Baker** in Boston, and helped **Mason** by teaching in the Boston schools before 1845. He then moved to New York where he was organist of the Church of the Strangers and taught at the Institute for the Blind. Among his blind students was Fanny Crosby (1820-1915) who provided him with both sacred and secular texts. During the time when **Stephen Foster's** songs gained popularity, **Root** set words of Crosby in a similar style. In some of these early compositions **Root** used the German translation of his name as a pseudonym, **Friedrich Wurzel**.

    2.   In 1859 **Root** went to Chicago to join the publishing firm (established in 1858) of his brother Ebenezer T. Root and Chauncey M. Cady. The company was completely destroyed in the catastrophic Chicago fire of 1871. Although they rebuilt the company the original plates of many songs were destroyed in the fire.

    3.   During the period of **Root's** residence in Chicago (1859-1871) he developed a lasting reputation for songs inspired by the Civil War. Among approximately 50 war songs that he wrote, the most popular are *The Battle Cry of Freedom*, 1861; *The Vacant Chair*, 1861, a favorite in both the North and the South, printed in Georgia and Virginia; *Just before the Battle, Mother*, 1862, and *Tramp! Tramp! Tramp!* 1864, of which 10,000 copies were sold the first year.

    4.   In 1850 **Root** studied in Paris and later in 1886 he visited England. The University of Chicago conferred on him the Doctor of Music degree in 1872.

    5.   A list of **Root's** compositions in his autobiography is long; however most of his works are no longer in use. His gospel song tunes include *Where are the Reapers?, Ring the Bells of Heaven*, and the children's song *When He Cometh*. **Root** also wrote several cantatas, instruction books and collections of Sunday school songs and church music.

        a.   *The Haymakers*, Boston 1857 (an operatic cantata)

        b.   *How long wilt thou forget me?* 1857 (*BCAC*, p. 97)

        c.   *Sabbath Hymn and Tune Book*, 1859

           1) *Shining Shore* (*AH*, p. 505)

        d.   *Diapason*, 1860

           1) *Cottage* (*AH*, p. 421)

        e.   *The Triumph*, 1868

           1) *The Beauteous Day* (*AH*, p. 391)

        f.   *Model Organ Method: A Book of Graded Instruction*, Cincinnati, 1873

        g.   *Choir and Congregation: A Collection of Music on a New Plan*, 1875

           1) *Trust* (*AH*, p. 486)

        h.   *David, the Shepherd Boy*, a cantata in ten scenes, Cincinnati, 1882

        i.   *Snow-White and the Seven Dwarfs*, a juvenile cantata, Cincinnati, 1888

BIBLIOGRAPHY

Books

1. Birge, Edward Bailey. *The History of Public School Music in the United States*. Philadelphia: Oliver Ditson Co., 1939.
2. Epstein, Dena J. *Music Publishing in Chicago Before 1871: The Firm of Root & Cady, 1858-1871*. Detroit: Information Coordinators, 1969; reprint: New York: Da Capo Press, 1970.
3. Foreman, Grant. *Sequoia*. Norman: University of Oklahoma Press, 1938; reprint: 1970.
4. Hall, Jacob Henry. *Biography of Gospel Song and Hymn Writers*. New York: Fleming H. Revell Co., 1914; reprint: New York: AMS Press, 1971.
5. Hastings, Thomas. *Dissertation on Musical Taste*. Albany, NY: Websters and Skinner, 1822; reprint: New York: Johnson Reprint Corporation, 1968; New York: Da Capo Press, 1974.
6. –––––––*The History of Forty Choirs*. New York: Mason Brothers, 1854; reprint: Ann Arbor: University Microfilms, 1956; New York: AMS Press, 1976.
7. Johnson, H. Earle. *Hallelujah, Amen!: The Story of the Handel and Haydn Society of Boston*. Boston: Bruce Humphries Publishers, 1965.
8. Mason, Henry Lowell. *Hymn-Tunes of Lowell Mason, A Bibliography*. Cambridge, MA: The University Press, 1944.
9. Mason, Lowell. *Manual Exercises for Singing Schools to be Used in Connexion with the "Manual of the Boston Academy of Music," for Instruction in the Elements of Vocal Music*. Boston: G. W. Palmer & Co., 1838. (a set of 66 large charts)
10. –––––––*Musical Letters from Abroad*. New York: Mason Brothers, 1854; reprint: New York: Da Capo Press, 1967.
11. Mason, William. *Memories of a Musical Life*. New York: The Century Co., 1901.
12. *Memorial of Oliver Shaw*, ed. Frederic Denison, Albert A. Stanley and Edward K. Glezen. Providence: J. A. & R. A. Reid, 1884. (Catalog of published works, pp. 35-46)
13. Rich, Arthur Lowndes. *Lowell Mason: The Father of Singing Among the Children*. Chapel Hill: The University of North Carolina Press, 1946.
14. –––––––*Lowell Mason, Music Educator*. Ann Arbor: University Microfilms, 1972.
15. Root, George Frederick. *The Story of a Musical Life–An Autobiography*. Cincinnati: The John Church Co., 1891; reprint: New York: Da Capo Press, 1970.
16. Stevenson, Robert. "Church Music: A Century of Contrasts," in *One Hundred Years of Music in America*, ed. Paul Henry Lang. New York: G. Schirmer, 1961, pp. 80-108.
17. Webb, George J., and Chester G. Allen. *Vocal Culture: A Complete Method of Theory and Practice*. New York: Biglow and Main, 1871.
18. Wienandt, Elwyn A., and Robert H. Young. *The Anthem in England and America*. Riverside, NJ: The Free Press, 1970.
19. Williams, Thomas. *A Discourse on the Life and Death of Oliver Shaw*. Boston: C. C. P. Moody, 1851; reprint in microfilm (negative): Washington, DC: Library of Congress, 1944; microfilm (positive): Ann Arbor: University Microfilms, 1956.

Articles

1. Ellis, Howard. "Lowell Mason and the Manual of the Boston Academy of Music." *Journal of Research in Music Education* 3 (1955), pp. 3-10.
2. Epstein, Dena J. "Music Publishing in Chicago Before 1871: The Firm of Root and Cady, 1858-1871." *Notes* (June, 1944), pp. 3-11; (September, 1944), pp. 43-59; (December, 1944), pp. 16-26; (March, 1945), pp. 124-148; (June, 1945), pp. 201-226; September, 1945), pp. 310-324; (December, 1945), pp. 80-108; (March, 1946), pp. 193-214.

3.   Flueckiger, Samuel L. "Why Lowell Mason Left the Boston Schools." *Music Educators Journal* 22 (1936), pp. 20-23.
4.   Fowells, Robert M. "Public School Music in San Francisco, 1848-1897." *Journal of Research in Music Education* 11 (1963), pp. 63-74.
5.   Garbett, Arthur Selwyn. "America's First Great Musical Pioneer." *Etude* 60 (May 1942), p. 310.
6.   Hitchcock, H. Wiley. "An Important American Tune-Book." *JAMS* 8 (1955), pp. 225-226.
7.   Johnson, H. Earle. "George K. Jackson, Doctor of Music (1745-1822)." *MQ* 29 (1943), pp. 113-121.
8.   Norton, Albert Charles. "Pioneers in Music Education." *Music Journal* 16 (March, 1958), pp. 22-23.
9.   Rich, Arthur Lowndes. "Lowell Mason, Modern Music Teacher." *Music Educators Journal* 28 (January, 1942), pp. 22-24.
10.   Sabin, Robert. "Early American Composers and Critics." *MQ* 24 (1938), pp. 210-218.
11.   Scanlon, Mary Browning. "Lowell Mason's Philosophy of Music Education." *Music Educators Journal* 28 (January, 1942), pp. 24, 25, 70.
12.   ————"Pioneer Music Maker." *Music Educators Journal* 27 (November, 1941), pp. 18-21.
13.   ————"Thomas Hastings". *MQ* 32 (1946), pp. 265-277.
14.   Southern, Eileen J. "Musical Practices in Black Churches of Philadelphia and New York *ca.* 1800-1844." *JAMS* 30 (1977), pp. 296-312.
15.   Sunderman, Lloyd Frederick. "The Era of Beginnings in American Music Education (1830-1840)." *Journal of Research in Music Education* 4 (1956), pp. 33-39.
16.   ————"Lowell Mason, Father of American Music Education." *Journal of Musicology* (November, 1944), p. 6.
17.   Thayer, Alexander Wheelock. "Lowell Mason." *Dwight's Journal of Music* 39 (November 22, 1879), pp. 186-187; (December 6, 1879), pp. 195-196.
18.   Upton, William Treat. "Secular Music in the United States 150 Years Ago." *Papers of the American Musicological Society* (Annual Meeting, 1941), pp. 105-111.
19.   Yont, Rose M. "Introduction of Music in 19th Century U. S. Universities." *Woodwind World* 11, No. 5 (1972), pp. 21-22.

Music

1.   Baker, Benjamin Franklin. *Baker's Church Music. Collection of Hymn Tunes, Chants, Sentences and Anthems.* Boston: J. P. Jewett & Co., 1855.
2.   ————*The Choral; A Collection of Church Music Adapted to the Worship of All Demoninations.* Boston: Otis, Broaders & Co., 1847. (with I. B. Woodbury)
3.   Bradbury, William Batchelder. *The Alpine Glee Singer; A Complete Collection of Secular and Social Music.* New York: M. H. Newman & Co., 1850.
4.   ————*Bright Jewels for the Sunday School.* New York: Bigelow & Main, 1869.
5.   ————*Daniel, or The Captivity and Restoration.* A Sacred Cantata. New York: Mason Brothers, 1954.
6.   ————*Flora's Festival: A Musical Recreation for Schools, etc.* New York: M. H. Newman & Co., 1847.
7.   ————*The Golden Censer: A Musical Offering to the Sabbath Schools.* New York: W. B. Bradbury, 1864.
8.   ————*Golden Chain of Sabbath School Melodies.* New York: Ivison, Phinney & Co., 1861.
9.   ————*Golden Shower of Sunday School Melodies.* Rochester, NY: E. Darrow & Bro., 1862.

10.   Bradbury, William Batchelder. *The Jubilee: An Extensive Collection of Church Music for the Choir, the Congregation, and the Singing-School.* Also the sacred cantata, *Esther, The Beautiful Queen*. New York: Mason Brothers, 1857.

11.   ————*The Key-Note.* New York: Mason Brothers, 1863.

12.   ————*The Metropolitan Glee Book.* New York: Newman & Ivison, 1852.

13.   ————*The Psalmodist.* New York: M. H. Newman, 1844.

14.   ————*The Singing Bird; Progressive Music Reader.* New York: Ivison, Phinney & Co., 1852.

15.   ————*The Young Melodist; A Collection of Social, Moral and Patriotic Songs.* New York: M. H. Newman, 1846.

16.   Hastings, Thomas. *The Manhattan Collection of Psalm and Hymn Tunes and Anthems.* New York: Ezra Collier & Co., 1838.

17.   ————*Musica Sacra: or Springfield and Utica Collections United.* Utica: W. Williams, 1819. (with Solomon Warriner)

18.   ————*The New York Choralist: Collection of Psalm and Hymn Tunes.* New York: M. J. Newman & Co., 1877. (with W. B. Bradbury)

19.   ————*The Presbyterian Psalmodist.* Philadelphia: Presbyterian Board of Publications, 1852.

20.   ————*Selah: A Collection of Psalm and Hymn Tunes.* New York: A. S. Barnes & Co., 1856.

21.   Mason, Lowell. *Book of Chants Consisting Mostly of Selections from the Sacred Scriptures, Adapted to Appropriate Music, and Arranged for Chanting. Designed for Congregational Use in Public or Social Worship.* Boston: J. H. Wilkins & R. B. Carter, 1842.

22.   ————*The Boston Academy's Collection of Church Music.* Boston: Carter, Hendee & Co., 1835.

23.   ————*The Boston Glee Book.* Boston: J. H. Wilkins & R. B. Carter, and Jenks and Palmer, 1844; reprint: New York: Da Capo Press, 1977. (with George J. Webb).

24   ————*The Boston Handel and Haydn Society Collection of Church Music, Being a Selection of the Most Approved Psalm, and Hymn Tunes, Anthems, Sentences, Chants, &c.* Boston: Richardson & Lord, 1822; reprint: New York: Da Capo Press, 1973 (Earlier American Music, v. 15)

25.   ————*The Boston School Song Book Published Under the Sanction of the Boston Academy of Music.* Boston: J. H. Wilkins & R. B. Carter, 1841.

26.   ————*Cantica Laudis. The American Book of Church Music.* New York: Mason and Law, 1850. (with George J. Webb)

27.   ————*Carmina Sacra: or Boston Collection of Church Music.* Boston: J. H. Wilkins & R. B. Carter, 1841; New York: Mason Brothers, 1855.

28.   ————*The Cherokee Singing Book.* Boston: Alonzo P. Kennick, 1846. (with George Guess)

29.   ————*The Choir, or Union Collection of Church Music.* Boston: Carter, Hendee & Co., 1833.

30.   ————*The Harp: A Collection of Choice Sacred Music.* Cincinnati: Moore, Wilstach & Baldwin, 1841. (with Timothy Mason)

31.   ————*Juvenile Lyre; or Hymns and Songs, Religious, Moral and Cheerful, Set to Appropriate Music, for the Use of Primary and Common Schools.* Boston: Richardson, Lord & Holbrook, 1831.

32.   ————*The Juvenile Lyre.* Boston: J. H. Wilkins and R. B. Carter, 1836. (with Elam Ives)

33.   ————*The Juvenile Psalmist, or The Child's Introduction to Sacred Music.* Boston: Richardson, Lord & Holbrook, 1829.

34.   ————*The Hallelujah. A Book for the Service of Song in the House of the Lord.* New York: Mason Bros, 1854.

35.   Mason, Lowell. *The Juvenile Singing School*. Boston: J. H. Wilkins & R. B. Carter, 1837. (with George J. Webb)

36.   –––––––*Lyra Sacra, Consisting of Anthems, Motetts, Sentences, Chants, &c*. Boston: Richardson, Lord and Holbrook, 1832.

37.   –––––––*Manual of the Boston Academy of Music, for Instruction in the Elements of Vocal Music, on the System of Pestalozzi*. Boston: Carter, Hendee and Co., 1834.

38.   –––––––*The Modern Psalmist. A Collection of Church Music*. Boston: J. H. Wilkins & R. B. Carter, 1841.

39.   –––––––*Musical Exercises for Singing Schools*. Boston: Kidder and Wright, 1838.

40.   –––––––*The New Carmina Sacra: or Boston Collection of Church Music*. Boston: Rice and Kendall Co., 1854.

41.   –––––––*The New Sabbath Hymn and Tune Book, for the Service of Song in the House of the Lord*. Hartford: Hamersley & Co., 1872.

42.   –––––––*The Psaltery, A New Collection of Church Music*. Boston: Wilkins, Carter & Co., 1845. (with George J. Webb)

43.   –––––––*The Sabbath Hymn Book*. New York: Mason Bros.; Boston: Mason & Hamlin, 1858.

44.   –––––––*The Sacred Harp: or Beauties of Church Music*. Boston: Shepley and Wright, 1841. (with Timothy Mason)

45.   –––––––*The Sacred Harp or Eclectic Harmony*. Cincinnati: Truman and Smith, 1835. (with Timothy Mason)

46.   –––––––*The Song-Garden*. A Series of School Music Books. Boston: Ditson & Co., 1864.

47.   –––––––*Spiritual Songs*. Boston: Carter, Hendee & Co., 1834. (with Thomas Hastings)

48.   McCurry, John Gordon. *The Social Harp: A Collection of Tunes, Odes, Anthems, and Set Pieces, Selected from Various Authors*. Philadelphia: Collins, 1855; reprint: Athens: Georgia University Press, 1973.

49.   Riley, Edward. *Riley's Flute Melodies*, 2 vols., 1816, 1820. reprint: New York: Da Capo Press, 1973.

50.   Shaw, Oliver. *The Gentleman's Favorite Selection of Instrumental Music*. Dedham, MA: H. Mann, 1805.

51.   –––––––*Melodia Sacra*. Providence, RI: Miller and Hutchens, 1819.

52.   –––––––*The Providence Selection of Psalm and Hymn Tunes*. Dedham, MA: H. Mann, 1815.

53.   –––––––*The Social Sacred Melodist*. Providence: The Author, 1835.

54.   –––––––*Thanksgiving Anthem*. Dedham, MA: H. Mann, 1809.

55.   *Social Hymn and Tune Book: for the Lecture Room, Prayer Meeting, Family Circle, and Mission Church*. Philadelphia: Presbyterian Publication Committee, 1865.

56.   Webb, George James. *The American Glee Book*. Boston: Jenks and Palmer, 1841.

57.   –––––––*The Boston Chorus Book*. Boston: Wilkins, Carter & Co., 1846. (with Lowell Mason)

58.   –––––––*The Common School Songster*. Boston: Jenks and Palmer, 1842.

59.   –––––––*The Glee Hive*. New York: Mason & Law, 1851. (with Lowell Mason)

60.   –––––––*The Little Songster: Consisting of Original Songs for Children, Together with Directions for Teachers*. Boston: J. H. Wilkins & R. B. Carter, 1840.

61.   –––––––*The Massachusetts Collection of Psalmody*. Boston: J. H. Wilkins & R. B. Carter, 1840.

62.   –––––––*The New Odeon*. New York: Mason Brothers, 1855. (with Lowell Mason)

63.   –––––––*The Odeon: A Collection of Secular Melodies*. Boston: J. H. Wilkins & R. B. Carter, 1837. (with Lowell Mason)

64.   –––––––*The Young Ladies' Vocal Class-Book*. Boston: Jenks and Palmer, 1842.

65.   –––––––*Vocal Technics: A Progressive Course of 75 Exercises*. Boston: Oliver Ditson, n. d. (with Chester G. Allen)

66. Woodbury, Isaac Baker. *The Boston Musical Education Society's Collection of Church Music*. Boston: Saxton, Pierce and Co., 1843. (with Benjamin F. Baker)
67. ————*The Choral. A Collection of Church Music*. Boston: Otis, Broaders & Co., 1847. (with Benjamin F. Baker)
68. ————*The Cythara*. New York: F. J. Huntington & Mason Bros., 1854.
69. ————*The Dulcimer: or the New York Collection of Sacred Music*. Boston: W. J. Reynolds and Co., 1850.
70. ————*The Settlement of Jamestown*, selected from the most celebrated operas . . . by the author, 1856.
71. ————*The Thanksgiving*. New York: F. J. Huntington, 1857.

From **The Easy Instructor** by Little and Smith, c. 1798

THE

BOSTON HANDEL AND HAYDN SOCIETY

COLLECTION OF CHURCH MUSIC.

A page from the fourth edition, 1826, by Lowell Mason

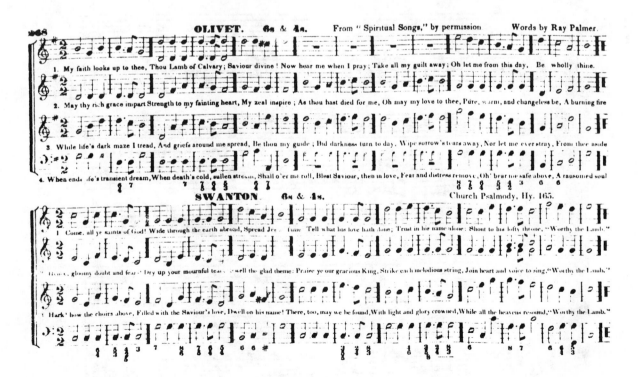

From **The Choir** by Lowell Mason, 1834

Original edition of
"From Greenland's Icy Mountains" by Lowell Mason, 1824

down their golden sand; From many an ancient river, From many a palmy plain, They call us to de _ liv _ _ _ er Their land from errors chain.

2.

What tho' the spicy breezes blow soft o'er ceylon's isle;
Tho'ev'ry prospect pleases and only man is vile;
In vain with lavish kindness the gifts of God are strown;
The heathen in his blindness bows down to wood and stone.

3.

Shall we, whose souls are lighted by wisdom from on high,
Shall we to men benighted the lamp of life deny?
Salvation! O Salvation! The joyful sound proclaim,
Till earth's remotest nation has learnt Messiah's name.

4.

Waft, Waft, ye winds his story, and you, ye waters, roll,
Till, like a sea of glory, it spreads from pole to pole;
Till o'er our ransom'd nature the lamb for sinners slain,
. . . . reigns to reign.

FOLK HYMNS AND MUSIC OF THE SHAKERS

Early Development of Folk Hymns
Music of the Southern Folk Hymns — Southern Collections of Folk Hymns
Gospel Songs — Music of the Shakers

I. **Early Development of Folk Hymns**

    A. Religious dissension in Europe before the American Revolution
        1. The dissension of Protestant groups with institutionalized religion, particularly the Church of England, led many to come to America to gain religious as well as political freedom.
            a. The Episcopalians were strong in Virginia and North Carolina, and the Puritans were centered in New England.
    B. Religious dissension in America
        1. A revival movement began among dissension groups of various denominations in America, Presbyterians, Baptists and Methodists, who extended their work in the South. This movement grew rapidly, especially among the Baptists in Massachusetts. About 1740 began the period of the "Great Awakening" led by the evangelistic preachers **Jonathan Edwards** (1703-1750) and **George Whitefield** (1714-1770).
            a. The orthodox groups and the revivalists stood opposed to each other in regard to music as well as in other things.
                1) The Psalm tunes, sung in the New England churches, were entirely unsatisfactory to the revivalists.
                2) The singing schools, which began as early as 1720, were also a protest against New England psalmody.
            b. Rhymed versions of the Psalms and hymns by **Isaac Watts**, a dissenter, were used as texts by the revivalists.
        2. Following the Revolution religious freedom became even more widely realized, especially among the Baptists and Methodists.
            a. The Baptists, for instance, split into new groups such as the Free Will Baptists and Merry Dancing Baptists. Some of the latter joined the Shaker movement.
            b. Hymn texts were written praising the virtues of the various groups. These hymn texts were published without tunes until about 1805.
        3. About 1800 a new revival movement, which often led to mass hysteria, broke out in Kentucky, and inter-denominational camp meetings were instituted which often lasted for weeks.
            a. Revival songs were needed and, as none were available, portions of familiar secular music were used. The leader sang a phrase and the people repeated the text and tune.
                1) Revival songs, also known as chorus songs, refrain songs or spiritual songs, were not included in hymnals until nearly 1840.

II. **Music of the Southern Folk Hymns**

    A. Texts of early folk hymns and religious songs were first adapted to ballads, fiddle tunes, jigs and other secular sources.
        1. Many of the tunes had their origin in the British Isles and had been brought to this

country by the early settlers.

2. Folk hymns are related to folk songs, but differ in that they are written down, harmonized, and the composers are often known.

B. The earliest collections of harmonized tunes which contained folk hymns appeared first in New England and then in the Middle West and South from about 1815.

1. In addition to folk hymns, the singing school books generally contained Psalm tunes, fuging tunes, odes and anthems.

 a. There was much borrowing from other collections, particularly those by **Billings, Holden, Kimball, Swan** and **Tans'ur**.

2. *The Christian Harmonist*, Salem, Massachusetts, 1804, by **Samuel Holyoke**

 a. This was written for Baptist churches; it contains folk-like music set to folk texts. It was used only in New England.

3. *The Christian Harmony: or, Songster's Companion*, Exeter, New Hampshire, 1805, by **Jeremiah Ingalls**

 a. This collection contains 80 tunes with texts. It was not much used in New England, but became popular in the South.

C. Notation (shape-notes, patent-notes, buckwheat notes, character notes)

1. Most of the early hymnals were printed in the four-shape notation system. At least 38 collections were published before 1856.

 a. A four-syllable (*fa, sol, la, mi*) solmization of the scale is given in **Thomas Morley's** (1557-1602) *A Plaine and Easie Introduction to Practicall Musicke*, 1597.

2. Collections using the four-shape system followed the notation developed by **William Little** and **William Smith** in *The Easy Instructor*, Philadelphia, 1801. **Andrew Law's** system used the same four syllables, but with a square for "*faw*" and a triangle for "*law*" and without the use of a staff. **Little** and **Smith's** notation is as follows:

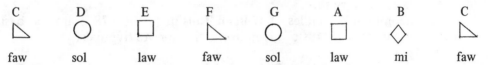

a. "Flat" keys are minor and "sharp" keys are major.

b. The scale begins with "*faw*" in every "sharp" key and with "*law*" in every "flat" key.

c. The note values are the same as in conventional notation.

d. The order of voices is treble (top line), counter (using the alto "cliff"), tenor (singing the melody) and bass.

e. The parts are all written on separate staffs with some variation of the order.

f. Accidentals are rarely used in shape-note notation.

3. Seven-shape notation system

 a. As early as 1832 an effort was made to introduce a seven-shape notation system. In 1846 **Jesse B. Aikin** published *The Christian Minstrel* in Philadelphia. He used seven different shapes with the syllables *do, re, mi, fa, sol, la, si*. A variety of shape-notes was used in different collections.

 b. The seven-shape system at first paralleled the four-shape system, but by the turn of the twentieth century the seven-shape system was generally used.

 1) *Southern Harmony* and the *Original Sacred Harp* are published today in the original four-shape system.

 2) Hymnals of the Southern Baptist Church are published in both the seven-shape and conventional notations.

D. Characteristics of the musical style of Southern folk hymns

1. The music was largely in three parts at first, but alto parts were soon added to many of the songs.

 a. All parts except the bass were sung by both men and women resulting in four real parts with the upper three doubled at the octave.

2. Melody
   a. The melody is in the tenor except when the word "Air" is printed before the top staff.
   b. Many melodies are pentatonic, especially those in minor.
      1) The fourth and seventh degrees are omitted in major.
      2) The second and sixth degrees are omitted in minor.
   c. Hexatonic melodies omit the fourth or seventh degree in major and the sixth degree in minor.
   d. The Ionian, Aeolian, Mixolydian and Dorian modes are found.
   e. The tunes printed in minor are often sung modally, and even in major the singers alter the notes by ear. The use of the Aeolian minor is frequent, especially at cadences.
   f. Repetition of characteristic melodic figures is common. The melodies are often of wide range.
   g. The second and third phrases are sometimes similar (A B B' A; A B B' C).
      1) Other forms include A B; A A A'B; A A' B C; A B A C; A B C D.
   h. Non-harmonic passing tones are used.
   i. Melodic intervals larger than a fifth are rarely found, except between phrases.

3. Harmony
   a. The so-called "dispersed harmony" often has parallel fifths and octaves, even in the outer parts.
   b. Consonant intervals are fourths, fifths and octaves.
   c. The third is frequently omitted in the final cadence.
   d. Half cadences often occur on chords in second inversion.
   e. Modulation is very rare.
   f. The theoretical principles of **William Tans'ur** (1706-1783) are the basis of many of the "Rudiments of Music" given in the shape-note hymnals.

4. Counterpoint
   a. There is a primitive form of counterpoint with some attempt at canonic imitation.
   b. Dissonance sometimes results from the voice leading of independent lines.

E. Manner of singing
   1. The leader "pitches out" the song (gives the tonic pitch) and it is first sung with the syllables then with the text. The singers often beat time with an up and down motion similar to the "tactus" in Renaissance music. No accompaniment is used. All the parts except the bass are sung by both men and women.
   2. Singing schools were organized by a traveling "singing master" and lasted one or two weeks. The singing master taught the people how to read music with the aid of the four syllables and usually used his own collection of music.
   3. Numerous singing "conventions" were organized to provide opportunity for massed singing.
      a. Only a few singing conventions still remain, including those in Benton, Kentucky; Birmingham, Alabama; and Atlanta, Georgia.
      b. The usual procedure at a "convention" today is to sing every song in the book before any song is repeated; the convention is advertised as "all-day singing with dinner on the ground."
   4. Ornamentation
      a. The melodies are freely ornamented.
      b. The singer often adds a high, or a low, grace note before going to a lower melody note.
      c. At the end of a phrase a leap of an octave might be taken falsetto.
      d. There is frequent use of slides, scoops and anticipations.
      e. Coloring of the intervals by the singers sometimes results in "neutral thirds;" partic-

ularly in untutored groups may neutral thirds and sevenths be heard.

5. Meter

    a. The meter is often free in performance. This freedom is necessary at times to give the singer a chance to breathe, because of the use of ornamentation, because of the greater importance of the words, or because of the adaptation of an old tune to a new text.

    b. The variations in interpretation of the same tune are often reflected in the printed versions during the period from 1810 to 1840.

III. Southern Collections of Folk Hymns in Four-Shape Notation

A. **John Wyeth**, *Repository of Sacred Music, Part Second*, Harrisburg, Pennsylvania, 1813

    1. **John Wyeth** (1770-1858) borrowed his shape notes from **Little** and **Smith**. This collection, although not published in the South, was a source for many harmonized tunes used in Southern folk hymnody.

B. *Kentucky Harmony or A Choice Collection of Psalm Tunes, Hymns, and Anthems in Three Parts*, Harrisonburg, Virginia, 1816

    1. This is the first Southern collection to contain harmonized tunes. Of the 146 tunes, 111 are included in *The Missouri Harmony*. The *Kentucky Harmony* had a strong influence on *The Social Harmony*, 1835, and *The Sacred Harp*, 1844; it was the source for many folk hymns found in later collections.

    2. The book is divided into three parts: Part I includes an introduction, rudiments and general observations, along with 56 hymns. Part II (pp. 36-96) contains "the more lengthy and elegant pieces, commonly used in concert or singing societies" (12 anthems and 2 odes). Part III (pp. 97-136) includes several anthems and odes "of the first eminence." The second section of Part III includes several fuging pieces.

        a. Concerning the organization of the various parts, the following is from the section on "General Observations:" "The proper proportion of the parts is generally said, to be 3 on the bass, 1 on the tenor, 1 on the counter, and 2 on the treble; but I think two on bass sufficient for the other proportions, particularly in flat keyed tunes" (p. xi).

    3. Among the tunes are some common ones: *China*, p. 20; *Windham*, p. 13; *Lenox*, p. 9; *Poland*, p. 33; **Billings'** *Easter Anthem*, p. 101.

C. *The Missouri Harmony, or a collection of Psalm tunes, Hymns, and Anthems*, St. Louis, 1820; Cincinnati, 1833.

    1. Compiled by **Allen D. Carden**, this collection is made up of settings mostly in four parts; sixteen pages are devoted to the "Ground and Rudiments of Music."

    2. Folk hymns included are *Rockbridge* (p. 22), *Ninety-Third* (p. 31), *Glasgow* (p. 47) and *Morality* (p. 54). Several hymns are often included in present day hymnals: *Consolation* (p. 25; *MinA*, p. 249; *Hymnal*, No. 483); *Silver Street* (p. 69; *Hymnal*, No. 552), *Arlington* (p. 71; *Hymnal*, No. 325).

    3. The compiler "acknowledges himself indebted to Mr. 'Wyeth's Respository, part second' for many of the rules and remarks contained in this introduction."

D. *The Southern Harmony, and Musical Companion containing a choice Collection of Tunes, Hymns, Psalms, Odes, and Anthems*, Philadelphia, 1835, 1847, 1854

    1. **William Walker**, A. S. H (Author of *Southern Harmony*) (1809-1875) was the compiler of this collection and harmonizer of many of the tunes. He was of Welsh descent and lived in Spartanburg, South Carolina, where he became known as "singin' Billy." His *Southern Harmony* became exceedingly popular in singing schools, especially in the rural sections of the South. Over 600,000 copies were sold before the Civil War.

        a. **Walker** published his *Christian Harmony* in the seven shape-note system in 1866, after the Civil War, but it did not become popular.

    2. The 335 songs, mostly in three parts, are principally folk hymns with a few "Psalms" and "Odes and Anthems."

    a.   Many of the songs were used in *The Sacred Harp*, 1844.

    b.   An unusual feature of the notation is the use of ⊃ or ⊅ for 4/4 time, but sung two beats to the bar.

3.   Many songs are taken from *The Missouri Harmony* and other collections.

    a.   *Captain Kidd* (p. 50; *Missouri Harmony*, p. 57) retained the title of the ballad describing the hanging of Captain Kidd in 1701.

    b.   *Evening Shade* (p. 46; *Missouri Harmony*, p. 56) was a popular fuging tune.

    c.   *Happy Land* (p. 89) is a hexatonic melody with the fourth omitted.

4.   *The Good Old Way* (p. 156; *MinA*, p. 254) by **William Walker** is an example of a revival song with a chorus refrain.

5.   Ornamentation of a melody may be seen in *Kedron* (p. 3; *MinA*, p. 251), one of the most popular tunes, and in the *Ninety-Third Psalm* (p. 7).

E.   *Original Sacred Harp* (Denson Revision, 1936)

1.   *The Sacred Harp* by **Benjamin Franklin White** and **E. J. King** was published in Philadelphia in 1844. This collection contains much material from earlier shape-note collections, particularly **Walker's** *Southern Harmony*, and was widely used. The fifth edition of *The Sacred Harp*, 1911, was revised and enlarged by **Joe S. James**.

2.   The Denson Revision of 1936 was based on the fifth edition by **James**.

    a.   Many of the early *Sacred Harp* songs, however, were restored and a number of newly composed fuging tunes were added. Many of the less popular songs were omitted.

3.   The music, written in four-shape notation, is mostly in four parts.

    a.   Some of the borrowed music which was originally in three parts has had the fourth part (alto) added.

    b.   The tunes are given to the tenor voice as in other collections.

    c.   Dyadic harmony is used in pentatonic folk hymns.

4.   Several melodies are borrowed from secular sources.

    a.   *Sweet Affliction* (p. 145; *Southern Harmony*, p. 259) uses the well-known song *Go tell Aunt Tabby* for the first half of the melody.

    b.   *Plenary* (p. 162; *Southern Harmony*, p. 262; *MinA*, p. 255) is *Auld Lang Syne*.

5.   Modal melodies (tenor voice)

    a.   Mixolydian: *The Converted Thief* (p. 44; *Southern Harmony*, p. 9; *MinA*, p. 252)

    b.   Dorian (the D-flat is sung as D-natural): *Wondrous Love* (p. 159; *Southern Harmony*, p. 252; *MinA*, p. 257)

    c.   Phrygian: *The Hebrew Children* (p. 133; *Southern Harmony*, p. 266; *MinA*, p. 253)

6.   Pentatonic melodies

    a.   Fourth and seventh tones omitted: *New Britain [Amazing Grace]* (p. 45; *Southern Harmony*, p. 8; *MinA*, p. 256)

    b.   Second and sixth tones omitted: *Restoration* (p. 312; *Southern Harmony*, p. 5)

7.   Hexatonic melodies

    a.   Sixth tone omitted: *Tribulation* (p. 29; *Southern Harmony*, p. 119)

    b.   Seventh tone omitted: *Primrose* (p. 47; *Southern Harmony*, p. 3; *MinA*, p. 250)

F.   *The Social Harp, A Collection of Tunes, Odes, Anthems, and Set Pieces*, Philadelphia, 1855

1.   Compiled by **John Gordon McCurry**, this collection contains 222 pieces, about half of them new, and they are printed in the four shape-note system (*me, faw, sole, law*). Not only does it contain the usual section on "Rudiments of Music" (pp. 5-15) but also a "Dictionary of Musical Terms" (p. 16).

2.   *Adeste Fidelis [Portuguese Hymn]*, (p. 40)

G.   *The Revivalist*, Troy, New York, 1868, 1869

1.   Compiled by **Joseph Hillman** (1833-1890), this collection contains 265 hymns, enlarged to 554 hymns the following year. It was the most popular collection of evangelistic hymns printed during the latter half of the nineteenth century.

a.   This book was used extensively in campmeetings. Most of the campmeeting song books contain only texts and are of pocket size.

b.   The first campmeetings were held by Presbyterians and the Methodists followed very soon.

2.   Included in this collection are hymns representative of many earlier compilations and composers: **Billings**, *Majesty*, p. 95; **Swan**, *China*, p. 179; **Mason**, *Hamburg*, p. 188; **Read**, *Windham*, p. 237; **I. B. Woodbury**, *Rockport*, p. 291.

H.   Other collections of four shape-note hymn books

1.   *Choral-Music*, Harrisonburg, Virginia, 1816, **Joseph Funk**

2.   *The Methodist Harmonist*, New York, 1821, **B. Waugh** and **T. Mason**

3.   *The Ohio Sacred Harp*, Cincinnati, 1834, **Lowell Mason** and **Timothy Mason**

4.   *The Harmonist*, New York, 1837, **T. Mason** and **G. Lane**

5.   *Union Harmony*, Maryville, Tennessee, 1837, **William Caldwell**

6.   *Hesperian Harp*, Philadelphia, 1848, **William Hauser**

I.   Collections of seven shape-note hymn books

1.   *Norristown New and Improved Music Teacher*, Norristown, Pennsylvania, 1832, **D. Somer**

2.   *Christian Minstrel*, Philadelphia, 1846, **Jesse B. Aikin**

3.   *Harp of Columbia*, Knoxville, Tennessee, 1848, **W. H.** and **M. L. Swan**

4.   *Christian Harmony*, Philadelphia, 1866, **William Walker**

5.   *The New Harp of Columbia*, Nashville, Tennessee, 1867, **M. L. Swan**

6.   *Olive Leaf*, Philadelphia, 1878, **William B. Houser**

IV.   Gospel Songs

A.   Although at first only different in notation, the music in the seven shapes gradually changed in character as well.

1.   Music now printed in the seven shapes is largely of poor quality; it combines a "gospel" text with stereotyped music having a catchy rhythmic movement.

2.   Thousands of copies of collections of gospel songs are published annually in the South. Singing schools, taught by the compilers of the collections, are still held in rural sections of the South and West. All night singing of a commercial nature takes place in many larger centers in the South.

a.   The *Blessed Hope* collection uses the following shape-notes. These are the same as in **Aikin's** collection of 1846.

do   re   mi   fa   sol   la   ti

B.   Composers and song leaders

1.   **Charles C. Converse** (1832-1918), *What a Friend We Have in Jesus*

2.   **William H. Doane** (1832-1915), *Saved by the Blood of the Lamb*

3.   **William G. Fischer** (1835-1912), *I Love to Tell the Story*

4.   **Hart P. Danks** (1834-1903), *Silver Threads Among the Gold*; *Not Ashamed of Jesus*

5.   **Philip P. Bliss** (1838-1876), *Rescue the Perishing*

6.   **Ira D. Sankey** (1840-1908), *The Ninety and Nine*

7.   **Homer Rodeheaver** (1880-1955), *Brighten the Corner Where You Are*

V.   Music of the Shakers

A.   History of Shakerism (1776-1876)

1.   Shakerism originated in the English Quaker Church and the earlier "French Prophets" or Camisards. The religious beliefs of these revivalists included violent bodily motions.

a.   They were known as the "United Society of Believers in Christ's Second Appearing," "Shaking Quakers" and "Shakers."

2. The Society of Shakers was founded in Manchester, England, in 1772 by Ann Lee, called "Mother Ann."

3. Ann and eight followers came to America in 1774 and in 1776 finally settled in Niskeyuna, later known as Watervliet, New York.

    a. Religious revivalism was prevalent at that time, and Shakerism spread to New England and Eastern New York State. The central church was at New Lebanon, New York. Eleven colonies were established in Massachusetts, Maine, New Hampshire, Connecticut and New York. After 1800 communities were established in Kentucky and Ohio (one near Cleveland on Shaker Heights). For a short period of time a community existed near Vincennes, Indiana, and in 1827 a community was organized at Sodus Point, New York, later removed to Son Yea in Livingston County. During the second quarter of the nineteenth century at the height of their popularity, the total membership was about 6,000.

    b. Of the seventeen Societies established only three remained at the mid-twentieth century: at Sabbathday Lake, New Gloucester, Maine; Canterbury, New Hampshire; and Hancock, Massachusetts.

    c. The Shaker brothers and sisters lived separately on communal farms. They made furniture and other household articles, and developed many labor-saving devices. Even a simple task was a consecrated act.

B. Religious beliefs

1. The Shakers believed in Divine revelation, the millenium, celibacy, formal confession, separation and equality of the sexes, and in the second coming of Christ (in the person of Ann Lee, a masculine-feminine Deity).

2. Dancing and bodily movements were considered to be an act of praise and a part of Divine worship.

    a. Marches, shuffles and dance songs were sung to express the "inner spirit." The "Holy Squares," filled with symbolism, were their highest dance ritual.

3. Between 1830 and 1860 the ritual was most colorful and the public was invited to the services. Persecution and ridicule, however, eventually led to the closing of the services to all except Believers.

C. Shaker music

1. Early tunes were sometimes derived from New England Psalmody and many religious and secular tunes were adapted or rewritten by the few who knew music.

    a. The first hymnal, *Millennial Praises*, which contains 140 compositions, was compiled by **Seth Young Wells** and published in 1813, but the songs and dances go back to 1781.

    b. Gradually the songs became more lively and folk-like, and some English folk tunes appeared.

2. During the Great Revival (1837-1847) "gifts" began to be "received" by the laity, both young and old, through "visions."

    a. The "gifts" included songs, messages and presents from the spirit world.

    b. The "visions" were accompanied by shaking, whirling and dancing, and came from Mother Lee, the Saviour, Saints and Angels.

    c. The songs "received" were notated in manuscript books and learned by the congregations by rote.

        1) Some tunes had metrical form, but many were meaningless repetitions of short phrases or syllables. Tunes were frequently the basis for improvisation.

        2) Some songs were "received" from Indian, Negro and Chinese spirits as well as in unknown tongues.

3. Instrumental music was not allowed; the Shaker voice was "God-given and God-tuned."

D. Notation
1. The first known tune books were written in the usual round-note notation.
2. An attempt at a new musical notation was made about 1820 when singing classes were organized.
    a. Various types of letter notation were experimented with, including shape notes, and a method was finally standardized at New Lebanon.
3. The first seven letters of the alphabet were used with lines above or below the letters to indicate eighth, sixteenth and thirty-second notes.

    a. Whole note: A d. Eighth note: $\bar{a}$

    b. Half note: a' e. Sixteenth note: $\overset{=}{a}$

    c. Quarter note: a

4. Meter (mode) was indicated by special signs at the beginning of the piece:

$$\| = 4/4 \qquad \mathbb{H} = 2/4 \qquad \mathbb{H} = 3/4 \qquad \phi = 6/8 \qquad \varphi = 3/8$$

    a. Some tunes changed meter frequently.
5. Tempo was indicated by the numbers 1 to 4.
    a. 1 = Adagio; 2 = Largo; 3 = Allegro; 4 = Presto.
    b. The tempo was determined by a "speediometer." "A bullet attached to a string 39 1/2 inches long will very nearly vibrate seconds."
    c. Various lengths were given for various tempos.
6. All major scales had c for a basic note; all minor scales had d for a basic note (Dorian).
7. Harmonized tunes were rare until about 1860.

BIBLIOGRAPHY

Books

1. Andrews, Edward Deming. *The Gift to be Simple. Songs, Dances and Rituals of the American Shakers.* New York: J. J. Augustin, 1940; reprint: New York: Dover Publications, 1962.
2. Brink, Carol. *Harps in the Wind; the Story of the Singing Hutchinsons.* New York: Macmillan, 1947; reprint: New York: Da Capo Press, 1980.
3. Brown, Thomas. *An Account of the People Called Shakers.* Troy, NY: Parker and Bliss, 1812; reprint: New York: AMS Press.
4. Bruce, Dickson D. *And They All Sang Hallelujah: Plain-Folk Camp-Meeting Religion, 1800-1845.* Knoxville: Tennessee University Press, 1974.
5. Cook, Harold E. *Shaker Music: A Manifestation of American Folk Culture.* Lewisburg, PA: Bucknell University Press, 1972.
6. Epstein, Dena J. *Sinful Tunes and Spirituals: Black Folk Music to the Civil War.* Urbana: University of Illinois Press, 1977.
7. Herzog, George. *Research in Primitive and Folk Music in the United States.* Washington, DC: American Council of Learned Societies, Bulletin No. 24, April, 1936.
8. Jackson, George Pullen. *Another Sheaf of White Spirituals.* Gainesville: University of Florida Press, 1952.
9. ———————*Down-East Spirituals and Others.* New York: J. J. Augustin, 1953.
10. ———————*Spiritual Folk Songs of Early America.* New York: J. J. Augustin, 1937; reprint: Gloucester, MA: Peter Smith Publishers, 1975.
11. ———————*The Story of the Sacred Harp, 1844-1944.* Nashville: Vanderbilt University

Press, 1944.

12.   ──────*White and Negro Spirituals, Their Life Span and Kinship.* New York: J. J. Augustin, 1944; reprint: New York: Da Capo Press, 1975.

13.   ──────*White Spirituals in the Southern Uplands.* Chapel Hill: The University of North Carolina Press, 1933; reprint: New York: Dover Publications, 1965.

14.   Lowens, Irving. "John Wyeth's *Repository of Sacred Music, Part Second* (1813): A Northern Precursor of Southern Folk-Hymnody," in *Music and Musicians in Early America.* New York: W. W. Norton, 1964, pp. 138-155.

15.   Morley, Thomas. *A Plaine and Easie Introduction to Practicall Musicke.* London: P. Short, 1597; ed. R. Alec Harman. New York: W. W. Norton, 1952; facsimile: Westmead, England: Gregg International Publishers, 1971.

16.   Nettl, Bruno. *Folk and Traditional Music of the Western Continent.* Englewood Cliffs, NJ: Prentice-Hall, Inc., 1973.

17.   Patterson, Daniel Watkins. *The Shaker Spiritual.* Princeton: Princeton University Press, 1979.

18.   Sharp, Cecil James. *English Folk-Song, Some Conclusions.* London: Simpkin, 1907; Novello, 1936; Methuen, 1954.

Articles

1.   Andrews, Edward Deming. "Shaker Songs." *MQ* 23 (1937), pp. 491-508.

2.   Buchanan, Annabel Morris. "A Neutral Mode in Anglo-American Folk Music." *Southern Folklore Quarterly* 4 (1940), pp. 77-92.

3.   Downey, James C. "Revivalism, the Gospel Song and Social Reform." *Ethnomusicology* 9 (1965), pp. 115-125.

4.   Eskew, Harry. "William Walker, 1809-1875: Popular Southern Hymnist." *The Hymn* 15 (1964), pp. 5-13.

5.   Hall, Roger L. "Shaker Hymnody—or American Communal Tradition." *The Hymn* 27 (1976), pp. 22-29.

6.   Horn, Dorothy D. "Dyadic Harmony in the Sacred Harp." *Southern Folklore Quarterly* 9 (1945), pp. 209-212.

7.   ──────"Shape-Note Hymnals and the Art Music of Early America." *Southern Folklore Quarterly* 5 (1941), pp. 251-256.

8.   Lowens, Irving. "John Wyeth's *Repository of Sacred Music*, Part Second: A Northern Precursor of Southern Folk Hymnody." *JAMS* 5 (1952), pp. 114-131.

9.   Lumpkin, Ben Gray. "Folksongs of the Early 1830's." *Southern Folklore Quarterly* 33 (1969), pp. 116-128.

10.   Maultsby, Portia Katrenia. "Music of Northern Independent Black Churches During the Ante-Bellum Period." *Ethnomusicology* 19 (1975), pp. 401-420.

11.   Metcalf, Frank J. "The Easy Instructor." *MQ* 23 (1937), pp. 89-97.

12.   Morgan Catharine. "Sacred Folk Song in America." *American Guild of Organists Quarterly* 12 (1967), pp. 54-60.

13.   Pierce, Edwin H. "Gospel Hymns and Their Tunes." *MQ* 26 (1940), 355-364.

14.   Reichenbach, Herman. "The Tonality of English and Gaelic Folksong." *ML* 19 (1938), pp. 269-279.

15.   Seeger, Charles. "Contrapuntal Style in the Three-Voice Shape-Note Hymns." *MQ* 26 (1940), pp. 483-493.

16.   Stevenson, Robert. "Ira D. Sankey and Gospel Hymnody." *Religion in Life* 20, No. 1 (Winter, 1950-1951).

17.   Terri, Salli. "The Gift of Shaker Music." *Music Educators Journal* 62 (September, 1975), pp. 22-35.

Music

1. Black, Eleanora, and Sidney Robertson, compilers. *The Gold Rush Song Book: Comprising a Group of Twenty-Five Authentic Ballads as They Were Sung by the Men Who Dug for Gold in California During the Period of the Gold Rush of 1849*. San Francisco: The Colt Press, 1940.

2. Carden, Allen D. *The Missouri Harmony*. Cincinnati: Phillips and Reynolds, 1820; reprint: New York: Da Capo Press, in preparation. (Earlier American Music)

3. Ingalls, Jeremiah. *The Christian Harmony*. Exeter, NH: 1805; reprint: New York: Da Capo Press, 1980. (Earlier American Music, v. 22)

4. Jackson, George Pullen. *Down-East Spirituals and Others*. New York: J. J. Augustin, 1937; reprint: New York: Da Capo Press, 1975. (300 songs supplementary to *Spiritual Folk-Songs of Early America*)

5. ———*Spiritual Folk-Songs of Early America*. New York: J. J. Augustin, 1937; reprint: Gloucester, MA: Peter Smith Publishers, 1975.

6. ———*White Spirituals in the Southern Uplands: The Story of the Fasola Folk, Their Songs, Singings, and "Buckwheat Notes."* Chapel Hill: The University of North Carolina Press, 1933.

7. *Kentucky Harmony, or A Choice Collection of Psalm Tunes, Hymns, and Anthems. In three parts, taken from the most eminent authors, and well adapted to Christian churches, singing schools, or private societies*, ed Ananias Davisson. 1816; reprint: Minneapolis: Augsburg Press, 1976.

8. Krohn, Ernst Christopher. *Missouri Music*. New York: Da Capo Press, 1971. (reprinted from *A Century of Missouri Music*. St. Louis: Privately printed, 1924)

9. Lomax, Alan. *The Folk Songs of North America in the English Language*. Garden City, NY: Doubleday & Co., 1975.

10. Lomax, Alan, and John A. Lomax. *American Ballads and Folk Songs*. New York: Macmillan, 1934.

11. ———*Folk Song in U. S. A.* New York: Duell, Sloan & Pearce, 1947.

12. McCurry, John Gordon. *The Sacred Harp, A Collection of Tunes, Odes, Anthems, and Set Pieces*. Philadelphia: T. K. Collins, 1855; reprint: ed. Daniel W. Patterson and John F. Garst. Athens: University of Georgia Press, 1973.

13. ———*The Social Harp*. Philadelphia: T. K. Collins, 1855; reprint: Athens: University of Georgia Press, 1973.

14. *Millennial Praises Containing a Collection of Gospel Hymns, in Four Parts; Adapted to the Day of Christ's Second Appearing*, compiled by Seth Young Wells. Hancock: Josiah Tallcott, Junior, 1813.

15. *The New Harmonia Sacra. A Compilation of Genuine Church Music*, 22nd edition, ed. Joseph Funk and sons. Dayton, VA: Shenandoah, 1959.

16. Niles, John Jacob. *More Songs of the Hill-Folk*. New York: G. Schirmer, 1936.

17. ———*Seven Kentucky Mountain Tunes*. New York: G. Schirmer, 1929.

18. ———*Songs of the Hill-Folk*. New York: G. Schirmer, 1934.

19. ———*Ten Christmas Carols from the Southern Appalachian Mountains*. New York: G. Schirmer, 1935.

20. Sankey, Ira David. *Gospel Hymns, Nos. 1 to 6 Complete*. New York: 1895; reprint: New York: Da Capo Press, 1972. (Earlier American Music, v. 5)

21. *Shaker Music: Inspirational Hymns and Melodies Illustrative of the Resurrection Life and Testimony of the Shakers*. Albany: Weed, Parsons, 1875; reprint: New York: AMS Press, 1974.

22. White, Benjamin Franklin, and E. J. King. *The Sacred Harp*. Philadelphia: S. C. Collins for White, Massengale & Co., Hamilton, Georgia; reprint: Nashville: Broadman, 1968.

23.   White, Benjamin F. *Original Sacred Harp, Denson Revision*. Cullman, AL: Sacred Harp
       Publishing Co., 1967.
24.   Walker, William. *The Southern Harmony*. Philadelphia: E. W. Miller, 1835; reprint:
       New York: Hastings House, 1939; Los Angeles: Pro Musicamericana, 1966.
25.   Wyeth, John. *Wyeth's Repository of Sacred Music. Part Second*. Harrisburg: John
       Wyeth, 1820; New York: Da Capo Press, 1964.
26.   Yoder, Don. *Pennsylvania Spirituals*. Lancaster, PA: Pennsylvania Folklife Society, 1961.

AN OFFERING OF PRAISE.

2 Through the loud sounding trump I'll proclaim the glad word,
   Heaven's arches resound while I praise the Lord;
   For the gates of salvation are open to me,—
   I will shout and I'll sing, praise the Lord! I am free.

3 In the regions of bliss I have found an abode,
   I am owned of my Savior, O praise the Lord!
   I am free to acknowledge my good Mother Ann,
   For I'm saved by her word,—praise the Lord! Amen.

Canterbury, N. H.

A Shaker hymn from
A Sacred Repository of Anthems and Hymns, 1852

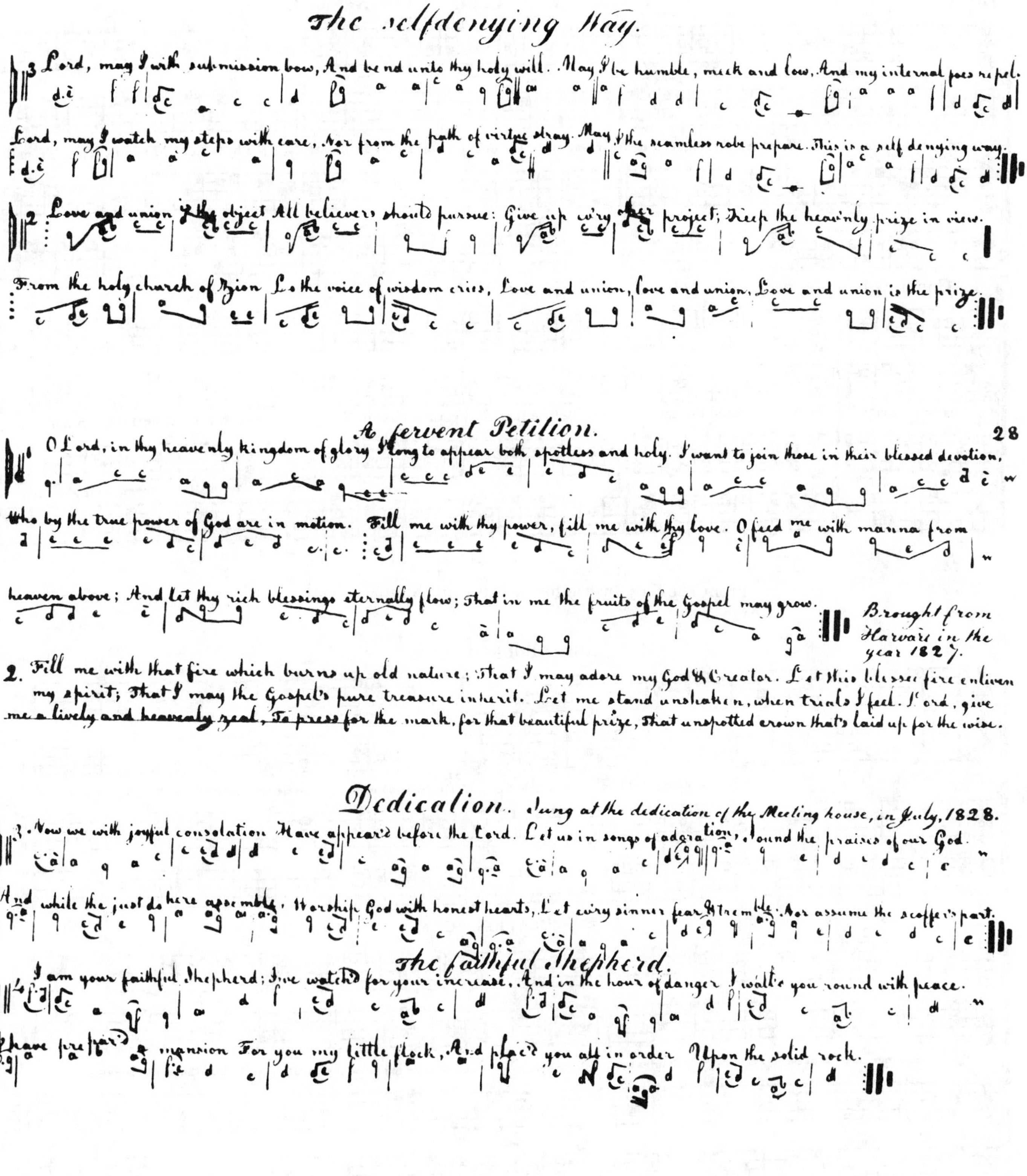

Three Shaker hymns in manuscript

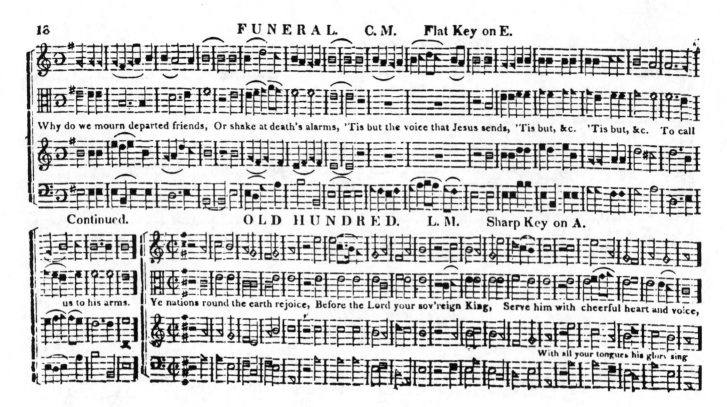

From **The Easy Instructor** by Little and Smith (Albany, 1810)

From **The Missouri Harmony** by Allen D. Carden, 1846

GENERAL OBSERVATIONS.

Obs. 1. Care should be taken that all the parts (when singing together) begin upon their proper pitch. If they are too high, difficulty in the performance, and perhaps discords will be the consequence; if too low, dullness and langour. If the parts are not united by their corresponding degrees, the whole piece may be run into confusion and jargon before it ends, and perhaps the whole occasioned by an error in the pitch of one or more parts, of only one semitone.

2. Each one should sing so soft, as not to drown the teacher's voice; and each part so soft, as will permit the other parts to be distinctly heard. If the teacher's voice cannot be heard, it cannot be imitated; and if the singers of any one part are so loud that they cannot bear the other parts because of their own noise, the parts are surely not rightly proportioned, and ought to be altered.

3. The bass should be sounded full and bold; the tenor regular and distinct; the counter clear and plain, and the treble soft and mild, but not faint. The tenor and treble may consider the German flute, the sound of which they may endeavor to imitate if they wish to improve the voice.

4. The high notes, quick notes, and slurred notes, of each part, should be performed softer than the low notes, long notes, and single notes of the same parts.

5. Learners should sing all parts somewhat softer than their leaders do, as it tends to cultivate the voice, and give an opportunity of following in a piece with which they are not well acquainted: but a good voice may be soon much injured by singing too loud.

6. All the notes included by one slur, should be sung at one breath if possible.

7. All notes (except some in syncopation) should be fairly articulated; and in applying the words, great care should be taken that they be properly pronounced, and not torn in pieces between the teeth. Let the mouth be freely opened, the sound come from the lungs,* and not be entirely formed where they should be only distinguished, viz: on the end of the tongue. The superiority of vocal to instrumental music is, that while one only pleases the ear, the other informs the understanding.

8. When notes of the tenor fall below those of the bass in sound, the tenor should be sounded full and strong and the bass soft.

9. There are but few long notes in any tune, but what might be swelled with propriety. The swell is one of the greatest ornaments to vocal music, if rightly performed. All long notes of the bass should be swelled, if the other parts are singing short or quick notes at the same time. The swell should be struck plain upon the first part of the note, increase to the middle and then decrease or die away like the sound of a bell.

*The organs of a man's voice (or the lungs) is in form somewhat like a tube, about one fourth of an inch in diameter, and possesses power sufficient to divide a note or tone of music into one hundred equal parts.

10. The common method of beating the two first modes of common time is as follows: for the first beat, bring down the end of the fingers to whatever is used for beating upon; for the second bring down the heal of the hand; for the third, raise the hand a few inches; and for the fourth, raise the hand up nearly as high as the shoulder in readiness for the next measure.

For the triple time mood, let the two first be the same as the two first of common time; and for the third, raise the hand a little higher than for the third beat of common time, when it will be in readiness for the next measure.

For the third and fourth moods of common time, and the two moods of compound time, there is just one motion down and one up for each measure; with this difference, for the common time moods there is no resting for the hand; but in compound time, the resting is double the length of the motion.

11. Learners should beat by a pendulum, or by counting seconds, until they can beat regular time, before they attempt to beat and sing both at once; because it perplexes them to beat, name and time the notes all at once, until they have acquired a knowledge of each by itself.

12. While first learning a tune, it may be sung somewhat slower than the mood of time requires, until the notes can be named, and truly sounded without looking on the book.

13. Some teachers are in the habit of singing too long with their pupils. It is better to sing but six or eight tunes at one time, and inform the learners concerning the nature and disposition of the pieces, and the manner in which they should be performed, and continue at them until they are understood, than to skim over 40 or 50 in one evening, and at the end of a quarter of schooling, perhaps few, besides the teacher, know a flat keyed piece from a sharp keyed one; what part of the anthems, &c. require an emphasis; or how to give the pitch of any tune which they have been learning, unless some person informs them. It is easy to name the notes of the piece, but if requires attention and practice to sing one.

14. Too long singing at one time, injures the lungs.†

15. I have found by experience, that learners will soon know when to sing soft and when strong, if they are led, by the teacher making a larger motion in beating where emphatical words or notes occur, than where others do.

†A cold or cough, all kinds of spirituous liquors, violent exercise, bile upon the stomach, long fasting, the veins overcharged with impure blood, &c. &c. are destructive to the voice of one who is much in the habit of singing. A frequent use of spirituous liquors will speedily ruin the best voice.

A frequent use of some acid drink, such as purified cider, elixir of vitriol with water vinegar, &c. if used sparingly are strengthening to the lungs.

From **The Missouri Harmony** by Allen D. Carden, 1846.

From **The Missouri Harmony** by Allen D. Carden, 1846

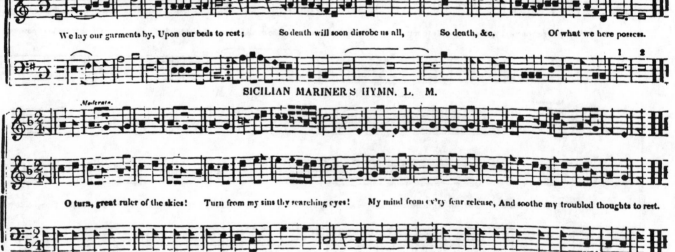

From **The Missouri Harmony** by Allen D. Carden, 1846.

OUTLINE X

SECULAR MUSIC (1800-1860)

Concert Life — Song Composers
Minstrel Shows
Stephen Foster — Louis Gottschalk — John S. Dwight

I. **Concert Life**

  A. Philadelphia, New York and Boston continued to develop as musical centers in the early nineteenth century.

    1. Concerts included songs and ballads, operatic selections, orchestral pieces and instrumental solos.

  B. Music Societies, formed by the leading musicians, helped to raise the music standards.

    1. The New York Sacred Musical Society encouraged the performance of large sacred works; the Society, under the direction of **Ureli Corelli Hill**, gave the first complete American performance of **Handel's** *Messiah* with orchestral accompaniment in 1831.

    2. The New York Philharmonic Society was organized in 1842 largely as the result of the efforts of **Ureli Corelli Hill** (1802-1875), a Connecticut violinist who was their president for six years (1842-1848). He played in the orchestra until 1873 and conducted a few of the concerts.

      a. The first program was given in the Apollo Rooms at 410 Broadway on December 7, 1842; three conductors directed the program as follows:

PART I.

Grand Symphony in C minor . . . . .Beethoven
Scena, from Oberon . . . . Weber
Madame Otto
Quintette in D Minor . . . . .Hummel

PART II.

Overture to Oberon . . . . Weber
Duett—from Armida . . . . .Rossini
Madame Otto and Mr. C. E. Horn
Scena, from Fidelio . . . . .Beethoven
Mr. C. E. Horn
Aria Bravura—from Belmont and Constantia . . . . .Mozart
Madame Otto
New Overture in D. . . . . Kalliwoda

The Vocal Music will be directed by Mr. Timm.

      b. During the first ten years only three programs were given each season. The programs were increased to four each season during the following sixteen years (1852-1868).

  C. Several outstanding European concert pianists not only presented recitals but also gave support and encouragement to the development of musical organizations.

1. **Henry Christian Timm** (1811-1892)
    a. **Timm**, who settled in the United States in 1835, was a pianist and organist in Boston and New York. He was president of the New York Philharmonic Society for sixteen years (1847-1863). As a composer he wrote for piano, including four-hand transcriptions, organ and choir.
2. **William Scharfenberg** (1819-1895)
    a. **Scharfenberg**, a pupil of **Johann Nepomuk Hummel** (1778-1837) in Weimar, arrived in New York in 1838 and immediately became involved in musical activities. In addition to being a prominent piano teacher, he served the New York Philharmonic Society in several offices: secretary, vice-president, treasurer, and in 1863 succeeded **Timm** as president. For many years he did excellent editorial work for the G. Schirmer music publishing firm.

D. Operas by **Rossini, Weber, Paisiello, Bellini** and **Donizetti**, and excerpts from **Wagner's** *Tannhäuser* were heard in New York in the first half of the nineteenth century. The English-type ballad-opera, not to be compared with grand opera, continued to be presented and new airs and choruses were introduced.

1. **John Bray** (1782-1822)
    a. *The Indian Princess; or, La Belle Sauvage* (*EAM*, v. 11), a ballad-opera, was presented at the Chestnut Street Theatre in Philadelphia on April 6, 1808. Generally only the main arias of a ballad-opera were published, but in this case the entire score was printed.
2. In the early part of the nineteenth century the French population of New Orleans was supporting an attractive opera series. By 1810 the New Orleans Theater boasted a permanent opera company which was unrivaled in America. Their touring troupe (1827-1833) played in New York, Philadelphia and Baltimore to enthusiastic audiences who favorably compared their productions to those from Europe.
3. **Manuel del Popolo Vicente Garcia** (1775-1832), a famous Spanish tenor who sang in Madrid, Paris, London and Italy, brought his own opera troupe to New York. On November 29, 1825, he introduced at the Park Theatre a repertoire of 11 Italian operas with **Rossini's** *The Barber of Seville*, the first foreign language opera in New York; other composers represented were **Mozart, Zingarelli** and himself. During the following ten months they gave 79 performances before returning to Europe.
4. **Lorenzo da Ponte** (real name is **Emanuele Conegliano**) (1749-1838), **Mozart's** librettist (*Le nozze de Figaro, Così fan tutte, Don Giovanni*), was active in New York from 1805. In his last years (after 1825) he was a teacher of Italian literature and language at Columbia University. The Italian Opera House, built as a result of **da Ponte's** efforts, was opened (to run only two seasons) in November, 1833.
5. Another attractive opera house, the Astor Place Opera House, under the direction of Ferdinand Palmo, was built and opened in 1847. It also failed because of poor management. Not until the opening of the New York Academy of Music in 1854 was opera on the road to permanency in America.

II. Song Composers

A. Concerts of ballads and popular songs were a favorite type of musical entertainment, and foreign and American composers wrote a large number of these songs.
1. **Charles Edward Horn** (1786-1849)
    a. **Horn** came from London in 1833 and was active in Boston and New York as a singer, pianist, conductor and composer of opera, oratorio and songs. He was also one of the founders of the New York Philharmonic Society (1842); in 1848 he became the conductor of the Boston Handel and Haydn Society.
    b. **Horn** and his wife were prominent in ballad concerts and often appeared on concert programs given by others.

  c. Songs: *A Southern Refrain* (*PAS*, p. 3); *What can a Poor Maiden do?* (*PAS*, p. 6)

2. **Joseph Philip Knight** (1812-1887)

  a. **Knight**, an English organist, clergyman and song writer, had an unusual ability in developing a lyrical melody. Although he was in the United States for only two years (1839-1841), he met with great popular success.

  b. His best known songs, written in the United States, are *Rocked in the Cradle of the Deep* and *Why Chime the Bells so Merrily?*

  c. Songs: *The New Year's Come* (*PAS*, p. 8); *Oh! Lord, I have Wandered* (*PAS*, p. 11)

3. **Henry Russell** (1812-1900)

  a. **Russell**, an English singer and composer, studied in Italy and had a few lessons with **Giaochino Rossini** (1792-1868). He came to America in 1833 and became organist of the First Presbyterian Church in Rochester, New York (1833-1841). He then returned to England where he was extremely popular as a singer and composer of ballads.

  b. His best known songs are *Woodman, Spare that Tree* (*PAS*, p. 13) and *The Old Arm Chair* (*MinA*, p. 313; *PAS*, p. 17).

4. **John Hill Hewitt** (1801-1890)

  a. **Hewitt**, the American-born son of **James Hewitt**, wrote about 300 songs and is known as the "father of the American ballad."

  b. Songs: *The Minstrel's Return from the War* (*PAS*, p. 28); *The Knight of the Raven Black Plume* (*PAS*, p. 31); *All Quiet Along the Potomac To-Night* (*MinA*, p. 297; *PAS*, p. 34)

5. **Septimus Winner** [**Alice Hawthorne**] (1827-1902)

  a. Born in Philadelphia, **Winner** learned the violin, opened a music store in Philadelphia and gave lessons on the violin, banjo and guitar.

  b. He wrote about 200 volumes of music, many of them instructive "methods" for 23 different instruments, including the accordion, concertina, reed organ, clarionet, fife flute, piccolo, pianoforte and guitar. He made 2,000 arrangements for violin and piano.

  c. Among his songs is the famous *Listen to the Mocking Bird*, 1854 (*MinA*, p. 318; *PAS*, p. 43) which sold 20 million copies in his lifetime; he sold the copyright for only $5.

  d. Another song, *Whispering Hope*, became very popular in the United States.

6. **Henry Clay Work** (1832-1884)

  a. **Work** was born in Middletown, Connecticut, on October 1, the son of an anti-slavery supporter. He was a printer and a self-taught musician who got his start in the minstrel shows of **E. P. Christy**. In 1854 **Work** went to Chicago where he contracted with the publishing firm of [E. T.] Root & [C. M.] Cady; he continued to study and composed many songs.

   1) American commercialism of the mid-nineteenth century gave phenomenal advertising to *"Kingdom Coming,"* a new song in 1862. It sold 8,000 copies in three months.

  b. All of **Work's** printing plates were destroyed in the great Chicago fire of 1871; he returned to the east to Philadelphia. In Vineland, New Jersey, he published *The Upshot Family*, a collection of 43 songs, 29 of which appear in *EAM*, v. 19.

  c. **Work** returned to Chicago in 1875 and again contracted with the Root & Cady printing firm. With the publishing of other songs he gained a great following.

  d. **Work** composed 75 songs, many of which became very popular during his time.

   1) The subjects of his songs include Civil War songs, story-telling and temperance ballads and minstrel songs.

   2) Songs: *Marching through Georgia* (*EAM*, v. 19, p. 18; *MinA*, p. 304; *CWS*, p. 34); *Grandfather's Clock* (*EAM*, v. 19, p. 178); *Kingdom Coming* (*EAM*, v. 19, p. 162; *CWS*, p. 145)

III. Minstrel Shows

A. Minstrel shows were becoming increasingly popular and minstrel songs, mostly in imitation of the Negro's style of singing, appeared in large numbers (*B* 43, pp. 429-491).

   1. Blackface minstrelsy spread to California by the mid-century; troupes went to South America and England and enjoyed great success throughout the eastern United States. There were many competitors and imitators with a variety of programs.

   2. The era of blackface minstrelsy can be divided into three periods: 1) the highly successful period of the 1840's, 2) from 1850 to 1857, a period of decline, and 3) a period of more formal organization and maturity which brought the minstrel show to a grand conclusion (1857-1870). Isolated talents continued performing to about 1900.

   3. The minstrel show was generally made up of three parts: 1) white songs, sentimental ballads and instrumental pieces; 2) in a more Negro flavor characterized by both musical and choreographic virtuoso acts and often comical and satirical operatic imitations (burlesque), and 3) songs and patter concerning the southern plantation.

      a. The "walk-around" was the finale for the show. Alternating solo and small group, the company sang and danced in grotesque and boisterous steps with hand clapping in the final number, accompanied with instruments.

   4. In the 1840's the troupe frequently was made up of five blackfaced performers, each with his own instrument (bones, fiddle, banjo, triangle and tambourine). One of the "end-men" (often the tambourine) acted as the master-of-ceremonies, but later the leadership shifted to the center in the person of an interlocutor.

      a. The banjo was a long-necked gourd, cut in half, with the bowl covered with coon skin. It generally had four strings.

      b. The bones, two for each hand, were taken from cattle ribs.

      c. The jawbone, also used, was from an ox, horse or sheep. By rapidly striking or scraping the teeth a tremolo effect was created similar to the sound of the clicking bones.

      d. The triangle was a U-shaped iron clevis for hitching horses to a plow. Suspended on a string, the clevis was struck with a pin.

   5. Among the many troupes, the most prominent in the field were those of **Dan Emmett** and **E. P. Christy.**

      a. **Daniel Decatur Emmett** (1815-1904)

         1) **Emmett** was born in Mt. Vernon, Ohio. In 1834 he joined the army and spent the following three years as a fife and drummer in the military bands. In 1840 he made his début with the Cincinnati Circus Company by singing and playing the banjo in blackface impersonations. Two years later he was employed by the Spauldings North American Circus. In 1843 **Emmett** joined the Virginia Minstrels which made their début at the New York Bowery Amphitheatre and later played in London. From 1858 to 1866 **Emmett** was with Dan Bryant's Minstrels.

         2) On March 7, 1843, the Virginia Minstrels opened at the Masonic Temple in Boston with the following "Ethiopian Concert."

PART I

```
Air —    Johny Bowker . . . . . . . . . . . . . . . . . . . . . . . . . . . by the Band
Song—    Old Dan Tucker, a Virginian Refrain, in which is described
         the ups and downs of Negro life . . . . . .Full Chorus by the Minstrels
Song—    Goin Ober de Mountain, or the difficulties between
         Old Jake and his Sweet Heart. . . . . . . . . . . . . . . . .Full Chorus
Song—    Old Tar River—or the incidents attending
         a Coon Hunt. . . . . . . . . . . . . . . . . . . . . . . . . . . .Full Chorus
A Negro Lecture on Locomotives . . . . . . . . . . . . . . . . .by Billy Whitlock
         in which he describes his visit to the Wild Animals,
         his scrape with his Sweetheart, and show[s] the
         white folks how the Niggers raise Steam.
```

Part II

Song— Uncle Gabriel—or a chapter on Tails . . . . Full Chorus
Song— Boatman Dance—a much admired Song, in imitation
of the Ohio Boatman . . . . Full Chorus
Song— Lucy Long—a very fashionable song which has never failed
to be received with unbounded applause . . . . Full Chorus
Song— Fine Old Colored Gemman—a Parody, written by Old Dan Emmett,
who will, on this occasion, accompany himself on the Banjo,
in a manner that willl make all guitar players turn pale with delight.

    3) **Emmett** composed 62 songs and tunes (*B* 43, pp. 313-426).
      a) *Dixie's Land [Dixie]*, 1859 (*MinA*, p. 276; *B* 43, p. 359; *CWS*, p. 13)
        (1) A typical "walk-around," *Dixie* is **Emmett's** most popular song, composed during his tenure with Bryant's Minstrels. It achieved such tremendous success and popularity that it was adopted as a Confederate war song even though **Emmett** was a Northerner.
      b) Other famous songs by **Emmett** include *The Road to Richmond* (*B* 43, p. 370), *Turkey in the Straw (Old Zip Coon)* and *Old Dan Tucker.*
      c) *Old Dan Emmit's [sic] Original Banjo Melodies*, Boston, 1843; 2nd series, 1844 (23 songs in all)
      d) *Songs of the Virginia Minstrels A Correct Edition of the Celebrated Songs of the Virginia Minstrels, Originally Composed and Sung by Them at Their Concerts*, Boston, 1843
      e) *Fife Instructor: Being a Thorough and Progressive Method, Embracing The Rudiments Of Music And a Complete Collection of All the Calls and Tunes as used in the Regular Army of the United States*, published as part of George B. Bruce, *The Drummer's and Fifer's Guide, or Self-Instructor*, 1862
  b. **Edwin Pearce Christy** (1815-1862)
    1) **Christy** was born in Philadelphia; in Buffalo (1842) he organized and was a performer in a small minstrel troupe. For about ten years from 1846 the troupe was centered in New York. In 1847 the troupe gave a benefit concert for **Stephen Foster** in Cincinnati; the program included *"Oh! Susanna."* From then on they specialized in premièring **Foster** "Ethiopian" songs. After retiring from New York in 1854, **Christy** was in San Francisco for a short time. **Christy's** troupe presented songs, parodies, comic skits and short plays.

IV. Stephen Collins Foster (1826-1864)

  A. **Foster** was born on July 4 near Pittsburgh of well-to-do parents who were descendants of pre-Revolution settlers from Great Britain. His father was prominent in politics, a member of the Pennsylvania State Legislature. **Stephen**, in a family of eleven, was the youngest to live beyond infancy. His only interest was in writing songs.
    1. At the age of 14, while attending Athens Academy in Bradford County, Pennsylvania, he composed his first work, *The Tioga Waltz* for three flutes, for a school program.
    2. After an unsuccessful attempt at college **Foster** returned home to Pittsburgh and spent the next five years (1841-1846) composing songs and studying French and German.
      a. His first song, *Open Thy Lattice, Love* (*EAM*, v. 12, p. 3; *SSF*, p. 46; *FSB*, p. 108; *FAS*, p. 2), 1843, was published in Philadelphia, 1844.
    3. In 1846 **Foster** tried to enroll in West Point but spent the next three years in Cincinnati as a bookkeeper for a steamboat agency. Several songs achieved great popularity during this time: *Oh! Susanna* (*EAM*, v. 14, No. 17; *FSB*, p. 88; *SSF*, p. 79), 1848; *Old Uncle Ned* (*FAS*, p. 5; *FSB*, p. 104; *SSF*, p. 25), 1848; *Nelley was a Lady* (*EAM*, v. 14, p. 15; *FAS*, p. 8; *FSB*, p. 80; *SSF*, p. 90).

4. The most successful years were spent in Pittsburgh (1850-1855): *Camptown Races* (*EAM*, v. 14, No. 8; *FAS*, p. 15; *FSB*, p. 14; *SSF*, p. 88), 1859; *Old Folks at Home* (*EAM*, v. 14, No. 20; *FAS*, p. 29; *FSB*, p. 100; *SSF*, p. 43), 1851; *Massa's in de Cold Ground* (*EAM*, v. 14, No. 10; *FAS*, p. 32; *FSB*, p. 63; *SSF*, p. 72), 1852; *My Old Kentucky Home* (*EAM*, v. 14, No. 13; *FAS*, p. 35; *FSB*, p. 67; *SSF*, p. 12), 1853; *Jeanie with the Light Brown Hair* (*EAM*, v. 12, p. 36; *FAS*, p. 46; *FSB*, p. 53; *SSF*, p. 21), 1854; *Come Where My Love Lies Dreaming* (*EAM*, v. 12, p. 42; *FAS*, p. 49; *FSB*, p. 18; *SSF*, p. 15), 1855; "The Last Song ever written by Stephen C. Foster Composed but a few days previous to his death" was *Beautiful Dreamer* (*EAM*, v. 12, p. 89; *FSB*, p. 5; *SSF*, p. 86), 1864.

5. Even after his songs achieved great popularity, **Foster** was unable or unwilling to protect his rights. He led a troubled existence and died in poverty at the age of 38. His purse contained just thirty-eight cents and a piece of paper with the pencilled words "Dear friends and gentle hearts."

6. **Foster** wrote 201 songs and instrumental pieces, all in the major mode. The songs may be separated for two main purposes: 1) for household parlor use (*EAM*, v. 12) and 2) for use as stage songs, mostly in dialect for minstrel shows, particularly **Christy's** shows (*EAM*, v. 14). They reveal his great gift for melody; sometimes they are happy, sometimes sentimental and always simply harmonized.

    a. The basic harmonic background is often I - IV - V - I or merely the alternation of I - V with secondary chords occasionally appearing. Other patterns are I - IV - I - V (half cadence), I - IV - I - V - I.

    b. The subjects of **Foster's** songs are concerned with the American home, slavery, life on the rivers, plantation life, political campaigns and Southern battlefields. The musical antecedent of the **Foster** songs in reality is the Anglo-Celtic folksong and owes little if anything to the music of slavery.

    c. Gospel songs: *When our earthly sun is setting* (*AH*, p. 361); *Who has our Redeemer heard?* (*AH*, p. 362)

7. *The Social Orchestra*, New York, 1853 (*EAM*, v. 13)

    a. This is a collection of 85 popular melodies arranged as solos, duets, trios and quartets for flutes or violins. In addition to songs and dances there are several European melodies, including **Schubert's** *Serenade* (*EAM*, v. 13, p. 80).

8. Piano: *Holiday Schottisch* (*BCAK*, p. 34)

V.   Louis Moreau Gottschalk (1829-1869)

A. **Gottschalk**, one of the first American piano virtuosi, was born in New Orleans on May 8. At the age of five he studied with François Letelier, organist at the St. Louis Cathedral in New Orleans. By the age of seven **Gottschalk** was playing at Mass as a substitute for his teacher. When **Gottschalk** was twelve he applied for entrance to the Paris Conservatory but was denied; he then studied (1841-1846) piano privately with **Karl [Charles] Hallé** (1819-1895) and **Camille-Marie Stamaty** (1811-1870); he also studied composition. In 1845 (age 16) he gave a successful concert in the Salle Pleyel, after which **Chopin** predicted he would become the "king of pianists." In 1850 **Gottschalk** toured Switzerland and the following year Spain where he won the enthusiastic praise of Queen Isabella II.

1. On these tours **Gottschalk** played some of his own piano compositions and, as a composer, was hailed as the first genuine musical mouthpiece from America. The *Louisiana Trilogy* (*Bamboula, La savane, Le bananier*), in which are melodies and rhythms reminiscent of songs of the Louisiana Creoles, gained for **Gottschalk** an enviable reputation throughout Europe.

    a. *Bamboula, danse de nègres*, 1845 (*PW*, v. 1, p. 87; *PMG*, p. 3)

        1) Two traditional characteristics of a *bamboula* are the habanera rhythm and the cakewalk figure, both used effectively by **Gottschalk**.

     b.   *La savane, ballade Créole* (The savanna), 1848 (*PW*, v. 5, p. 51; *PMG*, p. 39)

         1)   **Gottschalk** uses a portion of an attractive Creole song, *Lolotte*.

     c.   *La Bananier, chanson nègre* (The banana tree), 1845 (*PW*, v. 1, p. 103; *PMG*, p. 19)

  2. While in Spain **Gottschalk** probably composed his brilliant *fantaisie grotesque, The Banjo* (*PW*, v. 1, pp. 109, 123; *PMG*, p. 25)

  3. Among his pieces that show the influence of his tenure (almost two years) in Spain are the Spanish caprice, *La jota Aragonesa*, 1852 (*PW*, v. 3, p. 223; *PMG*, p. 69), also arranged for piano four-hands (*PW*, v. 3, p. 229); the caprice *Minuit à Séville* (Midnight in Seville), 1856 (*PW*, v. 4, p. 39; *PMG*, p. 85); the concert etude *Manchega*, 1856 (*PW*, v. 3, p. 273; *PMG*, p. 75).

B.   Early in 1853 **Gottschalk** returned to the United States; he played a recital in New York and afterward refused a generous contract from P. T. Barnum. Nevertheless, during the 1855-1856 concert season he played 80 concerts in New York. Meanwhile he composed his religious meditation, *The Last Hope*, 1854 (*PW*, v. 3, p. 241; *PMG*, p. 245).

C.   **Gottschalk** went to Cuba in 1857 and spent five years wandering throughout the Caribbean, living the life of a vagabond. During this time he gathered materials which he used in several "souvenirs" of the Caribbean.

  1. The Cuban dance, *La Gallina* (The hen) (*PW*, v. 2, p. 245; *PMG*, p. 125), also arranged for four hands (*PW*, v. 2, p. 253)

  2. The grand concert caprice, *Souvenir de la Havane* (*PW*, v. 5, p. 169; *PMG*, p. 159)

D.   Having returned to the United States for the concert season of 1862-1863, **Gottschalk** played and conducted his own works on 1,100 programs in the United States and Canada. This was during the Civil War, but he continued to draw capacity audiences. In 1865 he took a tour of South America, playing 60 concerts in Peru, several concerts in Montevideo and Buenos Aires. In Montevideo he organized a festival of over 300 performers and included for the orchestra his own *Marche Solennelle* (dedicated to the Emperor of Brazil) and the descriptive symphony *Montevideo*. **Gottschalk** continued on to Rio de Janeiro and organized three grand festivals with 800 performers. He was too weak to conduct the second concert. After about two weeks he was taken to a higher elevation, to the suburb of Tijuca; there he died on December 18, 1869. He was buried in Rio de Janeiro, but late in 1870 his remains were removed to Greenwood Cemetery, New York.

E.   **Gottschalk** was a significant character in America's music; not only was he able to captivate and exite his listeners, but more importantly his significance lies in the fact that he incorporated native American materials into his music about 50 years before other composers realized this tremendous resource.

F.   Included in his works are 2 operas, 2 symphonic poems, about 15 songs and some 100 pieces for the piano, several arranged for four hands.

  1. *The Dying Swan* (*PW*, v. 2, p. 189; *BCAK*, p. 42)

  2. *Morte!!* (She is dead), Lamentation, 1868 (*PW*, v. 4, p. 73; *PMG*, p. 257)

VI.   John Sullivan Dwight (1813-1893)

A.   **Dwight**, an American musician and critic of high standards, was born and lived his life centered in Boston. He is often called "the father of American musical criticism." After graduating from Harvard in 1832 he continued study toward the ministry, graduating from Harvard Divinity School in 1836. In 1837 he was one of the founders of the Harvard Musical Association (not connected with Harvard University), which is still active.

B.   His ministerial pursuits became non-productive so he gave up his pastorate in Northampton and joined the Brook Farm Community based on socialistic teachings. There he taught Latin and music, and wrote for the *Harbinger* (1845-1847). **Dwight** returned to Boston in 1848, devoted himself to writing and proceeded to establish his *Journal of Music*.

  1. The *"Journal"* was a weekly periodical devoted to the object of bringing the music of

the past into the present. During this period in American music history when the light, frivolous, affected and sentimental styles were captivating the public, **Dwight** eloquently plead for quality, intelligence and meaning in music and performance. He was uncompromising in promoting and maintaining the highest musical standards. To his way of thinking, there was no more supreme music than that of **Beethoven**; **Bach** and **Mozart** were not far behind.

2, Forty-one volumes (1852-1881) of the *"Journal"* were published. Not only did they contain critiques of concerts and new works but various significant articles or series appeared.

  a. **Dwight** championed **Bach's** music; in the issues from October, 1855, to January, 1856. he published an English translation of Forkel's biography of **Bach**, the first English translation published in America and the first known scholarship on **Bach** in the United States. Another English translation had appeared in London in 1820.

  b. In 1852 (April 24 to June 19) there appeared **Franz Liszt's** series on the life of **Frederic Chopin**. Other valuable articles are the historical essays by the **Beethoven** biographer, Alexander Wheelock Thayer.

  c. The *"Journal"* is a most important source for musical information and events during the thirty-year period of its publication.

C. A number of attempts were made in New England to found musical periodicals, but none of them survived more than a few years at most.

1. *Euterpeiad: or, Musical Intelligence*, Boston, 1820-1823
2. *Lyre: or, New York Musical Journal*, New York, 1824-1825
3. *Euterpeiad: or, Album of Music, Poetry, and Prose*, New York, 1830-1831
4. *Musical Review and Record of Musical Science, Literature and Intelligence*, New York, 1838-1839
5. *American Journal of Music and Musical Visitor*, Boston, 1840-1846
6. *Musical World*, New York, 1849-1860
7. *The New York Weekly Review*, 1850-1873, was variously named: *Choral Advocate and Singing Class Journal*, 1850-1851; *Musical Review and Choral Advocate*, 1852-1853; *New York Musical Review and Gazette*, 1855-1860, and *The New York Musical Review and Musical World*, 1860-1864.

  a. *The New York Musical Review and Musical World* was published fortnightly by the **Mason** brothers; **Theodore Hagen** became publisher with the issue of July 5, 1862.

BIBLIOGRAPHY

Books

1. *The American Musical Magazine*, vol. 1, nos. 1-12 [May, 1786-September, 1787],ed. A[mos] Doolittle and D[aniel] Read. reprint: Scarsdale, NY: Annemarie Schnase, 1961; Ann Arbor: University Microfilms, 1961.
2. *The American Musical Magazine*, vol. 1, nos. 1-2 [October, 1800-January, 1801], Northampton, Massachusetts; reprint: Ann Arbor: University Microfilms, 1961.
3. Arpin, Paul. *Life of Louis Moreau Gottschalk*, tr. Henry C. Watson. New York, 1853.
4. Austin, William W. *"Susanna," "Jeanie" and "The Old Folks at Home": The Songs of Stephen C. Foster from His Time to Ours*. New York: Macmillan, 1975.
5. Claghorn, Charles Eugene. *The Mocking Bird; the Life and Diary of Its Author, Septimus Winner*. Philadelphia: The Magee Press, 1937.
6. Clarke, Garry E. "Louis Moreau Gottschalk," in *Essays on American Music*. Westport, CT: Greenwood Press, 1977, pp. 49-72.
7. Cooke, George Willis. *John Sullivan Dwight; Brook-Farmer, Editor, and Critic of Music; A Biography*. Boston: Small, Maynard and Co., 1898; reprint: New York: Da Capo

Press, 1969.

8. Da Ponte, Lorenzo. *Memorie*, 4 vols. New York: 1823-1827; Philadelphia: J. B. Lippin-
    cott, 1929; reprint: New York: Dover Publications, 1967. (*Memoirs of Lorenzo da
    Ponte*, tr. Elisabeth Abbott. New York: Orion Press, 1959)

9. Doyle, John G. *Louis Moreau Gottschalk (1829-1869): A Bibliographical Study and Cata-
    log of Works*. Detroit: The College Music Society, 1981.

10. Dwight, John Sullivan. *Dwight's Journal of Music, a Paper of Art and Literature*, 41 vols.
    Boston: Edward L Balch, 1853-1881; reprint: New York: Johnson Reprint Corpor-
    ation and Arno Press, 1968.

11. Erskine, John. *The Philharmonic Symphony Society of New York, Its First Hundred
    Years*. New York: Macmillan, 1943.

12. *The Euterpeiad or Musical Intelligencer*, ed. John Rowe Parker. New York: Da Capo
    Press, 1974.

13. Fenner, Theodore. *Leigh Hunt and Opera Criticism; The "Examiner" Years, 1808-1821*.
    Lawrence: University Press of Kansas, 1972.

14. Fitzlyon, April. *The Libertine Librettist, A Biography of Mozart's Librettist, Lorenzo da
    Ponte*. London: J. Calder, 1955; New York: Abelard-Schuman, 1957.

15. Fors, Luis Ricardo. *Louis Moreau Gottschalk*. Havana: La Propaganda Literaria, 1880;
    microfilm: New York: New York Public Library, 1970.

16. Foster, Morrison. *My Brother Stephen*. Indianapolis: Privately Printed for the Foster
    Hall Collection, 1932.

17. Foster, Stephen Collins. "Letters to E. P. Christy," in *The American Composer Speaks, a
    Historical Anthology, 1770-1965*, ed. Gilbert Chase. Baton Rouge: Louisiana State
    University Press, 1966, pp. 53-57.

18. Fuld, James J. *A Pictorial Bibliography of the First Editions of Stephen C. Foster*. Phila-
    delphia: Musical Americana, 1957.

19. Galbreath, Charles B. *Daniel Decatur Emmett, Author of "Dixie."* Columbus, Ohio:
    F. J. Heer, 1904.

20. Gottschalk, Louis Moreau. "From the Notes of a Pianist," in *The American Composer
    Speaks; a Historical Anthology, 1770-1965*, ed. Gilbert Chase. Baton Rouge: Louisi-
    ana State University Press, 1966, pp. 58-65.

21. ──────*Notes of a Pianist*, ed. Jeanne Behrend. Philadelphia: J. B. Lippincott, 1881.

22. Hamm, Charles. *Yesterdays: A History of American Popular Song*. New York: W. W.
    Norton, 1979.

23. Harwell, Richard Barksdale. *Confederate Music*. Chapel Hill: University of North Caro-
    lina Press, 1950.

24. Hoffman, Richard. *Some Musical Recollections of Fifty Years*. New York: Charles Scrib-
    ner's Sons, 1910.

25. Hodges, Fletcher, Jr. *A Pittsburgh Composer and His Memorial*. Pittsburgh: Historical
    Society of Western Pennsylvania, 1938.

26. ──────*Swanee Ribber and a Biographical Sketch of Stephen Collins Foster*. White
    Springs, Florida: The Stephen Foster Memorial Association, 1958.

27. Howard, John Tasker. *Stephen Foster, America's Troubadour*. New York: Thomas Y.
    Crowell, 1953.

28. Huggins, Coy Elliott. *John Hill Hewitt: Bard of the Confederacy*. Ann Arbor: University
    Microfilms, 1964.

29. Huneker, James Gibbon. *The Philharmonic Society of New York and Its Seventy-Fifth
    Anniversary. A Retrospect*. New York: Printed for the Society, 1917.

30. Jackson, Bruce. *The Negro and His Folklore in Nineteenth-Century Periodicals*. Austin,
    TX: Texas University Press, 1967.

31. Katz, Bernard. *The Social Implications of Early Negro Music in the United States*. New
    York: Arno Press and The New York Times, 1969.

32. Kmen, Henry. *Music in New Orleans: The Formative Years, 1791-1841*. Baton Rouge:

Louisiana State University Press, 1966.

33. Levy, Lester G. *Grace Notes in American History; Popular Sheet Music from 1820 to 1900*. Norman: Oklahoma University Press, 1967.

34. Locke, Alain LeRoy. *The Negro and His Music*. Washington, DC: The Associates in Negro Folk Education, 1936; reprint: New York: Arno Press, 1969.

35. Loggins, Vernon. *Where the Word Ends: The Life of Louis Moreau Gottschalk*. Baton Rouge: Louisiana State University Press, 1977.

36. Lowens, Irving. "American Democracy and American Music (1830-1914)," in *Music and Musicians in Early America*. New York: W. W. Norton, 1964, pp. 264-271.

37. ––––––"A Check-List of Writings About Music in the Periodicals of American Transcendentalism (1835-1850)," in *Music and Musicians in Early America*. New York: W. W. Norton, 1964, pp. 311-321.

38. ––––––"Our First Matinee Idol: Louis Moreau Gottschalk," in *Music and Musicians in Early America*. New York: W. W. Norton, 1964, pp. 223-233.

39. ––––––"Music and American Transcendentalism (1835-1850)," in *Music and Musicians in Early America*. New York: W. W. Norton, 1964, pp. 249-263.

40. Malone, Bill C. *Southern Music: American Music*. Lexington: University Press of Kentucky, 1979.

41. Milligan, Harold Vincent. *Stephen Collins Foster, A Biography of America's Folk-Song Composer*. New York: G. Schirmer, 1920; reprint: New York: Gordon Press, 1977.

42. Morneweck, Evelyn Foster. *Chronicles of Stephen Foster's Family*, 2 vols. Pittsburgh: University of Pittsburgh Press, 1944; reprint: Port Washington, NY: Kennikat Press, 1973.

43. Nathan, Hans. *Dan Emmett and the Rise of Early Negro Minstrelsy*. Norman: University of Oklahoma Press, 1962.

44. Offergeld, Robert. *Centennial Catalogue of the Published and Unpublished Compositions of Louis Moreau Gottschalk*. New York: Zill-Daris Publishing Co., 1970.

45. Perkins, Charles C., and John S. Dwight. *History of the Handel and Haydn Society, of Boston, Massachusetts, 1815-1890*. Boston: Alfred Mudge, 1883-1893; reprint: New York: Da Capo Press, 1977.

46. Purdy, Claire Lee. *He Heard America Sing; the Story of Stephen Foster*. New York: Julian Messner, 1940.

47. Russell, Henry. *The Passing Show*. Boston: Little, Brown & Co., 1926.

48. ––––––*Cheer! Boys, Cheer! Memories of Men and Music*. London: J. Macqueen, 1895.

49. Russo, Joseph Louis. *Lorenzo da Ponte, Poet and Adventurer*. New York: Columbia University Press, 1922; reprint: New York: AMS Press, 1966.

50. Seymour, Mary Alice Ives (Octavia Hensel, pseudonym). *Life and Letters of Louis Moreau Gottschalk*. Boston: Oliver Ditson, 1870; reprint: New York: AMS Press.

51. Smith, Sarah B. *A Tribute to Stephen Collins Foster*. Louisville, KY: Kentucky Lithographing Co., 1976.

52. Sonneck, Oscar George Theodore, and Walter R. Whittlesey. *Catalogue of the First Editions of Stephen C. Foster*. Washington, DC: Library of Congress Government Printing Office, 1915; reprint: New York: Da Capo Press, 1971.

53. Southern, Eileen. *The Music of Black Americans*. New York: W. W. Norton, 1971.

54. Spaeth, Sigmund G. *Weep Some More, My Lady*. New York: Doubleday, Page & Co., 1927; reprint: New York: Da Capo Press, 1980.

55. Toll, Robert C. *Blacking Up. The Minstrel Show in Nineteenth-Century America*. New York: Oxford University Press, 1974.

56. Walters, Raymond. *Stephen Foster: Youth's Golden Gleam; A Sketch of His Life and Background in Cincinnati, 1846-1850*. Princeton: Princeton University Press, 1936.

57. Waters, Edward N. "John Sullivan Dwight, First American Critic of Music," in *Dwight's Journal of Music*, vol. 1. reprint edition: New York: Johnson Reprint Corporation

and Arno Press, 1968, pp. vii-xiii.

58. Weichlein, William J. *A Checklist of American Music Periodicals, 1850-1900*. Detroit: Information Coordinators, 1970.

59. Wintermute, H. Ogden. *Daniel Decatur Emmett*. Mount Vernon, Ohio: n. p., 1955.

60. Wolf, Edwin. *American Song Sheets, Slip Ballads, and Poetical Broadsides, 1850-1870; A Catalogue of the Collection of the Library Company of Philadelphia*. Philadelphia: Library Co., 1963.

61. Wolfe, Richard J. *Secular Music in America 1801-1825; A Bibliography*, 3 vols. New York: New York Public Library, 1964.

Articles

1. "Black Musicians and Early Ethiopian Minstrelsy." *Black Perspectives in Music* 3, No. 1 (1975), pp. 77-99.

2. Epstein, Dena J. "Slave Music in the United States Before 1860; A Survey of Sources." *Notes* 20 (1963), pp. 195-212, 377-390.

3. Hill, Richard S. "The Mysterious Chord of Henry Clay Work." *Notes* 10 (1953), pp. 211-225, 367-390.

4. Hinton, James. "Mozart in America." *Opera* (London) 7 (1956), pp. 207-212, 343-346.

5. Howard, John Tasker. "The Literature of Stephen Foster." *Notes* 1, No. 2 (1944), pp. 10-15.

6. –––––––"Louis Moreau Gottschalk, as Portrayed by Himself." *MQ* 18 (1932), pp. 120-133.

7. –––––––"Newly Discovered Fosteriana." *MQ* 21 (1935), pp. 17-24.

8. Jackson, George Pullen. "Stephen Foster's Debt to American Folk-Song." *MQ* 22 (1936), pp. 154-169.

9. Johnson, H. Earle. "Early New England Periodicals Devoted to Music." *MQ* 26 (1940), pp. 153-161.

10. Lindstrom, Carl E. "The American Quality in the Music of Louis Moreau Gottschalk." *MQ* 31 (1945), pp. 356-370.

11. Loewenberg, Alfred. "Lorenzo da Ponte in London, A Bibliographical Account of His Literary Activity, 1793-1804." *Music Review* 4 (1943), pp. 171-189.

12. Lowens, Irving. "The First Matinee Idol: Louis Moreau Gottschalk." *Musicology* 2, No. 1 (1948), pp. 23-34.

13. –––––––"Writings About Music in the Periodicals of American Transcendentalism, 1835-1850." *JAMS* 10 (1957), pp. 71-85.

14. Nathan, Hans. "Dixie." *MQ* 35 (1949), pp. 60-84.

15. –––––––"Early Banjo Tunes and American Syncopation." *MQ* 42 (1956), pp. 455-472.

16. –––––––"Two Inflation Songs of the Civil War." *MQ* 29 (1943), pp. 242-253.

17. Norton, M. D. Herter. "Haydn in America (before 1820)." *MQ* 18 (1932), pp. 309-337.

18. O'Handley, Marie. "Early Music Periodicals in New York City." *Listen* 1 (1964), pp. 5-7.

19. Rubin, Libby. "Louis Moreau Gottschalk and the 1860-61 Opera Season in Cuba." *Inter-American Music Bulletin* (July-October, 1970), pp. 1-7.

20. Southall, Geneva. "Blind Tom: A Misrepresented and Neglected Pianist-Composer." *Black Perspectives of Music* 3 (1975), pp. 141-159.

21. "The Rival Dixies." *Literary Digest* 47 (July 26, 1913), pp. 134-135.

22. Thompson, Donald. "Gottschalk in the Virgin Islands." *Yearbook for Inter-American Music Research* 6 (1970), pp. 95-103.

23. Waters, Edward N. "John Sullivan Dwight, First American Critic of Music." *MQ* 21 (1935), pp. 69-88.

Music

1. Bray, John, and James Nelson Barker. *The Indian Princess or, La Belle Sauvage*. Philadelphia, 1808; reprint: New York: Da Capo Press. (Earlier American Music, v. 11)
2. Christy, Edwin Pearce. *Christy's Plantation Melodies*, 5 vols. Philadelphia: Fischer & Bro., 1855.
3. –––––––*The Christy's Minstrels' Song Book*. New York: Da Capo Press, in preparation. (Earlier American Music)
4. Emmett, Daniel Decatur. *Fife Instructor: Being a Thorough and Progressive Method, Embracing The Rudiments Of Music And a Complete Collection of All the Calls and Tunes as Used in The Regular Army of the United States Published as Part of George B. Bruce. The Drummer's and Fifer's Guide, or Self-Instructor*. New York: Firth, Pond & Co., 1862.
5. Foster, Stephen Collins. *Album of Songs*, ed. Harold Vincent Milligan. New York: G. Schirmer, 1921.
6. –––––––*Foster Hall Reproductions, Songs, Compositions and Arrangements by Stephen Collins Foster 1826-1864*, 3 vols. Indianapolis: Josiah Kirby Lilly, 1933.
7. –––––––*Forty Stephen Foster Songs*, compiled by Elmer Griffith Sulzer. Chicago: Hall & McCreary, 1934.
8. –––––––*Household Songs*. New York: Da Capo Press, 1973. (Earlier American Music, v. 12)
9. –––––––*Minstrel-Show Songs*. New York: Da Capo Press, 1979. (Earlier American Music, v. 14)
10. –––––––*The Social Orchestra*. New York: Firth, Pond and Co., 1853; reprint: New York: Da Capo Press, 1973. (Earlier American Music, v. 13)
11. –––––––*Songs of Stephen Foster*, ed. Will Earhart and Edward B. Birge. Pittsburgh: University of Pittsburgh Press, 1941.
12. –––––––*Stephen Foster Song Book*, ed. Richard Jackson. New York: Dover Publications, 1974.
13. –––––––*A Treasury of Stephen Foster*, ed. John Tasker Howard. New York: Random House, 1946.
14. Gottschalk, Louis Moreau. (*PW*) *The Piano Works of Louis Moreau Gottschalk*, 5 vols., ed. Vera Brodsky Lawrence. New York: Arno Press & The New York Times, 1969.
15. –––––––*The Little Book of Louis Moreau Gottschalk*, ed. Richard Jackson and Neil Ratliff. New York: New York Public Library, 1976.
16. –––––––*Piano Music by Louis Moreau Gottschalk*, ed. Jeanne Behrend. Bryn Mawr, PA: Theodore Presser, 1956.
17. –––––––*Piano Music of Louis Moreau Gottschalk*, ed. Richard Jackson. New York: Dover Publications, 1973. (26 pieces from original editions)
18. Harwell, Richard Barksdale, ed. *Confederate Music*. New York: Broadcast Music, 1951.
19. *Old Dan Emmit's Original Banjo Melodies*. Boston: Charles H. Keith, 1843; 2nd series, 1844.
20. *Piano Music from New Orleans, 1851-1898*, ed. John Baron. reprint: New York: Da Capo Press, 1980.
21. *Slave Songs of the United States*, ed. William Francis Allen, Charles Prickard Ware, and Lucy McKim Garrison. New York: A. Simpson, 1867; reprint: New York: Peter Smith, 1929, 1951; new piano arrangements and guitar chords by Irving Schlein. New York: Oak Publications, 1965.
22. *Songs of the Virginia Minstrels A Correct Edition of the Celebrated Songs of the Virginia Minstrels, Originally Composed and Sung by Them at Their Concerts*. Boston: Charles H. Keith, 1843.
23. Work, Henry Clay. *Songs*. New York: Da Capo Press, 1974. (Earlier American Music, v. 19)

24.   Winner, Septimus. *Accordeon Method, Winner's Improved; Containing the Rudiments of Music* . . . Philadelphia: C. H. Davis, Winner and Schuster, 1854.
25.   ——————*New Method for Reed Organ or Melodeon* . . . Cleveland: S. Brainard's Sons, 1877.
26.   ——————*Winner's New Method for the Pianoforte*. Cleveland: S. Brainard's Sons, 1872.

The Germania Musical Society in 1853

From the original edition of
"My Old Kentucky Home, Good-Night!" by Stephen Foster, 1853

OUTLINE XI

FOREIGN MUSICIANS ABOUT 1850

Musical Life
Foreign Virtuosi — The German Influence
Louis A. Jullien

I. Musical Life

A. There was a real musical life in most of the larger cities by the middle of the nineteenth century. The sensational foreign virtuosi who came to America about that time achieved great success, especially in the western cities where not much music had been heard.
  1. Concerts, except in the larger centers, were generally regarded as a popular entertainment, sometimes on the level of a minstrel show or circus, and eccentric personalities were exploited.
  2. Opera with its elaborate spectacle was attractive to the American concert-goer. Italian opera, which was the favorite of mid-nineteenth century audiences, was displaced by German opera under the leadership of **Leopold Damrosch** (1832-1885) in the later part of the century. Oratorio also received a great impetus with the founding of the New York Oratorio Society in 1874.
    a. **Wagner's** *Die Meistersinger, Der Ring des Nibelungen* and *Tristan und Isolde* were presented for the first time in America (Metropolitan Opera House) during the 1884-1885 opera season.

II. Foreign Virtuosi

A. Violinists
  1. **Ole Bornemann Bull** (1810-1880)
    a. **Bull** was born near Bergen, Norway, on February 5; he studied violin with **Ludwig Spohr** (1784-1859) in Kassel, Germany (1829), but returned to Norway rather disenchanted. Later in 1831 he heard the great Italian virtuoso **Niccolò Paganini** (1782-1840) in Paris and was strongly influenced by him.
    b. **Bull** made five very successful tours of the United States between 1843 and 1879. In 1852 he attempted to establish a Norwegian colony on Kettle Creek in Potter County, Pennsylvania, called "Oleana," but it failed because of his incompetence in business affairs.
    c. **Bull** developed an unusual style of playing with an almost level bridge and flat fingerboard, which enabled him to play all four strings at once. At a concert in Rochester, New York, in 1844 one number was a "Quartette, composed for four instruments, and performed on one, by Ole Bull."
    d. His concerts consisted mostly of his own compositions on American themes and arrangments of Norwegian folk tunes; his spectacular and bizarre style attracted an enthusiastic public. However, **Dwight** in his *Journal of Music* wrote disparagingly of **Bull's** improvisations, demanding "at least one snatch of melody from Mozart" or other major violin work. Henry Wadsworth Longfellow wrote of **Bull** in his *Tales of the Wayside Inn*.
    e. Music for violin and piano
      1) *Ein Sennenbesuch* (A mountain visit), from *Et Saeterbesög* (*M* 2, p. 143)
      2) *Saeterjentens Sondag* (Shepherd Girl's Sunday) (*M* 2, p. 148)
      3) *Adagio Religioso*, Op. 1 (*M* 2, p. 150)

2. **Eduard Hoffman Reményi** (1830-1898)
   a. **Reményi** was born in Hungary on July 17. He studied violin with **Joseph Böhm** (1795-1876) at the Vienna Conservatory (1842-1845) and in 1848 was banished from Austria for participation in the Hungarian Revolution. After wandering for some time in America he returned to Europe in 1853 and became solo violinist to Queen Victoria of Great Britain in 1854. In 1860 he was pardoned and appointed solo violinist to the Emperor of Austria.
   b. In 1865 he began a series of concert tours, first through France, Germany and the Low Countries, then to England in 1877 and through Canada, the United States and Mexico in 1878. In 1886 he made a world tour playing in Japan, China and South Africa. On another American tour he died of a stroke in San Francisco.
   c. **Reményi** had a brilliant technique and is said to have played with vigor and passion. He made skillful transcriptions of compositions by **Bach, Schubert, Chopin** (Polonaises, Waltzes, Mazurkas) and others, and composed a violin concerto and solo violin pieces.

B. Pianists
   1. **Henri Herz** (1803-1888)
      a. **Herz** was born in Vienna on January 6. He was taught by his father and later by **Franz Hünten** (1793-1878) in Coblenz, Germany. At the age of thirteen (1816) **Herz** entered the Paris Conservatory and studied with **Anton Reicha** (1770-1836) among others. Later having gained a fine reputation as a teacher and concert artist he was appointed professor of piano at the Paris Conservatory (1842-1874). **Herz** began his tours in 1831 through Germany, in 1834 in London and during 1845 to 1851 in the United States, Mexico and the West Indies.
      b. **Herz** was known as a brilliant performer and was a fashionable teacher and composer. His florid piano compositions (over 200) catered entirely to popular taste; they include variations, ballades, one concerto, marches, dances, polonaises, divertimentos and rondos. Many of them were printed in Paris.
   2. **Sigismond Thalberg** (1812-1871)
      a. **Thalberg** was born in Geneva on January 8. He studied piano in Vienna with **Johann Nepomuk Hummel** (1778-1837) and others. In 1830 he made a successful tour through Germany, was appointed court pianist in Vienna in 1834, and in 1835 studied piano in Paris with **Friedrich W. M. Kalkbrenner** (1785-1849). He was highly acclaimed throughout Europe and Russia. In 1855 and 1856 he toured Brazil and the United States.
      b. He was a brilliant but superficial pianist and was at his best as an interpreter of salon music.
         1) A feature of his pianistic style, widely imitated, was to play a central melody with the thumb of either hand, surrounding it with brilliant figurations. **Liszt**, admiring his legato, said he could play the violin on the piano.
      c. Included in his compositions are nocturnes, caprices, sonatas, fantasies on operas and piano studies.

C. Singers
   1. **Maria Felicità Malibran** (1808-1836)
      a. **Malibran** was born in Manchester England, on March 24. She was the daughter of **Manuel del Popolo Vicente García** (1775-1832), a famous tenor and singing teacher with whom she studied, and the sister of **Manuel Patricio Rodriquez Garcia** (1805-1906), the distinguished Spanish vocal teacher who wrote the popular treatise on singing *Traité complet de l'art du chant*, 1847. She became a famous dramatic contralto and made her operatic début in London at the age of seventeen (1825).
      b. The family spent two years (1825-1827) in New York where she became a popular operatic favorite, singing in such operas as *Othello, Don Giovanni, Tancredi* and two operas with **da Ponte** librettos composed for her by her father. The **Garcia** troupe

made their début in New York with a performance of **Rossini's** *The Barber of Seville*.

   c.   In addition to becoming a famous singer, she also was an excellent pianist and composed many pieces for the piano. For the remainder of her life she enjoyed immense success in London, Paris and several cities in Italy. **Malibran's** first marriage proved unsuccessful and a few months before her death she had married the famous Belgian violinist **Charles de Bériot**, with whom she had concertized.

2.   **Henriette Sontag** (1806-1854)

   a.   **Sontag** was born in Coblenz on January 3; she often played children's parts on the stage. In 1820 at the age of 14 she sang in Italian and German opera in Vienna. In 1823 she sang the title role in *Euryanthe* by **Weber** and in 1824 in Vienna she was the soprano soloist in the first performances of **Beethoven's** *Missa Solemnis* and *Ninth Symphony*. Until 1828 she had a successful operatic career singing in London, Paris and Berlin. For the next twenty years she gave up her operatic singing but gave solo concerts while traveling with her husband on diplomatic missions. She resumed her operatic career in 1848.

   b.   She sang in New York (1852-1853) in operas and concerts with sensational success. In Mexico where she was singing opera in 1854 she died in a cholera epidemic.

3.   **Jenny Lind** (1820-1887)

   a.   **Jenny Lind** was born in Stockholm on October 6; she became a world-famous soprano and was known as the "Swedish Nightingale." She made her début as Agatha in **Weber's** *Der Freischütz* at the Swedish Royal Opera House in Stockholm at the age of 17 on March 7, 1838. In the ensuing three years she appeared in opera regularly twice weekly in such roles as Pamina in **Mozart's** *The Magic Flute*, Julia in **Spontini's** *Vestale*, Donna Anna in **Mozart's** *Don Giovanni* and Lucia in *Lucia di Lammermoor* by **Donizetti**. She sang the role of Alice in **Meyerbeer's** *Robert de Normandie* 73 times. In addition to opera, **Lind** also sang solo parts for the Stockholm Harmonic Society in productions of **Haydn's** *Creation* and *The Seasons* and **Mendelssohn's** *St. Paul*. In 1840 she was appointed Court Singer to the Swedish King, Karl Johan. In all, up to 1841, **Lind** sang 447 performances at the Royal Theater.

   b.   In 1841 **Lind** went to Paris to study with **Manuel García** who gave her a background in "scientific" singing. During that year she did no public singing. **Meyerbeer** wrote the part of Viekla in his *Ein Feldlager in Schlesien* (The Camp in Silesia) for **Lind**. When **Lind** was away in Stockholm during part of the time of the rehearsals, the understudy became jealous and wanted the part. Upon **Lind's** return she unselfishly insisted, against **Meyerbeer's** wishes, that the understudy sing the role, but the unsuccessful opera ran only a few days. Not until **Lind** sang the role several years later in 1847 did the opera become very successful.

   c.   **Lind** made her Berlin début on December 15, 1845, in *Norma*, following her first appearance in Leipzig in a Gewandhaus concert with **Mendelssohn** as accompanist. By the time of **Lind's** Vienna début, April 18, 1846, her fame had become phenomenal. Her mainland reputation had preceded her to London where she made a sensational début in March, 1847, and reached the pinnacle of her fame.

   d.   **Jenny Lind** toured the United States in 1850-1852 with **Phineas Taylor Barnum**, the showman circus manager, as her impresario. He exploited her as he did his circus attractions, and she soon became a sensation in America. When **Lind** sailed into New York harbor on September 1, 1850, a crowd of thirty to forty thousand people enthusiastically greeted her. **Barnum's** contract stipulated a guarantee of $1,000 for each of 150 concerts and an additional half of all in excess of $5,500 likewise for each of the concerts.

   e.   **Jenny Lind's** first concert in America was given September 11, 1850, in New York. A prize of $200 had been offered by **Mr. Barnum** for a song to be called "Greeting to America." The winning entry was written by Bayard Taylor. Tickets for the concert were sold at auction. The first ticket was bought by a hatmaker for $225. The total sale was over $25,000 and **Jenny Lind** contributed $10,000 to charity. The Fire Department Fund received $3,000 and the Musical Fund Society $2,000. The remaining $5,000 was divided equally among ten charities, several of them concerned with women.

1) This was the largest audience **Jenny Lind** had ever faced, but in spite of some nervousness at the beginning of the concert, **Miss Lind** made a tremendous success and was ranked by the New York press as the foremost artist to have yet visited America.

2) The program of her first concert was as follows:

CASTLE GARDEN
First Appearance of Mademoiselle Jenny Lind,
on
WEDNESDAY EVENING, 11th SEPTEMBER, 1850

Programme.

Part I.

Overture (Oberon) . . . . Weber.
Aria "Sorgete," (Maometto Secondo,) . . . . Rossini.
Signor Belletti.
Scena and Cavatina, "Casta Diva" (Norma) . . . . Bellini.
Mademoiselle Jenny Lind.
Duet on two Piano Fortes, ... Benedict.
Messieurs Benedict and Hoffman.
Duetto, "Per piacer alla Signora," (Il Turco in Italia,) . . . . Rossini.
Mademoiselle Jenny Lind and Signor Belleti.

Part II.

Overture, (The Crusaders.) . . . . Benedict.
Trio for the Voice and two Flutes, composed expressly for
Mademoiselle Jenny Lind, (Camp of Silesia,) . . . . Meyerbeer.
Mademoiselle Jenny Lind.
Flutes, Messrs. Kyle and Siede.
Cavatina "Largo ad Factotum," Il Barbiere, ... Rossini.
Signor Belletti.
The Herdsman's Song, more generally known as The Echo Song,
Mademoiselle Jenny Lind.
The Welcome to America, written expressly for this occasion,
by Bayard Taylor, Esq. . . . . Benedict.
Mademoiselle Jenny Lind.

Conductor, ... M. Benedict.
The Orchestra will consist of Sixty Performers, including the first Instrumental talent in the country.
Price of Tickets Three Dollars. Choice of places will be sold by Auction, at Castle Garden.
Doors open at six o'clock. Concert to commence at eight o'clock.
No checks will be issued.
Mdlle. Jenny Lind's Second Grand Concert, will be given at Castle Garden, on Friday evening, 13th instant.
Chickering's Grand Pianos will be used at the first Concert.

3)   The public was in ecstacy; newspapers could not find enough superlatives; books and pictures of **Jenny Lind** were sold out as quickly as they were printed.

f.   In Boston tickets for **Jenny Lind's** concert also went by auction; they began at $250 and went as high as $625. Henry Wadsworth Longfellow, professor at Harvard University, commented about her: "She is very feminine and lovely. Her power is in her presence, which is magnetic, and takes her audience captive before she opens her lips. She sings like the morning star: clear, liquid heavenly sounds . . . There is something very fascinating about her; a kind of soft wildness of manner, and sudden pauses in her speaking, and floating shadows over her face."

g.   When **Jenny Lind** arrived in Philadelphia an uproarous crowd outside her hotel window demanded seeing her, but she was indisposed with headache. Thereupon the ingenius **Barnum** had **Lind's** traveling companion, Josephina Ahmansson, dress in **Jenny Lind's** clothes; he presented her on the balcony and the cheering crowd was satisfied, not being the wiser.

1)   The reserved Philadelphia audience was frigid toward **Jenny Lind** as she began her concert, but the barrier was soon broken down and the audience became as excited as those in New York and Boston.

h.   In November, 1850, **Lind's** tour took her down the eastern coast (Washington, D. C., Mt. Vernon, Wilmington, Richmond, Charleston) to Havana, Cuba. She returned through New Orleans, up the Mississippi and Ohio Rivers to Nashville, Cincinnati, Pittsburgh and Rochester on the Erie Canal.

1)   **Jenny Lind** was invited personally by President and Mrs. Fillmore to visit the White House.

2)   In Rochester, New York, on July 22, 1851, she sang the following songs on a mixed program: "*Come unto Him* (*Messiah*), **Handel**; two arias from *La Sonnambula*, **Bellini**; "*The Bird's Song,* " **Taubert**; "*Comin' through the Rye.*"

i.   Up to May, 1851, **Jenny Lind** gave 93 concerts in America under the sponsorship of **P. T. Barnum.** She gave another 40 concerts on her own but found the experience more exhausting. She had netted $176,675 and **Barnum** had made $535,486. **Jenny Lind** left the United States on May 29, 1852, with her new husband (married February 5, 1852), Otto Goldschmidt. Although she often sang on the mainland of Europe, they made their home in England. In 1894 to honor **Jenny Lind** a bust and plaque were placed posthumously in the Poet's Corner of Westminster Abbey, London.

III.   The German Influence

A.   The Revolution in Central Europe in 1848 caused many fine German musicians to come to America. These, in contrast to the virtuosi, came to America to live, settling not only in Boston, New York and Philadelphia, but also in Cincinnati, St. Louis, Milwaukee and other inland cities.

1.   These well-trained musicians dominated American musical life until 1900 as composers, teachers and solo performers; many also played in orchestral and chamber groups, and performed in choral organizations.

a.   **Alfred Jaëll** (1832-1882), a celebrated French pianist, appeared as a child prodigy in Venice. He studied with **Ignaz Moscheles** (1794-1870) in Vienna and toured the United States in 1852-1854. He was known as a sensitive interpreter of **Chopin's** works and was praised by **Liszt.**

b.   **Otto Dresel** (1826-1890) was a pupil of **Ferdinand Hiller** (1811-1885) in Cologne and **Felix Mendelssohn** (1809-1847) in Leipzig. **Dresel** was very influential in performing German music for American audiences. He published a few songs and piano pieces.

c.   **William Scharfenberg** (1819-1895), with **Dresel** and **Jaëll**, played the *Concerto* for three claviers by **Bach** in Boston on March 5, 1853 (Dwight's *Journal of Music*, v. 2, pp. 174-175).

    d.   Piano concertos by **Mendelssohn** (1844) and **Chopin** (1846) and **Mendelssohn's** violin concerto (1849) were heard.

    2.   The complete dominance of German music affected the native composers, who studied with German teachers in this country and often went to Germany to complete their education.

B.   The Germania Musical Society

    1.   The twenty-four members of the Germania Musical Society under the direction of **Carl Bergman** (1821-1876) arrived in New York in 1848 for an extended tour. Although at first the receipts were rather discouraging in New York, Philadelphia and Baltimore, Boston was most enthusiastic and supportive. The orchestra devoted themselves to playing works by **Wagner, Beethoven, Weber, Spohr, Mozart, Haydn** and **Mendelssohn,** as well as the usual descriptive fantasias for popular appeal.

        a.   In 1853 the Society performed the first complete symphony—**Beethoven's** *Second*— to be heard in Chicago, and the first complete symphony—**Beethoven's** *Sixth*— to be heard in Pittsburgh.

        b.   The orchestra exemplified the characteristic qualities of European orchestras: well-trained and disciplined, precise, concern for detail and sensitive expression. Many outstanding soloists performed with the orchestra: pianists **Alfred Jaëll** and **Otto Dresel,** violinists **Ole Bull** and the child prodigy **Camilla Urso,** vocalists **Adelina Patti** and **Henriette Sontag.**

    2.   After six years (1848-1854) the Society disbanded and many of the musicians became prominent conductors, teachers and performers in Baltimore, Boston, New York, Philadelphia, Syracuse and Chicago. For thousands the first contact with genuine orchestra music was through the concerts of the Germania Musical Society.

IV. Louis Antoine Jullien (1812-1860)

A.   **Jullien** was born in Sisteron, France, on April 23, the son of a bandmaster. He went to Paris (1833) to study composition with **Adolphe-Clair Le Carpentier** (1809-1869) and **Jacques-François Halévy** (1799-1862) at the Paris Conservatory. Without taking a degree he left the Conservatory and began conducting dance music. In 1846 he wrote the *British Army Quadrilles* for orchestra and four military bands to be performed in the Covent Garden Theatre, London. In 1849 he conducted three large concerts of 400 players, three choruses and three military bands.

B.   In 1853 P. T. Barnum contracted with him for a series of concerts in the United States.

    1.   One of **Jullien's** biggest successes was on June 15, 1854, at the Crystal Palace in New York. Before a large audience he presented *The Fireman's Quadrille* during which, as flames burst from the stage, firemen raced through the hall with water pouring from the nozzles of their hoses.

    2.   At times **Jullien** was presented with white kid gloves on a silver platter to conduct **Beethoven;** at other times he used a jeweled baton. On occasion at a climactic moment he would seize the concertmaster's violin and bow or take a piccolo from his velvet coat and dramatically play with the orchestra. After an exhausting conducting experience he would faint into a throne-like velvet chair.

C.   **Jullien** was a sensational conductor and his programs included music from the classics, American music and popular airs. While in the United States **Jullien** conducted 214 concerts in less than a year. He pioneered in the practice of conducting with a baton. In spite of his extravagant showmanship, he helped in the development of national consciousness through his playing of music by native American composers.

    1.   Among the American compositions on his programs was **William Henry Fry's** *Santa Claus Symphony*, a piece of program music portraying snow storms, trotting horses,

sleigh bells and cracking whips.

D.   **Jullien** returned to London in 1854 but financial failure overtook him there. In 1859 he returned to Paris where he was confined in prison for a month for theft. The following year he was placed in an insane asylum and died shortly thereafter.

BIBLIOGRAPHY

Books

1.   Benét, Laura. *Enchanting Jenny Lind*. New York: Dodd, Mead, & Co., 1939.
2.   Bull, Inez. *Ole Bull Returns to Pennsylvania; the Biography of a Norwegian Violin Virtuoso and Pioneer in the Keystone State*. New York: Exposition Press, 1961.
3.   Bull, Sara Chapman. *Ole Bull, A Memoir; with Ole Bull's "Violin Notes," and Dr. A[lpheus] B[enning] Crosby's Anatomy of the Violinist*. Boston: Houghton, Mifflin, 1886; reprint: Kennebunkport, ME: Longwood Press, 1977.
4.   Bulman, Joan. *Jenny Lind, A Biography*. London: James Barrie, 1956.
5.   Carse, Adam. *The Life of Jullien: Adventurer, Showman-Conductor and Establisher of the Promenade Concerts in England and a History of Those Concerts up to 1895*. Cambridge, England: Heffer, 1951.
6.   Cavanah, Frances. *Jenny Lind and Her Listening Cat*. New York: Vanguard, 1961.
7.   Chorley, Henry Fothergill. *Thirty Years' Musical Recollections*. New York: Alfred A. Knopf, 1926.
8.   Davison, James William. *Music During the Victorian Era, From Mendelssohn to Wagner*. London: William Reeves, 1912.
9.   Hack, Gwendolyn Kelley, and George P. Upton. *Edouard Reményi, Musician, Litterateur, and Man*. Chicago: A. C. McClurg & Co., 1906.
10. Headland, Helen. *Ole Bull, Norwegian Minstrel*. Rock Island, IL: Augustana Book Concern, 1949.
11. ——————*The Swedish Nightingale; A Biography of Jenny Lind*. Rock Island, IL: Augustana Book Concern, 1940.
12. Herz, Henri. *Mes Voyages en Amérique*. Paris: Achilles Fauré, 1866 (*My Travels in America*, tr. Henry Bertram. Ann Arbor: Edwards Brothers, 1963)
13. Holland, Henry, and William Smyth Rockstro. *Memoir of Madame Jenny Lind-Goldschmidt: Her Early Art-Life and Dramatic Career, 1820-1851*, 2 vols. New York: Charles Scribner's Sons, 1893; reprint: Kennebunkport, ME: Longwood Press, 1978; New York: AMS Press.
14. Lind-Soldschmidt, Jenny Maria. *The Lost Letters of Jenny Lind*, tr. W. Porter Ware and Thaddeus C. Lockard, Jr. London: Gollancz, 1966.
15. Loesser, Arthur. *Men, Women, and Pianos; a Social History*. New York: Simon and Schuster, 1954.
16. Maretzek, Max. *Crotchets and Quavers or Revelations of an Opera Manager in America*. New York: S. French, 1855; reprint: New York: Da Capo Press, 1966.
17. Maude, Jenny M. *The Life of Jenny Lind: Briefly Told by Her Daughter, Mrs. Raymond Maude*. London: Cassell, 1926; reprint: New York: AMS Press, 1977.
18. Nathan, Isaac. *Memoirs of Mme. Maria Malibran de Bériot*. London, 1836.
19. Reményi, Eduard. *Notes and Reflections of an Artist on Japan, Its People and Its Art*. n. p., 1886.
20. Riviére, Jules Prudence. *My Musical Life and Recollections* [Jullien]. London: S. Low, Marston & Co., 1893.
21. Rosenberg, Charles G. *Jenny Lind in America*. New York: Stringer and Townsend, 1851; reprint: New York: AMS Press.
22. Russell, Frank. *Queen of Song, The Life of Henriette Sontag, Countess de Rossi*. New

York: Exposition Press, 1964.

23. Ryan, Thomas. *Recollections of an Old Musician*. New York: E. P. Dutton, 1899.

24. Schonberg, Harold C. *The Great Pianists*. New York: Simon & Schuster, 1963.

25. Slonimsky, Nicolas. *A Thing or Two About Music*. New York: Allen, Towne & Heath, 1948, pp. 226-235.

26. Smith, Mortimer Brewster. *The Life of Ole Bull*. Princeton: Princeton University Press, 1943; reprint: Westport, CT: Greenwood Press, 1973.

27. Wagenknecht, Edward C. *Jenny Lind*. Boston: Houghton, Mifflin, 1931; reprint: New York: Da Capo Press, 1980.

28. Ware, W. Porter, and Thaddeus C. Lockard, Jr. *Jenny Lind, the First Superstar*. Chicago: Greatlakes Living Press, 1977.

29. ————*P. T. Barnum Presents Jenny Lind*. Baton Rouge: Louisiana State University Press, 1980.

30. Weber, Erwin. *Jenny Lind Chapel*. Rock Island, IL: Augustana College, 1975.

31. Werner, Morris Robert. *Barnum*. New York: Harcourt, Brace & Co., 1923.

Articles

1. Comettant, Oscar. "Musical America 1850 as Seen Through a French Squint." *Music Educators Journal* 55 (1969), pp. 43-46.

2. Douël, Martial. "Chopin and Jenny Lind." *MQ* 18 (1932), pp. 423-427.

3. Ellsworth, Ray. "Jenny Lind and Ole Bull in America." *HiFi Review* 15 (September, 1965), pp. 58-62.

4. Engel, Carl. "Again La Fayette and Maria Malibran." *Chesterian* 40 (January-February, 1925).

5. Flory, Joseph H. "Jenny Lind (Her Arrival in America)." *Musart* 18, No. 3 (1976), pp. 24-26.

6. Johnson, H. Earle. "The Germania Musical Society." *MQ* 39 (1953), pp. 75-93.

7. Mussulman, Joseph Agee. "Mendelssohnism in America." *MQ* 53 (1967), pp. 335-346.

8. Olson, Ivan Walter. "Music and Germans in Nineteenth Century Richmond." *Journal of Research in Music Education* 14, No. 1 (1966), pp. 27-32.

9. Prod'homme, Jacques-Gabriel. "La Fayette and Maria Malibran." *Chesterian* 34 (September, 1919).

10. Rogers, Francis. "Henriette Sontag in New York." *MQ* 28 (1942), pp. 100-104.

11. Sabin, Robert. "Early American Composers and Critics." *MQ* 24 (1938), pp. 210-218.

12. "Six Unpublished Letters From La Fayette to Maria Malibran." *Chesterian* 40 (March-April, 1925).

Music

1. Bull, Ole. *Violin Instruction Book; A Complete School for the Violin*. Boston: Keith's Music Publishing House, 1845; New York: Mark H. Newman, 1845.

2. Headland, Helen. *Ole Bull, Norwegian Minstrel*. Rock Island, IL: Augustana Book Concern, 1949. (Music for violin and piano: *Ein Sennenbesuch* (A mountain visit) from *Et Saeterbesog*, p. 143; *Saeterjentens Sondag* (Shepherd Girl's Sunday), p. 148; *Adagio Religioso*, Op. 1, p. 150.

3. Herz, Henri. *New and Complete Piano-Forte School Conducting the Student from the First Elements of Music to the Highest and Most Refined Styles of Performance*. New York: J. F. Nunns, 1844.

4. ————*Collection of Scales and Exercises for the Pianoforte*, new and augmented edition. New York: G. Schirmer, 1894.

5. Thalberg, Sigismond. *Home, Sweet Home! Air anglais varie pour le piano*, Op. 72. New York: G. Schirmer, 1857.

Nº 31.
THE TOWER OF BABEL
OR LANGUAGE CONFOUNDED.

SINFONIA CANONICALE, or the Symphony of Indefinite Perplexity.(M.S.)
MOST RESPECTFULLY & HUMBLY DEDICATED TO HIS IMPERIAL HIGHNESS,
STEPHAN, Vice Roy of BOHEMIA, &c.&c.

Nº 2.
JOHANNISBERG,
OR THE FESTIVAL OF THE VINTAGERS ON THE RHINE.
Grand Divertissement champêtre, pour l'Orchestre.(M.S.) Most respectfully & humbly Dedicated to
HIS SERENE HIGHNESS,
PRINCE GEORGE DE METTERNICH,

Nº 33.
THE ELKHORN PYRAMID, OR
THE INDIANS' OFFERING TO THE SPIRIT OF THE PRAIRIES, *Fantaisie Mystique.*
Pour l'Orchestre.(M.S.) Most respectfully & humbly Dedicated to
HIS SERENE HIGHNESS,
MAXIMILIAN, PRINCE DE WIED, &c.&c.

Nº 34.
TO THE SPIRIT OF BEETHOVEN.
GRANDE SINFONIA caratteristica.(In Manoscritto) Most respectfully & humbly Dedicated to
His Serene Highness,
Prince FERDINAND OF LOBKOWITZ, &c.&c.

Nº 35.
THE EMPRESS QUEEN AND THE MAGYARS.
SINFONIA PATRIOTICO-DRAMATICA, *Piena Orchestra.(M.S.)* A tribute to the MEMORY OF THE
EMPRESS, MARIA THERESIA, *Designed to portray the following* HISTORICAL INCIDENTS:
THE CONVOCATION OF THE DIET AT PRESBURG *on the 11th of September AD. 1741.*
MARIA THERESIA'S APPEAL AND CHIVALRIC RESPONSE OF THE HUNGARIAN MAGNATES.
Most respectfully & humbly Dedicated to Her Imperial Majesty.
CAROLINE AUGUSTA, *Empress of Austria, Queen of Hungaria, &c.&c.&c.&c.*

Nº 36.
LIKEWISE.
The fair Daughters of the Western World.
Capriccio leggiadro, scherzevole, per Grande Orchestra.

Nº 37.
The War of the Elements & the Thunders of Niagara,
SCENA MAGNIFICA E GRAN CAPRICCIO STREPITOSO, *per Piena Orchestra.(M.S.) Also:*
Nº 38.
THE WASHINGTONIAD OR THE DEEDS OF A HERO.
AN AMERICAN FESTIVE OUVERTURE, *For full Orchestra.(M.S.) Most respectfully & humbly*
DEDICATED TO HIS MAJESTY, LOUIS PHILIPPE, KING OF THE FRENCH &c.&c.&c.
Nº 39.
THE DEDICATION WALTZ.
(Printed.)

A page from the **Presentazioni Musicali** from
Anthony Philip Heinrich's collection of music dedicated
to Empress Elizabeth Amelie Eugenie of Austria

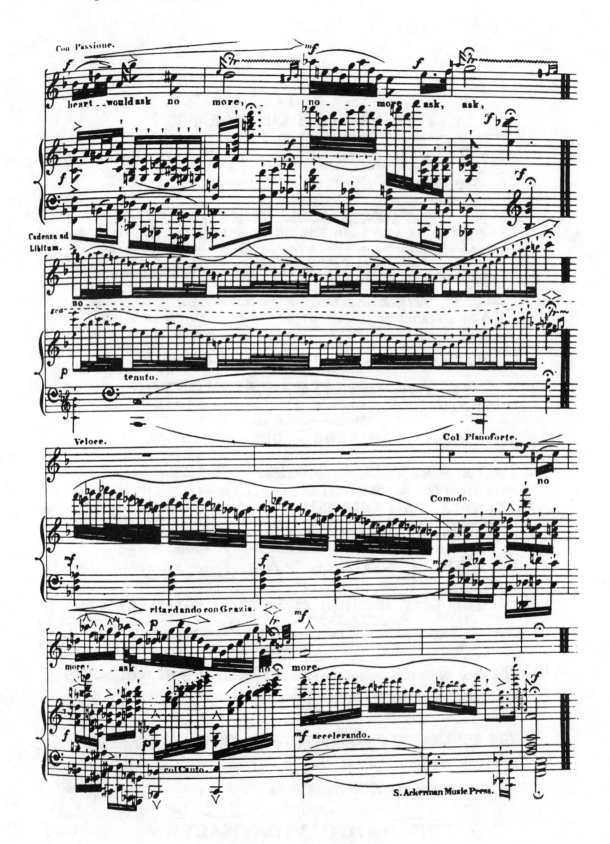

The concluding measures of the song
"Love's Enchantment" by Anthony Philip Heinrich, 1850

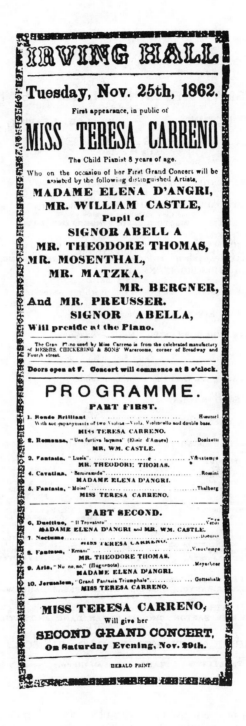

Program of the début of Teresa Carreño

17

THURSDAY AFTERNOON, JUNE 6, 1889,
At 1.30 o'clock.
ORGAN CONCERT — — W. J. D. LEAVITT, ORGANIST.

PROGRAMME.
At 2.30 o'clock.

1. OVERTURE. — "Leonore, No. 3" . . . . *Beethoven*
   GILMORE'S BAND.

2. ARIA FOR TENOR. — From "The Iron Mask" . . . . . . *A. Thomas*
   HERR DE DANCKWARDT.

3. QUARTETTE FOR FRENCH HORNS. — "Annie Laurie" . . *Dudley Buck*
   From the arrangement for male voices.
   MESSRS. WESTON, CASO, RINGER, AND ZILM.

4. "GLORIA." — From Twelfth Mass . . . . *Mozart*
   **SUNG BY THE RE-UNION CHORUS OF SINGERS FROM NEW ENGLAND
   CHORAL SOCIETIES THAT PARTICIPATED IN THE JUBILEE OF 1869,
   ACCOMPANIED BY THE ORGAN AND GILMORE'S BAND.**

5. RHAPSODIE HONGROISE, No. 12 . . . . *Liszt*
   GILMORE'S BAND.

6. ARIA FOR BASSO. — "She Alone Charmeth my Sadness." . . . . *Gounod*
   MR. WHITNEY.

7. SCOTCH SYMPHONY (Two Movements only) . . . . *Mendelssohn*
   GILMORE'S BAND.

8. CAVATINA FOR SOPRANO. — "Una Voce poco fa" . . . . . . *Rossini*
   MME. STONE-BARTON.

9. MORCEAUX DE SALON. — Valse Caprice . . . . *Rubinstein*
   GILMORE'S BAND.

10. CAVATINA. — "Ah, Quel Giorno" (Semiramide) . . . . *Rossini*
    MISS CAMPBELL.

11. CORNET SOLO (Selected) . . . . *Liberati*
    SIGNOR LIBERATI.

12. POPULAR FANTAISIE. — "Le Carnival de Venise" . . . . . . *Paganini*
    GILMORE'S BAND.

The following Soloists will each play a variation of his own composition on the above theme: —

1. EUPHONIUM	. . . .	SIGNOR RAFFAYOLO
2. CLARINET	. . . .	SIGNOR STENGLER
3. FLUGEL HORN	. . . .	HERR RITZE
4. PICCOLO	. . . .	SIGNOR DE CARLO
5. SAXOPHONE	. . . .	MONS. LEFEBRE
6. CORNET	. . . .	MR. B. C. BENT
7. FLUTE	. . . .	MR. JOHN COX
8. ORPHEON	. . . .	MR. HARRY WHITTIER
9. BASSOONS	. . . .	MESSRS RUPP and CAVANAGH
10. OBOE	. . . .	SIGNOR DE CHIARRI
11. CORNET	. . . .	MR. CHAS. PETIT
12. PETIT CLARINET	. . . .	MATUS UR
13. BASS ANTONIOPHONE	. . . . . .	MR. ELDEN BAKER
14. TROMBONE	. . . .	MR. WILSON
15. BASS CLARINET	. . . .	ERNST WEBER

GILMORE'S BAND.

13. QUARTETTE. — From "Martha" . . . . *Flotow*
    **MME. STONE-BARTON, MISS CAMPBELL, MESSRS. DANCKWARDT
    AND WHITNEY.**

14. NATIONAL AIR. — "Star Spangled Banner" . . . . *Key*
    **SOLO BY MME. BARTON; CHORUS, ORGAN, BAND, AND ARTILLERY
    ACCOMPANIMENT.**

MUSICAL DIRECTOR, P. S. GILMORE.

The STEINWAY PIANO used at all Gilmore Concerts.

A program given in Boston by Gilmore's Band,
commemorating the twentieth anniversary of the
Peace Jubilee of 1869

OUTLINE XII

MUSIC FROM 1850 TO 1900

American Nationalism — Civil War Songs — Music in the West
Expansion of American Concert Interests
William Mason — Theodore Thomas — Patrick S. Gilmore
John Philip Sousa — Dudley Buck — Frederick Grant Gleason

I.   **American Nationalism**

    A.   In the years immediately prior to the Civil War there were three American composers (**Heinrich, Fry** and **Bristow**) who were working in the larger musical forms of opera, symphony, oratorio and overture, as well as in the lesser forms for piano and songs. In their attempts to establish a native American style, each of them encouraged the performance of native American music and each contributed substantially to the repertoire.

        1.   Many of their compositions were performed for capacity audiences and received enthusiastic acclaim. On the other hand, few if any of their compositions lived beyond their day.

            a.   Was **Dwight** too severe when he printed in his *Journal*, "The appreciative music lovers, learned or unlearned, professional or amateur, who love Beethoven's music and do not love Fry's have not been apt to recognize the classical affinity. The value of a symphony is settled by the public."

        2.   The products of these composers may have made use of American subjects but, in actuality, their music remained rooted in the concepts and styles of European music, whether it be the German symphonic tradition or the operatic culture of France and Italy.

    B.   **Anthony Philip Heinrich** (1781-1861)

        1.   Although born in Bohemia, **Heinrich** considered himself an American; he emigrated to the United States and settled in Philadelphia in 1810. This eccentric musician was one of the earliest to champion American music. In 1817 he walked from Philadelphia to Pittsburgh and then traveled down the Ohio River to Kentucky. On November 12, 1817, in Lexington **Heinrich** conducted the first known performance of a **Beethoven** symphony (No. 1) in America. Inspired by the frontier and the grandeur of the new nation, he composed, without a knowledge of harmony, his first pieces for piano and voice.

            a.   *The Dawning of Music in Kentucky, Or The Pleasures of Harmony in the Solitudes of Nature*, Op. 1 (*EAM*, v. 10, pp. 4-269)

              1)   *The Musical Bachelor* (*EAM*, v. 10, p. 67)

            b.   *The Western Minstrel*, Op. 2 (*EAM*, v. 10, p. 270)

        2.   In 1827 he traveled to London, played violin in an orchestra and studied theory. After a return to the United States in 1832, he again went to England and Germany in 1834 and on to Austria the following year. In 1836 he had pieces performed in Dresden, Prague, Budapest, Graz and in France. **Heinrich** returned to America and settled in New York in 1837. His compositions enjoyed immense popularity and many piano works and songs were published.

        3.   In addition to songs and piano pieces he composed oratorios and a large number of showy, descriptive and programmatic orchestral works based on American subjects, particularly the Indians and scenic wonders. He was known by his admirers as the "Beethoven of America" and in 1846 conquered New York, Boston and Philadelphia with festivals of his own compositions. The following "Complimentary Concert" was

presented in Boston on June 13, 1846. There was an orchestra of sixty and a chorus of fifty performers.

PROGRAMME.

Part First

1.–TECUMSEH, OR THE BATTLE OF THE THAMES–a Martial Ouver–
  ture–for full Orchestra.
  Introduction–The Indian War Council.
  Allegro Eroico–The Indian War Dance–Advance of the Americans–
  Skirmishing–Battle, and fall of Tecumseh, ... A. P. Heinrich

2.–"IMOINDA,"–An Indian Love Song,–Miss Stone, ... A. P. Heinrich

3.–CAVATINA,–"Una Voce poco fa,"–Mrs. Shirley, ...Rossini

4.–SONG,–"The Parting,"–Miss Stone, ... A. P. Heinrich

5.–"CORO DI CACCIA," OR HUNTING CHORUS,–"The Yager's Adieu,"–
  with Orchestral Accompaniments;   vocal soli parts by Miss Stone,
  Miss Emmons, Mrs. Rametti, and Mr. Richardson, ... A. P. Heinrich

Part Second.

1.–OUVERTURE,–"To the Pilgrims,"–Full Orchestra, with Trumpet
  Obligato by Mr. Bartlett,–comprising the following Tableaux:
  1st–Adagio Primo,–The Genius of Freedom slumbering in the forest
  shades of America.
  2nd–Adagio Secondo,–She is awakened into life by those moving
  melodies, with which nature regales her votaries in her primeval
  solitude.
  3d–Marcia,–The efforts of power to clip the young eagle of liberty.
  4th–Allegretto Pollacca,–The joyous reign of universal freedom and
  universal intelligence, ... A. P. Heinrich
2.–"WE WANDER IN A THORNY MAZE,"
  A sacred song,–from the Oratorio of the Pilgrims,–Miss Stone,
  . . . . A. P. Heinrich
3.–SONG,–"I dearly love the sea,"–Mrs. Franklin, ... G. F. Hayter
4.–DUETTO SCHERZANTE,–"The Valentine,"–Mrs. Franklin and
  Miss Stone, ... A. P. Heinrich
5.–OUVERTURE,–"Der Freischütz," . . . . Von Weber

C.   **William Henry Fry** (1813-1864)
  1.   Fry, a music critic and composer, was born in Philadelphia on August 10 and died in the West Indies; he was buried in New York. His first grand opera, *Aurelia the Vestal*, written in 1841, was never performed. His second opera, *Leonora*, 1845, was the first publicly performed grand opera by an American. The libretto is in English but the music, modeled on **Meyerbeer** and **Donizetti**, lacks distinction and individuality. It was unsuccessfully revived in 1858 in Italian translation. Fry's third opera, *Notre Dame of Paris*, was staged in Philadelphia the year of Fry's death. **Theodore Thomas** made his début as an opera conductor at this performance.
  2.   For six years (1846-1852) **Fry** was the European correspondent for the *New York Tribune* and on his return to the States he continued with the *Tribune* and championed native American music. In 1852-1853 he gave a series of notable lectures admonishing

American composers to break from European domination and American audiences to recognize native composers. He said, "A composer in this country may as well burn his compositions for any opportunity he has for making himself heard. Our Opera Houses and Musical Societies are worse than useless so far [as] they foster American Art, that art which elevates artists here above the level of provincial beggars."

3. Fry also wrote symphonies (*Santa Claus [Christmas] Symphony*, 1853; *Hagar in the Wilderness*, a sacred symphony, 1854; *Niagara Symphony*, 1854) which were played by **Jullien**. The *Evangeline Overture* was composed in 1860 and the *Macbeth Overture* with chorus in 1862. For chorus he wrote *Stabat Mater*, 1855, and a Mass in E-flat.

4. **Fry** claimed that the Philharmonic Society of New York had not played a single American work during its first eleven years, a remark that touched off a long controversy.

5. *Leonora*, Philadelphia, 1845
   a. Aria: *My triumph's nigh* (*MinA*, p. 341)
   b. Aria: *Ev'ry doubt and danger over* (*MinA*, p. 344)
   c. Aria: *Return to me, ah brother dear* (*PAS*, p. 45)

D. **George Frederick Bristow** (1825-1898)
   1. **Bristow** was born in Brooklyn, New York, on December 19. He studied violin with **Ole Bull** and played violin in the New York Philharmonic Society (1843-1879). During this time he was also conductor of the New York Harmonic Society (1851-1863), the Mendelssohn Society (1867-1871) and St. George's Chapel (1854-1860). **Bristow** contributed much to the musical education of New Yorkers.
   2. Not unlike **Heinrich** and **Fry**, **Bristow** used American subject matter in his compositions but composed in the typical European styles, particularly that of **Mendelssohn**. He was a champion of the American composer and pointed out that the New York Philharmonic Society had played only one American piece, his own.
      a. The Society made an official statement regarding its policy, which was that one American work might be performed each season if submitted to and approved by its committee.
   3. Among his 120 compositions, the five symphonies are probably his best works. The *Niagara Symphony*, 1893, for soloists, chorus and orchestra is a reflection of the **Beethoven** "Ninth."
   4. The opera *Rip Van Winkle*, 1855, was the second American grand opera composed. Written in light opera style, it is completely undistinguished.
      a. *Vivandiere Song* (*PAS*, p. 47)
   5. Other works include four overtures, two string quartets, many piano pieces, *Mass in C*, 1885; the oratorio *Daniel*, 1866; and the cantatas *The Pioneer*, 1872; *The Great Republic* and *Ode to the American Union*, 1880.
   6. *Geo. F. Bristow's New and Improved Method for the Reed or Cabinet Organ*, New York, 1887
   7. *Bristow's Two-part Vocal Exercises, designed for the use of Schools or Private Classes*, Op. 75, New York, 1890
   8. *The Cantilena; a Collection of Songs, Duets, Trios and Quartettes*, New York, 1861
      a. *Knisely* (*AH*, p. 589)

II. **Songs of the Civil War**

A. During the War between the States (1861-1865) songs were sung everywhere: at home, in the camp, on the battlefield.
   1. There are patriotic songs which called forth a nationalistic enthusiasm or exaggerated hatred, depending on one's focus.
      a. *Dixie's Land [Dixie]* (*MinA*, p. 276; *CWS*, p. 13), written and used by **Daniel Decatur Emmett** (1815-1904), became a sensation. In the presidential race of 1860 the music was adapted to a campaign song for Abraham Lincoln; the follow-

ing spring the South seceded. The song was soon taken over by the South.

b.   *The Battle Hymn of the Republic* (*MinA*, p. 296; *CWS*, p. 5), adopted by the Northerners, was written by the social reformer Julia Ward Howe (1819-1910) and "Adapted to the favorite Melody of 'Glory, Hallelujah' " (*MinA*, p. 294). This vigorous campmeeting or Sunday School tune, attributed to the Southerner **William Steffe**, appeared in 1856 and has been set with many different texts, among them "*John Brown's Body*."

c.   *The Bonnie Blue Flag* (*CWS*, p. 17; *PAS*, p. 37) is "A Southern Patriotic Song, Written, Arranged, and Sung at his 'Personation Concerts' by Harry Macarthy, the Arkansas Comedian."

d.   Other patriotic songs include *The Battle Cry of Freedom* (*CWS*, p. 1) and *Maryland! My Maryland!* (*CWS*, p. 21) set to the German Christmas tune "*O Tannenbaum*."

2.   Songs depicting the life of the soldiers were numerous; many are marching songs, others are more meditative.

a.   *Marching Through Georgia* (*MinA*, p. 304; *CWS*, p. 34; *EAM*, v. 19, p. 18) by **Henry Clay Work** speaks of the Union General William Sherman's march through the South toward the Atlantic in the summer of 1864.

b.   *Tramp! Tramp! Tramp! or the Prisoner's Hope* (*CWS*, p. 46) by **George F. Root** reveals a prisoner's thoughts of home with mother, the futile cry of victory and the wish for freedom.

c.   *Tenting on the Old Camp Ground*, 1862 (*MinA*, p. 299; *CWS*, p. 58) by **Walter Kittredge** was sung by both sides.

d.   *Just before the Battle, Mother* (*CWS*, p. 49) by **George F. Root**; *All Quiet along the Potomac To-Night* (*MinA*, p. 297; *CWS*, p. 62; *PAS*, p. 34), set by **John Hill Hewitt** who was active in the Confederate cause.

3.   To counterbalance the songs about the soldiers' life, there were many songs written concerning the domestic scene, the anxiety, bravery and sorrow of those at home.

a.   "*Weeping Sad and Lonely*" or "*When this cruel war is over*" (*CWS*, p. 104; *PAS*, p. 40), set by **Henry Tucker**, was sung by both the North and the South.

b.   *When Johnny Comes Marching Home* (*MinA*, p. 302; *CWS*, p. 113), dedicated to the Army and Navy of the Union, was written by **Louis Lambert [Patrick Gilmore]** and popularized by his band.

c.   *The Vacant Chair, or We Shall Meet but We Shall Miss Him* (*CWS*, p. 117) by **George F. Root** on Thanksgiving Day, 1861, honors the memory of "our noble Willie" who "strove to bear our banner thro' [*sic*] the thickest of the fight."

III.   Music in the West

A.   There was very little music in the West before 1850 except in Chicago, New Orleans, Cincinnati, St. Louis and Milwaukee, where Music Societies had been founded in the earlier part of the century.

B.   Concerts, a music school, Music Societies and theatres began to appear in Chicago after 1833.

1.   In 1847 music was studied in the Chicago public schools, only ten years after **Lowell Mason's** system was introduced in Boston.

2.   In 1850 grand opera was performed and orchestral music was initiated.

3.   **Theodore Thomas** made his first Chicago appearance in 1869 with his Central Park Garden Orchestra. San Francisco had opera in 1853.

4.   **Brahms'** *Symphony No. 2*, composed in the summer of 1877, was played by the Musical Society of Milwaukee on December 10, 1878.

C.   European virtuosi traveled from East to West in the late nineteenth century, but had little influence on the development of native music. **William [Johann Heinrich Wilhelm] Steinway [Steinweg]**, one of the sons of the famous piano builder, **Henry [Heinrich**

Engelhard] Steinway, made it possible for many European pianists to tour the United States; he frequently offered Steinway Hall for concerts free of charge, even to supplying the programs.

1. In spite of their efforts to play good music, the programs of these foreign artists had to include variations on popular tunes, operatic potpourris and sentimental pieces. Generally concerts included more than one artist or else the soloist was assisted by an ensemble, vocal or instrumental.

    a. **Anton Rubinstein** (1820-1894) played 215 concerts in the United States during the 1872-1873 concert season; he was paid about $40,000. Solo recitals were rare at that time; **Rubinstein** played a series of seven historical piano recitals in New York which drew large audiences, but he refused to return to America, even for $2,500 a concert.

        1) In addition to his solo recitals **Rubinstein** also presented concerts with the famous Polish violinist **Henri Wieniawski** (1835-1880); they played the **Beethoven** *Kreutzer Sonata* some 70 times while on tour in the United States.

        2) After **Rubinstein** returned to Europe, **Wieniawski** continued his tour, including California. One of his favorite display pieces was the *Carnival of Venice*.

    b. **Henri Vieuxtemps** (1820-1881), the celebrated Belgian violinist, toured the United States first in 1844-1845; he made two more visits to America, one in 1857 with the virtuoso pianist **Sigismond Thalberg** (1812-1872) and another with **Kristina Nilsson** (1843-1921), the Swedish soprano, in 1870.

        1) **Vieuxtemps** charmed his audiences with *The Arkansas Traveler* and *Money Musk*.

    c. **Hans von Bülow** (1830-1894) gave 193 concerts during his tour of the United States in 1875-1876. He returned to America in 1889-1890. He played the world première of the **Tchaikovsky** *Concerto, No. 1,* for piano in Boston and gave a series of recitals playing the **Beethoven** piano sonatas.

    d. **Ignace Jan Paderewski** (1860-1941), the eminent Polish pianist, made his first appearance in America in New York in 1891 and followed it with 116 more concerts; **William Steinway** had guaranteed him $30,000 for 80 concerts. **Paderewski's** variations on *Yankee Doodle* became very popular.

        1) In 1900 **Paderewski**, recognizing the sad situation for struggling American composers, established a trust fund of $10,000 which would offer a $1,000 prize triennially to a worthy American composer. **Horatio Parker** received the first prize for his cantata *A Star Song* (1901).

    e. **Teresa Carreño** (1853-1917), Venezuelan pianist, made her début in New York in 1862 as a child prodigy. She later studied with **Louis Gottschalk** (1829-1869), and in Paris with **Georges Mathias** (1826-1910) and **Anton Rubinstein** (1820-1894). She also had success as an opera singer, composer and conductor. She contributed a great deal in securing early appreciation of the music of her pupil, **Edward MacDowell**, by playing it on her programs.

IV. **Expansion of American concert interests**

    A. **William Mason** was a leader in the development of American music and systematic study and instruction of the piano. In the area of orchestral organization and touring, **Theodore Thomas** did much to give the American audiences throughout the country a stable diet of high quality orchestral music. **Patrick Gilmore** with his colossal concerts and **John Philip Sousa** through his many disciples were very influential in bringing about a great interest in band music, particularly in the military bands and in the schools. **Dudley Buck** was instrumental in encouraging the larger forms of choral composition and **F. G. Gleason** was instrumental in developing an organization to promote and protect the American composer.

B.   **William Mason** (1829-1908)
   1.   **William Mason**, son of **Lowell**, had the advantages of being brought up in a musical home.   He was a well-trained musician of high standards and wide experience.   In 1849 he went to Leipzig where he studied with **Ignaz Moscheles** (1772-1844), **Moritz Hauptmann** (1792-1868) and **Ernst Richter** (1808-1879);   in 1853-1854 he studied piano with **Franz Liszt** (1811-1886) in Weimar.   While in Europe he gave concerts in many countries and had the opportunity to meet the leading musicians of the day, among them **Berlioz, Rubinstein, Wieniawski, Joachim**, the young **Brahms, Rémenyi, Schumann** and **Wagner**.
   2.   **Mason** returned to America in 1854 and began his career as a piano virtuoso, giving some of the first serious piano recitals in this country.   However, he began to devote himself more and more to teaching and became the foremost piano teacher of his time.   His piano method, *Touch and Technic*, is still used.
   3.   In 1855 he organized with **Theodore Thomas** the Mason and Thomas Chamber Music Soirées which for thirteen years continued to present significant chamber music works to American audiences.   In 1872 he received the Doctor of Music degree from Yale College.
   4.   **Mason** composed more than 50 virtuoso piano pieces and wrote several instruction books.
       a.   *A Method for the Piano-forte*, New York, 1867, with **E. S. Hoadley**
          1)   This includes European fingering and a dictionary of musical terms.
       b.   *A System of Technical Exercises for the Piano-forte*, Boston, 1878
       c.   *Touch and Technic; for artistic piano playing*, Philadelphia, 1889
       d.   *A Primer of Music*, New York, 1894, with **W. S. B. Mathews**
   5.   When he was 18 and 19 years of age respectively, he compiled two books of part songs and glees, no doubt under the influence of his father.
       a.   *The Social Glee Book: being a selection of glees and part songs, by distinguished German composers; never before published in this country: together with original pieces*, Boston, 1847
       b.   *Fireside Harmony: a new collection of glees and part songs*, Boston 1848.
C.   **Theodore Thomas** (1835-1905)
   1.   **Thomas** came from Germany to New York in 1845 at the age of nine and helped support his family by playing the violin. He played in **Jullien's** orchestra in 1853, and appeared as a concert violinist with **Thalberg** and others. He also played in the New York Philharmonic Society in 1854.
   2.   In 1862 he organized an orchestra and, through his high standards and planned education of the public in good orchestral music, laid the foundation for the great orchestras of today.
       a.   **Thomas** gave the first American performance of **Wagner's** *Overture to the Flying Dutchman*.
       b.   From 1868 to 1875 he gave his famous series of concerts in Central Park Garden; he conducted 1,227 concerts in these eight seasons.
   3.   Beginning in 1869 **Thomas** traveled from one end of the country to the other with his Theodore Thomas Orchestra, and his influence for good music was felt everywhere.   He met with considerable criticism, however, from those who thought he played too much "classical" music.
       a.   In Keokuk, Iowa, he conducted a program which included **Wagner's** *Overture to Tannhäuser*, the second movement of **Beethoven's** *Fifth Symphony* and **Weber's** *Invitation to the Dance*. The latter was arranged for orchestra by **Berlioz** and a note to that effect was placed under the title of the work in the program. The critic of Keokuk, however, interpreted this as applying to all three pieces. His review in the local paper the next morning was as follows: "The first piece was that fine trilogy which **Hector Berlioz** with exquisite art made from **Wagner, Beethoven, and Weber.**

"The thought of **Hector Berlioz**, evidently, in arranging the trilogy was to put after the passionate action of the one, the ocean-like, star-like, measureless calm of the symphony. After you have bathed in that luxury and languor long enough, there comes **von Weber's** *Invitation to the Dance*. Oh, there has been nothing heard in Keokuk like this trilogy."

4. From 1866 **Thomas** conducted the Brooklyn Philharmonic. In 1872 he helped to organize the Cincinnati Festival and became its conductor. For a year and a half he was director of the College of Music in Cincinnati but did not remain because of certain College policies. **Thomas** was the music director of the Philadelphia Centennial Exposition in 1876 and the Chicago World's Fair in 1893. In 1877 he was elected conductor of the New York Philharmonic; this caused him to subordinate his own orchestra. **Thomas** adopted the plan of the Cincinnati Festival of choral and orchestra concerts in other cities. In New York in 1882 he organized a festival in which a chorus of 3,000 singers and an orchestra of 300 players performed for an audience of 8,000. In 1883 he toured from coast to coast with his orchestra; they gave 74 concerts in 74 days in 30 cities.

5. An effort to establish an American Opera Company in New York in 1885 was a financial failure. He organized the Chicago Symphony in 1891 and conducted it almost to the time of his death.

6. His programs usually included selections from the classics, works of contemporary American composers and a few pieces of the lighter type. The following typical program (first part) was given in 1873.

PROGRAMME

First Part

```
OVERTURE        )
SCHERZO         )
INTERMEZZO      ) — Midsummer Night's Dream. . . . Mendelssohn
NOCTURNE        )
WEDDING MARCH   )


ARIA, "In diesen heil'gen Hallen," Magic Flute . . . . . . . . . . Mozart
                Mr. Myron W. Whitney


SELECTIONS, 1st Act Lohengrin . . . . . . . . . . . . . . . . . . Wagner


OVERTURE, Leonore No. 3 . . . . . . . . . . . . . . . . . . Beethoven


SOLO for Harp, Grand Studio, ad imitazione del
    Mandolina . . . . . . . . . . . . . . . . . . . . . . . . . . . . Parish Alvars
                Mr. A. Lockwood


SONG, A Mariner's Home's the Sea. . . . . . . . . . . . . . . . Randegger
                Mr. Myron W. Whitney


WALTZ, Publicisten . . . . . . . . . . . . . . . . . . . . . . . . . . Strauss


OVERTURE, Hunyadi Laszlo. . . . . . . . . . . . . . . . . . . . . Erkel
```

D.   New musical organizations (1875-1900)
1.   The last quarter of the nineteenth century saw many new artistic developments and organizations in the United States.
2.   The New York Philharmonic-Symphony Society had been organized in 1842. A second orchestra in New York City, the New York Symphony Society, was established in 1878; the Boston Symphony Orchestra, 1881; the Chicago Symphony Orchestra under **Theodore Thomas**, 1891; the Cincinnati Symphony and the Pittsburgh Symphony, 1895 (**Victor Herbert** was the second conductor of the Pittsburgh Symphony); the Philadelphia Orchestra, 1900; the Minneapolis Symphony Orchestra, 1903; the St. Louis Symphony Society, 1907; and the San Francisco Symphony Orchestra in 1911.
3.   During the third quarter of the nineteenth century the operatic center in New York was the Academy of Music which opened in 1854 with a performance of **Bellini's** *Norma*.
   a.   By 1880 the idea of having a special, well-equipped theater for opera developed into positive plans and the Metropolitan Opera House was inaugurated on October 22, 1883, with a performance of **Gounod's** *Faust*.
      1)   Included on the roster of "greats" during the 1890's are Jean and Edouard de Reszke, Lillian Nordica, Emma Eames, Ernestine Schumann-Heinck, Nellie Melba, Marcella Sembrich, Lilli Lehmann and Adelina Patti.
   b.   In 1889 the Auditorium for the Chicago Opera Company was opened. Within the next few years every major opera company of the country performed in Chicago. New Orleans and San Francisco hosted touring opera companies regularly.
4.   Choral festivals took on great interest in St. Louis where in 1880 the St. Louis Choral Society was founded; it combined with the orchestra and was renamed the St. Louis Choral Symphony Society (1893).
5.   Philadelphia had its second May festival in 1884; among the works performed were **Mendelssohn's** *Elijah* and **Verdi's** *Requiem*. Cincinnati had already established its biennial May Festival in 1873. The Ann Arbor May Festivals of the University of Michigan began in 1893 and the Bethlehem Bach Choir (Bethlehem, Pennsylvania) founded in 1898 includes a performance of **Bach's** *B minor Mass* in each festival.
6.   The Chautauqua Institution of New York was founded in 1874 by the Methodist Episcopal Church. Cultural programs by symphony orchestras, opera singers and solo instrumentalists were offered each summer. The summer school of music, art and dance, organized shortly after 1874, has continued to the present and is now associated with the State University of New York.
7.   A variety of music societies and federations had their beginnings in the musical explosion of the "nineties."
   a.   The National Federation of Music Clubs grew out of a meeting at the Chicago World's Fair, 1893. The Music Teachers' National Association, interested primarily in music education, was organized in 1876. In 1896 the American Guild of Organists, the national organization of organists, was founded. The Music Division of the Library of Congress, Washington, D. C., was organized in 1897 and it has since become one of the largest and most significant music related collections in the world.
E.   **Patrick Sarsfield Gilmore** (1829-1892)
1.   **Gilmore** was born in Ballygar, Galway County, Ireland, on December 25. His early interest in band music was evident at the age of sixteen when he became a cornetist in a Galway band. In 1848 he went to Canada but soon moved to Boston where he conducted local bands and opened a music store. In 1859 he organized the famous Gilmore's Grand Boston Band. In 1861 he and his band enlisted in the Union Army; in 1863 he wrote the popular song *When Johnny Comes Marching Home* (*MinA*, p. 302; *CWS*, p. 113) under the pseudonym **Louis Lambert**. Other of his Civil War songs are *Freedom on the Old Plantation, The Spirit of the North* and *Good News from*

Home. **Gilmore** made many transcriptions and arrangements for band.

2.　After the Civil War **Gilmore** was stationed in New Orleans where he gave many concerts.　One concert in the city square included 5,000 voices, 500 bandsmen and a trumpet and drum military corps. *Hail Columbia* was sung accompanied by a battery of cannon firing on each beat of the drums and the ringing of church bells in the vicinity.

3.　He staged supercolossal performances, especially at two enormous music festivals held in Boston.

　　a.　The five-day Great National Peace Festival, commemorating the peace after the Civil War, was described as "the grandest musical festival ever known in the history of the world."　It required an orchestra of 1,000 (led by **Ole Bull**), a chorus of 10,000 and six bands, one with a bass drum 25 feet in diameter.　In addition there was a powerful organ, cannons, bells and 100 red-shirted firemen pounding anvils during the *"Anvil Chorus"* from **Verdi's** *Il Trovatore*.　(see **Dwight's** *Journal of Music*, v. 29 (1869), pp. 55, 57, 60, 71, 72, 93)

　　b.　The ten-day World's Peace Jubilee (1872) was even more stupendous with an orchestra of 2,000 and a chorus of 20,000.　**Franz Abt, Johann Strauss II** (brought over from Europe for this festival) and **Carl Zerrahn** (German-born conductor of the Boston Handel and Haydn Society for 42 years) were among the international cast of conductors.　**Strauss** conducted (?) his *Blue Danube Waltz* with the aid of 100 assistant conductors.　He described the result as an "unholy row," but they all managed to finish together.　He described the situation: "There I stood at the raised desk, high above all the others.　Suddenly a cannon-shot rang out, a gentle hint for us twenty thousand to begin playing *The Blue Danube*.　I gave the signal, my hundred assistant conductors followed me as quickly and as well as they could and then there broke out an unholy row such as I shall never forget.　As we had begun more or less simultaneously, I concentrated my whole attention on seeing that we should finish together too!　Thank Heaven, I managed even that.　It was all that was humanly possible."

4.　After the Jubilee **Gilmore** went to New York and organized a band of 65 players.　This concert band toured throughout the United States, Canada and later in Europe (1878).　During the 1880's the band was a summer attraction at Manhattan Beach.

F.　**John Philip Sousa** (1954-1932)

1.　**Sousa** was born on November 6 in Washington, D. C., of a Portuguese father and German mother.　He studied violin, theory, composition and band instruments.　At the age of thirteen he enlisted in the United States Marine Band.

2.　In 1876 he went to Philadelphia to the American Centenary celebration to play first violin under **Jacques Offenbach** during his American tour.　**Sousa** conducted the United States Marine Band from 1880 until 1892.　After **Gilmore's** death in 1892, **Sousa** formed his own band.　This band, which included nineteen of **Gilmore's** best musicians, became world-famous and was in constant demand, beginning with the Chicago World's Fair in 1893.　He made several tours of Europe (1900, 1901, 1903, 1905) where he was held in high esteem and received many decorations.　In 1910-1911 he made a tour around the world.　In 1973 **Sousa** was posthumously elected to the Hall of Fame for Great Musicians.

3.　**Sousa's** published compositions number several hundreds, but he is most famous for his 136 marches which have earned for him the title "The March King."　Many of these marches were inspired by particular events, such as *The Washington Post*, written to celebrate a prize given by the newspaper. *Semper Fidelis* was adopted as the official march of the United States Marine Corps.　**Sousa's** celebrated *Stars and Stripes Forever* is known and loved throughout the world.

　　a.　**Sousa** also wrote 11 comic operas (operettas), 70 songs, 11 waltzes, 11 suites, 14 humoresques, 20 fantasias and 332 arrangements.　In addition he wrote 5 novels and an autobiography. In the late 1890's he had the first upright Sousaphone built to his own specifications.

4. **Sousa's** skill in training musicians had an important influence in the development of band music in America.

    a.   Many of the 500 musicians who received training in his band became conductors and teachers throughout the country.

        1)   A large number of compositions were written by these men and others to fill the needs of the estimated 18,000 bands, amateur and professional, in the United States at the turn of the century.

    b.   **Giuseppe Creatore** (1871-1952) and **Arthur Pryor** (1870-1942) were well-known band masters in the early part of the twentieth century.

5. *The Trumpet and Drum*, 1886

G. **Dudley Buck** (1839-1909)

1. **Buck** was born on March 10 in Hartford, Connecticut; he studied in Leipzig and Dresden (1858-1859) with **Moritz Hauptmann** (composition), **Johann Schneider** (organ) and **Ignaz Moscheles** (piano). He studied in Paris in 1861-1862 and returned to America in 1862 and became organist of Park Church, Hartford. He later held church positions in Chicago (St. James), Boston (St. Paul's) and Brooklyn (Holy Trinity Church, 1875-1903). During his tenure in Boston (1871-1875) he taught at the New England Conservatory of Music and later in Brooklyn became director of the Apollo Club.

    a.   In 1875 **Theodore Thomas** invited **Buck** to act as assistant conductor of the Central Park Garden Concerts.

2. **Dudley Buck** was a pioneer in the larger forms of choral composition and was one of the first American composers to achieve national recognition, particularly with his church music. Among his works are the comic opera *Deseret*, 1880, the opera *Serapis*, the *Forty-Sixth Psalm* for chorus and orchestra, 112 anthems, canticles and hymns.

    a.   *God of Our Fathers* (*AH*, p. 285)

    b.   He had a wide influence on church music through his pupils, some of whom were **Harry Rowe Shelley** (1858-1947), **John Hyatt Brewer** (1856-1931), **William Harold Neidlinger** (1863-1924) and **Raymond Huntington Woodman** (1861-1943).

    c.   **Buck's** music was written largely for popular appeal and, although better than much church music of his time, is rarely heard today. His inaugural lecture for the Department of Organ in the College of Music of Boston University gave considerable impetus to the study of organ in this country.

3. *Buck's New and Complete Dictionary of Musical Terms*, Boston, 1873

4. *Illustrations in Choir Accompaniment with hints in Registration*, New York, 1877

H. **Frederick Grant Gleason** (1848-1903)

1. **Gleason** was born on December 17 in Middletown, Connecticut; his first musical studies were with **Dudley Buck** in Boston. In 1869 **Gleason** entered the Leipzig Conservatory where he studied harmony with **Ernst Richter** (1808-1879) and piano with **Ignaz Moscheles** (1794-1870); he also studied piano in Berlin with **Oscar Raif** and in London. On returning to the United States he settled for a time in Connecticut where he held several positions as organist; in 1876 he moved to Chicago where he taught piano, orchestration and composition.

2. **Gleason** became one of the most honored musicians in the Chicago area. He was editor of the *Musical Bulletin* from 1871 and was music editor for the *Chicago Tribune* (1884-1889). In 1896 he organized and became the first president of the Manuscript Society, an organization for promoting and protecting new compositions by American composers.

3. **Gleason's** works, many of which were championed by conductor **Theodore Thomas**, include two operas: *Otho Visconti* (posthumously performed, 1907) and *Montezuma*, never performed. The *leitmotif*, full-textured orchestration and rich harmonies betray

his German study experience. These devices are quite apparent in his cantatas: *God Our Deliverer*, *The Culprit Fay*, *Praise Song of Harmony* and the *Auditorium Festival Ode*, written in 1889 for the opening of the Auditorium Theater in Chicago.

4. In addition to two symphonic poems, *Edris* and *The Song of Life*, **Gleason** wrote several songs, piano and organ pieces, a piano concerto and two Services for the Episcopal Church.

5. *Gleason's Motette Collection*, Chicago, 1875

BIBLIOGRAPHY

Books

1. Bergmann, Leola Nelson. *Music Master of the Middle West: The Story of F. Melius Christiansen and the St. Olaf Choir*. Minneapolis: The University of Minnesota Press, 1944; reprint: New York: Da Capo Press, 1968.

2. Bernard, Kenneth A. *Lincoln and the Music of the Civil War*. Caldwell, Ohio: Caxton Printers, 1966.

3. Bierley, John. *John Philip Sousa, American Phenomenon*. New York: Appleton-Century-Crofts, 1973.

4. Bierley, Paul E. *John Philip Sousa: A Descriptive Catalog of His Works*. Urbana: University of Illinois Press, 1973.

5. Broder, Nathan. "The Evolution of the American Composer," in *One Hundred Years of Music in America*, ed. Paul Henry Lang. New York: G. Schirmer, 1961, pp. 25-35.

6. Buck, Dudley. *Buck's New and Complete Dictionary of Musical Terms*. Boston: Oliver Ditson, 1873.

7. ————*Illustrations in Choir Accompaniment (with Hints in Registration)*. New York: G. Schirmer, 1877; 6th edition, 1903.

8. ————*The Influence of the Organ in History*. London: William Reeves, 1882; reprint: Saint Clair Shores, MI: Scholarly Reprints, 1976.

9. Darlington, Marwood. *Irish Orpheus: The Life of Patrick Gilmore*. Philadelphia: Olivier-Maney-Klein, 1950.

10. Davis, Ronald Leroy. *A History of Opera in the American West*. Englewood Cliffs, NJ: Prentice-Hall, 1965.

11. ————*Opera in Chicago*. New York: Appleton-Century, 1966.

12. Foner, Philip S. *American Labor Songs of the Nineteenth Century*. Urbana: Illinois University Press, 1975.

13. Fry, William Henry. "Prefatory Remarks to Leonora," in *The American Composer Speaks; A Historical Anthology, 1770-1965*, ed. Gilbert Chase. Baton Rouge: Louisiana State University Press, 1966, pp. 46-52.

14. Gallo, William K. *The Life and Church Music of Dudley Buck*. Ann Arbor: University Microfilms, 1969.

15. Gilmore, Patrick Sarsfield. *Gilmore's Famous Band Concerts*. New York: Sackett & Wilhelms Lithoprinting Co., 1892.

16. ————*History of the National Peace Jubilee and Great Musical Festival, Held in the City of Boston, June, 1869, to Commemorate the Restoration of Peace Throughout the Land*. New York: Lee, Shepard, and Dillingham, 1871.

17. Glass, Paul. *Singing Soldiers—A History of the Civil War in Song*. New York: Da Capo Press, 1968.

18. Goldin, Milton. *The Music Merchants; the Colorful Chronicle of the Impresarios, Entrepreneurs and Patrons Who Popularized Serious Music in America*. New York: Macmillan, 1969.

19. Goldman, Richard Franko. "Band Music in America," in *One Hundred Years of Music in*

America, ed. Paul Henry Lang. New York: G. Schirmer, 1961, pp. 128-139.

20.   ————"John Philip Sousa," in *Selected Essays and Reviews, 1948-1968*, ed. Dorothy Klotzman.   Brooklyn: Institute for Studies in American Music, 1980 (ISAM Monograph, No. 13), pp. 208-224.

21.   ————*The Wind Band*. Boston: Allyn & Bacon, 1961.

22.   Graber, Kenneth. *William Mason: An Annotated Bibliography*. Detroit: The College Music Society. (In preparation)

23.   Hall, Florence Marion. *The Story of the Battle Hymn of the Republic*. New York: Harper & Bro., 1916.

24.   Hart, Philip. *Orpheus in the New World. The Symphony Orchestra as an American Cultural Institution*. New York: W. W. Norton, 1973.

25.   Heaps, Porter W., and Willard A. *The Singing Sixties; the Spirit of Civil War Days Drawn From the Music of the Times*. Norman: Oklahoma University Press, 1960.

26.   Heinrich, Anthony Philip. "Preface to *The Dawning of Music in Kentucky* and Letter to Mr. Seaton, Mayor of Washington, D. C.," in *The American Composer Speaks; a Historical Anthology, 1770-1965*, ed. Gilbert Chase. Baton Rouge: Louisiana State University Press, 1966, pp. 41-45.

27.   *A Hundred Years of Music in America, An Account of Musical Effort in America*, ed. William Smyth Babcock Mathews. Chicago: G[ranville] L. Howe, 1889.

28.   Kolodin, Irving. *The Metropolitan Opera 1883-1966. A Candid History*. New York: Alfred A. Knopf, 1968.

29.   Lair, John. *Songs Lincoln Loved*. New York: Duell, Sloan, & Pearce, 1954.

30.   Lingg, Ann M. *John Philip Sousa*. New York: Henry Holt & Co., 1954.

31.   Lowens, Irving. "The Triumph of Anthony Philip Heinrich," in *Music and Musicians in Early America*. New York: W. W. Norton, 1964, pp. 203-211.

32.   ————"William Henry Fry: American Nationalist," in *Music and Musicians in Early America*. New York: W. W. Norton, 1964, pp. 212-222.

33.   Mason, William. *Memories of a Musical Life*. New York: The Century Co., 1901; reprint: New York: AMS Press, 1970.

34.   Milinowski, Marta. *Teresa Carreno*. New Haven, CT: Yale University Press, 1940.

35.   Miller, Philip L. "Opera, the Story of an Immigrant," in *One Hundred Years of Music in America*, ed. Paul Henry Lang. New York: G. Schirmer, 1961, pp. 53-79.

36.   Morrison, Theodore. *Chautauqua: A Center for Education, Religion, and the Arts in America*. Chicago: University of Chicago Press, 1974.

37.   Mueller, John Henry. *The American Symphony Orchestra: A Social History of Musical Taste*. Bloomington: Indiana University Press, 1951; reprint: Westport, CT: Greenwood Press, 1976.

38.   Mueller, John Henry, and Kate Hevner. "Trends in Musical Taste," in *Indiana University Publications*, Humanities Series, No. 8. Bloomington: Indiana University, 1942.

39.   Otis, Philo Adams. *The Chicago Symphony Orchestra: Its Organization, Growth, and Development, 1891-1924*. Chicago: Clayton F. Summy Co., 1924.

40.   Root, George Frederick. *The Musical Curriculum*. Chicago: Root & Cady, 1865.

41.   ————*The Story of a Musical Life*. Cincinnati: The John Church Co., 1891.

42.   Russell, Charles Edward. *The American Orchestra and Theodore Thomas*. New York: Doubleday, Page, and Co., 1927.

43.   Seltnam, William H. *Metropolitan Opera Annals, A Chronicle of Artists and Performances*. New York: The H. W. Wilson Co., 1947.

44.   Shanet, Howard. *Philharmonic: A History of New York's Orchestra*. Garden City, NY: Doubelday & Co., 1975.

45.   Simon, Mina Lewiton. *John Philip Sousa, the March King*. New York: Didier, 1944.

46.   Slonimsky, Nicolas. "The Plush Era in American Concert Life," in *One Hundred Years of Music in America*, ed. Paul Henry Lang. New York: G. Schirmer, 1961, pp. 109-127.

47.   Smart, James R. *The Sousa Band: A Discography*. Washington, DC: Library of Congress, 1970.

48. Sousa, John Philip. *Marching Along; Recollections of Men, Women and Music*. Boston: Hale, Cushman & Flint, 1928, 1941.

49. ––––––*Through the Years with Sousa*. New York: Thomas Y. Crowell, 1910.

50. *Theodore Thomas: A Musical Autobiography*, 2 vols., ed. George Putnam Upton. Chicago: A. C. McClurg & Co., 1905; reprint: New York: Da Capo Press, 1964.

51. Thomas, Rose Fay. *Memoirs of Theodore Thomas*. New York: Moffat, Yard & Co., 1911; reprint: Freeport, NY: Books for Libraries Press, 1971.

52. Thompson, Helen M. "The American Symphony Orchestra," in *One Hundred Years of Music in America*, ed. Paul Henry Lang. New York: G. Schirmer, 1961, pp. 36-52.

53. Trotter, James M. *Music and Some Highly Musical People*. Boston: Lee and Shepard; New York: Charles T. Dillingham, 1881; reprint: New York: Johnson Reprint Corporation, 1968. (Includes Black musicians and composers)

54. Upton, George Putnam. *Musical Memories: My Recollections of Celebrities of the Half-Century, 1850-1900*. Chicago: A. C. McClurg & Co., 1908.

55. Upton, William Treat. *Anthony Philip Heinrich: A Nineteenth-Century Composer in America*. New York: Columbia University Press, 1939; reprint: New York: AMS Press, 1967.

56. ––––––*The Musical Works of William Henry Fry, in The Collections of the Library Company of Philadelphia*. Philadelphia: The Free Library of Philadelphia, 1946.

57. ––––––*William Henry Fry: American Journalist and Composer-Critic*. New York: Thomas Y. Crowell, 1954; reprint: New York: Da Capo, 1974.

58. Wise, Arthur, and Francis A. Lord. *Bands and Drummer Boys of the Civil War*. New York: T. Yoselof, 1966; reprint: New York: Da Capo Press, 1979.

59. Hall, Harry H. *A Johnny Reb Band from Salem: The Pride of Tarheelia*. Raleigh, NC: North Carolina Confederate Centennial Commission, 1963; reprint: New York: Da Capo Press, 1980.

Articles

1. Behrend, Jeanne. "Early American Choral Music." *Choral Guide* 8 (1955), p. 22.

2. Damrosch, Walter. "Hans von Bülow and the Ninth Symphony." *MQ* 13 (1927), pp. 280-293.

3. Dwight, John Sullivan. "Mr. Fry and His Critics." *Dwight's Journal of Music* 4 (February 4, 1854), pp. 140-142.

4. Engel, Lehman. "Songs of the American Wars." *Modern Music* 19 (1942), pp. 147-152.

5. Felts, Jack H. "Some Aspects of the Rise and Development of the Wind Band During the Civil War." *Journal of Band Research* 3, No. 2 (1967), pp. 29-33.

6. Fennell, Frederick. "The Civil War: Its Music and Its Sounds." *Journal of Band Research* 4, No. 2 (1968), pp. 36-44; 5, No. 1 (1968), pp. 8-14; 5, No. 2 (1968), pp. 4-10; 6, No. 1 (1968), pp. 46-58.

7. ––––––"Hardy Perennial: Bands in the Open." *MA* 81 (July, 1961), pp. 14-17.

8. Hamm, Charles. "The Chapins and Sacred Music in the South and West." *Journal of Research in Music Education* 8 (1960), pp. 91-98.

9. Henderson, William J. "Walter Damrosch." *MQ* 18 (1932), pp. 1-8.

10. Jackson, M. Y. "Folklore in Slave Narratives Before the Civil War." *New York Folklore Quarterly* 11 (Spring, 1955), pp. 14-19.

11. Kraft, Ivor. "Music for the Feeble-Minded in Nineteenth-Century America." *Journal of Research in Music Education* 11 (1963), pp. 119-122.

12. Leighton, George R. "Bandmaster Gilmore." *American Mercury* 30 (1933), pp. 172-183.

13. Loft, Abram. "Richard Wagner, Theodore Thomas and the American Centennial." *MQ* 37 (1951), pp. 184-202.

14. Lowens, Irving. "Music in the American Wilderness." *Etude* 74 (September, 1956), pp. 13, 20.

15. ––––––"The Triumph of Anthony Philip Heinrich." *Musicology* 1 (1947), pp. 365-373.

16.   ——————"William Henry Fry: Fighter for American Music." *Musicology* 2 (1948), pp. 162-173.

17.   Maddy, Joseph Edgar. "The First School Orchestras." *The Instrumentalist* 10 (1956). p. 17.

18.   Mintz, Donald M. "The Civil War and Music." *MC* 163 (July, 1961), pp. 9-13.

19.   Nash, Ray. "For Love or Money." *MA* 49 (February 25, 1929), pp. 18-19, 57.

20.   Rice, Edwin T. "Thomas and Central Park Garden." *MQ* 26 (1940), pp. 143-152.

21.   Salter, Sumner. "Early Encouragements to American Composers." *MQ* 18 (1932), pp. 76-105.

22.   Saerchinger, César. "Musical Landmarks in New York." *MQ* 6 (1920), pp. 69-90, 227-256.

23.   Saunders, William. "The American Opera." *ML* 13 (1932), pp. 147-155.

24.   Stopp, Jacklin B. "The Secular Cantata in the United States: 1850-1919." *Journal of Research in Music Education* 17 (1969), pp. 388-398. (Includes list)

25.   Wagner, John W. "Some Early Musical Moments in Augusta." *Georgia Historical Quarterly* 16 (1972), p. 529.

26.   Warner, Frank M. "Three Civil War Songs." *New York Folk Quarterly* 17 (1961), pp. 90-95.

Music

1.   Berger, Kenneth Walter. *The March King and His Band*. New York: Exposition Press, 1957.

2.   Bristow, George F. *Bristow's Two-Part Vocal Exercises*. New York: J. Van Loan, 1890.

3.   ——————*Geo. F. Bristow's New and Improved Method for the Reed or Cabinet Organ*. New York: R. A. Saalfield, 1887.

4.   ——————*Rip van Winkle*. New York: G. Schirmer, 1882; reprint: New York: Da Capo Press, 1981. (Earlier American Music, v. 25)

5.   Buck, Dudley. *The Coming of the King*, cantata for Advent and Christmas-tide. New York: G. Schirmer, 1895.

6.   ——————*Golden Legend*, symphonic cantata for solos, chorus and orchestra. Cincinnati: The John Church Co., 1908.

7.   *Civil War Song Anthology*, ed. Henry S. Humphreys. Cincinnati: Willis Music Co., 1963.

8.   *The Civil War Songbook, Complete Original Sheet Music for 37 Songs*, ed. Richard Crawford. New York: Dover Publications, 1977.

9.   Heinrich, Anthony Philip. *The Dawning of Music in Kentucky Or the Pleasures of Harmony in the Solitudes of Nature (Opera Prima); The Western Minstrel (Opera Seconda)*. Philadelphia: 1820; reprint: New York: Da Capo Press, 1973. (Earlier American Music, v. 10)

10.   Levy, Lester S. *Sousa's Great Marches in Piano Transcription*. New York: Dover Publications, 1975.

11.   Mason, William. *Fireside Harmony; A New Collection of Glees and Part Songs*. Boston: Tappan, Whittemore and Mason, 1848.

12.   ——————*A System of Technical Exercises for the Piano-forte*. Boston: Oliver Ditson, 1878.

13.   ——————*Touch and Technic; for Artistic Piano Playing*. Philadelphia: Theodore Presser, 1889.

14.   Mason, William, and E. S. Hoadley. *A Method for the Piano-forte*. New York: Mason Bros., 1867.

15.   Mason, William, and W. S. B. Mathews. *A Primer of Music*. New York: John Church Co., 1894.

16.   Mason, William, and Silas A. Bancroft. *The Social Glee Book: Being a Selection of Glees and Part Songs, by Distinguished German Composers; Never Before Published in This*

Country: Together with Original Pieces. Boston: Wilkins, Carter & Co., 1847.

17. *Piano Music in Nineteenth-Century America.* Chapel Hill, NC: Hinshaw Music, 1975.

18. *A Program of Early and Mid-Nineteenth Century American Songs*, ed. John Tasker Howard. New York: J. Fischer, 1931.

19. *The Rebel Songster; Songs the Confederates Sang*, ed. Manly Wade Wellman. Charlotte: Heritage, 1959.

20. *Songs of the Civil War*, ed. Irwin Silber. New York: Columbia University Press, 1960.

21. Sousa, John Philip. *National, Patriotic and Typical Airs of All Lands.* Philadelphia: H. Coleman, 1890; New York: Carl Fischer, 1890.

22. ————*Sousa's Great Marches in Piano Transcription.* New York: Dover Publications, 1975.

23. ————*The Trumpet and Drum. A Book of Instruction for the Field-Trumpet & Drum.* New York: Carl Fischer, 1886; reprint: W. F. L. Drum Co., 1954.

24. ————*Sousa's 21 Best Marches: in Their Original Piano Parlour Editions*, ed. Robert Kail. Carlstadt, NJ: Lewis Music Publishing Co., 1975.

Interior of the Great Coliseum, built expressly for the Peace Jubilee of 1869.
Looking from the Conductor's Stand toward the Chorus and Orchestra.

OUTLINE XIII

JOHN KNOWLES PAINE AND THE BOSTON GROUP

John Knowles Paine
Boston Group: George Chadwick, Arthur Foote
Horatio Parker, Arthur Whiting, Mrs. H. H. A. Beach

American music had become thoroughly Germanized by the Germans who settled in America and the migration of many competent American composers to Germany. On their return, these men began to write in the larger forms which they had learned abroad and took their place with eminent European composers of their time. **John Knowles Paine** is the first American composer of works in larger forms whose music is still heard today.

I. **John Knowles Paine** (1839-1906)

    A. Life

        1. **Paine** was born into a musical family in Portland, Maine, on January 9. His first music studies were with a resident musician, **Hermann Kotzschmar** (1829-1909). In 1858 **Paine** went to Berlin and studied counterpoint and organ with **Karl Haupt** (1810-1891) and others. He played many organ recitals in Germany and returned to America in 1861. The following year he was appointed as instructor in music at Harvard College and to the first professorship in music in an American institution of higher education in 1875. He remained there until a year before he died, although not without opposition to music receiving credit on an academic basis. He received an honorary Master of Arts degree from Harvard (1869) and a Doctor of Music degree from Yale in 1890.

           a. With **Paine's** appointment to the full professorship at Harvard (1875) the first department of music in an American university was established and credit for work in a music department was granted for the first time; undergraduate credit had been offered the four years previously. The Harvard University Department of Music under **Paine's** directorship became a model for other music departments throughout the country.

           b. During his tenure of 43 years at Harvard University, **Paine** had many pupils who were to become famous and make significant contributions in the development of music in America: **Arthur Foote** (1853-1937), **Sumner Salter** (1856-1944), **Frederick S. Converse** (1871-1940), **John Alden Carpenter** (1876-1951), **Edward Burlingame Hill** (1872-1960), **Blair Fairchild** (1877-1933) and **Daniel Gregory Mason** (1873-1953). Among his music history students were **Richard Aldrich** (1863-1937), **Archibald T. Davison** (1883-1961), **Olin Downes** (1886-1955), **Hugo Leichtentritt** (1874-1951), **Henry Finck** (1854-1926) and **Henry Lee Higginson** (1834-1919).

           c. **Paine** composed over 100 works for University activities and functions: inaugurations, graduations, plays, concerts, etc. He made Harvard a center of culture attracting such personages as Henry Wadsworth Longfellow, James Russel Lowell, John Greenleaf Whittier, George Santayana, Oliver Wendell Holmes, Frederick Jackson Turner and Ralph Waldo Emerson.

           d. Harvard can boast of the nation's oldest orchestra with an unbroken performance record. It was founded in 1808 and was known as the Pierian Sodality Orchestra.

        2. In 1861 **Paine** gave a series of organ recitals which included the major works of **Bach**, not often heard at that time. In 1867 he toured Germany and conducted his *Mass* in

D for soli, chorus and orchestra at the Berlin Singakademie. During 1870-1871 he gave a series of 18 public lectures on the development of music. He, along with **George Chadwick** and **Arthur Foote**, was one of the founders of the American Guild of Organists (1896). Many of his larger works (Mass, oratorio, symphonies, cantatas) were performed during his lifetime; the Boston Symphony Orchestra and the Thomas Orchestra frequently played his works and several were published by Breitkopf & Härtel in Leipzig.

3. **Paine** was instrumental in having the famous Walcker organ built for the Boston Music Hall; it is now installed in Metheun. The opening recital was played by six organists.

PROGRAMME

Part I.

1. Ode, recited by Miss Charlotte Cushman.
2. Opening of the Organ, by Herr Friedrich Walcker, son of the eminent
    Organ-builder, E. F. Walcker, of Ludwigsburg, (Kingdom of Wurtemburg.)
3. (a.) Grand Toccata in F . . . . Bach
    (b.) Trio Sonata in E flat: for two Manuals and Pedal:
          1. Allegro moderato. 2. Adagio. 3. Allegro . . . . Bach
                    By John K. Paine, Organist
            at the West Church, Boston, and Musical Instructor
                    at Harvard University.
4. Grand Fugue in G minor. . . . . Bach
                    By W. Eugene Thayer, of Worcester.

Part II.

1. Grand Double Chorus: "He led them through the deep," and Chorus:
    "But the waters overwhelmed their enemies," from "Israel in Egypt"
    . . . . Handel
                    By George W. Morgan,
                Organist at Grace Church, New York.
2. Grand Sonata in A, No. 3: Con moto maestoso — Andante tranquillo —
    fugue — maestoso . . . . Mendelssohn
            By B. J. Lang, Organist of the Old South Church
                and of the Handel and Haydn Society.
3. (a.) "Lamentation in Parasceve" . . . . Palestrina
          "Kyrie" and "Sanctus," from a Mass. . . . . Palestrina
    (b.) Movement from the Anthem, "O give thanks" . . . . Purcell
                    By Dr. S. P. Tuckerman,
                Organist at St. Paul's Church.
4. Offertorium in G. . . . . Lefébure-Wély
                    By John H. Willcox, Organist
                at the Church of the Immaculate Conception.
5. Hallelujah Chorus . . . . Handel
                    By G. W. Morgan

4. **Paine** continued fostering an interest in the **Bach** works; the two succeeding recitals following the opening recital on November 2, 1863, included five major organ works by **Bach**: *Prelude and Fugue in A minor, Christ the Lord to Jordan came, Fugue in D major, Prelude and Fugue in C major* and *"St. Ann's" Fugue.*

B.   Music
1.   **Paine's** compositions include two symphonies, an oratorio, cantatas, several symphonic poems (*The Tempest*, 1876; *An Island Fantasy*, 1888; *Poseidon and Amphitrite*, 1903; *Lincoln*, 1905 [unfinished]), several *a cappella* men's choruses and the incidental music to Sophocles' *Oedipus tyrannus* (1881). Also there are several songs including two groups of four songs each, some chamber works (string quartet, two piano trios, violin sonata) and several organ works (three sets of variations, two preludes and a fantasy on *"Ein feste Burg"*) (*ROL*, v. 1).

   a.   He was commissioned by **Theodore Thomas** to write a *Centennial Hymn* (*AH*, p. 506) on a text by John Greenleaf Whittier for the Philadelphia Centennial Exposition, 1876. He also wrote the *Columbus March and Hymn* for the Chicago 1893 Columbian Exposition, *Hymn of the West* for the St. Louis 1904 Louisiana Purchase Centennial Exposition and *Song of Promise*, a cantata for soprano solo, chorus and orchestra, for the Cincinnati May Festival, 1888. *The Nativity* (1883) is a cantata for soprano, alto, tenor and bass soloists, chorus and orchestra for the Boston Handel and Haydn Society.

   b.   He wrote much program music in German romantic style. In his earlier works he shows the influence of **Schumann** and **Mendelssohn** and later, in spite of himself, of **Brahms** and **Wagner**.

   c.   His music is characterized in general by a strong rhythmic sense, regular phrases, powerful climaxes, a strong sense of tonality, correct harmonic structure marked by an increase of chromaticism, good counterpoint, straight-forward melodic lines and sensitive orchestration.

   d.   *Oedipus tyrannus*, Boston, 1881; Leipzig, 1903
      1)   **Paine** composed a prelude, incidental music (six choruses, one a male chorus) and a postlude to Sophocles' tragedy for a performance in the original Greek by students of Harvard University in 1881.
      2)   The *Prelude* in C minor is scored for woodwinds in pairs, four horns, two trumpets, three trombones, timpani and strings.

   e.   *Symphony*, No. 1 in C minor, Op. 23, 1875 (*EAM*, v. 1)
      1)   The symphony was introduced by **Theodore Thomas** in Boston in 1876; his orchestra consisted of 40 members. The symphony was later published (1908) in Leipzig by Breitkopf & Härtel. It contains four movements and is scored for full orchestra, including four horns and three trombones.

   f.   *Symphony* No. 2 in A major, Op. 34 (*In the Spring*), 1880
      1)   The instrumentation of this program music is colorful and effective.
      2)   Movement I: Introduction, Adagio sostenuto (*The Departure of Winter*); Allegro ma non troppo (*The Awakening of Nature*)
      3)   Movement II: Scherzo (*May-Night Fantasy*) depicts bird songs and lively nature.
      4)   Movement III: Adagio (*A Romance of Springtime*), in the form of a rondo
      5)   Movement IV: Allegro giojoso (*The Glory of Nature*) in sonata form. There is a grand chorale-like theme of Thanksgiving.

   g.   *Azara*, grand opera in three acts, 1886-1900; published in Leipzig, 1901
      1)   Based on the medieval story of Aucassin and Nicolette, the opera libretto was written by **Paine**; it was performed in concert version in Boston in 1903 and 1907, but never had a stage performance.

   h.   Hymn: *Devotion* (*AH*, p. 490)

2.   H. Wiley Hitchcock has said that **Paine** is "the first American composer to have been thoroughly trained in Europe and to have mastered the Austro-Germanic style of Romantic symphony and symphonic poem, chamber music, cantata, and opera; and [is characterized] as the leader, on his return, of a new wave of American music based on that style."

II. **The Boston Group**

A. This group of musicians—**George Chadwick, Arthur Foote, Horatio Parker, Arthur Whiting**—living about the same time in Boston and considered musical heirs to **John Knowles Paine**, were known as the Boston "Classicists" or the "New England Academicians;" they flourished generally from 1880 to the first World War. They were united by their common musical interests, personal friendships and backgrounds. **Mrs. H. H. A. Beach** is usually included in the group, although she was not actually a member of the Boston Group.

1. They met from time to time for critical consideration of each other's works. With the exception of **Whiting**, they were important teachers of theory and composition; with the exception of **Foote**, they all either studied or concertized in Europe.

2. Although their personal styles vary, common characteristics of their music are strong rhythms, use of classical forms, regularity of phrase structure, German romanticism as particularly typified by the music of **Brahms**, and adherence to academically correct harmony and counterpoint.

B. **George Whitefield Chadwick** (1854-1931)

1. **Chadwick** was born in Lowell, Massachusetts, on November 13. His early studies were with **Dudley Buck** (1839-1909), **George Whiting** (1840-1923) and **Eugene Thayer** (1838-1889) in Boston. For one year (1876) **Chadwick** was head of the music department at Olivet College, Olivet, Michigan. He went to Germany in 1877 where he studied at the Leipzig Conservatory with **Carl Reinecke** (1824-1910) and **Salomon Jadassohn** (1831-1902); in 1879 he went to Munich to study composition and organ with **Josef Rheinberger** (1839-1901). **Chadwick** attained rapid success at the Leipzig Conservatory.

a. The best compositions were presented at the annual conservatory concert; in the concert of 1879 **Chadwick** had two pieces presented: *String Quartet* No. 2 in C major and the concert overture *Rip Van Winkle*.

b. In 1879 **Chadwick** traveled to France in the company of several American students of painting who had come under the influence of the American painter Frank Duveneck (1848-1919) residing in Munich. **Chadwick** considered studying with **César Franck** (1822-1890) but returned to Munich to continue his study with **Rheinberger**.

2. **Chadwick** settled in Boston in 1880 as organist at the South Congregational Church and taught harmony and composition at the New England Conservatory. He was appointed director there in 1893 and became an important figure in the field of music education.

a. **Chadwick** brought about a number of innovations at the Conservatory: opera workshops, a student orchestra for playing new works and the study of harmony and orchestration based on the actual music.

3. **Chadwick** received honorary degrees from Yale University (M. A.) in 1897 and from Tufts College (LL. D.) in 1905; he was a member of the National Academy and National Institute of Arts and Letters, and was awarded a gold medal in 1928. He was the director-conductor of the Worcester (1889-1899) and Springfield (1897-1901) Festivals.

4. Among his pupils, some of whom had studied with **Paine**, were **Horatio Parker** (1863-1919), **Arthur Whiting** (1861-1936), **Sidney Homer** (1864-1953), **William Grant Still** (1895-1978), **Frederick S. Converse** (1871-1940), **Henry Hadley** (1871-1937), **Daniel Gregory Mason** (1873-1953), **Arthur Shepherd** (1880-1958), **Edward Burlingame Hill** (1872-1960) and **Paul White** (1895-1973).

a. **Chadwick** wrote an important theory text, *Harmony, A Course of Study*, 1897.

5. **Chadwick** began releasing the hold the German conservative style had on American musical expression. Evidence of this may be noted in the French impressionism of

his lyric drama *Judith* and the suggestion of native materials in his second symphony (*EAM*, v. 4).

    a.   A Negro melody appears in the Scherzo; this is nine years before **Dvořák's** example of simulated native melodic material.

6.   **Chadwick's** compositions include three symphonies (C major, 1882; B-flat major, 1883-1885; F major, 1894), overtures (*Thalia*, 1883; *The Miller's Daughter*, 1884; *Melpomene*, 1887; *Adonais*, 1900; *Euterpe*, 1904; *Anniverary Overture* for the Norfolk Festival, 1922), symphonic poems (*Cleopatra*, 1905; *Angel of Death*, 1917), five string quartets, three operas (*Tabasco*, 1894; *Judith*, 1901; *The Padrone*, 1912), several large choral works and about 115 published songs.

    a.   Hymn: *Eaton* (*AH*, p. 666)

7.   **Chadwick** was a sophisticated, yet eclectic and versatile composer. His style is characterized by rhythmic vitality and freedom, colorful orchestration, attractive melodic lines and harmony, and counterpoint that is more virile and less sentimental than some others of his group.

8.   *Symphonic Sketches*, 1895-1904

    a.   In this realistic musical suite bits of poetry appear opposite each of the four movements: 1) *Jubilee*, 2) *Noël*, 3) *Hobgoblin* (Hallowe'en scene), 4) *A Vagrom Ballad*.

    b.   In the *Jubilee* **Chadwick** uses pentatonic and modal tunes, the habañera rhythm, cross accents, succession of different meters, syncopation, brassy orchestration and noisy percussion. He combines Anglo-Saxon melody with the Afro-Caribbean beat.

       1)   **Gottschalk** first blended these elements to produce the typical American sound. **"Jelly Roll" Morton** is said to have invented jazz by using these same elements, but this took place later.

    c.   The *Vagrom Ballad* reflects the realistic life of the hobo.

9.   *Judith*, 1901 (*EAM*, v. 3)

    a.   This opera was premièred at the Worcester Choral Festival in September, 1901, in a concert performance; it may also be staged.

    b.   The story is that of the biblical Judith, an Israelitish widow who entices Holofernes, the Assyrian chief, to dine with her. She gets him drunk, beheads him with his own sword and presents his head to Israel's chief, Ozias.

10.   *Padrone*, 1912

    a.   This opera was refused by the Metropolitan Opera Company. It is a realistic portrayal of frightened and illiterate Italian immigrants to America, exploited by Catani the *padrone* (political boss), a master of lust and treachery.

11.   *Tam O'Shanter*, a symphonic ballad, 1915

    a.   The ballad makes use of pentatonic and modal scales, syncopation, off-beat effects, open intervals of octaves, fifths and fourths; it reflects the Anglo-Saxon Celtic background; it does not make use of the Afro-Caribbean beat and habañera.

12.   During this period a group of songs would often be included in instrumental, symphony or ensemble, concerts. **Chadwick's** songs show the influence of **Schubert** and **Schumann**; some are strophic, others are through-composed.

    a.   *Told in the Gate* (*EAM*, v. 16, pp. 53-105), on poems of Arlo Bates, a contemporary poet in Boston.

       1)   The 12 songs are on pseudo-oriental narrative poems and their setting is in old Persia at the time of Omar Khayyam.

       2)   *Sweetheart, Thy Lips are Touched with Flame* (*EAM*, v. 16, p. 53; *ASA*, p. 117)

       3)   *Oh, Let Night Speak of Me* (*EAM*, v. 16, p. 93; *ASA*, p. 118)

    b.   *A Flower Cycle* (*EAM*, v. 16, pp. 1-51)

       1)   A cycle of 12 songs, each representing a different flower.

    c.   Other songs include: *Allah gives light in darkness* (Henry Wadsworth Longfellow) (*CSA*, p. 12); *The Danza* (Arlo Bates) (*CSA*, p. 14); *Ballad of trees and the master* (Sidney Lanier).

13. *Caprice*, No. 2 for piano (*BCAK*, p. 59)

C.   **Arthur William Foote** (1853-1937)

1.   **Foote** was born in Salem, Massachusetts, on March 5. He studied with **Paine** at Harvard and received the first Master of Arts degree in music conferred in America (1875). Through the encouragement of **Benjamin J. Lang** (1837-1909) **Foote** turned from a business career to become a professional musician. He was organist at the First Unitarian Church in Boston for 32 years (1878-1910). **Foote** was one of the founders of the American Guild of Organists (1896) and was its national president from 1909 to 1912. He taught privately and at the New England Conservatory and performed professionally as a concert pianist.

2.   From 1881 to 1900 **Foote** organized series of chamber music concerts and was often pianist with the Kneisel String Quartet.

    a.   The Kneisel Quartet (1886-1917), under the leadership of the first violinist **Franz Kneisel** (1865-1926), gave performances of high quality and gained an international reputation for presenting chamber music; they brought before the public in Boston, New York and other American cities the major string quartet literature from **Haydn** to the Romantics. **Kneisel** was also concertmaster of the Boston Symphony Orchestra (1885-1905).

3.   **Foote** was one of the few important composers of his time who did not go to Europe to study; he did, however, attend the Wagner Festival at Bayreuth in 1876 and had a few piano lessons with **Stephen Heller** (1813-1888) in Paris in 1883. He was a member of the National Insitute of Arts and Letters and a Fellow of the American Academy of Arts and Sciences. He was one of the editors of *The American History and Encyclopedia of Music*, 12 volumes.

4.   **Foote's** compositions include eight works for full or string orchestra (no symphonies) (overture: *In the Mountains*, 1887; a cello concerto, 1894; *Four Character Pieces after Omar Khayyám*, 1912; the Lisztian symphonic poem *Francesca da Rimini*, 1893) and several works for chorus *a cappella* and with orchestra (*The Farewell of Hiawatha* for men's chorus, 1886; *The Wreck of the Hesperus*, 1887; *The Skeleton in Armor*, 1891). There are many pieces for piano, about 30 for organ (*ROL*, v. 2) and some 150 songs. **Foote's** interest in chamber music is evident with numerous pieces for various combinations of instruments: three string quartets (No. 1 in G minor, 1883; No. 2 in E major, 1894; No. 3 in D major, 1910), two piano trios (No. 1 in C minor, 1882; No. 2 in B-flat major, 1909), a piano quartet, 1890; a piano quintet, 1897; and several pieces for violin and piano, and cello and piano.

    a.   **Foote** has written some important theory texts.

5.   **Foote's** style is highly refined, lyrical and basically harmonic; earlier works show the influence of **Brahms**. His music is melodically and rhythmically interesting; he makes some use of modes and, in choral music, of the *leitmotif* after **Wagner**.

    a.   *Suite* (Prelude, Pizzicato, Fugue), Op. 63 for string orchestra, 1907 (*EAM*, v. 24)

       1)   This was played many times by **Sergei Koussevitsky** (1874-1951) and the Boston Symphony Orchestra in concert, and radio audiences were very enthusiastic about it.

       2)   The *Prelude* in E major is based entirely on the first phrase of eight notes with much use of imitation.

       3)   The *Pizzicato* in A minor is interrupted by an *Adagietto* in F major played *arco* with strings muted.

       4)   The *Fugue* in E minor is thoroughly worked out but without the use of augmentation, inversion, etc. The first four notes of the theme are heard often by themselves and a long pedal point appears at the last return of the theme.

    b.   *A Night Piece* for flute and strings, 1918

    c.   *Serenade* in E, Op. 25, for string orchestra (*EAM*, v. 24)

D. **Horatio William Parker** (1863-1919)
1. **Parker** was born in Auburndale, Massachusetts, on September 15; he began the study of piano and organ at the age of fourteen; became a church organist at sixteen and was one of **Chadwick's** first pupils in composition. He studied at the Hochschule für Musik in Munich (1882-1885) with **Josef Rheinberger** (1839-1901) and perfected his contrapuntal style.
    a. While in Munich he composed many works including *Ballad of a Knight and His Daughter* for chorus and orchestra (1884); *King Trojan*, a ballad for tenor and baritone soloists, chorus and orchestra (1885) and *Symphony* in C (1885).
2. **Parker** returned to New York and taught at the Cathedral School of St. Paul and St. Mary in Garden City (1886-1890), the General Theological Seminary (1892) and the National Conservatory of Music in New York (1892-1893) where **Dvořák** was director. He became organist at St. Luke's Church in Brooklyn (1885-1887), St. Andrew's Church in Haarlem (1887-1888), Holy Trinity Church in Manhattan (1888-1893) and Trinity Church in Boston (1893-1902). **Parker** conducted several choral societies in various cities; in 1894 he received an honorary Master of Music degree from Yale University. That same year he accepted the Battell Professorship of the Theory of Music at Yale University which he maintained until his death; he became the Dean of the School of Music at Yale in 1904. He organized and conducted the New Haven Symphony Orchestra (1895-1918) and its Choral Society (1903-1914). **Parker** was awarded a Doctor of Music degree by Cambridge University, England, in 1892.
3. **Parker's** students include **Douglas Moore** (1893-1969), **Quincy Porter** (1897-1966), **Charles Ives** (1874-1954), **Edward Shippen Barnes** (1887-1958) and **Seth Bingham** (1882-1972).
4. **Parker's** reputation as a composer was established during the 1890's. His compositions include as his main contribution some 50 choral works for various combinations of voices and instruments composed for a variety of occasions; included also are some 25 anthems and services with organ accompaniment. In addition he wrote 10 orchestral works, five of which were composed in Munich, an organ concerto (1902), some 115 songs, plus 50 *Kate Greenaway Songs* (1878) and 61 songs in *The Progressive Music Series for Basal Use in Primary, Intermediate and Grammar Grades* (1914). Organ pieces number 30, including *Sonata* in E-flat major (1908); there are 20 piano pieces. The chamber music consists of a string quartet (1885), a string quintet (1894) and two suites, one for piano, violin and cello (1893) and one for piano and violin (1894). The six stage works include a masque (*Cupid and Psyche*, 1916) and two operas (*Mona*, 1910; *Fairyland*, 1914). Included also are a number of hymns: *Parker* (*Hymnal*, No. 63; *Pixham* (*Hymnal*, No. 150; *AH*, p. 685); *Garden City* (*Hymnal*, No. 175); *Jubilate* (*Hymnal*, No. 350; *Mount Sion* (*Hymnal*, No. 390; *AH*, p. 690); *Pro Patria* (*AH*, pp. 538, 679); *Clovelly* (*AH*, p. 624); *Mission* (*AH*, p. 681); *King of Glory* (*AH*, p. 731).
5. **Parker's** style is facile but somewhat uneven in quality. He is most successful in choral music; his harmony and counterpoint are inclined to be academic and sometimes commonplace.
    a. *Hora Novissima, The Rhythm of Bernard de Morlaix on the Celestial Country* (Cometh earth's latest hour, or Day of judgment), Op. 30, for soli, chorus, organ and orchestra (*EAM*, v. 2)
    1) Considered to be **Parker's** masterpiece, the oratorio has been widely performed and "at once took rank among the best works on this side of the Atlantic," according to the *New York Times*. The performance of the work under his direction in England brought several commissions for other similar works for English festivals and culminated in the honorary doctorate from Cambridge. Since 1897 over 178 performances have been given with full orchestra and many more with piano and organ. In 1899 it was performed at the Three Choirs Festival in Wor-

cester, England, the first American composition to be heard there. Inspired by the **Handel** and **Mendelssohn** oratorio tradition, it was composed for the Church Choral Society of New York to be used in choral festivals.

   b.   The text was translated by **Parker's** mother from the twelfth century Latin hymn of Bernard de Morlaix, a monk in the Abbey of Cluny in France.

   c.   The oratorio is divided into two parts and contains 11 numbers; each part closes with a grand chorus incorporating the solo quartet. There is one double chorus and an aria for each of the four soloists. The work contains some vigorous, effective writing with skillful handling of massed effects, fugal style, texture and hymn-like themes.

   d.   *"Pars mea"* (*EAM*, v. 2, p. 35) shows skillful contrapuntal writing and *"Spe modo vivetur"* (*EAM*, v. 2, p. 29) reveals **Parker's** sensitivity to the text with its use of 3/4, 4/4, 5/4, 2/4 and 3/2 time.

6.   *Mona*, 1910

   a.   The opera won a $10,000 prize offered by the Metropolitan Opera House. **Parker's** opera *Fairyland* (1915) also won a $10,000 prize offered by the National Federation of Music Clubs. The librettos of both operas were by Brian Hooker, professor of English at Yale University. *Mona*, the third opera by an American to be performed at the "Met," was never revived after the first season (1912).

   b.   The story deals with Mona, princess of Britain during the Roman invasion (*c*. 100 A. D.), who is torn between her love for the son of the Roman governor and hatred of the Roman conquerors.

   c.   *Fairyland* was performed six times in Los Angeles in 1915 but has not been heard since.

E.   **Arthur Battelle Whiting** (1861-1936)

   1.   **Whiting** was born in Cambridge, Massachusetts, on June 20. At the New England Conservatory he studied piano with **William H. Sherwood** (1854-1911), composition with **George Chadwick** (1854-1931) and harmony with **Louis Maas** (1852-1889); he went abroad and studied composition with **Josef Rheinberger** (1839-1901) and others for two years (1883-1885). On his return to the United States **Whiting** lived in Boston for ten years and then settled in New York (1895) where he was a concert pianist. After 1907 he organized series of chamber music concerts at various universities including Yale, Harvard, Columbia and Princeton; in 1911 he inaugurated a series of concerts of early music in which he played the harpsichord, **Constance Edson** the violin, **Georges Barrère** the flute and **Paul Kéfer** the viola da gamba.

   a.   **Arthur Whiting** is the nephew of **George Elbridge Whiting** (1842-1923), composer and organist. **George Whiting** studied with **William Thomas Best** (1826-1897) in Liverpool (1863) and **Karl Haupt** (1810-1891) in Berlin (1874). He taught at the New England Conservatory until 1879, at the Cincinnati College of Music (1879-1882) and again at the New England Conservatory (1883-1897). He was organist of several churches, was well known as an organ teacher and composed many works, including two instruction books for organ and several organ pieces.

   2.   **Arthur Whiting's** compositions are comparatively few.

   a.   They include a *Concert Overture* (1886), a piano concerto (1888), *Fantasie* for piano and orchestra (1897), *Suite* for strings and four horns (1891) and incidental music for *The Golden Cage—a dance pageant* for orchestra (1926).

   b.   **Whiting's** chamber music includes a piano quintet, a string quartet, a piano trio and a *Sonata* for violin.

   c.   For the piano there is a *Suite moderne*; *Three Characteristic Waltzes*; *Six Bagatelles* and for instruction purposes, *Melodious Technical Studies* and *Pianoforte Pedal Studies*.

   d.   **Whiting** also composed many anthems and songs, including the *Barrack Room Ballads* and some settings from the *Rubáiyát of Omar Khayyám*.

F.   **Mrs. H. H. A. Beach [Amy Marcy Cheney]   (1867-1944)**
  1.   **Mrs. Beach** was born in Henniker, New York, September 5. Her early musical studies
         were with teachers in Boston: piano with **Ernest Perabo** (1845-1920) and theory with
         Junius W. Hill (1840-1916); she was largely self-taught in counterpoint and composi-
         tion. At the age of 16 (1883) she made her début in Boston as a pianist playing the
         Moscheles *Concerto in G minor*. In 1885 she married Dr. Henry Harris Aubrey Beach,
         a renowned surgeon.
  2.   **Mrs. Beach** toured Europe with great success and introduced her own compositions in
         Hamburg, Leipzig and Berlin (1911-1915). On her return to the United States she de-
         voted herself to composition and some concert work.
  3.   In 1892 **Mrs. Beach's** first important work (*Mass* in E-flat) was performed by the
         Boston Handel and Haydn Society for which it was composed. In 1896 her *Symphony
         in e* (*Gaelic*), Op. 32, was played by the Boston Symphony Orchestra under the direc-
         tion of **Emil Paur** (1855-1932). The symphony was the first American symphony by a
         woman as well as the first composition by a woman to have been played by the Boston
         Symphony Orchestra. Her reputation was enhanced considerably when it was played
         also in Hamburg and Leipzig and received with high acclaim. **Mrs. Beach** often spent
         summers at the MacDowell Colony where she wrote the opera, *Cabildo*, 1932, and the
         Piano Trio, 1938.
  4.   **Mrs. Beach** was the leading representative of the late nineteenth-century Romantic
         style fostered by **George Chadwick**, **Arthur Foote** and others of the Boston Group.
         The influence of **Brahms** and **Wagner** is strong with occasional impressionistic hints of
         late **MacDowell** and **Debussy**. She had a natural gift for melody; her instrumental
         works demonstrate complex harmonies, frequent modulations, half-diminished chords,
         pedal points and use of folk tunes.
  5.   Included in her works are 120 songs for which she is best known, 68 anthems and
         larger choral works, including 12 with orchestra, some 70 piano pieces, 12 chamber
         works, a symphony (*Gaelic*), a piano concerto, two arias for orchestra, an opera and
         music for the church.
    a.   Her best known songs are *The Year's at the Spring, Ah, Love but a Day* and *Ecstacy*
           on Robert Browning poems.
    b.   Important choral works include *Benedictus es Domini* (1924), *The Canticle of the
           Sun*, Op. 123 (1925), *The Chambered Nautilus*, Op. 66 (1907) and *Christ in the
           Universe*, Op. 139 (1931).
    c.   *Scottish Legend*, Op. 54, No. 1 for piano (*BCAK*, p. 80)
  6.   **Mrs. Beach** received commissions to compose *Festival Jubilee*, Op. 17, for chorus and
         orchestra for the dedication of the Women's Building at the Columbian Exposition
         [Chicago World's Fair] in 1892; *Song of Welcome* for the Omaha Trans-Mississippi
         Exposition in 1898 and *Panama Hymn* for the Panama-Pacific Exposition in San
         Francisco, 1915.

BIBLIOGRAPHY

Books

1. Chadwick, George Whitefield. *Commemorative Tribute to Horatio Parker*. New York: American Academy of Arts and Letters, 1922.
2. –––––––*Harmony, A Course of Study*. Boston: B. F. Wood Music Co., 1925; reprint: New York: Da Capo Press, 1975.
3. –––––––*Horatio Parker*. New Haven, CT: Yale University Press, 1921; reprint: New York: AMS Press, 1971.
4. Cipolla, Wilma Reid. *A Catalog of the Works of Arthur William Foote, 1853-1937*. Detroit: Information Coordinators, 1980.
5. Clarke, Garry E. "The American-European," in *Essays on American Music*. Westport, CT: Greenwood Press, 1977, pp. 73-86.
6. *Dramatic Compositions Copyrighted in the United States, 1870-1916*. Washington, DC: U. S. Copyright Office, 1918; reprint: New York: Johnson Reprint Corp., 1968.
7. Epstein, Dena J. "Amy Marcy Cheney Beach," in *Notable American Women, 1607-1950*, v. 1. Cambridge, MA: Harvard University Press, 1971, pp. 117-119.
8. Fay, Amy. *Music-Study in Germany*. New York: Macmillan Co., 1897.
9. Foote, Arthur William. *An Autobiography*. Norwood, MA: Privately printed at the Plimpton Press, 1946.
10. Foote, Arthur William, and Walter R. Spalding. *A Key to the Exercises in Modern Harmony in Its Theory and Practice*. Boston: Arthur P. Schmidt Co., 1936.
11. Foote, Arthur William, and Walter R. Spalding. *Modern Harmony in Its Theory and Practise*. Boston: Arthur P. Schmidt Co., 1905; republished as *Harmony*. Evanston, IL: Arthur P. Schmidt Co., 1969.
12. Foote, Arthur William. *Modulation and Related Harmonic Questions*. Boston: Arthur P. Schmidt Co., 1919.
13. –––––––*Some Practical Things in Piano Playing*. Boston: Arthur P. Schmidt Co., 1909.
14. Goetschius, Percy. *Mrs. H. H. A. Beach. Analytical Sketch*. Boston: Arthur P. Schmidt Co., 1906.
15. Hughes, Rupert. *American Composers; Being a Study of the Music of This Country, and of Its Future, with Biographies of the Leading Composers of the Present Time*. Boston: L. C. Page & Co., 1900, 1914, 1918, 1921, 1929.
16. Kearns, William. *Horatio Parker: A Bio-Bibliographical Study*. Detroit: The College Music Society. (In preparation)
17. Paine, John Knowles. *The History of Music to the Death of Schubert*. Boston: Ginn & Co., 1907; reprint: New York: Da Capo Press, 1971.
18. Rosenfeld, Paul. "The End of the Kneisel Quartet," in *Musical Chronicle (1917-1923)*. New York: Harcourt, Brace & Co., 1923, pp. 20-26.
19. Semler, Isabel Parker. *Horatio Parker: A Memoir for His Grandchildren*. New York: G. P. Putnam's Sons, 1942; reprint: New York: Da Capo Press, 1973; New York: AMS Press, 1975.
20. Southard, Lucian H., and George Elbridge Whiting. *The Organist*. Boston: Oliver Ditson, 1868.
21. Spalding, Walter Raymond. *Music at Harvard; A Historical Review of Men and Events*. New York: Coward-McCann, 1935.
22. Throll, Josephine. "Hora Novissima," in *The American History and Encyclopedia of Music*, v. [8], ed. William Lines Hubbard. New York: Irving Squire, 1910, revised, 1924, pp. 249-252.
23. Upton, William Treat. *Art-Song in America. A Study in the Development of American Music*. Boston: Oliver Ditson, 1930.

24. Wilson, George Henry. *The Boston Musical Year Book and Musical Year in the United States*, vols. 1-3. Boston: G. H. Ellis, 1884-1886.

25. *Women in American Music: A Bibliography of Music and Literature*, ed. Adrienne Fried Block and Carol Neuls-Bates. Westport, CT: Greenwood Press, 1979.

26. Rosenfeld, Paul. "The Fate of 'Mona'," in *Musical Chronicle (1917-1923)*. New York: Harcourt, Brace & Co., 1923, pp. 54-60.

Articles

1. Adams, Juliet A. Graves (Mrs. Crosby Adams). "An American Genius of World Renown: Mrs. H. H. A. Beach." *Etude* 46 (January, 1928), pp. 34, 61, 69.

2. "An American Composer's Triumph in Russia [Henry F. Gilbert]." *Current Opinion* 60 (May, 1916), pp. 330-331.

3. Beach, Mrs. H. H. A. "The Twenty-Fifth Anniversary of a Vision (The MacDowell Colony)." *ProMTNA* 27 (1932), pp. 45-48.

4. ————"Emotion Versus Intellect in Music." *ProMTNA* 26 (1931), pp. 17-19.

5. Broekhaven, J. van. "Mona: A Thematic Analysis." *Musical Observer* 6 (April, 1912). p. 22.

6. Brooks, Benjamin A. "The 'How' of Creative Composition: a Conference with Mrs. H. H. A. Beach." *Etude* 61 (March, 1943), pp. 151, 208, 209.

7. Cowen, Gertrude F. "Mrs. H. H. A. Beach, the Celebrated Composer." *MC* 60 (June 6, 1910), pp. 14-15.

8. Dart, Harold. "An Introduction to Selected New England Composers of the Late Nineteenth Century." *Music Educators Journal* 60 (November, 1973), pp. 47-53, 89-92.

9. Dwight, John S. "The History of Music (Lecture by John Knowles Paine)." *Dwight's Journal of Music* 30 (December 31, 1870), pp. 371-372.

10. Elder, Dean. "Where was Amy Beach All These Years? An Interview with Mary Louise Boehm." *Clavier* 15 (December, 1976), pp. 14-17.

11. Elson, Louis C. "John Knowles Paine." *Etude* 24 (March, 1906), pp. 104, 105.

12. Engel, Carl. "George W. Chadwick." *MQ* 10 (1924), pp. 438-457.

13. Foote, Arthur W. "A Bostonian Remembers." *MQ* 23 (1937), pp. 37-44.

14. ————"The Relation of Consonance to Dissonance." *Etude* 55 (1937), pp. 504, 542.

15. ————"Rhythm and Accent." *Etude* 51 (1933), pp. 653, 709, 722.

16. Goldman, Richard Franko. "Those Forgotten American Composers." *HiFi/Stereo Review* 20 (February, 1968), pp. 114-115.

17. H. A. S. "At 74 Mrs. Beach Recalls Her First Critics." *MC* 123 (May 15, 1941), p. 7.

18. "Horatio Parker." *MT* 43 (1902), pp. 586-592.

19. Howe, M. A. DeWolfe. "John Knowles Paine." *MQ* 25 (1939), pp. 257-267.

20. Hughes, Edwin. "The Outlook for the Young American Composer: An Interview with the Distinguished American Composer, Mrs. H. H. A. Beach." *Etude* 33 (1915), pp. 13-14.

21. Jacobi, Frederick. "Homage to Arthur Foote." *Modern Music* 14 (1937), pp. 198-199.

22. Langley, Allan Lincoln. "Chadwick and the New England Conservatory of Music." *MQ* 21 (1935), pp. 39-52.

23. Macdougall, Hamilton C. "Arthur Foote's Life Comes to Its Close." *Diapason* 28 (May, 1937), p. 3.

24. ————"George W. Chadwick: An Appreciation of a Distinguished Life." *Diapason* 22 (May, 1931), p. 8.

25. Mason, Daniel Gregory. "Arthur Whiting." *MQ* 23 (1937), pp. 26-36.

26. Mathews, John Lathrop. "Harvard University (Interview with John Knowles Paine)." *Music* 9 (1896), pp. 644-649.

27. Mathews, William Smyth B. "German Influence upon American Music as Noted in the Works of Dudley Buck, J. K. Paine . . ." *The Musician* 15 (1910), p. 160.

28. "Mrs. Beach's Compositions." *MC* 70 (March 24, 1915), p. 37.

29. "Mrs. H. H. A. Beach Honored." *Musical Leader* 72 (May 25, 1940), p. 9.

30. "Mrs. H. H. A. Beach in Boston." *MC* 119 (December 30, 1914), p. 9.

31. "New Gems in the Old Classics." *Etude* 22 (1904), p. 51.

32. "Professor John Knowles Paine (Obituary Notice)." *MC* 18 (1906), pp. 19, 20; *MT* 47 (1906), p. 395.

33. Peeler, Clare W. "American Woman Whose Musical Message Thrilled Germany." *MA* 20 (October 17, 1914), p. 7.

34. P[eyser], H[erbert] F. "New Beach Quintet Played in New York." *MA* 15 (December 9, 1911), p. 19.

35. Rorick, William C. "The Horatio Parker Archives in the Yale University Music Library." *Fontes Artis Musicae* 26 (1979), pp. 298-304.

36. Rosenfeld, Paul. "One of the Parents [Horatio Parker]." *Modern Music* 19 (1942), pp. 215-221.

37. Smith, David Stanley. "A Study of Horatio Parker." *MQ* 16 (1930), pp. 153-163.

38. Smith, Rollin. "American Organ Composers." *Music/The AGO-RCCO Magazine* 10 (August, 1976), p. 18.

39. ———"American Organ Composers: Arthur Foote." *Music/The AGO-RCCO Magazine* 10 (May, 1976), p. 38.

40. ———"American Organ Composers: George Whitefield Chadwick." *Music/The AGO-RCCO Magazine* 10 (April, 1976), p. 39.

41. ———"American Organ Composers: Horatio Parker." *Music/The AGO-RCCO Magazine* 10 (June, 1976), pp. 34-35.

42. ———"American Organ Composers: John Knowles Paine." *Music/The AGO-RCCO Magazine* 10 (February, 1976), pp. 31-32.

43. Steinberg, Judith Tick. "Women as Professional Musicians in America, 1870-1900." *Yearbook for Inter-American Musical Research* 9 (1973), pp. 95-133.

44. Stevenson, Robert. "American Musical Scholarship: Parker to Thayer." *19th Century Music* 1 (1978), pp. 191-210.

45. Stopp, Jacklin B. "The Secular Cantata in the United States: 1850-1919." *Journal of Research in Music Education* 17 (1969), pp. 388-398.

46. Strunk, W. Oliver. "Works of Horatio W. Parker." *MQ* 16 (1930), pp. 164-169.

47. Tuthill, Burnet C. "Mrs. H. H. A. Beach." *MQ* 26 (1940), pp. 297-310.

48. Whiting, Arthur. "The Lesson of the Clavichord." *New Music Review* 8 (January, 1909), p. 69.

49. Wilson, Arthur. "A Conversation on Musical Conditions in America." *The Musician* 17 (January, 1912), pp. 1-2.

50. Yellin, Victor F. "Chadwick, American Musical Realist." *MQ* 61 (1975), pp. 77-97.

Music

1. Beach, Mrs. H. H. A. *Ah, Love But a Day!* (Browning songs, No. 2). Boston: Arthur P. Schmidt, 1900.

2. ———*The Canticle of the Sun*, Op. 123, for soli, chorus and orchestra. Boston: Arthur P. Schmidt, 1928.

3. ———*Ecstacy*. (Song Album No. 1). Boston: Arthur P. Schmidt, 1891.

4. ———*Five Improvisations*, for piano. Boston: Arthur P. Schmidt.

5. ———*Quintet in F-sharp Minor*, Op. 67, for piano, 2 violins, viola and violoncello. Boston: Arthur P. Schmidt, 1909; reprint: New York: Da Capo Press, 1979. (Earlier American Music)

6. ———*Suite*, for two pianos, four hands. Cincinnati: John Church Co., 1924.

7. ———*Symphony (Gaelic) in E Minor*, Op. 32. Leipzig: Breitkopf & Härtel, 1897.

8. ———*Theme and Variations*, for flute and string quartet, Op. 80. New York: G. Schirmer, 1920.

9.   Beach, Mrs. H. H. A. *The Year's at the Spring* (song). Boston: Arthur P. Schmidt, 1928.

10. Chadwick, George Whitefield. *Judith*: lyric drama for soli, chorus and orchestra. New York: G. Schirmer, 1901; reprint: New York: Da Capo Press, 1972. (Earlier American Music, v. 3)

11. ──────*Noël*. A Christmas pastoral for soli, chorus and orchestra. London: Novello & Co., 1909; reprint: New York: Da Capo Press, in preparation. (Earlier American Music)

12. ──────*Quartet No. 4 in E minor*. New York: G. Schirmer, 1902.

13. ──────*Rip Van Winkle*. Overture for orchestra. Boston: C. C. Birchard, 1930.

14. ──────*Song Album*, 15 Selected Songs for soprano or tenor. Boston: Arthur P. Schmidt, 1886.

15. ──────*Song Album*, 17 Songs for alto or baritone. Boston: Arthur P. Schmidt, 1890.

16. ──────*Songs of Brittany*. Boston: Arthur P. Schmidt, 1890.

17. ──────*Songs* to poems by Arlo Bates; *A Flower Cycle* and *Lyrics from "Told in the Gate."* Boston: Arthur P. Schmidt, 1892; Leipzig: Breitkopf & Härtel, 1892; reprint: New York: Da Capo Press, 1980. (Earlier American Music, v. 16)

18. ──────*Symphony No. 2 in B-flat Major*, Op. 21. Boston: Arthur P. Schmidt, 1888; reprint: New York: Da Capo Press, 1972. (Earlier American Music, v. 4)

19. ──────*Symphony No. 3 in F Major*. Boston: Arthur P. Schmidt, 1896.

20. ──────*Tam O'Shanter*. Symphonic ballade for orchestra. Boston: Boston Music Co., 1917.

21. Foote, Arthur William. *Francesca da Rimini*, Op. 24. Symphonic prologue. Boston: Arthur P. Schmidt, 1892.

22. ──────*The Organ Works of Arthur Foote*, ed. Wayne Leupold. Dayton, OH: McAfee Music Co., 1977. (Romantic Organ Literature Series, v. 2)

23. ──────*Quintet in A minor*, Op. 38, for piano and strings. Leipzig: Breitkopf & Härtel, 1898.

24. ──────*Sonata in G minor*, for violin and piano. Boston: Arthur P. Schmidt, 1890.

25. ──────*Suite in E major*, Op. 63 and *Serenade in E major*, Op. 25, for string orchestra. Leipzig: Breitkopf & Härtel, 1909; reprint: New York: Da Capo Press, 1981. (Earlier American Music, v. 24)

26. ──────*Trio in B major*, Op. 65, for piano, violin and violoncello. Boston: Arthur P. Schmidt, 1909.

27. Paine, John Knowles. *Azara*, an opera. Leipzig: Breitkopf & Härtel, 1901.

28. ──────*Centennial Hymn*, for chorus and orchestra. Boston: Oliver Ditson Co., 1930.

29. ──────*The Complete Organ Works of John Knowles Paine*, ed Wayne Leupold. Dayton, OH: McAfee Music Corp. 1975. (The Romantic Organ Literature Series, v. 1)

30. ──────*The Nativity*, Op. 39, for chorus, soli, and orchestra. Boston: Arthur P. Schmidt, 1903.

31. ──────*Oedipus Tyrannus of Sophocles*, for male chorus and orchestra. Boston: Arthur P. Schmidt, 1908.

32. ──────*St. Peter*, an oratorio. Boston: Oliver Ditson Co., 1872.

33. ──────*Shakespeare's Tempest*, symphonic poem. Leipzig: Breitkopf & Härtel, 1907.

34. ──────*Symphony No. 1*, Op. 23. Leipzig: Breitkopf & Härtel, 1908; reprint: New York: Da Capo Press, 1972. (Earlier American Music, v. 1)

35. ──────*Symphony No. 2*, Op. 34 in A major (Spring Symphony). Boston: Arthur P. Schmidt, 1880; reprint: New York: Da Capo Press, in preparation. (Earlier American Music)

36. Parker, Horatio William. *Concerto*, for organ and orchestra. London: Novello, 1903.

37. ──────*Fairyland*, an opera. New York: G. Schirmer, 1914.

38. ──────*Hora Novissima, The Rhythm of Bernard De Morlaix on the Celestial Country*, Op. 30, for soli, chorus and orchestra. London: Novello, 1893; reprint: New York: Da Capo Press, 1972. (Earlier American Music, v. 2)

39.   Parker, Horatio William. *The Legend of St. Christopher*, for soli, chorus, orchestra and organ: London: Novello, Ewer & Co., 1898.

40.   ———————*Mona*, an opera. New York: G. Schirmer, 1911.

41.   ———————*A Star Song*, for solo, quartet, chorus and orchestra. Cincinnati: John Church Co., 1902.

42.   ———————*Suite*, Op. 35, for piano, violin and violoncello. New York: G. Schirmer, 1904.

43.   Whiting, Arthur Battelle. *Fantasy*, Op. 11, for piano and orchestra. New York: G. Schirmer, 1897.

44.   ———————*Floriana*, for solo voices and piano. New York: G. Schirmer, 1901.

45.   ———————*The Golden Cage*, for small orchestra. New York: G. Schirmer, 1926.

46.   ———————*Melodious Technical Studies for the Pianoforte for Strength and Independence of the Fingers*. New York: G. Schirmer, 1905.

47.   ———————*Pianoforte Pedal Studies*. New York: G. Schirmer, 1904; 1917.

48.   ———————*Suite Moderne*, Op. 15, for piano. New York: G. Schirmer, 1900.

49.   Whiting, George Elbridge. *Whiting's First Six Months on the Organ*. Boston: Russell & Co., 1870.

OUTLINE XIV

CONTEMPORARIES OF THE BOSTON GROUP

Ethelbert Nevin – Henry F. Gilbert
Music of American Folklore
Edward MacDowell

I. **Ethelbert Woodbridge Nevin** (1862-1901)

    A. **Nevin** was born on November 25 of Scotch ancestry at Edgeworth, near Pittsburgh, on his father's country place called "Vineacre." In 1877 he went to Europe to study piano with **Franz Böhme** (1828-1898) of Dresden. A year later he returned to Pittsburgh; then in 1881 he went to Boston to study with **Benjamin J. Lang** (1837-1909) and **Stephen A. Emery** (1841-1891). He settled in Pittsburgh in 1883 as a pianist and teacher, but returned to Europe to study piano with **Karl Klindworth** (1840-1916) and **Hans von Bülow** (1830-1894) and composition with **Otto Tiersch** (1838-1892).

    B. In 1886 **Nevin** came back to the United States and made his début as a pianist in Pittsburgh. From 1891 to 1897 he spent most of his time in Europe studying, performing and teaching. In 1891 he went to Paris, spent about a year, and then on to Berlin for about eight months. After a brief return to America in 1892, **Nevin** took a trip to Algiers (1894) and spent time in Florence, Venice and Paris (1895). In October, 1897, he established himself in New York; his last years were marked with a nervous disorder and declining health. He died at the age of 38.

    C. **Nevin's** compositions are largely short piano pieces (about 45) and songs (about 75). In addition to the cantata *The Quest* (published posthumously in 1902) he wrote 12 choruses, two of which are for male voices, and *Floreane's Dream*, a pantomime which makes use of melodies later used in the suite *A Day in Venice*. His compositions reveal a lyrical gift for melody; they are mostly of the sentimental, salon-type of music.

        1. *Sketchbook*, Op. 2, Boston, 1888

           a. This collection of 7 songs, 5 piano pieces and one mixed chorus with violin obbligato was immediately successful and brought **Nevin's** music before the public.

        2. *Water Scenes*, Op. 13, Boston, 1891

           a. The suite contains five pieces for piano including the very famous *Narcissus*, Op. 13, No. 4.

        3. *A Day in Venice*, Op. 25, Cincinnati, 1898

           a. Written while **Nevin** was in Venice, these four piano pieces are reminiscent of Venetian life: 1) *Alba* (Dawn) (*BCAK*, p. 73), 2) *Gondolieri* (Gondoliers), 3) *Canzone Amorosa* (Love song) and 4) *Buona Notte* (Good night).

        4. **Nevin's** *The Rosary*, Boston, 1898, considered by many to be a perfect song, was his most successful song. Within three decades after his death almost three million copies had been sold. Ernestine Schumann-Heinck, the great operatic contralto, particularly identified with it and sang it with tremendous success in America and Europe. The song, *Mighty lak' a rose*, Cincinnati, 1901, a posthumous publication, likewise became very popular. It is a poem in Negro dialect by Georgia's poet laureate, Frank L. Stanton (1857-1927).

    D. In 1909 several years after **Ethelbert Nevin's** death, his widow, Anne Paul Nevin, rendered considerable service to American composers by lobbying among congressmen in Washington for the passage of the new Copyright Act, the last bill signed by retiring president Theodore Roosevelt.

II.   Henry Franklin Belknap Gilbert (1868-1928)

   A.   Life
1. **Gilbert** was born on September 26 in Somerville, Massachusetts. After hearing the violinist **Ole Bull**, who used well-played folk music on his recitals, **Gilbert** decided to study violin at the New England Conservatory; he also studied piano with **Arthur Whiting**. He became **MacDowell's** first American pupil in composition (1889-1892) and later spent several summers at the MacDowell Colony.
2. At the Chicago World's Fair in 1893 **Gilbert** met a Russian prince who discussed with him many details of Russian and Bohemian music based on folksongs, materials which had a tremendous influence on **Gilbert's** later works. **Gilbert** entered a variety of jobs and composed when he had opportunity. In 1895 he visited Paris and again in 1901 on learning of the very successful première (1900) of **Gustave Charpentier's** (1860-1956) popular opera *Louise*. The opera so impressed **Gilbert** that he decided to devote his whole time and energy to composition.
3. In 1902 **Gilbert** became associated with **Farwell** and his Wa-Wan Press. He began to employ Negro tunes and rhythms extensively in his compositions, many of which were published by the Wa-Wan Press. All the major orchestras played his music.
4. **Gilbert's** important contributions were for orchestra, piano and solo voice. In addition to his intense interest in folk and ethnic music, **Gilbert** also admired the contemporary French and Russian composers. He said, "It has been my aim from the first to write some American and un-European music; music which shall smack of our home-soil, even though it may be crude."

   B.   Compositions
1. *Negro Episode* for piano (1902) (*WWP*, v. 1, p. 114)
   - a.   This is his first piece based on Negro rhythms; it was later arranged for orchestra. It was praised by **Jules Massenet** (1942-1912) and hailed in France as the first appearance of truly native American music.
2. *Celtic Studies* (1905), four songs on Irish texts (*WWP*, v. 3, p. 110)
3. *Salammbô's Invocation to Tänith* (1902), aria for soprano and orchestra (*WWP*, v. 1, p. 100)
   - a.   The aria was first performed in New York (1906) with the Russian Symphony Orchestra and made **Gilbert** a favorite in Russia.
4. *Comedy Overture on Negro Themes* (1905)
   - a.   The *Overture* was originally intended as a prelude to an opera based on the Uncle Remus stories of Joel Harris. A performance by the Boston Symphony Orchestra in 1911 brought **Gilbert** into prominence. In 1914 it was performed by **Reinhold Glière** (1875-1956), eminent Russian composer and conductor, in Feodosia, Crimea, and Odessa.
5. *Dance in the Place Congo* (1906)
   - a.   This rhapsodic poem for orchestra was later arranged for ballet and produced at the Metropolitan Opera House in 1918.
   - b.   The music is based on fragments of Creole songs and dances as slaves may have used them in the old Place Congo in New Orleans. In the Preface **Gilbert** says that the Creole tunes are used "much after the manner of Grieg and Tchaikovsky."
   - c.   The work begins with semi-barbaric rhythms and a note of tragedy; the middle section is largely given over to the frenzied *Bamboula*, the principal dance of the slaves; the nine-o'clock bell is heard calling the slaves to quarters, and the music gradually grows more serious; after a final cry of revolt against slavery the composition ends in the mood of the beginning.
6. Other orchestral works making use of folk melodies and rhythms include *American-esque* (1909), *Negro Rhapsody* (1912), *American Dances in Rag-Time Rhythm* (1915).

7. **Gilbert's** songs include *The Lament of Deirdre* (1903) (*WWP*, v. 2, p. 38); *Pirate Song* 1902) (*WWP*, v. 1, p. 138); *Tell Me Where is Fancy Bred?* (1905) (*WWP*, v. 3, p. 145); two South American Gypsy songs: *La Montonéra* and *La Zambulidora* (1906) (*WWP*, v. 3, p. 191); *Orlamonde* (1907) (*WWP*, v. 4, p. 185) and *The Owl* (1910) (*WWP*, v. 5, p. 157).

III. Music of American Folklore

A. The music of the American Indians and Negroes and the folk music of mountaineers and cowboys, lumberjacks, sailors and others has had considerable influence on a number of American composers. One of the first to develop an interest in American folk music was the Bohemian composer **Antonin Dvořák**, who was in America from 1892 to 1895.

1. **Antonin Dvořák** (1841-1904)

   a. **Dvořák**, a teacher of composition at the Prague Conservatory, became very popular as a teacher and renowned as a composer, not only in his own country but also in England. Cambridge University bestowed on him an honorary Doctor of Music degree in 1891. He was appointed director of the National Conservatory in New York in 1892. During his three-year tenure in New York **Dvořák** became intensely interested in Negro spirituals and **Stephen Foster's** songs. **Dvořák** disallows any use of American tunes in his *From the New World Symphony*, Op. 95 (1893), yet does admit writing in the spirit of national American melodies.

   b. Among his students who capitalized on his interest in native American materials while he was at the National Conservatory in New York were **Rubin Goldmark, Harvey Loomis** and **Henry Burleigh**.

   1) **Harvey Worthington Loomis** (1865-1930)

      a) **Loomis**, interested in Indian music, arranged and published many works in the style of Indian melodies.

      b) *Lyrics of the Red-Man* for piano, Op. 76

         (1) Book I (*WWP*, v. 2, p. 22) includes: *Music of the Calumet; A Song of Sorrow; Around the Wigwam; The Silent Conqueror* and *Warrior's Dance*.

         (2) Book II (*WWP*, v. 2, p. 246) includes *Prayer to Wakonda; On the War Path; Ripe Corn Dance; Evening at the Lodge; The Chattering Squaw; Scalp Dance; The Thunder God and the Rainbow* and *The Warrior's Last Word*.

   2) **Henry [Harry] Thacker Burleigh** (1866-1949)

      a) **Burleigh**, a Black composer and singer, often sang slave songs to **Dvořák**. For more than half a century (1892-1946) he was baritone soloist at St. George's Church, New York. **Burleigh** gained wide recognition as a song writer and arranger of Negro spirituals.

      b) *Negro Spirituals arranged for solo voice* (1917-1922)

      c) *Let us cheer the weary traveler* (*AH*, p. 318)

   3) **Rubin Goldmark** (1872-1936)

      a) A teacher of piano and theory, **Goldmark** received many awards during his lifetime. For the last twelve years of his life he was head of the composition department at the Juilliard School of Music in New York. He often called on native materials for his works.

      b) *A Negro Rhapsody* for orchestra (1923)

      c) Song: *I have done, put by the lute* (*WWP*, v. 5, p. 91)

B. In addition to **Henry Gilbert** and those just mentioned, there were many composers writing during the first two decades of the twentieth century who drew on the musical materials of native America.

1. **Arthur Farwell** (1877-1952)

   a. **Farwell** was born on April 23 in St. Paul, Minnesota; he completed a degree in electrical engineering at Massachusetts Institute of Technology in 1893. Inspired by the performances of the Boston Symphony Orchestra and influenced by **Rudolf Gott** (1872-1911), an eccentric musician about whom he later wrote a symphony, **Farwell** began the study of theory with **Homer Norris** and composition with **George Chadwick**, both of Boston. **Edward MacDowell** encouraged the publication of some of his piano pieces and influenced him to study with **Engelbert Humperdinck** (1854-1921) and **Hans Pfitzner** (1869-1949) in Germany (1897-1899). He studied a short time with **Alexandre Guilmant** (1837-1911) in Paris before returning to the United States.

b.   Although he lectured for two years at Cornell University (1899-1901) his ambition was to create an atmosphere in which American music would contribute to and elucidate a "sense of the great awakening spirit of this nation." His ideals are expressed in his words: "This does not mean to exalt American music above its intrinsic worth. It does not mean to cast out great European work to make way for mediocre American work. It means to give the American composer adequate and fair trial at the hands of the American people everywhere.

   1)   In order to accomplish this he established the Wa-Wan Press (the name is taken from a ceremony of the Omaha Indians) in 1901. Eight volumes of music were published annually until 1907 when the publications were changed to monthlies.

   a)   Thirty-six composers, most of them in their twenties, are represented in the publications.

c.   **Farwell** moved to New York and joined the editorial staff of *Musical America* and also became supervisor of municipal concerts (1910-1913). The plates of the Wa-Wan Press were turned over to G. Schirmer in New York in 1912.

d.   Being influenced by his interest in community music, **Farwell** wrote music for several masques, pageants and outdoor occasions with audience participation.

   1)   Incidental music for *Joseph and His Brethren*, Op. 39 (1912); *Caliban by the Yellow Sand*, Op. 47 (1915), choruses and incidental music for the Shakespeare tercentenary; *The Evergreen Tree*, Op. 50 (1917), a Christmas masque; *Cartoon, or Once upon a Time Recently* (1948), an operatic fantasy of music in America; *Symphonic Song on "Old Black Joe,"* Op. 67, for audience and orchestra.

e.   In 1918-1919 **Farwell** was acting head of the music department at the University of California, Berkeley. For two years (1919-1921) he conducted the Santa Barbara Community Chorus which he founded, and in 1927 he went to Michigan State College where he taught theory until 1939. He ultimately settled in New York.

f.   **Farwell** was a prolific and eclectic composer who collected and used melodies from the American Indians, cowboys, Spanish-American communities, Black and Anglo-American folk singers. His chief contributions were for orchestra, chamber ensembles, piano and voice, including 39 settings of poems by Emily Dickinson. He often arranged his works for other media. He used polytonality in his *23 Polytonal Studies*, Op. 109.

   1)   *American Indian Melodies*, 10 pieces for piano (*WWP*, v. 1, p. 33)

   2)   *Folk Songs of the West and South: Negro, Cowboy, and Spanish Californian*, 6 songs (*WWP*, v. 3, p. 45)

   3)   *From Mesa and Plain: Indian, Cowboy, and Negro Sketches*, 5 pieces for piano (*WWP*, v. 3, p. 58)

   a)   *Prairie Miniature* from this set was arranged for wind quintet.

   4)   *Impressions of the Wa-Wan Ceremony of the Omahas*, Op. 21, 8 pieces for piano (*WWP*, v. 3, p. 242)

   5)   *Owasco Memories*, Op. 8, 5 pieces for piano, also arranged for piano trio (*WWP*, v. 4, p. 167)

g.   Orchestral works include *Dawn*, Op. 12, a fantasy on Indian themes, arranged from a piano piece (*BCAK*, p. 86; *WWP*, v. 1, p. 84) for piano and small orchestra; *The Domain of Hurakan*, Op. 15, from a piano piece (*WWP*, v. 1, p. 183); *Mountain*

Vision [Symbolistic Study, No. 6], Op. 37, from a piano piece arranged for two pianos and small orchestra; *The Gods of the Mountains*, Op. 52, a suite.

2.   **Charles Wakefield Cadman** (1881-1946)

a.   **Cadman**, born in Johnstown, Pennsylvania, on December 24, had his first formal musical training with **William Steiner** (organ), **Edwin L. Walker** (piano) and **Lee Oehmler** (theory); later he studied conducting with **Emil Paur**, conductor of the Pittsburgh Symphony Orchestra. In 1908 **Cadman** became conductor of the Pittsburgh Male Chorus and for two years (1908-1910) was music editor and critic for the *Pittsburgh Dispatch*.

b.   Because of an interest in the American Indians, **Cadman** spent the summer of 1909 recording tribal songs on the Omaha and Winnebago Indian reservations. From this experience he wrote and published *Four American Indian Songs* (1909). *At Dawning*, the first of the four songs was popularized by the famous Irish tenor **John McCormack** and it sold more than a million copies. *From the Land of the Sky Blue Water*, from the same set, also became very popular with the American public.

c.   In 1910 **Cadman** organized the "American Indian Music Talks," a series of lecture-recitals; in cooperation with the Omaha Indian Princess Tsianino Redfeather, a descendant of Tecumseh, **Cadman** toured America and Europe presenting American Indian music. In 1917 **Cadman** moved west to Los Angeles where he continued composing and teaching the remainder of his life. The University of Southern California presented him with an honorary doctorate in 1924 and he was one of the founders of the Hollywood Bowl.

d.   **Cadman's** music is not innovative nor particularly distinguished, but rather it is tuneful, obvious, at times sentimental and demonstrates a certain flair for the use of instruments. His contributions are chiefly in the realms of stage works (opera, operetta, radio score), orchestral pieces and vocal compositions, some 300 songs.

e.   Among his stage works are at least a dozen titles; the opera *Shanewis* (*The Robin Woman*) was produced at the Metropolitan Opera in 1918 and many performances followed in various places. *The Witch of Salem*, which includes one Indian character, deals with the burning of the witches in the early Massachusetts Colony.

f.   *The Thunderbird Suite* (1914) for orchestra makes use of Omaha Indian themes; *Dark Dancers of the Mardi Gras* for piano and orchestra premièred in the Hollywood Bowl in 1933, depicts the festivities of Blacks during the carnival in New Orleans. *Hollywood Suite* (1932) is a series of four contrasting tonal characterizations of 1) *Mary Pickford*, 2) *Charlie Chaplin*, 3) *To My Mother* and 4) *Hollywood Bowl*.

g.   Included in more than 300 songs are the song cycles: *Sayonara* (1913) on Japanese themes; *From Wigwam and Teepee* (1914) on Indian themes and *The Willow Wind* (1922) on Chinese poems.

3.   **Charles Sanford Skilton** (1868-1941)

a.   **Skilton** was born in Northampton, Massachusetts, on August 16; he finished his college work at Yale in 1889. In 1891-1893 he was at the Hochschule für Musik in Berlin and later studied with **Dudley Buck** (composition) and **Harry Rowe Shelley** (organ). For twelve years (1903-1915) **Skilton** was dean of the School of Fine Arts at the University of Kansas, Lawrence.

b.   In 1915 **Skilton** became interested in Indian music and later taught at the government Haskell Institute for the Indians. **Skilton** incorporated tribal melodies and folklore into his larger works.

c.   *Kalopin* (1927), an opera in three acts on the Indian legends surrounding the cause of the earthquake in New Madrid, 1811

d.   *The Sun Bride* (1930), a one-act Indian opera and *The Day of Gayomair* (1936), a two-scene opera

e.   The *Suite Primeval* for orchestra: the first part (1915), based on Indian themes, is made up of orchestral arrangements of *Deer Dance* and *War Dance*, originally composed for string quartet; the second part (1921) is based on four primitive songs: 1) *Sunrise Song* (Winnebago Indians), 2) *Gambling Song* (Rogue River Indians), 3) *Flute Serenade* (Sioux Indians) and 4) *Moccasin Game* (Winnebago Indians).

   f.   *Three Indian Sketches* for piano; *American Indian Fantasy* for organ

4.   **Frederick Jacobi** (1891-1953)

   a.   **Jacobi** was born in San Francisco on May 4; he spent most of his life in New York. He studied composition with **Rubin Goldmark** and later, after a period of time in Germany, with **Ernest Bloch**. For fourteen years (1936-1950) he taught at the Juilliard School of Music.

   b.   With deep interest **Jacobi** studied the music of the Pueblo Indians in Arizona and New Mexico about 1918. This furnished him with materials for his *String Quartet on Indian Themes* (1924). He tried to adapt the native music of the Indians to the art forms of the white man. *Indian Dances* for orchestra (1927-1928) also included Indian melodies.

   c.   In addition to writing in the classical style (chamber music, concertos for cello, 1932; for violin, 1939; and for piano, 1935 with orchestra) he also composed works based on Jewish motives and materials including several services: *Two Assyrian Prayers* (1923) for voice and orchestra, *Friday Evening Synagogical Service* (1930) and *Sabbath Evening Service* (1952).

5.   **Robert Nathaniel Dett** (1882-1943)

   a.   **Dett**, a famous Black American composer, pianist and conductor, was born in what is now known as Niagara Falls, Ontario, Canada, on October 11. In 1908 he graduated from Oberlin Conservatory and later studied at Columbia University, Howard University, Eastman School of Music, Harvard University, University of Pennsylvania and the American Conservatory in Chicago. In 1929 he studied with **Nadia Boulanger** (1887-1979) in France. For eighteen years (1913-1931) **Dett** was director of music at Hampton Institute in Virginia. As director of the Hampton Choir, **Dett** developed it into a prestigious organization with an enviable reputation throughout America and Europe. He received many prizes and awards.

   b.   **Dett** often spoke on the importance of Negro folk music and urged that "musical architects take the loose timber of Negro themes and fashion from it music . . . in choral form, in lyric and operatic works, in concertos and suites and salon music."

   c.   **Dett's** compositions include several large works for chorus and orchestra, five piano suites and two collections of spirituals.

      1)   Large choral works based on traditional Black themes: *Music in the Mine* (1916); *The Chariot Jubilee* (1922); *The Ordering of Moses* (1937) for soloists, chorus and orchestra, performed at the Cincinnati (1937) and Worcester (1938) Festivals and by the New York Oratorio Society (1939).

      2)   Five suites for piano are: *Magnolia* (1911); *In the Bottom* (1913) which includes *Juba Dance*, made famous by the Australian pianist **Percy Grainger** (1882-1961); *Enchantment* (1922); *The Cinnamon Grove* (1927); *Tropic Winter* (1938).

      3)   **Dett** arranged two collections of spirituals: *Religious Folksongs of the Negro* (1926) and *The Dett Collection of Negro Spirituals*, four volumes (1936).

      4)   *O ride on, Jesus* (AH, p. 316); *Oh, nobody knows de trouble I've seen* (AH, p. 320); *Roll, Jordan, roll* (AH, p. 321); *Lord, I want to be a Christian* (AH, p. 330)

6.   **William Grant Still** (1895-1978)

   a.   **Still**, highly regarded as the Dean of Black Composers, was born in Woodville, Mississippi, on May 11. He attended Wilberforce College and was influenced by Samuel Coleridge-Taylor (1875-1912) to study music. For a short time in 1916 he worked with the **W. C. Handy** (1873-1958) ensemble and then enrolled in Oberlin Conservatory. After service in the United States Navy during World War I, **Still** returned to Oberlin but shortly went to New York where he again did arranging and orchestrating for **Handy**, **Paul Whiteman** (1890-1967) and **Don Voorhees** in the popular field and studied with **Edgar Varèse** (1885-1965). **Still** spent several years with the Columbia Radio Network arranging and directing programs and in Hollywood directing film music.

b. **Still** was the recipient of many awards (Guggenheim Fellowship, 1924; Rosenwald Fellowship), commissions (League of Composers, *Kaintuck [Kentucky]*, 1935; Columbia Broadcasting System, *Lenox Avenue*, 1937; New York World's Fair, 1939) and prizes (Cincinnati Orchestra, 1944). He also received honorary doctorates from Howard University (1941), Oberlin (1947) and the University of Arkansas (1971); he was the first Black American to conduct a major American orchestra, the Hollywood Bowl Orchestra, 1936.

c. About the age of thirty, **Still** decided to devote himself to the development of the Negro idiom and he is best known for those nationalistic works which employ Negro and other American folk idioms. Included in his works are 7 operas, 4 ballets and many songs and piano pieces. For orchestra he wrote 6 symphonic poems, 6 suites and 5 symphonies. *From the Delta* and *Folk Suite* are for band.

d. The texture of **Still's** works is basically homophonic with modern dissonance applied to tertian harmony creating ninth and eleventh chords. Polytonality is rare and the occasional use of blues is evident.

e. *Afro-American Symphony*, 1931
1) This was the first symphony by a Black American composer to be performed by a major orchestra, the Rochester Symphony Orchestra.

f. Cantata: *And They Lynched Him on a Tree* (1940) is scored for contralto soloist, two choruses and orchestra; it was first performed by the New York Philharmonic-Symphony Orchestra (1940) under Artur Rodzinski (1892-1958).

g. Hymn: *All that I am* (*AH*, p. 805)

7. **David Wendell Fenstress Guion**

a. **Guion** was born on December 15, 1895, in Ballinger, Texas; he studied piano with **Leopold Godowsky** (1870-1938) in Vienna; he returned to the United States in 1915 and taught in several colleges in Texas. **Guion** settled in Pennsylvania and devoted many years to collecting and arranging American folk songs. He has made many choral arrangements of folk songs.

b. No doubt his musical reputation rests mostly on his piano arrangements of cowboy songs and Negro spirituals.
1) *Turkey in the Straw*; *Arkansas Traveler*; *Home on the Range*

c. The works for orchestra include *Shingandi*, an African ballet suite for large orchestra; *Southern Nights Suite*; *Alley Tunes*; *Sheep and Goats Walking to the Pasture*; *Mother Goose Suite* and *Suite for Orchestra*.

8. **John Powell** (1882-1963)

a. **Powell** was born on September 6 in Richmond, Virginia; he finished his college studies at the University of Virginia in 1902; during the following five years (1902-1907) he studied piano with **Theodor Leschetizsky** (1830-1915) in Vienna. On his return to the United States **Powell** toured the country as a concert pianist.

b. **Powell's** most important achievements lie in the field of ethnomusicology. He methodically gathered rural songs of the South, concentrating particularly on those of the Anglo-American heritage. However his use of a stylized form of Negro materials is apparent in some earlier works.
1) *Rapsodie Negre* (1918) for piano and orchestra
2) *Sonate Virginianesque* (1919) for violin and piano

c. **Powell** organized the Virginia State Choral Festivals and the annual White Top Mountain Folk Music Festivals. The Anglo-American rural song became a significant and integral part of many of **Powell's** compositions even though they are couched in a neo-Romantic style.
1) Overture: *In Old Virginia* (1921) for orchestra; *Natchez on the Hill* for orches-

tra; *Three Virginia Country Dances* (1932) for orchestra

2) *Five Virginia Folk Songs* for baritone and piano; *Twelve Folk Hymns*
3) Three piano sonatas: 1) *Sonate psychologique*, 2) *Sonate noble*, 3) *Sonata Teutonica*; suite for piano: *In the South*
4) *Symphony* in A (1947), commissioned by the National Federation of Music Clubs
5) Opera: *Judith and Holofernes*

IV.   Jazz

A.   Jazz, in general a twentieth century development, has its roots in a variety of idioms in the latter part of the nineteenth century.

1.   After the Civil War and the dissolution of military bands, a plentiful supply of second-hand instruments at extraordinarily cheap prices became available to the emancipated Blacks. They formed bands which not only accompanied street parades but also led funeral processions. This music (1870-1890) helped prepare the way for jazz.

2.   Ballroom dancing (to about 1890) had largely been accompanied with the "smooth, sweet" sounds of string orchestras, sometimes with piano. During the '90's the band was gradually introduced, syncopation and a certain rough tone quality was developed. The revolution of American popular music had begun.

a.   "Hot" rhythm of campmeeting spirituals, gospel songs and minstrel show music, ragtime, brass bands, and the inflections of the blues all had some influence on the development of jazz. New Orleans is often considered the region where jazz originally developed, however, elements of jazz may be noted in various sectors of the country (Chicago, Memphis, Kansas City, New York City).

2   b.   One of the earliest parade and dance bands was led by **Charles "Buddy" Bolden** (1868-1931), a barber turned cornetist. His band consisted of five to seven pieces (cornet, clarinet, valve trombone, guitar, bass and drums), and the slide trombone was used at times for glissandos. Several of his bandsmen went on to organize bands of their own.

c.   **Joseph "King" Oliver** (1885-1938) was born on a Louisiana plantation; he learned to play cornet early in life in New Orleans; he became a member of **"Buddy"** **Bolden's** band. In 1915 he organized his own band and after World War I went to Chicago where he had broader opportunities to play in night clubs and cafés. He developed his The Creole Jazz Band and in 1932 cut the first recordings by an all-Black band. Among his players was the trumpeter **Louis Armstrong** (1900-1971), whose performances were to be acclaimed worldwide.

3.   Another idiom that made a significant contribution to the early development of jazz in the first two decades of the twentieth century was ragtime.

a.   **Scott Joplin** (1868-1917)

1)   **Joplin** was born in Texarkana, Texas, and learned piano at an early age. He went to St. Louis in 1885 where he played piano in the "honky-tonks" and perfected his style of ragtime. In 1893 he went to the Chicago Columbian Exposition where he associated with other ragtime pianists.

2)   On his return to St. Louis he was encouraged to write down and publish some of the pieces he was playing. In 1896 **Joplin** moved across the river to Sedalia, Missouri, and organized the Queen City Negro Band; the instrumentation included a clarinet, cornet, baritone, E-flat tuba, drums and piano.

3)   In 1899 **Joplin** published the famous *Maple Leaf Rag*, which became a sensational success. In addition he published 38 other "rags."

b.   Characteristics of ragtime

1)   Persistent syncopation
2)   Regular harmonic figures, largely based on I, V, and IV, in duple time maintained in the left hand.

3) In the piano "rags" the characteristic rag figures are usually played by the right hand favoring a percussive tone.

   c.   Ragtime persisted for about twenty years (1900-1920) and was the principal music used in the Broadway musicals and vaudevilles.

4.   The "blues," which developed in the early part of the twentieth century, became an important ingredient of jazz; the "blues" technique is in general indebted to Black work songs and spirituals.

   a.   In contrast to the spirituals, the blues are generally slow solo songs with accompaniment.

   b.   They incorporate "blue" notes, notes that are unstable or are not in tune with the standard scale pitches (particularly the flatted third and seventh degrees of the major scale).

   c.   There is a tendency toward a declamatory style in a smooth, slow rhythm. The "break," an improvised instrumental interlude or cadenza, of about two measures was common.

   d.   **Ferdinand "Jelly Roll" Morton** (1885-1941), *Jelly Roll Blues*, 1905

   e.   **William Christopher Handy** (1873-1958), *Memphis Blues*, 1912; *St. Louis Blues*, 1919

V.   Edward Alexander MacDowell (1861-1908)

A. Life

1.   **MacDowell** was born in New York on December 18. At the age of fifteen (April, 1877) **MacDowell** and his mother sailed for Europe. With discouraging attempts at study in the Paris Conservatory, at Stuttgart and Wiesbaden, **MacDowell** went to Frankfurt in 1879 where he studied with **Joachim Raff** (1822-1882), director of the Conservatory and teacher of composition. Not wishing to return to the United States, **MacDowell** took a position for teaching piano at the Darmstadt Conservatory (1881) and composed while commuting on the train. Teaching responsibilities became too heavy so he resigned (1882); he went to Weimar and played his first piano concerto for **Franz Liszt** (1811-1886) who praised it. He recommended to Breitkopf & Härtel that they publish **MacDowell's** *Second Modern Suite*, Op. 14. The first and second suites were published by Breitkopf & Härtel in 1883.

2.   On a short return visit to New York in June, 1884, **MacDowell** married his former student, Marian Nevins. During the next four years the **MacDowells** made their home in Wiesbaden and made a few trips to England. **MacDowell's** time was spent in composing; his home became a meeting place for American musicians who encouraged him to return to America. **MacDowell** settled in Boston in 1888 after spending most of twelve years in Germany. He continued composing and playing recitals. His orchestral works were played by the Boston Symphony, the New York Philharmonic and the Chicago Symphony.

   a.   **MacDowell** returned to the United States as a successful composer, having received European acclaim for his compositions and performances, and having had his compositions introduced (1883) on American programs by the distinguished concert pianist **Teresa Carreño** (1853-1917).

3.   In 1896, after spending eight years in Boston, **MacDowell** became head of the new department of music at Columbia University, a distinction due "the greatest musical genius America has produced." Motivated by the possibilities of music education, he now devoted himself entirely to teaching and composition, writing many of his finest works. In the meantime **MacDowell** had become increasingly recognized as a teacher, composer and performer. In 1899 he became the first president of the newly formed Society of American Musicians and Composers.

4.   The professorship at Columbia University carries the title of Edward MacDowell Chair

of Music. In his last years he conceived the idea of an artists' colony at his summer home in Peterborough, New Hampshire. In 1902 **MacDowell's** health began to fail, and he resigned his position in 1904. His malady developed into insanity and ended in death in 1905. Shortly after the MacDowell Memorial Association was formed and the MacDowell Colony for American composers was established at his summer residence.

B.   Music

1.   **MacDowell's** music has a bold harmonic and noble melodic style of marked individuality. His themes are generally short and remarkably expressive; his rhythms have variety and strength. His works are well proportioned, and he is able to maintain a basic mood throughout a composition.

2.   **MacDowell** was regarded as a great American composer, but his music is not nationalistic. It shows a strong influence of **Schumann, Liszt, Wagner, Rubinstein** and especially **Grieg.**

3.   Included in his works are 42 songs with piano accompaniment and 16 collections of tone poems for piano. For orchestra there are two piano concertos and two suites, in addition to three symphonic poems. His more important works include the second suite, *Indian Suite* (1891), his last work for orchestra and an important landmark in American music; the second *Piano Concerto* in D minor, Op. 23 (1884); four piano sonatas: *Tragica* (1891), *Eroica* (1894), *Norse* (1899) and *Keltic* (1900).

4.   There are many short piano pieces and songs in the poetic vein.

   a.   Piano collections include: *Woodland Sketches*, Op. 51 (1896) (*EAM*, v. 8, pp. 1-45) which opens with *To a Wild Rose*; *Sea Pieces*, Op. 55 (1898) (*EAM*, v. 8, pp. 46-86); *Fireside Tales*, Op. 61 (1902) (*EAM*, v. 8, pp. 87-109); *New England Idyls*, Op. 62 (1902) (*EAM* v. 8, pp. 111-144).

   1)   *A. D. 1620*, Op. 55, No. 3 (*EAM*, v. 8, p. 59; *BCAK*, p. 68); *Starlight*, Op. 55, No. 4 (*EAM*, v. 8, p. 65; *BCAK*, p. 71)

   b.   The song collections include: *Six Love Songs*, Op. 40 (1890) (*EAM*, v. 7, pp. 1-15); *Eight Love Songs*, Op. 47 (1893) (*EAM* v. 7, pp. 17-35); *Four Songs*, Op. 56 (1898) (*EAM*, v. 7, pp. 37-46); *Three Songs*, Op. 58 (1899) (*EAM*, v. 7, pp. 47-57); *Three Songs*, Op. 60 (1902) (*EAM*, v. 7, pp. 59-68).

BIBLIOGRAPHY

Books

1.   Arvey, Verna. *William Grant Still*. New York: J. Fischer, 1939.

2.   Blesh, Rudi, and Harriet Janis. *They All Played Ragtime*, 4th rev. ed. New York: Oak Publications, 1971.

3.   Brawley, Benjamin. *The Negro Genius*. New York: Dodd, Mead & Co., 1937; reprint: 1966.

4.   Brown, Rollo Walter. *Lonely Americans*. New York: Coward-McCann, 1929; reprint: Freeport, NY: Books for Libraries Press, 1970.

5.   Burton, Frederick R. *American Primitive Music with Especial Attention to the Songs of the Ojibways*. New York: Moffat, Yard & Co., 1909. (Included in Part II: 28 Ojibway songs harmonized and provided with English words)

6.   Charters, Samuel Barclay. *The Country Blues*. New York: Rinehart, 1959.

7.   ————*Jazz: New Orleans, 1885-1963; An Index to the Negro Musicians of New Orleans*, rev. ed. New York: Oak Publications, 1963.

8.   Chilton, John. *Who's Who of Jazz: Storyville to Swing Street*. London: The Bloomsbury Book Shop, 1970; Philadelphia: Chilton Book Co., 1972.

9.   Cuney-Hare, Maude. *Negro Musicians and Their Music*. Washington, DC: The Associated

Publishers, 1936; Ann Arbor: University Microfilms, 1971.

10.   Downs, Olin. "Henry Gilbert: Nonconformist," in *A Birthday Offering to [Carl Engel]*, ed. Gustave Reese. New York: G. Schirmer, 1943, pp. 88-94.

11.   Ewen, David. *Panorama of American Popular Music; The Story of Our National Ballads and Folk Songs, the Songs of Tin Pan Alley, Broadway and Hollywood, New Orleans Jazz, Swing and Symphonic Jazz.* Englewood Cliffs, NJ: Prentice-Hall, 1957.

12.   Farwell, Arthur. *A Letter to American Composers.* Newton Center, MA: Wa-Wan Press, 1903.

13.   ——————"An Affirmation of American Music," in *The American Composer Speaks; A Historical Anthology, 1770-1965*, ed. Gilbert Chase. Baton Rouge: Louisiana State University Press, 1966, pp. 88-93.

14.   Fielder, Charles N. *Complete Musical Works of Charles Wakefield Cadman.* Los Angeles: Cadman Estate, 1951.

15.   F[urness], C[lifton] J[oseph]. "Gilbert, Henry Franklin Belknap," in *Dictionary of American Biography*, v. 7. New York: Charles Scribner's Sons, 1928-1937, p. 269.

16.   Gilbert, Mrs. Henry F. *Comment and Criticism on the Works of Henry F. Gilbert.* Cambridge, MA: Harvard University Press, 1928.

17.   Gilman, Lawrence. *Edward MacDowell. A Study.* New York: John Lane Co., 1908; New York: Da Capo Press, 1969.

18.   ——————*Phases of Modern Music.* New York: Harper & Bros., 1904; reprint: Freeport, NY: Books for Libraries Press, 1968.

19.   ——————*Nature in Music and Other Studies in the Tone-Poetry of Today.* New York: John Lane Co., 1907; reprint: New York: Arno Press.

20.   *A Guide to the Music of Arthur Farwell and to the Microfilm Collection of His Works*, ed. Brice Farwell. New York: Briarcliff Manor, 1972.

21.   Hadlock, Richard. *Jazz Masters of the Twenties.* New York: Macmillan, 1965. (Louis Armstrong, pp. 13-49)

22.   Handy, William Christopher. *Father of the Blues; An Autobiography by W. C. Handy.* New York: Macmillan, 1941.

23.   Hentoff, Nat, and Albert McCarthy. *Jazz, New Perspectives on the History of Jazz by Twelve of the World's Foremost Jazz Critics and Scholars.* New York: Rinehart, 1959; reprint: New York: Da Capo Press, 1975.

24.   Hier, Ethel Glenn. *The Boyhood and Youth of Edward MacDowell.* Peterborough, NH: Nubanusit Press, 1926.

25.   Howard, John Tasker. *Studies of Contemporary American Composers.* New York: J. Fischer & Bro., 1926.

26.   ——————*Charles Sanford Skilton.* New York: Carl Fischer, 1929.

27.   ——————*Ethelbert Nevin.* New York: Thomas Y Crowell, 1935.

28.   Jones, Max, and John Chilton. *Louis: The Louis Armstrong Story, 1900-1971.* London: Studio Vista, 1971.

29.   Lovell, Jr., John. *Black Song: The Forge and the Flame. The Story of How the Afro-American Spiritual Was Hammered Out.* New York: Macmillan, 1972.

30.   MacDowell, Edward. "Suggestions in Music," in *The American Composer Speaks, A Historical Anthology, 1770-1965*, ed. Gilbert Chase. Baton Rouge: Louisiana University Press, 1966, pp. 77-87.

31.   ——————*Critical and Historical Essays; Lectures Delivered at Columbia University.* Boston: Arthur P. Schmidt, 1912; reprint: New York: Da Capo Press, 1969.

32.   MacDowell, Marian Griswold. *Random Notes on Edward MacDowell and His Music.* Boston: Arthur P. Schmidt, 1950.

33.   McBrier, Vivian Flagg. *R. Nathaniel Dett: His Life and Works: 1882-1943.* Washington, DC: Associated Publishers, 1977.

34.   Morton, Ferdinand "Jelly Roll." "Jazz Music Comes from New Orleans," in *The American Composer Speaks; A Historical Anthology, 1770-1965*, ed. Gilbert Chase. Baton

Rouge: Louisiana State University Press, 1966, pp. 161-166.

35. Niles, John Jacob. *Singing Soldiers*. New York: Charles Scribner's Sons, 1927; reprint: Detroit: Singing Tree, 1968.

36. Page, Elizabeth Fry. *Edward MacDowell*. New York: Dodge Publishing Co., 1910.

37. Porte, John Fielder, *Edward MacDowell, A Great American Tone Poet; His Life and Music*. New York: E. P. Dutton, 1922; reprint: Ann Arbor: University Microfilms, 1970.

38. *Readings in Black American Music*, compiled by Eileen Southern. New York: W. W. Norton, 1971.

39. Rosenfeld, Paul. *Musical Portraits. Interpretations of Twenty Modern Composers*. New York: Harcourt, Brace and Howe, 1920; reprint: Freeport, NY: Books for Libraries Press, 1968.

40. Rublowsky, John. *Black Music in America*. New York: Basic Books, 1971.

41. Schafer, William, and Johannes Riedel. *The Art of Ragtime: Form and Meaning of An Original Black American Art*. Baton Rouge: Louisiana State University Press, 1973; reprint: New York: Da Capo Press, 1977.

42. Schuller, Gunther. *Early Jazz: Its Roots and Musical Development*. New York: Oxford University Press, 1968.

43. Shaw, Arnold. "Popular Music From Minstrel Songs to Rock 'n' Roll," in *One Hundred Years of Music in America*, ed. Paul Henry Lang. New York: G. Schirmer, 1961, pp. 140-168.

44. Skilton, Charles Sanford. *Modern Symphonic Forms*. New York: Caxton Institute, 1927. (*Fundamentals of Musical Art*, v. 14)

45. Sonneck, Oscar George T. *Catalogue of the First Editions of Edward MacDowell*. Washinton, DC: Government Printing Office, 1917; reprint: New York: Da Capo Press, 1971.

46. −−−−−−"MacDowell *versus* MacDowell," in *Suum Cuique Essays in Music*. New York: G. Schirmer, 1916, 1944; reprint: Freeport, NY: Books for Libraries Press, 1969, pp. 87-103.

47. Southern, Eileen. *The Music of Black Americans: A History*. New York: W. W. Norton, 1971.

48. Stearns, Marshall Winslow. *The Story of Jazz*. New York: Oxford University Press, 1956, 1972.

49. Thompson, Vance. *The Life of Ethelbert Nevin From His Letters and His Wife's Memories*. Boston: The Boston Music Co., 1913.

50. Waters, Edward N. "The Wa-Wan Press: An Adventure in Musical Idealism," in *A Birthday Offering to [Carl Engel]*, ed. Gustave Reese. New York: G. Schirmer, 1943, pp. 214-233.

51. White, Newman I. *American Negro Folk-Songs*. Cambridge, MA: Harvard University Press, 1928; reprint: Hatboro, PA: Folklore Associates, 1965.

52. *William Grant Still and the Fusion of Cultures in American Music*, ed. Robert Bartlett Haas. Los Angeles: Black Sparrow Press, 1972.

Articles

1. "A Birthday Offering to William Grant Still upon the Occasion of His 80th Anniversary." *Black Perspectives in Music* 3 (1975), pp. 133-238.

2. Brody, Elaine. "*Vive La France*: Gallic Accents in American Music from 1880 to 1914." *MQ* 65 (1979), pp. 200-211.

3. Brown, Rollo Walter. "A Listener to the Winds (MacDowell)." *MA* 49 (February 25, 1929), pp. 15, 60.

4. Cable, George W. "Creole Slave Songs." *The Century Magazine* 31 (1886), pp. 807-828.

5. −−−−−−"The Dance in the Place Congo." *The Century Magazine* 31 (1886), pp. 517-532.

6.   Cadman, Charles Wakefield. "The 'Idealization' of Indian Music." *MQ* 1 (1915), pp. 387-396.

7.   ———"Opportunities for the American Composer." *Etude* 61 (1943), pp. 705, 720.

8.   Campbell-Tipton. Louis. "Ethelbert Nevin." *Music* 19 (1901), pp. 572-576.

9.   Carter, Elliott. "American Figure, with Landscape." *Modern Music* 20 (1943), pp. 219-225.

10.   Cather, Willa. "The Man Who Wrote 'Narcissus'." *Ladies Home Journal* 17 (November, 1900), p. 11.

11.   "Charles Wakefield Cadman: An American Composer." *Musician* 20 (1915), p. 687.

12.   Currier, T. P. "Edward MacDowell as I Knew Him." *MQ* 1 (1915), pp. 17-51.

13.   de Lerma, Dominique Rene. "Dett and Engel: A Question of Cultural Pride." *Your Musical Cue* 7 (November, 1970), pp. 3-5.

14.   Dett, R. Nathaniel. "From Bell Stand to Throne Room." *Etude* 52 (1934), pp. 79-80.

15.   Diamond, David. "Frederick Jacobi." *Modern Music* 14 (1937), pp. 198, 199.

16.   Douglass, Fanny Howard. "A Tribute to William Grant Still." *Black Perspectives in Music* 2 (1974), pp. 51-53.

17.   Downes, Olin. "An American Composer [Henry F. Gilbert]." *MQ* 4 (1918), pp. 23-36.

18.   Erskine, John. "MacDowell at Columbia: Some Recollections." *MQ* 28 (1942), pp. 395-405.

19.   Farwell, Arthur. "Roy Harris." *MQ* 18 (1932), pp. 18-32.

20.   ———"Wanderjahre of a Revolutionist." *MA* (April 10, 1909).

21.   ———"The Zero Hour in Musical Evolution." *MQ* 13 (1927), pp. 85-99.

22.   Gilbert, Henry F. "The American Composer." *MQ* 1 (1915), pp. 169-180.

23.   ———"American Spirit." *Wa-Wan Press Monthly* 6 (1907), p. 21.

24.   ———"A Chapter of Reminiscences." *New Music Review* 20 (1921), pp. 54, 91.

25.   ———"Concerning Jazz." *New Music Review* 21 (1922), p. 438.

26.   ———"The Disease of Harmony." *New Music Review* 18 (1919), p. 269.

27.   ———"Folk Music in Art-Music; A Discussion and a Theory." *MQ* 3 (1917), pp. 577-601.

28.   ———"Humor in Music." *MQ* 12 (1926), pp. 40-55.

29.   ———"Indian Music." *New Music Review* 11 (1912), p. 56.

30.   ———"Notes on a Trip to Frankfurt in the Summer of 1927—With Some Thoughts on Modern Music." *MQ* 16 (1930), pp. 21-37.

31.   ———"Originality." *MQ* 5 (1919), pp. 1-9.

32.   ———"Personal Recollections of Edward MacDowell." *New Music Review* 11 (1912), p. 494.

33.   Gilman, Lawrence. "Orchestral Master Works (MacDowell: *Indian Suite*, No. 2, Op. 48)." *MA* 49 (February 25, 1929), p. 17.

34.   Goldberg, Isaac. "An American Composer." *American Mercury* 15 (November, 1928), pp. 331-335.

35.   Kramer, A. Walter. "An Important Addition to American Chamber Music." *MA* 20 (1914), p. 19.

36.   Longyear, Katherine E., and Rey Morgan Longyear. "Henry F. Gilbert's Unfinished 'Uncle Remus' Opera." *Yearbook for Inter-America Musical Research* 10 (1974), pp. 50-67.

37.   Lowens, Irving. "Edward MacDowell." *HiFi/Stereo Review* 19 (December, 1967), pp. 61-72.

38.   MacDowell, Marian. "MacDowell's 'Peterborough Idea'." *MQ* 18 (1932), pp. 33-39.

39.   McWhood, Leonard B. "Edward MacDowell at Columbia University." *ProMTNA* 18 (1923), pp. 71-77.

40.   Niles, John Jacob. "White Pioneers and Black." *MQ* 18 (1932), pp. 60-75.

41.   Porte, John Fielder. "Charles Wakefield Cadman: An American Nationalist." *Chesterian* 39 (1924), p. 223.

42.   Putnam, Natalie Alden. "Ten Ideas Gained from Study with Edward MacDowell." *Etude*

48 (1930), pp. 163, 164.

43.   Reed, Addison W. "Scott Joplin, Pioneer." *Black Perspectives of Music* 3 (1975), pp. 45-52, 269-277.

44.   Rogers, Francis. "Some Memories of Ethelbert Nevin." *MQ* 3 (1917), pp. 358-363.

45.   Sear, H. G. "Henry Franklin Belknap Gilbert." *Music Review* 5 (1944), pp. 250-259.

46.   Sinclair, Upton Beall. "Memories of Edward MacDowell." *Sackbut* (December, 1925), p. 127.

48.   ———"Recollections of Edward MacDowell." *Etude* 66 (1948), pp. 416, 444, 446, 453, 456.

49.   Slonimsky, Nicolas. "Composers of New England." *Modern Music* 7 (1930), pp. 24-27.

50.   Stanley, May. "R. N. Dett, of Hampton Institute, Helping to Lay Foundation for Negro Music of Future." *MA* 27 (July 6, 1918), p. 17.

51.   Steinberg, Judith Tick. "Women as Professional Musicians in the United States, 1870-1900." *Inter-American Music Research Yearbook* 9 (1973), pp. 95-133.

52.   Still, William Grant. "Are Negro Composers Handicapped? " *The Baton* 1, No. 2 (November, 1937).

53.   ———"The Structure of Music." *Etude* 68 (March, 1950), p. 17.

Music

1.   Burleigh, Harry T. *Negro Spirituals* arranged for solo voice, 2 vols. New York: G. Ricordi & Co., 1917-1922.

2.   *Classic Piano Rags: Complete Original Music for 81 Rags*, ed. Rudi Blesh. New York: Dover Publications, 1973.

3.   Dett, R. Nathaniel. *The Collected Piano Works of R. Nathaniel Dett*. Evanston, IL: Summy-Birchard, 1973. (Magnolia; In the bottoms; Enchantment; Cinnamon Grove; Tropic winter; Eight Bible vignettes)

4.   ———*The Dett Collection of Negro Spirituals*, 4 vols. Chicago: Hall & McCreary, 1936.

5.   Dett, R. Nathaniel, ed. *Religious Folk Songs of the Negro as Sung at Hampton Institute*. Hampton, VA: Hampton Institute Press, 1927; reprint: New York: AMS Press, 1972.

6.   *Favorite Songs of the Nineties: Complete Original Sheet Music for 89 Songs*, ed. Robert Fremont. New York: Dover Publications, 1973.

7.   Gilbert, Henry F. B. *Comedy Overture on Negro Themes*. New York: H. W. Gray, 1912.

8.   ———*Dance in the Place Congo*. New York: H. W. Gray, 1922.

9.   Gilbert, Henry F. B., ed. *One Hundred Folksongs from Many Countries*. Boston: C. C. Birchard, 1910.

10.   Joplin, Scott. *Collected Piano Works*, ed. Vera Brodsky Lawrence. New York: Dover Publications, 1971.

11.   MacDowell, Edward A. *Concerto No. 1*, Op. 15, for piano and orchestra. Leipzig: Breitkopf & Härtel, 1911.

12.   ———*Concerto No. 2*, Op. 23, for piano and orchestra. Leipzig: Breitkopf & Härtel, 1907.

13.   ———*Forest Idyls*, Op. 19, for piano. Leipzig: C. F. Kahnt, 1912.

14.   ———*From an Old Garden*, Op. 26. Six songs for voice and piano. New York: G. Schirmer, 1897.

15.   ———*Marionettes*, Op. 38, for piano. Boston: Arthur P. Schmidt, 1929.

16.   ———*Piano Pieces*. New York: Da Capo Press, 1972. (Earlier American Music, v. 8) Woodland Sketches, Op. 51; Sea Pieces, Op. 55; Fireside Tales, Op. 61; New England Idyls, Op, 62.

17.   ———*Rigaudon*, Op. 49, No. 2, for piano. Boston: Arthur P. Schmidt, 1894.

18.   ———*Scotch Poem*, Op. 31, No. 2, for piano. Boston: Arthur P. Schmidt, 1895.

19.   ———*Second Suite* (Indian), Op. 48. Leipzig: Breitkopf & Härtel, 1897.

20. MacDowell, Edward. *Six Idyls*, for piano. Boston: Arthur P. Schmidt, 1929.
21. ————*Sonata No. 1*, Op. 45 (Sonata Tragica), for piano. Leipzig: Breitkopf & Härtel, 1893.
22. ————*Sonata No. 2*, Op. 50 (Sonata Eroica), for piano. Leipzig: Breitkopf & Härtel, 1895.
23. ————*Sonata No. 3*, Op. 57 (Norse), for piano. Boston: Arthur P. Schmidt, 1900.
24. ————*Sonata No. 4*, Op. 59 (Keltic), for piano. Boston: Arthur P. Schmidt, 1901.
25. ————*Songs*, Op. 40, 47, 56, 58, 60. New York: Da Capo Press, 1972. (Earlier American Music, v. 7)
26. ————*Twelve Etudes*. Boston: Boston Music Co., 1950.
27. *More Favorite Songs of the Nineties: Complete Original Sheet Music for 62 Songs*, ed. Paul Charosh and Robert A. Fremont. New York: Dover Publications, 1975.
28. Nevin, Ethelbert. *Album of Favorite Songs*. New York: John Church Co., 1899.
29. ————*A Day in Venice*. Cincinnati: John Church Co., 1898.
30. ————*The Rosary*. Boston: Boston Music Co., 1900.
31. ————*Sketchbook*, Op. 2. Boston: Boston Music Co., 1888.
32. ————*Twenty-Six Favorite Compositions*, for voice and piano. Boston: Boston Music Co., 1943.
33. ————*Water Scenes*, Suite for piano. Boston: Boston Music Co., 1891.
34. *Ragtime Rarities: Complete Original Music for 63 Piano Rags*, ed. Trebor Jay Tichenor. New York: Dover Publications, 1975.
35. *The Wa-Wan Press*, 5 vols., ed. Vera Brodsky Lawrence. New York: Arno Press & The New York Times, 1970.

OUTLINE XV

THE EARLY TWENTIETH CENTURY

Charles Martin Loeffler — Charles Tomlinson Griffes
Frederick Shepherd Converse — Daniel Gregory Mason — Edward Burlingame Hill
Emerson Whithorne — Marion Bauer

I. **Charles Martin (Tornov) Loeffler** (1861-1935)

A. Life
   1. **Loeffler** was born in Mulhouse, Alsace; his boyhood was spent in Russia, Hungary and Switzerland. In 1875 he went to Berlin where he studied violin with Joseph Joachim (1831-1907) and then to the Paris Conservatory where he studied composition with the American-born Ernest Guiraud (1837-1892). **Loeffler** came to New York in 1881 and played in Leopold Damrosch's (1832-1885) Symphony Society. In 1882 he became second concertmaster with the newly-formed Boston Symphony Orchestra, at times appearing also as soloist. In the spring of 1883 he toured throughout America with the Theodore Thomas Orchestra. **Loeffler** became an American citizen at the age of 26; he resigned his position with the Boston Symphony Orchestra in 1903, but remained in Boston teaching and composing. He was the recipient of many awards, including being a member of the French Academy (1906), Chevalier in the French Legion of Honor (1919), member of the American Academy of Arts and Letters and receiving an honorary Doctor of Music degree from Yale University (1926).

B. Style
   1. **Loeffler's** style is highly refined and personal, although colored by French impressionism after **Debussy, Fauré** and **d'Indy**. He does not make use of "American" idioms, except in *Clowns* and the *Partita* for violin and piano, which show some jazz influence. In his later works he uses frequent alternations of duple and triple meter.
   2. The inspiration for much of his music comes from poems, dramas and texts from classic and modern sources.
   3. Gregorian chant is a strong influence in his mature style. *Canticum fratris solis* (1925), a setting for solo voice and chamber orchestra of the *Canticle of the Sun* by St. Francis, uses the liturgical themes *"Deo Gratias"* (*LU*, p. 53), *"Kyrie"* (*LU*, p. 80) and the Easter Introit *"Resurrexi"* (*LU*, p. 778). The songs also make use of modal melodies and are generally impressionistic with a spirit of mysticism touched with melancholy.

C. Music
   1. **Loeffler's** compositions include works for orchestra, often with a solo instrument, chorus with orchestra and *a cappella*, chamber music and songs.
   2. *The Pagan Poem*, 1907
      a. This is **Loeffler's** best-known work. It was first conceived as a piece of chamber music (1901), then arranged for two pianos and three trumpets (1903), and finally for symphony orchestra with piano. The Boston Symphony Orchestra gave the first performance in 1907.
      b. It is based on the eighth Eclogue of Virgil in which a Thessalian maiden tries, with the aid of sorcery, to win back her truant lover. The three obbligato trumpets, representing the call of the sorceress, are heard off-stage and gradually come nearer until they join the orchestra in the maiden's triumph.

3.   *Music for Four Stringed Instruments*, 1923
   a.   The work is in three movements and is dedicated to the memory of an American aviator who lost his life in World War I.
   b.   The beginning of the Easter Introit *"Resurrexi"* (*LU*, p. 778) appears in plainsong notation at the head of the score. This motive forms the principal melodic material of the quartet.
   c.   The second movement bears the title *"Le Saint Jour de Paques"* (Easter Sunday). The fourth string of the cello is turned down to A where it states the plainsong theme.
   d.   The third movement has many changes of tempo, one of which is marked "Tempo di Marcia."

4.   *String Quintet* in F major, 1894
   a.   A one-movement work, the *Quintet* is scored for the unusual combination of three violins, viola and cello.
   b.   There are three sections to the work; the second section begins (score, p. 18) with a recitative for viola and has a scherzo-like character with a development of earlier material. The third section (score, p. 29) is a shortened and varied recapitulation of the first section.

5.   The Boston Symphony Orchestra played several of **Loeffler's** works from manuscript, including *Les Veillées de l'Ukraine* (Evenings in the Ukraine) (1891), a suite for violin and orchestra; *Fantastic Concerto* (1894) for cello and orchestra; and *Divertimento* (1895) for violin and orchestra. **Loeffler's** published works for orchestra include *La Mort de Tintagiles* (The Death of Tintagiles), Op. 6 (1905) for orchestra and viola d'amore, from the drama by Maurice Maeterlinck; *La Villanella du Diable*, Op. 9 (1905), a symphonic poem for orchestra with organ; *Memories of My Childhood* (Life in a Russian Village) (1925), which reflects a certain modal sound of Russian and Ukrainian folksongs.

6.   **Loeffler's** published solo vocal output is chiefly organized in four groups: 1) *Four Melodies*, Op. 10 (1903) for voice and piano on poems of Gustave Kahn; 2) *Four Poems*, Op. 5 (1904) for voice, viola and piano; 3) another *Four Poems*, Op. 15 (1906) and 4) five *Irish Fantasies* (1922) for voice and orchestra.

7.   In addition to the *Music for Four Stringed Instruments*, other works for chamber groups are *Two Rhapsodies* (1905) for oboe, viola and piano after poems by Maurice Rollinat (*L'etang* [The pond] and *La Cornemuse* [The bagpipe]).

8.   Works for chorus include *Psalm 137* (By the Rivers of Babylon), Op. 3 (1907) for four-part women's chorus and organ, harp, two flutes and cello obbligato; *For one who fell in battle* (1911) for eight-part mixed chorus, *a cappella*; *Beat! Beat! Drums!* (1917) for unison men's chorus and orchestra.

II.   **Charles Tomlinson Griffes** (1884-1920)

A.   Life
   1.   **Griffes** was born in Elmira, New York, studied with local teachers and was organist at the Lutheran Church. In 1903 he went to Europe to study piano (Gottfried Galston, 1875-1950) and composition (Engelbert Humperdinck, 1854-1921). During this time he wrote works in the German romantic style; among them are several German songs, *Movement* for string quartet, *Symphonische Phantasie* for orchestra, *Sonata* in F minor for piano and three settings for five-part chorus: 1) *Passionlied, O Haupt voll Blut* (O sacred head), 2) *Lobe den Herrn* (Praise to the Lord) and 3) *Dies is der Tag* (This is the day).
   2.   **Griffes** returned to America in 1907 and for the next thirteen years (1907-1920) was director of the Hackley School for Boys in Tarrytown, New York. In 1916 he played the piano part in the first American performance of **Stravinsky's** *Petrouchka*.

B. Music
  1. **Griffes'** compositions include principally songs and piano pieces; there are a few stage works, chamber works and orchestral pieces, including one symphonic work for large orchestra.
  2. Five sets of teaching pieces for piano and songs were published under the name of **Arthur Tomlinson.**
      a. *Six Short Pieces* (1918), *Six Patriotic Songs* (1918), *Six Bugle-Call Pieces* (1918), *Six Familiar Songs* (1920), *Six Pieces for Treble Clef* (1920)
C. Style
  1. The harmonically conservative style of the German Romantics (**Brahms** and **Strauss**) influenced **Griffes** in his early works (1907-1910).
      a. *Five German Poems* make use of diatonic melodic lines and some added sixths.
  2. The influence of French impressionism and oriental and exotic music directed his style from 1910 to 1917.
      a. *Three Tone-Pictures*, Op. 5 (*The Lake at Evening*, 1911; *The Vale of Dreams*, 1912; *The Night Winds*, 1912)
          1) In the impressionistic style, these *Tone-Pictures* make use of augmented chords, chromatically added and altered tones, ostinato figures, whole-tone scales and gliding parallel chords.
      b. *Roman Sketches*, Op. 7, for piano: *The White Peacock* (1915), *Nightfall* (1916), *The Fountains of the Acqua Paola* (1916) (the pentatonic scale is used on page 1), *Clouds* (1916) (the chromatic scale appears in measure 12)
          1) *The White Peacock* (arranged for orchestra by the composer)
              a) There is use of cross rhythms, bitonality, alternating rhythms (3/2, 5/4, 7/4, 5/4), seventh, ninth and eleventh chords and chromatic scale lines (meas. 3). The first section makes unusual use of dominant and secondary dominant harmonies in a basic E major tonality.
      c. *The Pleasure Dome of Kubla Khan*
          1) Composed as a piano piece (1912), it was colorfully scored for orchestra by **Griffes** (1917) and revised by Frederick Stock (1919).
          2) It is a descriptive tone-poem based on the poem, *Kubla Khan* or *A Vision in a Dream* by Samuel Taylor Coleridge. **Griffes** uses the section describing the stately palace: "the sunny pleasure-dome with caves of ice, the miracle of rare device."
          3) Many impressionistic devices and oriental-type themes are used.
          4) The work is scored for 3 flutes, 2 oboes, English horn, 2 clarinets in A, bass clarinet in B-flat, 4 horns, 3 trumpets, 3 trombones, tuba, timpani, bass drum, cymbals, tambourine, gong, piano, celesta, 2 harps and strings.
          5) Introduction (meas. 1-15)
              a) Sacred Alph river and ice caverns.
          6) Part I (meas. 16-46)
              a) Palace gardens and fountains appear.
          7) Part II (meas. 47-138)
              a) Suggestions of revelry are heard.
          8) Part III (meas. 139-209)
              a) The dancing and revelry reach a climax.
          9) Coda (meas. 210-220)
              a) Return to the first mood.
  3. Strong influence of orientalism
      a. *Five Poems of Ancient China and Japan*, Op. 10 (1917)
          1) These make use of five- and six-tone scales.
      b. *Sho-jo*, a Japanese pantomime commissioned by Adolf Bolm for his Ballet-Intime, is scored for flute, oboe, clarinet, harp, Chinese drum, tam-tam, timpani and strings.

        1)   An oriental effect is achieved by using muted strings and harmonics to suggest quarter-tones.

   c.   *Two Sketches Based on Indian Themes* (1916-1917) for string quartet

        1)   The first sketch (lento e mesto) is of an eerie and fantastic mood.

        2)   The second sketch (allegro giocoso) makes use of primitive and sharply accented rhythms and ends in the style of a strenuous Indian dance.

  4.   Later works

   a.   The style marks a turning away from impressionism and programmatic writing. The influence of **Alexander Scriabin** (1872-1915) is apparent and modern harmonic devices appear. There is still some influence of orientalism to be found.

   b.   *Sonata for Piano* (December 1918-January 1919)

        1)   Three movements (the first two are connected); cyclical form

        2)   First movement (Feroce - Allegretto con moto)

           a)   Based on an oriental-sounding artificial scale (F - G-sharp - A - B-flat - C-sharp - D - E-flat)

           b)   Sonata-allegro form: Introduction (meas. 1-8); theme I (meas. 9-24); theme II (meas. 24-47). Development (meas. 48-79). Recapitulation (meas. 80)

           c)   The basic chord is built on fourths (F - B-flat - E-flat)

        3)   Second movement (Molto tranquillo)

           a)   A (meas. 1-36) – B (meas. 37-49) – A (meas. 50-56) – Coda

           b)   Use of plainsong-like theme, polytonal effects, harsh discords

        4)   Third movement (Allegro vivace)

           a)   A (meas. 1-42) – B (meas. 43-68) – A (meas. 69-125) – Coda for the entire sonata (meas. 126-223)

           b)   Devices include frequent changes of time signatures, use of polyrhythms and chords in fifths (B-flat - (D) - F-sharp - C-sharp).

           c)   Materials from the earlier movements return in the last movement.

   c.   *Poem* for flute and orchestra, 1918

        1)   This was written for Georges Barrère, flutist, who premièred it with the New York Symphony Orchestra under Walter Damrosch (1862-1950). It is scored for solo flute, 2 horns in E, snare drum, harp and strings. It is also published in an arrangement for flute and piano.

        2)   There is some use of modes.

   d.   *Three Preludes* for piano, 1919

        1)   These are **Griffes'** last completed works; they retain the abstract harmonies of the *Sonata* (1918), are confined to 32 measures or less and show a similarity to **Schoenberg** or **Scriabin**, but they never quite reach atonality.

III. Frederick Shepherd Converse (1871-1940)

  A. Life

    1.   **Converse**, who became a composer, teacher and administrator, was born in Newton, Massachusetts, on January 5. When he was ten years old he began studying the piano; showing considerable interest in composition, he entered Harvard College in 1889 and became a pupil of **John Knowles Paine** (1839-1906); in 1893 he graduated in music with highest honors. After an unsuccessful attempt at business, he continued his piano study and became a composition pupil of **George Chadwick** (1854-1931). For two years (1896-1898) **Converse** studied counterpoint, composition and organ in Munich under the guidance of **Josef Rheinberger** (1839-1901). On his return to the United States he taught harmony at the New England Conservatory (1900-1902) and then at Harvard University (1903-1907).

    2.   Having become active in the musical life of Boston, **Converse** helped to organize and administer the Boston Opera Company (1908-1914). During this time he produced

several operas;   among them was his own *The Pipe of Desire*, 1905. This opera was also produced at the Metropolitan Opera in New York, the first American opera to be performed there (March 18, 1910). A second opera, *The Sacrifice*, was presented in Boston the following year.

3.   **Converse** served in the Massachusetts State Guard during World War I and was a member of the National Committee on Army and Navy Camp Music.

4.   In 1920 he became chairman of the theory department at the New England Conservatory and was the Dean of Faculties from 1931 to 1938.

5.   He received the David Bispham Medal from the American Opera Society in Chicago (1926), an honorary doctorate from Brown University (1933) and in 1937 was elected to the American Academy of Arts and Letters.

B.   Music

1.   **Converse's** music was extensively performed during his lifetime. His early works, modeled on late German romanticism, reflect his European academic studies. The tone poem *Flivver Ten Million*, which celebrated the 10 millionth Ford car, made use of realistic modern materials after **Honegger's** *Pacific 231*.

   a.   Episodes depicted in this work are reminiscent of the American spirit: *Dawn in Detroit; The Birth of the Hero; May Night by the Roadside (America's Romance); The Joy Riders (America's Frolic); The Collision (America's Tragedy)* and *Phoenix Americanus*.

2.   In addition to the two operas that were performed, there are two operas that were not performed: *Beauty and the Beast* (1913) and *The Immigrants* (1914).

3.   Among his orchestral works are 6 symphonies and several tone poems: *Night and Day*, after Walt Whitman (1901); *Ormazd*, after the Persian Bundahesch (1911); *Ave atque vale* (1916); *Song of the Sea*, after Walt Whitman (1923); *Flivver Ten Million* (1926); *California* (1927) and *The Mystic Trumpeter* (1904).

   a.   The symphonic poems by **Converse** are some of the earliest successful compositions in that form among American composers. *The Mystic Trumpeter* is considered his most significant work.

4.   His chamber works include three string quartets, a *Septet* for clarinet, bassoon, horn, piano and string trio, a *Prelude and Intermezzo* for brass sextet, and a sonata each for violin and cello with piano.

5.   His piano works number about 24 pieces; his songs for solo voice and piano about the same number.

6.   There are several large choral works, including the oratorio *Job* (1906), the first American oratorio to be heard in Germany. Among his cantatas are: *The Peace Pipe* (1915), *The Answer of the Stars* (1919), and *Flight of the Eagle* (1930).

IV.   Daniel Gregory Mason (1873-1953)

A.   Life

1.   **Mason** was born in Brookline, Massachusetts, on November 20. He was a grandson of **Lowell Mason** (1792-1872) and a nephew of **William Mason** (1829-1908). His father, **Henry Mason** (1831-1890), was one of the founders of the Mason and Hamlin Piano Company. Before entering Harvard University **Mason** had some lessons with **Ethelbert Nevin**; at Harvard he studied with **John Knowles Paine** (1839-1906), whose lectures he found uninteresting; he graduated with a Bachelor of Arts degree in 1895. **Mason** then continued piano studies with **Arthur Whiting**, orchestration with **George Chadwick** in Boston and theory with **Percy Goetschius** in New York. Wishing to improve his composing techniques, in 1901 he went to Paris to study with **Vincent d'Indy** (1851-1931). **Mason** had become very much interested in writing about music; in 1902 his first book, *From Grieg to Brahms*, was published.

2.   In 1905 **Mason** was appointed as a lecturer at Columbia University; he was made an

assistant professor in 1910 and in 1929 became a MacDowell Professor, serving also as chairman of the music department until 1940; two year later he retired. **Douglas Moore** (1893-1969) succeeded **Mason** as chairman of the department (1940-1962).

3. **Mason** was an outstanding teacher; he lectured extensively and authored many books and articles. He received honorary doctorates from Tufts College (1929), Oberlin College (1931) and Eastman School of Music (1932); he was a member of the National Institute of Arts and Letters and received publication prizes from the Society for the Publication of American Music and the Juilliard Foundation.

4. **Mason's** works for orchestra include three symphonies, two preludes and fugues, a suite and an overture; he wrote many piano pieces and at least three pieces for organ; in addition to more than 70 songs, he composed for a variety of chamber groups.

B. Style

1. **Mason** believed that American music is "necessarily eclectic and cosmopolitan, and that the kind of distinctiveness to be looked for in it is individual rather than national." He was in no sense revolutionary and preferred the classic-romantic principles and forms of **Beethoven, Schubert, Brahms** and **Franck.** In regard to originality he stated, "Be original at your peril; if you wish immediate popularity, you must imitate current models." He wrote with sincerity and his craftsmanship is of the highest order. Many of his early works were revised for later publication.

2. Although he considered himself a conservative, he was not unaware of the trends of his time. He made some use of the whole-tone scale, triads with the added sixth, suggestions of polytonality, parallel open fifths and tone clusters of consecutive chromatic chords.

3. Various classic forms are used; sonata-allegro: *Sonata*, Op. 5, for violin and piano (1908); variation: *Variations on a Theme by John Powell* (1924) and *Variations on a Quiet Theme*, Op. 40 (1939), both for string quartet; fugue: *Prelude and Fugue*, Op. 12, for piano and orchestra (1914) and *Prelude and Fugue*, Op. 37, for strings (1939); overture: *Chanticleer* for orchestra (1926).

4. Borrowed themes are found in a number of compositions: *Yankee Doodle*, Op. 6, for piano (1911); *String Quartet on Negro Themes*, Op. 19, first movement: *You may bury me in the east,* second movement: *Deep river,* third movement: *O what do you say, seekers?, Shine, shine, I'll meet you in the morning* and *Oh, Holy Lord!* (1919); *Folksong Fantasy* on the English song *Fanny Blair,* op. 28, for string quartet (1927); *Suite after English Folksongs*, Op. 32, for orchestra (1933), uses *O no, John; A brisk young sailor; The two magicians; Arise, arise!* and *The rambling sailor; Two Chorale Preludes on Lowell Mason Tunes*, Op. 39, for organ (1941).

5. Cyclic treatment is found in the symphonies: No. 1 in C minor, Op. 11 (1914); No. 2 in A major, Op. 30 (1928); No. 3, *"A Lincoln Symphony,"* Op. 35 (1936). In the "Lincoln Symphony" descriptive titles suggest certain events in the "Emancipator's" life: movement I. "The Candidate from Springfield," II. "Massa Linkum," III. "Old Abe's Yarns," and movement IV. "1865, marcia funèbre." A popular tune of Civil War days, *Quaboag Quickstep*, forms the basis of the first movement and is turned into a funeral dirge in the last.

V. **Edward Burlingame Hill** (1872-1960)

A. **Hill** was born in Cambridge, Massachusetts, on September 9, the son of a chemistry professor at Harvard University and the grandson of a president (1862-1868) of Harvard. At Harvard **Hill** was a pupil of **John Knowles Paine**; he graduated *summa cum laude* in 1894. He studied organ with **Charles-Marie Widor** (1844-1937) in Paris, piano with **Arthur Whiting** and **Benjamin J. Lang** and composition with **George Chadwick** in Boston. Until 1908 **Hill** taught piano and theory in Boston, then was hired by Harvard University; from 1928 to 1940 **Hill** was chairman of the music department.

1. **Hill** devoted himself to instrumental works and many of them were premièred by the Boston Symphony Orchestra; almost no compositions for voice appeared.
   a. *Nuns of the Perpetual Adoration* for women's chorus and orchestra (1907) and *An Ode for the Fiftieth Anniversary of the Boston Symphony Orchestra* for chorus and orchestra (1930).
2. In his earlier works **Hill** makes use of various French impressionistic devices, rich and colorful orchestration.
   a. *Stevensoniana*, Suite I (1915), Suite II (1922), based on poems from Robert Louis Stevenson's *A Child's Garden of Verses*, and two symphonic poems: *The Fall of the House of Usher* (1919) and *Lilacs* (1926), which had many performances.
3. A brief but prudent acknowledgement of jazz was made in his *Jazz Studies* (1922) for two pianos and later in the *Concertino* (1931) for piano and orchestra, a three movement piece given to lively and vigorous materials.
4. The three symphonies (B-flat, 1927; C, 1929; G, 1936) bring out **Hill's** concepts of traditional form, texture and style. In these works, as **Hill** stated particularly concerning the third symphony, there is "no descriptive background, aiming merely to present musical ideas according to the traditional forms." Other orchestral works include *Waltzes* (1920), *Concertino* for piano and orchestra (1938) and *Concerto* for violin (1933).
5. Several chamber works are included: *Sonata* for flute and piano, *Sonata* for clarinet and piano (both in 1925), *Sextet* for wind instruments and piano (1934), a string quartet (1935) and a quartet for piano and strings (1937).
6. **Hill** wrote the music for two ballet-pantomimes: *Jack Frost in Midsummer* (1907) and *Pan and the Star* (1912).
7. **Hill's** book, *Modern French Music*, 1924, and many articles show his interest in the tonal materials of French impressionism.

VI. Emerson Whithorne (1884-1958)

A. **Whithorne** was born on September 6 in Cleveland, Ohio; he studied with **James H. Rogers** in Cleveland and at the age of 15 made two successful concert tours with the Chautauqua concerts. He spent three years (1904-1907) in Vienna as a piano student of **Theodor Leschetizsky** (1830-1915) and later with **Artur Schnabel** (1882-1951) and as a composition student of **Robert Fuchs** (1847-1927). In London (1907-1915) he taught piano and theory and also was the London correspondent and critic for *Musical America*. While in London he did research on oriental music in the British Museum and ultimately wrote several works based on Chinese and Japanese themes.
   1. *Two Oriental Pieces*, Op. 8, for piano; *Adventures of a Samurai*, Op. 17, a symphonic poem; *Quartettino Orientale*, Op. 21, a string quartet.
   2. Chinese themes were also incorporated into the ballet, *Sooner and Later*, Op. 37. The guitar, mandolin, tam-tam, gongs, celesta, muted trumpet and drums are used to imitate indigenous instruments.
B. For five years (1915-1920) **Whithorne** was editor of the *Arts Publication Society* in St. Louis. He then moved to New York, became an active member of the League of Composers and devoted himself mainly to composition. His compositions, although played frequently during his lifetime, have seldom been performed since.
C. Polytonality became evident in his *New York Days and Nights*, Op. 40, a suite for piano, later arranged for orchestra (1925). Natural sounds (piercing whistles, horns, strolling musicians, snatches of familiar tunes, gaiety and tragedy) reflect the programmatic elements of the movements: 1) *On the Ferry*, 2) *Chimes of St. Patrick's*, 3) *Pell Street*, describing Chinatown, 4) *A Greenwich Village Tragedy* and 5) *Times Square* with crowds, flashing lights and revelling.
   1. This was chosen to represent American music at the 1923 Salzburg Chamber Music

        Festival. It has been performed by jazz band as well as symphony orchestra.

D.   Syncopated rhythms (not jazz, **Whithorne** said) in restless and impulsive designs mingled with forceful thematic material are characteristics of *Poem*, Op. 43, for piano and orchestra; *Fata Morgana*, Op. 44, a symphonic poem and *Moon Trail*, Op. 53, a suite of four descriptive pictures: 1) *Death Valley*, 2) *The Devil's Kitchen*, 3) *Palos Verdes* and 4) *Surf at Malibu*.

E.   Two works on the poems of Black poet Countee Cullen, *Saturday's Child*, Op. 42, for mezzo-soprano, tenor and chamber orchestra and *The Grim Troubadour*, Op. 45, for medium voice and string quartet, are marked by strong rhythms.

F.   In addition to two symphonies (Op. 49, 1934; 1935) both introduced by the Cleveland Orchestra, there is a violin concerto, many songs and piano pieces. *Aeroplane*, Op. 38, originally written for piano (1921) and later arranged for orchestra (1926) is probably one of the earliest attempts at "machine music."

VII. Marion Eugenie Bauer (1887-1955)

A.   **Bauer** was born on August 15 in Walla Walla, Washington; she was educated in the schools of Portland, Oregon, and later (1932) received an honorary Master's degree from Whitman College in Walla Walla. She studied with **Nadia Boulanger** (1887-1980) and **Louis Campbell-Tipton** (1877-1921) in Paris and held various teaching positions: Mills College, Berkeley, California (1935), Carnegie Institute of Technology, Pittsburgh (1936, 1939), New York University (1926-1951), Juilliard School of Music (1940-1944) and the Institute of Musical Arts. Since 1928 she had lectured frequently at Chautauqua.

B.   She was the most distinguished woman composer of her time and had a strong inclination toward impressionism. She used a variety of national elements: American Indian materials in *Sun Splendor* (1926) for piano and also for orchestra and *Indian Pipes* (1928) for orchestra; African themes in *Lament on African Themes* (1928) for chamber orchestra.

C.   **Bauer's** main contribution is her book on contemporary composers and their music, *Twentieth Century Music*, 1933, revised in 1947.

BIBLIOGRAPHY

Books

1.   Ammer, Christine. "Marion Bauer," in *Notable American Women. The Modern Period*, ed. Barbara Sicherman and Carol Hurd Green. Cambridge, MA: Harvard University Press, 1980, pp. 68-69.

2.   Anderson, Donna K. *Charles T. Griffes, An Annotated Bibliography-Discography*. Detroit: The College Music Society, 1977. (*Bibliographies in American Music*, No. 3)

3.   Bauer, Marion. *Twentieth Century Music: How It Developed, How to Listen to It*. New York: G. P. Putnam's Sons, 1933; reprint: New York: Da Capo Press, 1978.

4.   *Boston Symphony Orchestra Programmes*. Boston: 1921-1922, pp. 1124-1132; 1935-1936, pp. 168, 177, 182; 1938-1939, p. 230 (Loeffler).

5.   Clarke, Garry E. "Charles Tomlinson Griffes," in *Essays on American Music*. Westport, CT: Greenwood Press, 1977, pp. 87-103.

6.   "From the Correspondence of Charles Martin Loeffler," in *A Birthday Offering to [Carl Engel]*. New York: G. Schirmer, 1943, pp. 155-160.

7.   Gilman, Lawrence. *Nature in Music and Other Studies in the Tone-Poetry of Today*. New York: John Lane Co., 1914; reprint: New York: Arno Press.

8.   Hill, Edward Burlingame. *Modern French Music*. Boston: Houghton Mifflin Co., 1924; reprint: New York: Da Capo Press, 1969; Westport, CT: Greenwood Press, 1970.

9.   Howard, John Tasker. *Charles Tomlinson Griffes*. New York: G. Schirmer, 1923.

10. Howard, John Tasker. *Emerson Whithorne*. New York: Carl Fischer, 1929.
11. Hughes, Rupert. *Contemporary American Composers*. Boston: L. C. Page, 1900.
12. Klein, Mary Justina. *The Contribution of Daniel Gregory Mason to American Music*. Washington, DC: Catholic University of America Press, 1957.
13. Maisel, Edward M. *Charles T. Griffes. The Life of an American Composer*. New York: Alfred A. Knopf, 1943.
14. Mason, Daniel Gregory. *The Appreciation of Music Series*, 5 vols. New York: H. W. Gray Co., 1907-1925.
    Volume I: *A Course of Study for Schools, Colleges, and General Readers*.
    Volume II: *Great Modern Composers*, with L. M. Mason. reprint: New York: Arno Press, 1968; Freeport, NY: Books for Libraries Press, 1968.
    Volume III: *Short Studies of Great Masterpieces*.
    Volume IV: *Music as a Humanity*.
    Volume V: *A Guide to Music for Beginners and Others*.
15. ————, editor. *The Art of Music*, 14 vols. New York: The National Society of Music, 1915-1917.
16. ————*Artistic Ideals*. New York: W. W. Norton, 1927.
17. ————*Beethoven and His Forerunners*. New York: Macmillan, 1904, 1930.
18. ————*The Chamber Music of Brahms*. New York: Macmillan, 1933; reprint: Ann Arbor: J. W. Edwards, 1950; New York: AMS Press, 1977.
19. ————*A Child's Guide to Music*. New York: Baker and Taylor Co., 1909.
20. ————*Contemporary Composers*. New York: Macmillan, 1918.
21. ————*The Dilemma of American Music, and Other Essays*. New York: Macmillan, 1928.
22. ————"The Dilemma of American Music," in *The American Composer Speaks; A Historical Anthology, 1770-1965*, ed. Gilbert Chase. Baton Rouge: Louisiana State University Press, 1966, pp. 118-131.
23. ————*Ears to Hear, A Guide to Music Lovers*. Chicago: American Library Association, 1925.
24. ————*From Grieg to Brahms. Studies of Some Modern Composers and Their Art*. New York: The Outlook Co., 1902; new and enlarged edition: New York: Macmillan, 1927; reprint: New York: AMS Press, 1971.
25. ————*From Song to Symphony. A Manual of Music Appreciation*. Boston: Oliver Ditson, 1924.
26. ————*Music and the Plain Man*. New York: H. W. Gray, 1923.
27. ————*Music as an International Language*. New York: American Association for International Conciliation, 1913.
28. ————*Music in My Time*. New York: Macmillan, 1938; reprint: 1970.
29. ————*A Neglected Sense in Piano-Playing*. New York: G. Schirmer, 1912.
30. ————*The Orchestral Instruments and What They Do; A Primer for Concert-Goers*. New York: H. W. Gray, 1909.
31. ————*The Quartets of Beethoven*. New York: Oxford University Press, 1947.
32. ————*The Romantic Composers*. New York: Macmillan, 1906.
33. ————*A Student's Guide to Music*. New York: H. W. Gray Co., 1909.
34. ————*Tune In, America. A Study of Our Coming Musical Independence*. New York: Alfred A. Knopf, 1931; reprint: New York: Arno Press, 1969.
35. Norman, Gertrude, and Miriam Lubell Shrifte. *Letters of Composers, An Anthology, 1603-1945*. New York: Alred A. Knopf, 1946; reprint: Westport, CT: Greenwood Press, 1979, p. 284 (Mason); pp. 282-283, 304-306 (Loeffler); pp. 307-308 (MacDowell); pp. 318-319 (Parker).
36. Rosenfeld, Paul. "Charles Loeffler," in *Musical Portraits. Interpretations of Twenty Modern Composers*. New York: Harcourt, Brace and Howe, 1920; reprint: Freeport, NY: Books for Libraries Press, 1968, pp. 257-266.

Articles

1. "Adolph Bohm Moving Spirit of Charming Organization. Chas. T. Griffes Writes Splendid Music for Itow." *Musical Leader* 34 (August 30, 1917), p. 211.

2. Bauer, Marion. "Charles T. Griffes as I Remember Him." *MQ* 29 (1943), pp. 355-380.

3. ———"Impressionists in America." *Modern Music* 4 (January-February, 1927), pp. 15-20.

4. Belt, Byron. "American Composers—Serendipitous Find (Sing Out, America)." *Music Journal* 34 (March, 1976), pp. 8-9.

5. Downes, Olin. "An American Composer [Daniel Gregory Mason]." *MQ* 4 (1918), pp. 23-36.

6. Engel, Carl. "Charles Martin Loeffler." *MQ* 11 (1925), pp. 311-330.

7. ———"Views and Reviews [Daniel Gregory Mason]." *MQ* 18 (1932), pp. 178-183.

8. ———"Views and Reviews [Charles Martin Loeffler]." *MQ* 21 (1935), pp. 368-375.

9. ———"Views and Reviews [Charles Tomlinson Griffes]." *MQ* 29 (1943), pp. 405-409.

10. Ewen David. "Charles M. Loeffler." *Chesterian* (July-August, 1935), p. 149.

11. Hammond, Richard. "Emerson Whithorne." *Modern Music* 8 (1931), pp. 23-28.

12. Hill, Edward Burlingame. "Charles Martin Loeffler." *Modern Music* 13 (1935), pp. 26-31.

13. Mason, Daniel Gregory. "The Artisti and His Fellows." *ML* 7 (1926), pp. 246.

14. ———"Artistic Ideals—Originality." *MQ* 13 (1927), pp. 1-13.

15. ———"Artistic Ideals— Spontaneity." *MQ* 12 (1926), pp. 315-326.

16. ———"Artistic Ideals— Universality." *MQ* 12 (1926), pp. 1-12; 13 (1927), pp. 345-358.

17. ———"Artistic Ideals— Workmanship." *MQ* 12 (1926), pp. 481-496.

18. ———"Brahms Third Symphony." *MQ* 17 (1931), 374-379.

19. ———"A Conservative Composer's Confession of Artistic Faith." *New York Times* (April 4, 1948), section II, p. 7:2.

20. ———"Dictator Conductors." *American Scholar* (October, 1941), pp. 447-454.

21. ———"Folk-Song and American Music (A Plea for the Unpopular Point of View)." *MQ* 4 (1918), pp. 323-332.

22. ———"A Glimpse of Lowell Mason." *New Music Review* 26 (January, 1927), p. 49.

23. ———"The Masons: Cultural Pioneers." *Music Digest* (December, 1946), p. 10.

24. ———"Memories of William Mason." *Etude* 54 (1936), p. 543.

25. ———"Our Musical Adolescence." *Harper's Magazine* 161 (1930), pp. 599-607.

26. ———"A Pragmatic Review of Harmony." *New Music Review* 10 (April, 1911), p. 242; (May, 1911), p. 306.

27. ———"Romanticism and Realism in Music." *New Music Review* 13 (1914), pp. 398-402.

28. ———"What Do We Mean By Classic? " *Etude* 50 (December, 1932), p. 845.

29. Peterkin, Norman. "Charles T. Griffes." *Chesterian* 30 (March, 1923), pp. 161-166.

30. Rosenfeld, Paul. "Griffes on Grand Street." *Modern Music* 18 (1940), pp. 27-30.

31. Rudhyar, Dane. "Griffes, Master of the Lied." *Singing* (June, 1927), p. 24.

32. Smith, George Henry Lovett. "Edward Burlingame Hill." *Modern Music* 16 (1939), p. 11-16.

33. Thompson, Randall. "The Contemporary Scene in American Music." *MQ* 18 (1932), pp. 9-17.

34. Tuthill, Burnet C. "Daniel Gregory Mason." *MQ* 34 (1948), pp. 46-60.

35. ———"Fifty Years of Chamber Music in the United States." *ProMTNA* 23 (1928), pp. 163-175.

36. Upton, William Treat. "The Songs of Charles T. Griffes." *MQ* 9 (1923), pp. 314-328.

37. Waters, Edward N. "New Loeffleriana." *Library of Congress Quarterly Journal.* (April-June, 1944), pp. 6-14.

Music

1.   Boda, Daniel. *The Music of Charles T. Griffes*. Ann Arbor: University Microfilms, 1967.

2.   Gleason, Frederick Grant. *Gleason's Motette Collection*. Chicago: F. S. Chandler & Co., 1875.

3.   Griffes, Charles Tomlinson. *By a Lonely Forest Pathway*, for voice and piano. New York: G. Schirmer, 1909, 1937.

4.   ————*Dance Song for Piano in the Early Grades*. New York: G. Schirmer, 1918.

5.   ————*Five Poems of Ancient China and Japan*, Op. 10, for medium voice and piano. New York: G. Schirmer, 1917.

6.   ————*Five German Poems* for voice and piano. New York: G. Schirmer, 1909.

7.   ————*Four German Songs*. New York: C. F. Peters, 1970.

8.   ————*Four Impressions*. New York: C. F. Peters, 1970.

9.   ————*Marching Song for Piano in the Early Grades*. New York: G. Schirmer, 1918.

10. ————*Piano Compositions*, Op. 5-7. New York: G. Schirmer, 1915-1917.
     Op. 5. Three Tone-Pictures: The Lake at Evening; The Vale of Dreams; The Night Winds.
     Op. 6. Fantasy Pieces: Barcarolle; Notturno; Scherzo.
     Op. 7. Roman Sketches: The White Peacock; Night Fall; The Fountain of the Acqua Paola; Clouds.

11. ————*The Pleasure-Dome of Kubla Khan*, symphonic poem for grand orchestra. New York: G. Schirmer, 1920.

12. ————*Poem* for flute and orchestra. New York: G. Schirmer, 1922.

13. ————*Sonata* for piano. New York: G. Schirmer, 1921.

14. ————*Symphony in Yellow*, Op. 3, No. 2, for mezzo-soprano and piano. New York: G. Schirmer, 1915.

15. ————*These Things Shall Be*, for unison chorus and piano. New York: G. Schirmer, 1917.

16. ————*Three Poems by Fiona MacLeod*, Op. 11, for voice and piano. New York: G. Schirmer, 1918.

17. ————*Three Preludes*, for piano. New York: C. F. Peters, 1967.

18. ————*Tone-Images*, Op. 3, for a mezzo-soprano voice and piano. New York: G. Schirmer, 1915.

19. ————*Two Poems*, by John Masefield, for medium voice and piano. New York: G. Schirmer, 1920.

20. ————*Two Rondels* for a soprano voice. New York: G. Schirmer, 1915.

21. ————*Two Sketches* for string quartet (based on Indian themes). New York: G. Schirmer, 1922.

22. Loeffler, Charles Martin. *Beat! Beat! Drums!* (Walt Whitman) for men's voices. Boston: C. C. Birchard, 1932.

23. ————*Canticum Fratris Solis* for soprano voice and orchestra. Washington, DC: The Library of Congress, 1929.

24. ————*Deux Rapsodies*, pour hautbois, alto et piano. New York: G. Schirmer, 1905.

25. ————*Evocation* on lines from the Select Epigram of the Greek Anthology by J. W. Mackail. Boston: C. C. Birchard, 1932.

26. ————*Five Irish Fantasies* for voice and orchestra. New York: G. Schirmer, 1935.

27. ————*Four Poems*, Op. 15, for voice and piano. New York: G. Schirmer, 1906.

28. ————*La mort de Tintagles*, for orchestra and viole d'amour. New York: G. Schirmer, 1905.

29. ————*La villanelle du diable*, Op. 9, for orchestra and organ. New York: G. Schirmer, 1905.

30. ————*Memories of My Childhood*. Poem for orchestra. New York: G. Schirmer, 1925.

31.   Loeffler, Charles Martin. *Music for Four Stringed Instruments*. New York: G. Schirmer, 1923.

32.   ————*Ode For One Who Fell in Battle*. Eight-part chorus for mixed voices a cappella. New York: G. Schirmer, 1911.

33.   ————*A Pagan Poem*. New York: G. Schirmer, 1909.

34.   ————*Partita* for violin and piano. New York: G. Schirmer, 1937.

35.   ————*Poem* for orchestra. New York: G. Schirmer, 1923.

36.   ————*Psalm 137* (By the rivers of Babylon), for four-part women's chorus. New York: G. Schirmer, 1907.

37.   ————*Quatre Melodies* pour chant et piano, Op. 10. New York: G. Schirmer, 1903.

38.   ————*Quatre poêmes* pour voix, alto et piano, Op. 5. New York: G. Schirmer, 1904.

39.   ————*Quintett in One Movement* for three violins, viola and violoncello. New York: G. Schirmer, 1938.

40.   ————*Serenade* pour voix, alto et piano. New York: G. Schirmer, 1904.

41.   ————*Violin Studies for the Development of the Left Hand*. New York: G. Schirmer, 1936.

42.   ————*The Wind Among the Reeds*; two poems by W. B. Yeats, for voice and piano. New York: G. Schirmer, 1908.

43.   Mason, Daniel Gregory. *Ballade* in E-flat, Op. 16, No. 2, for piano. Boston: Oliver Ditson, 1920.

44.   ————*Birthday Waltzes*, Op. 1. Boston: E. C. Schirmer, 1923.

45.   ————*Chanticleer*, Festival Overture, Op. 27. Boston: C. C. Birchard, 1929.

46.   ————*The Constant Cannibal Maiden*. New York: G. Schirmer, 1943.

47.   ————*Country Pictures* for piano, Op. 9; New York: Associated Music Publishers, 1914, 1942.

48.   ————*Divertimento* for two pianos, Op. 26A. New York: Carl Fischer, 1927; also arranged for woodwind quintet. New York: Carl Fischer, 1927; M. Witmark, 1936.

49.   ————*Elegy* in Free Variation-Form, Op. 2, for piano. London: Metzler & Co., 1902.

50.   ————*Fanny Blair, Folk-Song Fantasy* for string quartet, Op. 28. New York: Oxford University Press, 1930.

51.   ————*Five Children's Songs*, from "A Child's Garden of Verses" (Robert Louis Stevenson). Boston: Boston Music Co., 1899.

52.   ————*Four Songs*, Op. 4 (Mary L. Mason). Philadelphia: John Church Co., 1908.

53.   Mason, D. G., and Edward Burlingame Hill. *Granada*. Boston: Miles and Thompson, 1894.

54.   Mason, D. G. *Impromptu*, Op. 16, No. 1, for piano. Boston: Oliver Ditson Co., 1917.

55.   ————*Intermezzo* for string quartet, Op. 17. New York: Weaner-Levant, 1943.

56.   ————*Ländliche Bilder Für Pianoforte*, Op. 9. Leipzig: Breitkopf & Härtel, 1914.

57.   ————*Little John Bottlejohn*, trio for women's voices. Boston: Boston Music Co., 1915.

58.   ————*Ode to Big Business*, Op. 25, No. 1, for male voices. New York: G. Ricordi, 1927.

59.   ————*Passacaglia and Fugue*, Op. 10, for organ. New York: H. W. Gray, 1913.

60.   ————*Prelude and Fugue* for piano and orchestra, Op. 20. New York: J. Fischer, 1933.

61.   ————*Russians*, Op. 18, a cycle of songs for baritone and piano. New York: G. Schirmer, 1920.

62.   ————*Scherzo*, for two pianos, four hands. New York: Carl Fischer, 1931.

63.   ————*Sentimental Sketches* for violin, cello, piano, Op. 34. New York: J. Fischer, 1935.

64.   ————*Serenade* for string quartet, Op. 31. New York: J. Fischer, 1934.

65.   ————*Sonata* for clarinet, or violin, and piano, Op. 14. New York: Society for the Publication of American Music, 1920, 1946.

66.   ————*Sonata* in G minor for violin and piano, Op. 5. New York: G. Schirmer, 1913.

67.   ——————*Songs of the Countryside*, Op. 23 (A. E. Housman). New York: G. Ricordi, 1927.

68.   ——————*String Quartet on Negro Themes*, Op. 19. New York: G. Schirmer, 1930.

69.   ——————*Suite after English Folk Songs*, Op. 32. New York: G. Schirmer, 1936.

70.   ——————*Symphony No. 1 in C minor*, Op. 11. New York: Universal Edition, 1926.

71.   ——————*Symphony No. 3* (A Lincoln Symphony), Op. 35. New York: Juilliard, 1944.

72.   ——————*Three Pieces* for flute, harp and string quartet, Op. 13. New York: G. Schirmer, 1923.

73.   ——————*Three Preludes*, Op. 33, for piano. New York: E. B. Marks, 1943.

74.   ——————*Three Silhouettes*, Op. 21, for piano. New York: G. Schirmer, 1923.

75.   ——————*Three Songs* from "Nautical Lays of a Landsman," Op. 38 (Wallace Irwin). New York: G. Schirmer, 1943.

76.   ——————*The TreeToad*, Op. 25, No. 2, for female voices. New York: G. Ricordi, 1927.

77.   ——————*Two Chorale-Preludes on Hymn Tunes*, Op. 30, for organ. New York: J. Fischer, 1942.

78.   ——————*Variations on a Theme of John Powell* for string quartet, Op. 24. New York: Oxford University Press, 1928.

79.   ——————*When First My Way to Fair I Took* (A. E. Housman) for voice and piano. New York: M. Witmark, 1936.

GENERAL BIBLIOGRAPHY

Books

1. *American Bibliography. A Preliminary Checklist for 1801-1819*, 21 vols., compiled by Ralph R. Shaw and Richard H. Shoemaker. New York: The Scarecrow Press, 1958-1965.

2. *The American Composer Speaks: A Historical Anthology, 1770-1965*. Baton Rouge: Louisiana State University Press, 1966.

3. *The American History and Encyclopedia of Music*, v. [4], ed. William Lines Hubbard New York: Irving Squire, 1910; rev. ed., 1924; reprint: New York: AMS Press, 1976.

4. *American Music Before 1865 in Print and on Records. A Biblio-discography*. Brooklyn: Institute for Studies in American Music, 1976. (ISAM Monograph, No. 6)

5. Ammer, Christine. *Unsung: A History of Women in American Music*. Westport, CT: Greenwood Press, 1980.

6. Ayars, Christine Merrick. *Contributions to the Art of Music in America: By the Music Industries of Boston, 1640-1936*. New York: The H. W. Wilson Co., 1937; reprint: New York: Johnson Reprint Corp., 1969.

7. Barnes, Edwin Ninyon Chaloner. *American Music From Plymouth Rock to Tin Pan Alley*. Washington, DC: Music Education Publications, 1936.

8. Barzun, Jacques. *Music in American Life*. New York: Doubleday & Co., 1956.

9. *Bio-Bibliographical Index of Musicians in the United States of America Since Colonial Times*, 2nd ed. Washington, DC: Music Section, Pan American Union, 1956; reprint: New York: Da Capo Press, 1956.

10. Chase, Gilbert. *America's Music*. New York: McGraw-Hill Co., 1966.

11. *A Checklist of American Imprints for 1820-1833*, 15 vols., compiled by Richard H. Shoemaker. New York: The Scarecrow Press, 1964-1979.

12. Crawford, Richard. *American Studies and American Musicology: A Point of View and a Case in Point*. Brooklyn: Institute for Studies in American Music, 1975.

13. Daniel, Ralph T. *The Anthem in New England Before 1800*. Evanston: Northwestern University Press, 1966; reprint: New York: Da Capo Press, 1979.

14. Davis, Ronald L. *A History of Opera in the American West*. Englewood Cliffs, NJ: Prentice-Hall, 1965.

15. *Dictionary of American Biography*, 20 vols. New York: Charles Scribner's Sons, 1928-1937; 6 supplements, 1944-1980.

16. Douglas, Charles Winfred. *Church Music in History and Practice*. New York: Charles Scribner's Sons, 1937.

17. Edwards, Arthur C., and W. Thomas Marrocco. *Music in the United States*. Dubuque, IA: William C. Brown Publishers, 1968.

18. Ellinwood, Leonard. *The History of American Church Music*. New York: Morehouse-Gorham Co., 1953; reprint: New York: Da Capo Press, 1970.

19. Elson, Arthur. *Women's Work in Music*. Boston: L. C. Page Co., 1904; reprint: Portland, ME: Longwood Press, 1976.

20. Elson, Louis C. *History of American Music*. New York: Macmillan, 1904, 1915, 1925; reprint: New York: Burt Franklin, 1971.

21. Evans, Charles. *American Bibliography. A Chronological Dictionary of All Books, Pamphlets, and Periodical Publications Printed in the United States of America from . . . 1639 down to . . . 1820*, 12 vols. Chicago: Privately Printed, 1905-1934; reprint: New York: Peter Smith, 1941, 14 vols.

22. Ewen, David. *Music Comes to America*. New York: Thomas Y. Crowell Co., 1942; New York: Allen, Towne & Heath, 1947.

23.   *Famous Composers and Their Music*, 16 vols., ed. Theodore Thomas, John Knowles Paine, and Karl Klauser. Boston: J. B. Millet Co., 1901. (Vols. I-VI contain historical essays and illustrations; vols. VII-XVI contain music)

24.   Foote, Henry Wilder. *Three Centuries of American Hymnody*. Cambridge, MA: Harvard College, 1940; reprint: Hamden, CT: The Shoe String Press, 1961.

25.   Gould, Nathaniel Duren. *History of Church Music in America*. Boston: Gould and Lincoln, 1853; reprint: New York: AMS Press, 1972.

26.   *A Handbook of American Music and Musicians*, ed. F. O. Jones. Canaseraga, NY: F. O. Jones, 1886; reprint: New York: Da Capo Press, 1971.

27.   Heard, Priscilla S. *American Music 1698-1800: An Annotated Bibliography*. Waco, TX: Baylor University Press, 1975.

28.   Hipsher, Edward Ellsworth. *American Opera and Its Composers*. Philadelphia: Theodore Presser, 1927; reprint: New York: Da Capo Press, 1978.

29.   *A History of Song*, ed. Denis Stevens. New York: W. W. Norton, 1961.

30.   Hitchcock, H. Wiley. *Music in the United States*, 2nd edition. Englewood Cliffs, NJ: Prentice-Hall, 1974.

31.   Hixon, Donald L. *Music in Early America: A Bibliography of Music in Evans*. Metuchen, NJ: The Scarecrow Press, 1970.

32.   Horn, David. *The Literature of American Music in Books and Folk Music Collections: A Fully Annotated Bibliography*. Metuchen, NJ: The Scarecrow Press, 1977.

33.   Howard, John Tasker. *Our American Music*. New York: Thomas Y. Crowell, 1954.

34.   Howard, John Tasker, and George Kent Bellows. *A Short History of Music in America*. New York: Thomas Y Crowell, 1967.

35.   *Hymnal of the Protestant Episcopal Church in the United States of America*. New York: The Church Pension Fund, 1940.

36.   Jackson, Richard. *U. S. Bicentennial Music I*. Brooklyn: Institute for Studies in American Music, 1977. (ISAM Monograph, No. 1)

37.   Johnson, H. Earle. *First Performances in America to 1900*. Detroit: The College Music Society, 1979. (Bibliographies in American Music, No. 4)

38.   Julian, John A. *Dictionary of Hymnology: Origin and History of Christian Hymns*. London: Murray, 1919; reprint: New York: Gordon Press, 1977.

39.   Kaufmann, Helen L. *From Jehovah to Jazz; Music in America from Psalmody to the Present Day*. New York: Dodd, Mead & Co., 1937; reprint: New York: Arno Press, 1968; Port Washington, NY: Kennikat Press, 1969.

40.   Kingman, Daniel. *American Music: A Panorama*. New York: Schirmer Books, 1979.

41.   Lahee, Henry Charles. *Annals of Music in America: A Chronological Record of Significant Musical Events from 1640 to the Present Day*. Boston: Marshall Jones Co., 1922; reprint: New York: AMS Press, 1969.

42.   Lowens, Irving. *Bibliography of Songsters Printed in America Before 1821*. Worcester, MA: American Antiquarian Society, 1976.

43.   ——————*Music in America and American Music: Two Views of the Scene*. Brooklyn: Institute for Studies in American Music, 1978. (ISAM Monograph, No. 8)

44.   Longyear, Rey Morgan. *Nineteenth-Century Romanticism in Music*. Englewood Cliffs, NJ: Prentice Hall, 1969; 2nd edition, 1973.

45.   Mattfeld, Julius. *A Handbook of American Operatic Premières 1731-1962*. Detroit: Information Service, 1963.

46.   ——————*Variety Music Cavalcade 1620-1969. A Chronology of Vocal and Instrumental Music Popular in the United States*, 3rd edition. Englewood Cliffs, NJ: Prentice-Hall, 1971.

47.   Mellers, Wilfrid Howard. *Music in a New Found Land: Two Hundred Years of American Music*. London: Barrie and Rockliff, 1964; New York: Stonehill Publishing Co., 1975.

48.   *The National Cyclopedia of American Biography*, 59 vols. Clifton, NJ: James T. White & Co., 1898-1980.

49.   *National Music of America and Its Sources*. Boston: L. C. Page & Co., 1924; Detroit: Gale Research Co., 1974.

50.   *The New Grove Dictionary of Music and Musicians*, 20 vols., ed. Stanley Sadie. London: Macmillan, 1980.

51.   Ochse, Orpha. *The History of the Organ in the United States*. Bloomington: Indiana University Press, 1975.

52.   *One Hundred Years of Music in America*, ed. Paul Henry Lang. New York: G. Schirmer, 1961.

53.   Reynolds, William J. *A Survey of Christian Hymnody*. New York: Holt, Rinehart & Winston, 1963. (2nd edition with Milburn Price, *A Joyful Sound*. New York: Holt, Rinehart & Winston, 1978.

54.   Routley, Eric. *The Music of Christian Hymnody: A Study of the Development of the Hymn Tunes*. London: Independent Press, 1957.

55.   Rublowsky, John. *Music in America*. New York: Crowell-Collier Press, 1967.

56.   Sablosky, Irving L. *American Music*. Chicago: The University of Chicago Press, 1969.

57.   Scott, John Anthony. *The Ballad of America; The History of the United States in Song and Story*. New York: Bantam Books, 1966.

58.   Sonneck, Oscar George Theodore. *A Bibliography of Early Secular American Music (18th Century)*. Revised and enlarged by William Treat Upton. Washington, DC: Library of Congress, Music Division, 1945; reprint: New York: Da Capo Press, 1964.

59.   ———————*Early Concert Life in America (1731-1800)*. Leipzig: Breitkopf & Härtel, 1907; New York: Musurgia, 1949; reprint: New York: Da Capo Press, 1978.

60.   ———————*Suum Cuique: Essays in Music*. New York: G. Schirmer, 1916, 1944; reprint: Freeport, NY: Books for Libraries Press, 1969.

61.   Stevenson, Robert Murrell. *Patterns of Protestant Church Music*. Durham, NC: Duke University Press, 1953.

62.   ———————*Protestant Church Music in America. A Short Survey of Men and Movements From 1564 to the Present*. New York: W. W. Norton, 1966.

63.   Upton, William Treat. *The Art-Song in America. A Study in the Development of American Music*. Boston: Oliver Ditson Co., 1930; Supplement, 1938; reprint: New York: Johnson Reprint Corporation, 1969.

Music

AH   1.   *American Hymns Old and New*, ed. Albert Christ-Janer, Charles W. Hughes and Carleton Sprague Smith. New York: Columbia University Press, 1980.

BCAC   2.   *The Bicentennial Collection of American Choral Music*, ed. Mason Martens. Dayton, OH: McAfee Music Corporation, 1975.

BCAK   3.   *The Bicentennial Collection of American Keyboard Music (1790-1900)*, ed. Edward Gold. Dayton, OH: McAfee Music Corporation, 1975.

BCAM   4.   *The Bicentennial Collection of American Music*, v. 1, 1698-1900, ed. Elwyn A. Wienandt. Carol Stream, IL: Hope Publishing Co., 1974.

CAO   5.   *A Century of American Organ Music*, ed. Barbara Owen. Dayton, OH: McAfee Music Corporation, 1975.

CMCA   6.   *Christmas Music from Colonial America*, ed. Leonard Van Camp. New York: Galaxy Music Corporation, 1975.

      7.   *A Collection of Early American Keyboard Music*, ed. Anne McClenny and Maurice Hinson. Cincinnati: Willis, 1971; New York: Belwin-Mills, 1971.

CCAO   8. *A Collection of 19th Century American Organ Music*, ed. Janice Beck and D. Darrell Woomer. Cleveland: Cleveland Chapter of the American Guild of Organists, 1976.

        9. *Colonial Keyboard Tunes*, ed. James S. Darling. Williamsburg: Colonial Williamsburg Foundation, 1980.

EAM   10. *Earlier American Music*, 25 vols. to date, ed. H. Wiley Hitchcock. New York: Da Capo Press, 1972-

       11. *The Early American Songbook*, ed. Lee Vinson. Englewood Cliffs, NJ: Prentice-Hall, 1974.

       12. *Fifteen Anthems from America*, ed. Elwyn A. Wienandt and Robert H. Young. New York: J. Fischer (Belwin-Mills), 1970.

Hymnal 13. *The Hymnal of the Protestant Episcopal Church*. New York: The Church Pension Fund, 1940.

LEAM   14. *Landmarks of Early American Music*, ed. Richard Franko Goldman and Roger Smith. New York: G. Schirmer, 1943; reprint: New York: AMS Press, 1974.

       15. *Music for Patriots, Politicians, and Presidents. Harmonies and Discords of the First Hundred Years*, ed. Vera Brodsky Lawrence. New York: Macmillan, 1975.

MDGW   16. *Music from the Days of George Washington*, ed. W. Oliver Strunk and Carl Engel. Washington, DC: United States George Washington Commission, 1931; reprint: New York: AMS Press, 1970.

MinA   17. *Music in America. An Anthology from the Landing of the Pilgrims to the Close of the Civil War, 1620-1865*, ed. W. Thomas Marrocco and Harold Gleason. New York: W. W. Norton, 1964.

       18. *The New Liberty Bell: A Bicentennial Anthology of American Choral Music*, ed. James G. Smith. Champaign, IL: Fostco Music Press, 1976.

       19. *Our Earliest American Songs*, ed. Philip Weston. New York: Concord Music Co., 1941.

       20. *Popular Songs of the Nineteenth-Century America: Complete Original Sheet Music for 64 Songs*, ed. Richard Jackson. New York: Dover Publications, 1976.

PAS   21. *A Program of Early and Mid-Nineteenth Century American Songs*, ed. John Tasker Howard. New York: J. Fischer, 1931.

RRAM   22. *Recent Researches in American Music*, 7 vols. to date. Madison, WI: A–R Editions, 1977-

       23. Routley, Erik. *The Music of Christian Hymnody*. London: Independent Press, 1957.

       24. *Series of Old American Songs: Reproduced in Facsimile from Original and Early Editions in the Harris Collection of American Poetry and Plays*, ed. S. Foster Damon. Providence, RI: Brown University Library, 1936.

       25. *Spiritual Folk-Songs of Early America*, ed. George Pullen Jackson. New York: Dover Publications, 1964.

       26. *Yankee-Doodle-Doo: A Collection of Songs of the Early American Stage*, ed. Glenville Vernon. New York: Payson & Clarke, 1927; reprint: Detroit: Gale Research Co., 1972.

       27. *The Western Wind American Tune-Book*, ed. Lawrence Bennett. New York: Broude Brothers, 1974, 1975.

YONE   28. *Ye Olde New England Psalm-Tunes, 1620-1820, with Historical Sketch, Biographical Notes, and Hints on Performance*, ed. William Arms Fisher. Boston: Oliver Ditson Co., 1930; reprint: Bryn Mawr, PA: Theodore Presser Co., 1975.

INDEX